To Chr

May you

bat 1.000 in all

your endeavors

Al Pepper

18 DEC 2∅

Mendoza's Heroes
Fifty Batters Below .200

by Al Pepper

Art by Jon Gordon

Editor J. Thomas Hetrick

Pocol Press

POCOL PRESS

Published in the United States of America
by Pocol Press.
6023 Pocol Drive
Clifton, VA 20124
chrisandtom@erols.com
http://www.pocolpress.com
SAN: 253-6021

Copyright © 2002 by Al Pepper
http://www.mendozasheroes.com

Publisher's Cataloging-in-Publication

Pepper, Al.
    Mendoza's heroes : fifty batters below .200 / Al
Pepper ; art by Jon Gordon ; editor, J. Thomas Hetrick
-- 1st ed.
    p.cm.
    Includes bibliographical references and index.
    ISBN 1-929763-11-5

    1.   Baseball players--United States--Biography.
I. Hetrick, J. Thomas, 1957- II. Title.

GV865.A1P46 2002   796.357'092'2

Cover illustration and interior drawings by Jon Gordon.
http://www.artofjon.com

Cover illustration:
Top row (from left to right): Tony La Russa, Mario Mendoza, and Dan Briggs.
Middle row: Marty Castillo, Charlie Manuel. Bottom row: Adrian Garrett, Gair Allie, and Choo Choo Coleman.

Table Of Contents

Mendoza's Heroes: Allie to Zimmerman

Mario Mendoza	Frank Fernandez	Larry Murray
Gair Allie	Herman Franks	Jose Oliva
Frank Baker	Jim French	John O'Neill
Charlie Bastian	Jim Fuller	Larry Owen
Cramer Beard, Jr.	Adrian Garrett	Ray Oyler
Bill Bergen	John Gochnauer	Bill Plummer
Fred Buelow	Bobby Johnson	Luis Pujols
Dan Briggs	Steve Kiefer	Mike Ryan
Doug Camilli	Mike Laga	Dave Schneck
Marty Castillo	Tony La Russa	Bill Shipke
Clarence Coleman	Charlie Manuel	Anthony Smith
Bill Conroy	James McAvoy	Mike Stenhouse
Bob Davis	Mike McCormick	Ron Tingley
Brian Doyle	Tom McLaughlin	William Traffley
Oscar Dugey	Orlando Mercado	Bob Uecker
Henry Easterday	Charlie Metro	John Vukovich
Ernie Fazio	Rich Morales	Eddie Zimmerman

Acknowledgements

I would like to express my inestimable gratitude and appreciation to the following contributors. Without their assistance and support, you would not be reading *Mendoza's Heroes*:

My most highest thankfulness to the following major and minor league ballplayers for their contributions and insights: Brian Barsher, Cramer Beard, Dan Briggs, Doug Camilli, Tom Carroll, Brian Doyle, Herman Franks, Jim French, Frank Howard, Adrian Garrett, Mike Laga, Tony La Russa, Orlando Mercado, Charlie Metro, Larry Owen, John Pricher, Dave Schneck, Mike Stenhouse, and Denny Weiner.

Mr. Oscar Soria, sportswriter and Spanish-speaking broadcaster of the Arizona Diamondbacks, provided his personal experiences with Mario Mendoza while covering his games in the Mexican Pacific League.

Many members of the Society for American Baseball Research (SABR) provided me with their personal research on the players presented here, thus saving me countless man-hours and ensuring accurate facts. They are: Mark Amour, Adam Barth, Joey Beretta, Michael Bielawa, Stephen Boren, Bob Bowen, Michael Brannan, Merritt Clifton, Bill Deane, Joe Dittmar, Robert Fitts, Stuart Hodesh, Frank Gill, Russ Lake, Andy McCue, Wayne McElreavy, Michael Mavrogiannis, Stephen Milman, Jack V. Morris, Yoichi Nagata, Gary Plunkitt, Mike Richard, Tom Ruane, Bob Savitt, Terry Simpkins, Mark Simon, David Smith, Lyle Spatz, David Vincent, John Zajc, and Tom Zocco.

Patric Doyle, proprietor of the Professional Baseball Player Database; his product enabled me to research the minor league statistics of the featured players.

National Baseball Hall of Fame Librarian Jim Gates, and Bill Francis, a researcher, unearthed wondrous compilations of data for many of the pre-1950 ballplayers.

Ted Hathaway, of Rational Pastimes, compiled an extensive list of references and source documents of the players featured.

Bill Brody provided much insight and assistance in the tortuous nuances of submitting a correct book proposal.

Julian Tonning, my former boss and author of *Righting Words*, for giving me marvelous guidance and inspiration.

My father, Lenny, for introducing me to the great game of baseball.

Finally, my wife, Janice, for providing that special inspiration and support that only she can ever provide.

FOREWORD
by Mike Stenhouse

The only thing I find more astonishing than someone writing a book about below .200 hitters is that I am *in* a book about below .200 hitters! It just wasn't supposed to end up that way!

On my way to the Major Leagues, everything indicated success. In my genetic makeup, my father, Dave Stenhouse, was a 1962 American League All-Star. At the schoolboy level, I developed into Rhode Island's most heralded hitter since the legendary Nap Lajoie. At the collegiate level at Harvard, I was runner-up for the NCAA batting title and a first-team All-American in 1978. I may also be one of a select few players ever to be drafted #1 *twice*! It's an interesting story and one you can read about in this book. Then as a pro in the minor leagues in 1983, while playing Triple-A ball, I flirted with .400 for part of the season and was the American Association's MVP and Topps' Minor League Player of the Year. In 1984, in big-league camp with the Expos, I set a club record for Grapefruit League home runs. Things were truly looking good. But...

The Major Leagues was another story. You are probably aware of the challenges of hitting a $2^3/_4$-inch diameter sphere, being thrown from just over 20 yards away at a velocity of 95 MPH, with a thin piece of wood. Power hitting at the major-league level takes more than just strength and bat speed. It requires coordination of all of the major elements of the swing: hip rotation, head and arm position, and making contact with the ball on the proper swing path and at just the right spot over the plate. Most importantly, it takes near perfection and the ability to consistently replicate under pressure game conditions. It's hard enough to do this successfully as an everyday player. It's even harder for someone who, early in his career, was relegated to a role player, like me.

I had a very narrow window of opportunity to prove myself. Here is a sample of my competition in the outfield during my career: Andre Dawson, Tim Raines, Warren Cromartie, Kirby Puckett, Tom Brunansky, Mickey Hatcher, Jim Rice, Tony Armas, and Dewey Evans. Sitting in the dugout for long spells does not allow for memorable experiences on the field. You can't be a "Prime Time" (PT) player if you don't get playing time (pt). On those rare occasions when I did get a Major League "start," I can remember sitting around all day in a trance-like state and feeling like each at bat might be my last chance. I worried that I needed to hit a 7-run homer just to stay in the line-up.

If I could have snuck into a few more games, I always felt I could have progressed into a .290 hitter in the Major Leagues, with better than average power. But it didn't work out that way and I ended up batting .190 in my five-year career. While many people still compliment me for making it to "The Show," there is a personal degree of disappointment when you don't reach the potential you know you have.

I remained involved in the game for quite a while after I hung up the spikes. I was a TV and radio announcer for the Montreal Expos and for the Pawtucket Red Sox for 12 years. Other than running fantasy camps for the Expos and Red Sox, my playing days seemed a long-ago memory until I received an odd package, mailed to my house, a couple of years ago. The letter was from Al Pepper and it discussed his project to document the careers of the 50 greatest *below* .200 hitters of all time. He then announced that I held his honor of being designated as the 32nd-greatest below .200 hitter ever. That's all my family and friends had to hear. Thanks to Al, my new nickname is "Number 32."

While my initial thought was that this guy is either a crackpot or stalker, as a baseball researcher myself, I actually took interest in Al's project. We have talked on a couple of occasions and I shared some stories on what contributed to my big-league demise. Even a Harvard grad has to be impressed with Al's detailed and comprehensive account of my career, as well as his broad knowledge of the game. Not bad for someone who claims he can't even hit .200 in a coed, slow-pitch softball league.

There are plenty of great books on baseball out there. However, the vast majority of them focus on the very elite players of the game. Al's theme, presenting biographies of 50 players hitting below the so-called Mendoza Line, is quite unique. Some of the players we all have heard of, like Tony La Russa, Brian Doyle, Bob Uecker, and Choo Choo Coleman. There are a few I played against, such as Mike Laga, Marty Castillo, and Orlando Mercado. I was even a teammate of Danny Briggs while with Montreal. In fact, Briggs and I were vying against each other for a roster spot in AAA in 1982. Then there are those players who are baseball's equivalent of unknown soldiers. Where else are you going to read about Bill Bergen, the ancient catcher who batted .170, but was the greatest defensive backstop of his day, or Frank Fernandez, who actually was one of the game's better sluggers of the 1960s and early 1970s?

Mendoza's Heroes depicts not only how hard it is to make it to the Majors; but also, once there, how hard it is to stay. There were so many highly talented players who, given the right chance or with just one small break, might just have turned in a memorable career. I can say I am proud to be one of the "Heroes." There are more of us than there are super-stars.

"Nerve and love of the game for the game itself are strong points in a ballplayer's makeup."

-Bill Carrigan, Boston Red Sox catcher, 1906-1916

INTRODUCTION
Selection Criteria

Nearly everyone raised in the ESPN generation has heard the semi-trendy catch phrase: "He/she/it is below the Mendoza Line." Originally a baseball term, it's no longer used only in that sport's lexicon. This expression applies to a minimum acceptable numeric standard.

The Mendoza Line likely gets its name after Mario Mendoza, the 1970s journeyman infielder. Alas poor Mario, he of deft glove but marginal bat. His name might have uneventfully been passed to history, had not the great Kansas City Royals' infielder George Brett immortalized him in his famous quip: "The first thing I look for in the Sunday papers is to see who's below the Mendoza Line."

The Mendoza Line is set at a batting average of .200. This equates to one base hit per every five at bats. Players batting below the Mendoza Line are hitting .199 or less. That can be tolerated for a pitcher; teams pay pitchers to prevent runs, not create them. But generally for a catcher, definitely for an infielder, and most especially for an outfielder, the Mendoza Line equates to a statistical measurement of mediocrity. For batters, this is baseball's equivalent of the line of death.

Hundreds of hitters could not quite get untracked when called up to the big leagues. Failing to get on base in limited opportunities, they were sent back down to the minors. Many would never get a second chance. However, there exists a select legion of sub-.200 hitting ballplayers who stayed around long enough to make a lasting impression to the game. They survived countless roster cutdowns, wandered like nomads to stay in the league, and occupied niches that hardly led to riches. Their stories beg for telling. In these pages reside fifty of the most interesting. They are *Mendoza's Heroes.*

The question I hear from everyone (including ballplayers themselves) is, "How did you come up with this idea?" Well, have you ever wondered how a pitcher with an astronomically high earned run average or an outfielder with an infinitesimally low batting average, manages to play five years in the major leagues? I sure did.

From my earliest days as a fan of baseball (1968), I harbored an innate interest in the below .200 hitter. The less-than-stellar statistics on the reverse of a Rich Morales or Dave Adlesh baseball card fascinated me. Why was this? Maybe because my two favorite teams of the time, the Washington Senators and Philadelphia Phillies, always seemed to have five players each year flirt below .200. Perhaps it had something to do with my own limited ability to play the game. I could relate to Morales and Adlesh more than I could with the superstar bats of Bobby Bonds, Hank Aaron, and Carl Yastrzemski.

Fast forward to 30 years later. My job at that time required much writing. Enough people liked my work to encourage a personal project. A baseball book, specifically a Top-100 baseball players book, seemed a worthy project. While searching for the elusive formula to quantify the greatest players, I pored through the statistics of thousands of players. Though I automatically discarded hitters with batting averages below .200, I paused to examine closely at the record of one Bill Bergen, an early 20th century catcher. Bergen's .170 career batting average remains the *lowest* of any regular ballplayer in history. Yet, Bergen fielded stupendously. Then I wondered, "Using a subset of hitters with batting averages below .200, who are the best?"

What started as an article on the below .200 All-Star team, grew to a short book of 25 players, and eventually evolved into *Mendoza's Heroes*.

As I quickly discovered, interesting ballplayers do not necessarily equate to a linear function of batting average. The players herein may possess lower than normal batting averages, but they compensated this shortfall in other ways. Some fielded sensationally. Others established their legend as World Series saviors. Still others excelled in the minor leagues, amateur ball, or overseas baseball leagues. A few became famous coaches, managers, and even actors. A share of these players actually were productive men at the plate, if you delve deep enough into the numbers. That requires you to put faith in the heresy that as a statistic, batting average is not necessarily a bottom-line predictor.

The first chapter presents the etymology and history of the Mendoza Line. Chapter two offers a profile on the man behind the term—Mario Mendoza. Next, the player biographies appear in chronological sequence, interspersed with one hundred twenty five years worth of below .200 hitters covering five distinct eras in baseball history.

Not that any hitter is trying, but to be considered one of Mendoza's Heroes, in any era, the following eligibility criteria had to be met:

A. Players must have a batting average *below* .200.

B. Players must have a combined total of 200 career plate appearances playing for teams of an officially recognized major league.

C. The player must have played the majority of his games as a position player.

D. The player has not played a major league game since 1996. No active professional ballplayers are included.

Fifty biographical profiles detail each player's career and provide a glimpse of their lives outside the game of baseball. These narratives offer more than a rehashing of statistics. Quaint anecdotes and great moments are revisited. Colorful quotes abound; many obtained through my interviews with the players themselves. More often than not, these players emerge larger than life, each with a unique tapestry of accomplishments and experiences that make them as fascinating as the titans of the game. The intended effect provides a rollicking tour through baseball history, as seen and played by its lesser lights.

Mendoza's Heroes is not a "Hall of Shame" treatment or some other form of denigration. Though it is not my intent to place false laurels about their heads, I tend to praise these players, not bury them. Anyone playing at the major league level has accomplished something that few of us can even comprehend.

I assure you will find *Mendoza's Heroes* worth meeting and knowing. Whether you are a hard core "seamhead" or just a casual fan, you should find this work interesting reading, a useful reference, and mildly amusing. Please enjoy.

Chapter 1
THE CURIOUS ORIGINS OF THE MENDOZA LINE

According to *The New Dickson Baseball Dictionary*, the following is the definition of the term, Mendoza Line:

> Mendoza line. 1. The figurative boundary in the batting averages between those batters hitting above and below .215. It is named for shortstop Mario Mendoza whose career (1974–1982) batting average for the Pirates, Mariners, and Rangers was .215.
> 2. The figurative boundary in the batting averages between those batters hitting above and below .200.
> Usage Note. This clearly emerging term can have two slightly different meanings (.215 vs. .200), so it is important to make sure which Mendoza line is being referred to. However, it seems like the .200 line is used much more commonly than the .215 version.

A third definition, cited in the original *Rotisserie League Baseball* (1984), states:

> Named after former Pirate, Ranger, and Mariner shortstop Mario Mendoza, whose .215 lifetime batting average kept him at the bottom of the weekly batting averages. The Mendoza line is that boundary in the averages below which players cross into the Twilight Zone.

Based on this version, the Mendoza Line was a moving object—rising and falling on the fortunes of Mario Mendoza himself. With Mario not active as a player, this construes the Mendoza Line as something subjectively set by a sportswriter, announcer, or scout. It is not far-fetched, in today's game, for someone to set the Mendoza Line as high as .250.

So, is the line .200, .215, or none of the above? Based on a review of numerous different Mendoza Line citations, only one stated that the Mendoza Line is something other than a .200 batting average.

An overwhelming majority of references refer to one standard for the Mendoza Line. That is .200, the line of demarcation that separates rank-and-file hitters from the dreaded lot of .199 and below hitters. With most citations using the .200 version of the Mendoza Line, it is hoped that future editions of Dickson's and other references delete definitions of the Mendoza Line above the .200 standard.

Even before Mario Mendoza was born, there were other terms used for less-than-stellar hitters. In the 19th century, "tapperitis hitter" meant one who hits tappers. "Can't hit a balloon" and "Can't hit a bull in the ass with a shovel" harken the beginning of the 20th century. There's "buttercup hitter," first used in the 1930s. To "not hit one's weight," "a hole in your bat," and "out man," were others. "Ten o'clock hitter" defined players who hit the ball hard during morning batting practice but not during the game. "Banjo hitter," "ukulele hitter," and "Punch and Judy hitter," all describe light hitters; however, not necessarily inept batters, as it has the connotation of someone who can scratch-out cheap singles. Players with "warning track power" could belt the ball near the fence, but rarely enough to clear the boundary for a home run. "Aggressive hitters" were batters that often swung at pitches out of the strike zone, hampering their effectiveness. Players termed "All-American outs" indicate the limited nature of their batting skills. Of more recent vintage, a batter "on the Interstate" would mean that his .180 batting average would look like "I80" on old-fashioned scoreboard lights.

The Giants of the late 1960s sported the "Lanier-Mason Line," a play on the Mason-Dixon Line, which suggested a range of batting between Don Mason (.205 career average) and Hal Lanier (.228). The Tigers offered the "Ray Oyler Divide," named for the slick-fielding, light-hitting shortstop. Most likely, every team used a less-than-flattering term for lackluster hitting which came and went; mostly went. But, in just a span of 20 years, the Mendoza Line has jumped into the mainstream, and will most likely live as long as baseball.

Some uncertainty exists over who first described the mythical line. Pirates' fans claim that the late announcer Bob Prince came up with the term while Mendoza was batting .140 one year. Another source credits Johnny Bench. A minority insists that Christobal (Minnie) Mendoza is the actual Mendoza referred to in "Mendoza Line." Minnie Mendoza, a consistent .300 hitter in the minor leagues during the 1960s, finally made it with the Minnesota Twins in 1970. At age 36, Minnie managed just .188 in 16 games with the Twins that year. Though Minnie Mendoza batted below .200 in his brief career, no documented evidence appears to support the claim of anyone using the term Mendoza Line in the 1960s and early 1970s.

Most credit coinage of the term to George Brett, originally quoted in 1980: "The first thing I look for in the Sunday papers is who is below the Mendoza line." However, according to *Sports Illustrated* (Aug. 20, 1990), Mendoza's teammates on the 1979 Seattle Mariners, Tom Paciorek and/or Bruce Bochte, invented the term. Mendoza told *SI* that Paciorek was responsible. But Paciorek insisted otherwise, "It wasn't my idea. It was Bruce Bochte's. I got the credit, but I don't want it."

Mexican sportscaster Oscar Soria corroborates the *SI* story. The voice of the Mexican Pacific League's Hermosillo Naranjeros, Soria provided these comments concerning the Mendoza Line:

> I know Mario because he is the manager of the Obregon Yaquis in the Mexican Pacific League. I am a sportscaster in this league, I do the play-by-play of the Hermosillo team on TV, and that's the reason I know Mario very well. In an interview a few weeks ago, I asked Mario about the Mendoza line and he said that Tom Paciorek was the first to mention the phrase 'Mendoza Line' when he read the Sunday paper. Then George Brett heard about that and, years after that, Chris Berman quoted about the Mendoza line. Mario said that when Chris Berman mentioned it and people started to laugh, he was angry, but now he enjoys the fame of the phrase Mendoza line.

Bob Finnigan of the *Seattle Times* added this piece of testimony while writing a 2001 story on Bruce Bochte:

Wimpy, as Paciorek is known, revealed that Bookus, as Bochte was known, is the one who invented the term, "Mendoza Line," for a .200 batting average. "Most people credit me," said Paciorek, openly known as one of the game's zanies. "But it was Bruce. It was funny then, still is. But it was no knock on Mario (Mendoza), who's a great guy."

Based on the above statements, we all can be fairly certain that the originator of the "Mendoza Line" were his own teammates and not an outsider like Brett. However, to say, beyond the shadow of doubt, that it was Bruce Bochte, is questionable when Mendoza, himself, insists it was Tom Paciorek.

What does the term truly mean in the context of Brett's quote? To explain: most Sunday newspapers present the major league batting and pitching statistics. The format separately lists National League and American League hitters in order from highest to lowest batting average. Not every active player makes this list. To appear, a player must have a minimum number of plate appearances (different from an at bat) each week, based on his team's product of games played as of the previous Friday, multiplied by the constant, 3.1. Since Mario Mendoza was primarily a reserve with the Pittsburgh Pirates, he rarely would have appeared in this feature since he never had the requisite number of plate appearances.

While playing in the American League, Mendoza appeared as a regular from 1979 through 1981. Since Brett, Paciorek, and Bochte were all contemporaries of Mendoza during his American League days, it is conceivable that any of them would thumb through the Sunday edition of the newspaper, noting which rivals had a lower batting average than Mario Mendoza.

How did the term Mendoza Line become a piece of modern-day American jargon? The answer is intuitively simple: ESPN. The all-sports television network began its emergence near the conclusion of Mario Mendoza's playing days. Without sounding too much like a sociologist, *ESPN SportsCenter* has become such a cultural influence; it has injected many new buzzwords and catch phrases into our everyday speech. ESPN has even changed the way professional athletes play the game. Look at the present-day National Basketball Association. The slam-dunk and the long 3-point shot are highlighted on *SportsCenter* and its competitors. Basketball players, knowing the value in frequency of highlight film during contract negotiations, emphasize the perfection of these "circus shots" at the expense of 12-foot jump shots. This may explain why few players can hit a mid-range jump shot and NBA teams seldom break 100 points scored in a game anymore.

Baseball is not much different. Film highlights comprise home runs, strikeouts, and bench-clearing brawls after a hit batsman. Experts attribute the spike in recent home run hitting, in part, to modern-day player's mentality of getting a few seconds of highlight film—even at the expense of striking out 150 times a season.

With ESPN having such a cultural stranglehold on the American male population, it stands to reason that terms like, "Cool as the other side of the pillow," "He's gone below the Mendoza Line" and "Back...back...back...back...back," take on lives of their own. Day after day, talking heads such as Chris Berman, Dan Patrick, and others on the sports highlight shows use this jargon.

Born as a baseball term, Mendoza Line is no longer used solely in the sport's lexicon. Anything, with some type of minimum acceptable numeric standard, is rife for being a Mendoza Line. You see this expression applied to everything, from the stock market, to school grade point averages, to oil pressure, even to a U.S. Senators' statement on the competency of a federal Circuit Court. It has been uttered on prime time TV. There is even a rock group that goes by the name, *The Mendoza Line.*

"Shreveport of the Texas League named Mario Mendoza as its new manager. So there you go. The Mendoza Line is 32.5 degrees north latitude."

-Steve Rosenbloom, *Chicago Tribune*

Chapter 2
THE MARIO MENDOZA STORY

The man named for the most famous line since Mason and Dixon, Mario (Aizpuru) Mendoza, was born in Chihuahua, Mexico on December 26, 1950. The unusually named city (translates as "dry and sandy place") is about 250 miles south of El Paso and serves as the capital of the largest state in Mexico. Chihuahua was also the birthplace of all-time minor league home run king Hector Espino (with 484) and renowned actor Anthony Quinn.

While it is an exaggeration to say Mario Mendoza was born with a fielder's glove on his hand, he must have excelled as an infielder at a very tender age. Oscar Soria saw Mario play throughout his career. He recalls this inspirational story of Mario Mendoza's origins in professional baseball:

> A guy named Noga was the manager in Hermosillo. Mario was a rookie. He was trying to be the shortstop. Mr. Noga told Mario, "You have nothing to do in baseball; you are wasting your time." So Noga sent Mario to the Navojoa Mayos. [It was with this team] where he started to show his potential in this business and started his great career.

Mario Mendoza impressed scouts with his superior range, sure hands, fluid motion, and strong, accurate throws to first. Signed as a 19-year-old free agent by the Pittsburgh Pirates, Mendoza quickly showed his defensive prowess. Brian Barsher, also a shortstop on the Pirates' 1971 spring training roster, recalled that Mario Mendoza's quickness in getting to the ball and quick release in his throw were convincing enough to make Barsher try his luck as a catcher.

One of Mendoza's earliest influences was the legendary Roberto Clemente. Mendoza worked out with the great Pirate outfielder during the spring training sessions of 1971 and 1972. Mendoza and other Hispanic minor leaguers would listen to Clemente's prophetic advice on overcoming the hardships of making it into the majors. So enthralled Clemente became when talking to the prospects, he would often miss dinner and continue his lectures through the evening. Mendoza and Clemente might have been teammates, had Clemente's life not tragically ended following a December 31, 1972 plane crash while on a humanitarian mission.

Mario Mendoza progressed well on his way to the big leagues. He led Carolina League shortstops with 79 double plays for Salem in 1972. His high-water mark with the bat came in 1973. While playing Double-A ball at Sherbrooke (Quebec), Mendoza posted career bests with 8 home runs, a .268 batting average, and 30 stolen bases. Mendoza was also named All-Star shortstop of the Eastern League.

Mendoza joined the Pirates early in the 1974 season. On May 17, he collected his first three hits of his major league career (with two runs scored) in a win over Chicago.

For the season, Mendoza hit .221 in 91 games. The Pirates of 1974 won the NL Eastern Division, but lost to the Los Angeles Dodgers in the National League Championship Series. In his only postseason action, Mario Mendoza got a chance to start game three after regular shortstop Frank Taveras injured his hand. Mendoza came through with an RBI single during Pittsburgh's only win of the series. Playing in three games, Mendoza finished with one hit in five at bats—a .200 average.

Mario Mendoza played with Pittsburgh through 1978. Frank Taveras got the nod over Mendoza at shortstop primarily because of his superior speed as a baserunner. Indeed, Taveras stole as many as 70 bases in one season, but seats behind first base became a battle zone when grounders were hit to him. Those same balls would have been routine outs for Mendoza.

Not only an excellent defenseman for the Pirates, Mario Mendoza was also a quite versatile utility player, also playing second and third base. He even pitched a couple of innings against the Cardinals in 1977. Mendoza allowed a home run during that outing and a line drive that struck him on the belt buckle, nearly causing an embarrassing situation.

Though most of Mendoza's appearances with Pittsburgh came as late-inning defense, he had a few interesting moments with his bat. In the 1976 season opener, a ground single by Mario Mendoza in the 11th inning gave the Pirates a 5–4 victory over the Phillies. Another clutch performance by Mendoza that year saw him stroke a final-inning double to beat the Houston Astros. Mendoza blasted his first major league home run in 1978, against Jim Barr, in a 6–2 conquest of the San Francisco Giants.

Mendoza was traded with Odell Jones and Rafael Vasquez, to the Seattle Mariners on December 5, 1978, in exchange for fellow Mexican Enrique Romo, Rick Jones, and Tommy McMillan. With the Mariners, Mendoza finally found himself in a starter's role. He appeared in 148 games as the everyday shortstop, batting a light .198. He set a record for most games played in a season while batting below .200 (Steve Jeltz tied that mark in 1988). He did have some highlights at the plate. His only home run of the year was an inside-the-park shot. Against the New York Yankees on July 11, Mario went 2-for-4 with two runs scored and three RBI in a 16–1 Mariners' rout. He even led the team in an offensive statistical category—sacrifice bunts with 13.

To no one's surprise, Mendoza's defense was outstanding. *Total Baseball* rated him the third-best defensive player in the major leagues during the 1979 season. In an article entitled "M's Singing Praises of Mendoza's Glove Magic," appearing in *The Sporting News*, Seattle beat writer Hy Zimmerman wrote how pitchers were praising the amount of runs Mario Mendoza saved them. Hall of Fame second baseman Bill Mazeroski, a coach for Seattle that year, commented, "Mario Mendoza is the best shortstop in the American League." "That's praise from Caesar," added Zimmerman. *TSN* later featured a photo of Mendoza in the midst of executing a rather spectacular 4–6–3 twin killing.

Tom Paciorek, the alleged inventor of the Mendoza Line, stated that Mendoza was one of the Mariners' most popular players and something of a clubhouse wag. Mendoza targeted grizzled veteran Willie Horton. Though in his late thirties, Horton played every game at DH for the 1979 Mariners and clouted 29 home run balls. Mendoza was forever giving Horton a hard time on everything from his age to never playing the field. According to Paciorek, Willie Horton used to always say to Mario Mendoza, "Get away from me, you crazy Mexican!" Paciorek, while sitting next to a sleeping Horton on a bus ride, claims that the slugger woke up screaming, "Get away from me, you crazy Mexican!"

In 1980, while George Brett made one of the closest charges to .400 in years, Mario was on a quest of his own—to break .300. From June 8 to June 16, Mendoza hit safely in nine straight games to elevate his batting average to a stratospheric .325. During that roll, Mario Mendoza homered and singled against Boston (June 10). Three days later, he collected a three-hit game and scored the winning run over Baltimore. Though he cooled considerably, Mendoza still was something of an offensive force, knocking two home runs with a .245 average—both major league career highs.

On defense, Mendoza played outstanding as usual. It is ironic that George Brett, who has given Mario Mendoza all the notoriety a person could ever ask for, told *The Sporting News* how slick-fielding Mario turned the tables on him:

> I remember going into a series in Seattle, think I went 2-for-12 with two home runs, but hit the ball on the nose like 10 times. It was one of those streaks. I remember Mario Mendoza, the shortstop for the Mariners, making two or three diving stabs up the middle. When that starts happening, you think, "Geez, I wonder if it's in the stars." You're hitting line drives right at someone and guys are diving for balls and catching them.

Part of an 11-player transaction with Seattle and the Texas Rangers, Mario Mendoza joined the Rangers for the 1981 season. Mario was elated over the trade, telling *The Sporting News*, "I know there are a lot of Mexican people in the Dallas-Fort Worth area, and that's going to motivate me to play better." Honed by a winter of Mexican League play, Mendoza proceeded to beat out another shortstop hopeful in Mark Wagner during spring training.

During the strike-marred 1981 campaign, Mendoza enjoyed a good year for a good team. Traditionally branded as "klutzy," Texas' infield defense improved with Mendoza's consistently slick fielding. Mendoza also hit in the .270s and delivered some clutch RBI. With Mario Mendoza hitting, Texas surged to first in the American League West. Just $1^{1}/_{2}$ games behind Oakland on June 12, baseball's long labor dispute curtailed nearly 40 percent of the season and dashed the Rangers' hopes of their first title. Mendoza's batting average faded and he finished the year at .231.

Mendoza played briefly for Texas in 1982, ending his major league career at 31 years of age with nine years of big league service, a .215 batting average, and 4 home runs in just under 700 games. On defense, Mario Mendoza's .961 career fielding average is one of the 100 highest ever for a shortstop. One could speculate that Mendoza could have secured a Golden Glove or two had he been a regular performer.

Could Mario Mendoza have been a more dominant hitter? Hard to say. He seemed big enough; at 5'-11" and 180 pounds for most of his career, he was the same stature as Hank Aaron. Mario possessed decent speed as well. One observation about Mario Mendoza is that even in his rookie days, he wore rather thick glasses. Ted Williams claimed that his vision was so acute, that he could see the stitches of an inbound Bob Feller fastball. Perhaps, Mario Mendoza lost a few key milliseconds trying to visually lock-on to the baseball.

After his major league career, Mario continued to play professional baseball in Mexico, batting .291 during seven seasons in the Mexican Summer League. Mendoza also played 18 years of winter ball in the Mexican Pacific League before, during, and after his career in the "Great Leagues," as the Mexicans refer to our major leagues. Representing his country in five Caribbean Series tournaments, Mario performed with great intensity and emotion, with Mexico's national pride at stake. While playing in the Mexican Leagues during the mid-1980s, Mario Mendoza was the league's equivalent of Derek Jeter. As Mario Mendoza's son recalled during an interview, his father was nicknamed "*Elegante*." Others dubbed him "*Manos de Seda*" (Hands of Silk). Women appeared in droves at games, as much for Mendoza's good looks as his grace in the field. They compared him to a ballet dancer. He even had groupies.

In 2000, Mario Mendoza received the ultimate honor of *immortale* by his countrymen. He was elected into the Mexican League Hall of Fame (Hall FAMA), the "South of the Border" equivalent to Cooperstown.

Throughout the 1990s, Mario Mendoza remained active in professional baseball. He has scouted in Mexico and managed in the Anaheim Angels' minor league system from 1992 to 2000. Bill Bavasi, the former General Manager of the Angels, actively recruited Mendoza for this position. As the son of San Diego Padres' one-time owner, Buzzy Bavasi, Bill was apprenticing for a front office position by literally starting at the "ground floor," working with the Padres' grounds crew.

When the Pirates came to town, young Bavasi took an immediate liking to Mario Mendoza, who was always joking with the grounds crew and even helping them fix the field or wet it down before the game.

Near the end of his professional playing career, Mario received a surprise when ex-groundskeeper Bill Bavasi, now the Angels' Minor League Director, visited Mario Mendoza in Mexico. Mendoza recalled the event during a radio interview:

> Billy saw me playing winter ball when we were in Tijuana for a game. He told me that when I was ready to quit, he would like me to work for the Angels. He remembered me when I was with the Pirates, that I was an easygoing guy, and that I treat those grounds crew real well. He liked me and he always kept it in his head that if I ever wanted a coaching job, he was going to give me a chance.

Mendoza has managed as high as the AA-level while with Midland of the Texas League. Five times, Mendoza led his teams into the playoffs. While managing the Lake Elsinore Storm of the Class A California League in 2000, he had the opportunity to manage his son, Mario Mendoza, Jr., a promising minor league pitcher. His career managerial record, as of the completion of the 2000 season, was 579–662.

Fans who have seen Mario Mendoza managing in the minors describe him as one of the friendliest people in baseball. He actually comes over and talks to fans before ballgames. However, Mendoza has never been too keen on the term "Mendoza Line." A man who played the game with such intensity and passion deserves to be remembered by something better than a less-than-complimentary colloquialism.

While Mendoza was managing the Angels' farm team in Palm Springs in the early 1990s, he went after a fan that was making light of his hitting. In another episode of emotion, while managing the Cedar Rapids Kernels of the Midwest League in 1997, Mario Mendoza rushed out of the dugout and argued a questionable home run call. After the manager kicked and threw dirt at the field umpire, like Billy Martin, the arbiter ejected Mendoza.

Former Angels' minor league player, John Pricher, recalls playing for skipper Mario Mendoza:

> I played for Mario for several seasons while in the Angels' organization. He did not talk about the line much, if any, unless asked. He was not particularly fond of being remembered in that way. In 1992, while in Palm Springs, a crowd of fans walked over to the dugout; people can see down the step. He [Mario Mendoza] was sitting there one afternoon and an [insensitive] fan says, "Hey Mario, how about that Mendoza Line?" Mario responded, "I got your Mendoza Line." He was a great manager to play for and a friend. He is able to teach the game he loves. Sometimes, players that have to work hard for their roles make the best managers.

At the present time of writing, Mario Mendoza is the new manager of the Shreveport Swamp Dragons. The Texas League club is the Class AA affiliate of the San Francisco Giants.

In the final analysis, Mario Mendoza's batting statistics may not support the claim that he was an asset to a team. However, in his five years with Pittsburgh, the Pirates won their division twice and finished runner-up three times. Before his trade to Seattle, the Mariners finished 56–104. With Mendoza as the everyday shortstop, the Mariners improved to 67–95 and escaped the American League West cellar. When he arrived in Texas for the 1981 season, the Rangers were coming off a sub-par year. Mendoza took over as shortstop and Texas finished in second place, only 5 games behind Oakland. Sure-handed infielders, like Mario Mendoza, remain an important building block to a successful team.

"...And now the pitcher holds
the ball, and now he lets it go,
And now the air is shattered by
the force of Casey's blow..."

-Ernest Lloyd Thayer's *Casey At The Bat*

Chapter 3
YE OLDE EASY OUT
1876-1899

Origins of the Game

The true "Father of Baseball" was New York City surveyor Alexander Cartwright. Credit him for establishing the first set of rules for the game. Some of Cartwright's rules remain extant today. They include the establishment of 42 paces between bases (believed to equate to 90 feet), first and third base foul lines, three strikes constituting an out, and three outs comprising a team's half-inning.

On June 19, 1846, Cartwright's Knickerbockers club played what is believed to the first recorded game of baseball. The Knickerbockers faced the New York Nine at the Elysian Fields in Hoboken, New Jersey, a popular resort at the time. The mostly labor-class Nine put a deep hurting on the upper crust, more genteel Knickerbockers by a score of 23–1. Alexander Cartwright umpired the game and exacted a fine of six cents from a player who swore at him.

The game's popularity grew rapidly, with amateur teams forming from Maine to California. By 1857, the first baseball league, the National Organization of Baseball Players, formed with 25 amateur teams.

The first truly professional ball club was Harry Wright's 1869 Cincinnati Red Stockings. The team had a complement of ten players and a payroll of $9,500. The Red Stockings played 64 games against the best amateur teams of the day, Cincinnati winning them all. The Red Stockings' main contribution to the sport was through their promotion of baseball. Drawing over 200,000 fans, their profitability made way for the emergence of new professional teams.

The Beginning of Organized Major League Baseball

In 1871, baseball's first professional league, the National Association, began play. Yet, the disorganization of this federation rendered it as not recognized as a true major league. In 1876, the first bonafide major league, the National League, formed. It is the same venerable league in existence today—the one without the designated-hitter rule. The founding teams were located in Boston, Chicago, Cincinnati, Hartford, Louisville, New York, Philadelphia, and St. Louis.

The National League of the 1870s was as tumultuous in the front office as it was on the field. Several franchises folded without completing a single season. Similar to today's free agency, early major leaguers routinely jumped from team to team for better contracts. To counteract contract jumping, the league established the reserve clause in 1879.

The American Association of Base Ball Clubs formed in 1882. Their marketing strategy revolved around a basic 25-cent admission price, undercutting the National League prices of 50-cents. The American Association also allowed member clubs the option of selling alcohol and playing Sunday games. To lure quality talent, the American Association initially operated without a reserve clause. In addition, they admitted players blacklisted by the National League. An American Association innovation, that remains intact today, was the hiring of a salaried cadre of umpires.

In its maiden season, whether for the baseball or the beer, all six teams did well at the gate. Early stars of the Association included outfielder Pete Browning of Louisville, the original "Louisville Slugger." Browning was the first player to have a custom bat made for him by woodworker John Hillerich of Hillerich & Bradsby fame.

The Association expanded to eight clubs the next year. By opposing the National League's reserve clause, the American Association lured a number of disgruntled National Leaguers into its ranks. Thus strengthened, the 1883 American Association staged another profitable campaign, which saw the Philadelphia Athletics edge the St. Louis Browns by a single game.

By now, the National League understood that it had some valid competition from the so-called "Beer and Whiskey League." The two leagues negotiated the National Agreement of 1883, which recognized the American Association as a major league and instituted World Series play between the two leagues. In the compromise, the American Association instituted the reserve clause.

Rival Leagues

The ink on the agreement between the National League and American Association was barely dry when a new league made a bid for major league recognition. The Union Association of Base Ball Clubs began operations in the fall of 1883. The short-lived league was the brainchild of real-estate magnate Henry Lucas of St. Louis. Functioning as a minor league in previous years, Lucas announced the Union Association as one not bound by the reserve clause. Lucas was able to siphon some talent from the existing National League and American Association.

Lucas' league began play in 1884 with eight teams. His fatal mistake was stockpiling the best talent for the St. Louis Maroons' franchise—which he happened to manage. So, while St. Louis thrived on the field (94–19 won-lost record) and at the gate, franchises in hamlets like Altoona, Pennsylvania fared miserably. Half the Union teams went bankrupt before the season concluded. Even feebler teams replaced them. The Unions ceased operation after its only year of existence.

After the demise of the Union Association, National League and American Association owners of the 1880s perfected the abuse of player's rights. These tactics included contracts below fair value, no means to place grievance for unfair fines, and a reserve clause that gave owners free rein to trade, release, or blacklist players.

This malevolent environment gave rise to the Brotherhood of Professional of Base Ball Players. It was the first-ever player's union. The brotherhood, formed in the mid-

1880s, was the brainchild of John Montgomery Ward of the New York Giants. Not only a star infielder, Ward was also a Columbia University-trained lawyer.

In 1889, Ward's attempt to forge a collective bargaining agreement between players and owners went sour. Undaunted, Ward put Plan B into effect. He obtained financial backing from would-be owners to organize a rival league. Like the failed Union Association just six years earlier, the Players' League intended to compete directly against the National League (and, to a lesser extent, the reeling American Association). It began play in 1890.

The Players' League actually offered better quality baseball than the National League at the time. It might have succeeded. However, the manipulations of the wealthier National League ownership—off the field—doomed the renegade league. Dirty-pool tactics against the Players' League included scheduling National League games on the same dates as Players' League games, bribing PL players to jump ranks, and raiding the American Association and minor league rosters for players. The media of the day also had a play in the Players' League demise. The National League's ownership's coercion of the press, through threats to withdraw advertising, resulted in Players' League attendance figures being falsely understated with minimal press coverage of the games.

Most Players' League owners were sinking in red ink, while their attempts to secure buyouts from National League rivals were fruitless. The National League owners quickly divided and conquered, gaining individual buyouts from Players League owners for far less than fair value. The following year, the American Association succumbed. For the remainder of the century, the 12-team National League operated as the sole major league in existence.

The Players

As for the ballplayers, although a handful were college-educated men, most were quite rough around the edges. Rowdy ruffians and boisterous drunkards ruled the day. The style of play, particularly in the 1890s, would look like something out of a modern-day professional wrestling match. One umpire was not enough to monitor all this chaos. Games were typically a snafu of spiking, tripping, punching, pushing, and grabbing of baserunner's belts. On-field fisticuffs were so commonplace; fighting for the pennant took a literal meaning. To the ear, the game was raucous. Noisy and mean-spirited chatter by the players on the field and from the dugout was incessant. Unruly fans launched epithets at opposing team players. If that did not faze the visitors enough, the fans launched beer bottles instead. Moreover, angels help the umpires. Arbiters were especially abused and sometimes assaulted, both by fans and disgruntled players.

Baseball of that day was not totally dirty and barbaric. When played cleanly, the game was colorful and exciting. The development of many strategies, still employed today, took place in this era: the hit-and-run, bunting the runner to second, the suicide squeeze, hitting to the opposite field to advance a runner, the hook slide, and other run-creating plays.

The equipment and the overall mentality of the game were not conducive to hitting home runs with any regularity. Bats were still crudely-designed instruments and balls remained in play even while beaten into oblong shapes. The century's home run king, Roger Connor, needed 18 years to amass 138 home runs. A modern-day player can achieve that figure in three seasons. Most home runs were either inside-the-park "run homes" or the benefit of some ball park nuance, like the 180-foot right field wall in Chicago's Lake Front Park. The triple, rather than the home run, served as the gauge of hitting prowess in the 19th century.

Many stellar talents took the field in the 1880s and 1890s. Players of note include Wee Willie Keeler, who stroked over 200 hits in eight consecutive seasons and hit for a .424 batting average in 1897. Keeler's oft-quoted secret to his success: "I hit 'em where they ain't." Adrian "Cap" Anson, considered by many to be the best player of the era, was another extraordinary talent. A 22-year first baseman (and manager for most of that time) for the Chicago White Stockings, Anson amassed 1,879 RBI, still ninth best all-time. King Kelly, Bid McPhee, and Sam Thompson are other 19th century hitters enshrined in the Hall of Fame.

Standouts on the mound included Pud Galvin. He won 46 games one season and 360 games overall—the most of the century. Amos Rusie, "The Hoosier Thunderbolt," possessed a fastball so feared, that he was the chief catalyst in getting the pitching distance moved, in 1893, from 50 feet to the 60'-6" still used today.

Above all, the players were white, save the brief appearance of Moses Fleetwood Walker and brother Welday Walker. The Walkers played just one season, in 1884, during the height of the infamous Jim Crow era. As members of the Toledo Blue Stockings of the American Association that year, Fleet Walker hit .263 in 42 games. Welday went .222 in five appearances. Shortly after the debut of the Walkers, an unwritten agreement by the owners effectively barred African Americans from playing major league baseball.

The Mendoza Line in the 19th Century

An examination of the dynamics of sub-.200 hitters for each era will conclude each history lesson. In the 1880s, there were 44 position players, with a minimum of 200 plate appearances, who batted below .200 for their career. This is, by far, the most of any single decade. Likely, this is allowable due to the advantage pitchers had in the days of the 50-feet distance between home plate and the pitcher's mound. The presence of numerous new teams from rival leagues gave opportunities to hitters who might not otherwise have had business in a major league batter's box.

In the 1890s, the number of sub-.200 hitters with at least 200 plate appearances declined to just 10. The lengthening in the distance from home to the pitcher's mound helped. Whereas the composite National League batting average was just .245 in 1892, it skyrocketed to .280 in the first year of the 60'-6" pitching distance, and crested as high as .309 in 1894.

Billy The Bruise
William Traffley, C
1859-1908

Some folks simply write off ancient catcher Bill Traffley as a man who forgot to bring a bat to the Majors. With a career .175 batting average, it is hard to dispute such claims. However, Traffley's career is full of curious points and coincides with the very origins of major league baseball. He goes back so far, he might have played in *Jurassic Park.*

If you think today's pro football players are tough, your typical NFL lineman would not have half the cuts and bruises an 1880s vintage catcher endured. Bill Traffley goes back to the days when catchers received fastballs from 50 feet away without the luxury of shin guards, chest protectors, and helmets. The catcher's mitt, as we know it, was not available in Traffley's day. Instead, only a fingerless, lightly padded item protected the hand. It was common for a catcher to insert a piece of steak into their glove to assuage the impact of ball to bone. Even the catcher's masks were primitive in nature; so while Traffley didn't take the brunt of a fastball in the face; sharp metal wire, coated with a thin layer of dogskin, jammed into his flesh. Upon reading of Bill's defensive feats, appreciate that being a 19th century catcher required as much bravery as an ancient gladiator.

William Franklin Traffley was born before the Civil War—1859 in Staten Island. He was the second-ever of 30 players hailing from the New York borough to appear in the major leagues. The Traffley's moved to Chicago early in Bill's childhood. Though just a teenager, Bill played shortstop for several elite amateur clubs in the Windy City. He was also versatile enough to play just about any position on the field. While Bill was playing catcher one day, the legendary Cap Anson just happened to be taking in a game. Traffley impressed Anson with his aggressive play, powerful arm, and surprising speed. He invited Bill to practice with his Chicago White Stockings of the National League—just in its third year of existence. Infielder and manager Bob "Death to Flying Things" Ferguson approved and added young Bill to the roster.

Traffley's size belied his youth. A powerfully built 5'-11$\frac{1}{2}$" and 185 lb., he was one of the larger men on the diamond. Only Anson—a 19th century leviathan at 6-feet and 227 pounds, would dwarf Traffley. In photos and drawings, Traffley sported a rather prominent mustache, which made him look older. Bill started two games for Chicago, getting one hit, a run scored, and one RBI in nine at bats.

Traffley would never play another game in the National League. Over the next four seasons, he caught for the Union Pacific Club, a semi-professional outfit based out of Omaha. Traffley's skillful work behind the plate earned him a reputation as one of the best defensive players in the west. In a single nine-inning game, Traffley was credited with 21 putouts.

Bill returned to major league baseball with the 1883 Cincinnati Red Stockings of the American Association. The July 1883 edition of *The New York Clipper* profiled Traffley and commented, "His performance behind the bat has been especially brilliant, and stamps him as a decided acquisition to the present champion nine. One of his strong points as a catcher is his throwing to the bases, which is remarkable both for accuracy and speed, and makes it a matter of impossibility for the most adroit base-stealer to make headway in that direction."

Traffley may have been one the first backstops in history to exclusively catch for a specific pitcher. According to the *Clipper*, Traffley "filled that [catcher] position to the pitching of [Ren] Deagle."

Traffley played acceptably in his 30-game hitch with the Red Stockings. However, it was unlikely that Bill would usurp the incumbent catcher, Charles "Pop" Snyder. After all, Snyder also made out the line-up cards as manager of the team. Near the end of the season, Cincinnati declined rights on Bill Traffley.

From there, Bill went to the Baltimore Orioles. Playing on a semi-regular basis, Bill enjoyed his most wondrous years as a major leaguer. However, during the 1884 spring training exhibition season, things went rather badly for Traffley. In one game, Traffley allowed an unfathomable five passed balls. His overall play behind the plate was described as "weak" by the *New York Times*.

When the championship (regular) season rolled around, Bill came alive. In his very first game with Orioles, Traffley doubled in a run—later coming around to score—and was mentioned in the *Times* as the Baltimores best fielder in an 8–3 rout of the New York Metropolitans. More standout games followed for Bill. On May 14, he was credited with three double plays, two unassisted, in a single game. In a May 23 tilt between Baltimore and host Brooklyn, both clubs took a well-played scoreless tie into the ninth inning. With two aboard, Bill slammed a triple that brought home the winning runs in a 3–0 shutout of Brooklyn.

For the 1884 Baltimore Orioles, Traffley stroked six triples—a surprisingly high number for just a .176 hitter. On defense, though the backup backstopper played less than half of the team's total games, Bill finished third in the league in catcher's double plays with six.

As for Baltimore, they ended the season a strong 63–43. The team drew a rather zealous group of fans. In a June 12 game against Louisville, which ended in a 13-inning draw due to darkness, Bill Traffley and the rest of the Orioles found themselves surrounded by an outraged mob. The five hundred or so crazed cranks (fans, as they were referred back then) were hell-bent in taking their wrath out on umpire John Brennan for calling a Baltimore runner out at third in the tenth inning. To protect Brennan, players from both teams encircled him—bats locked and loaded—to keep the fans at-length. After that debacle, team management erected a barbed-wire fence around the field.

Even the press joined in the fervor of umpire-baiting. In an August 22 tilt against the Pittsburgh Alleghenys, the *Baltimore Herald* wrote: "Without a doubt the finest and most interesting game of ball ever played on the Oriole grounds was that between the Baltimores and the Alleghenys yesterday afternoon, in which the home team defeated 10 men, including the umpire, by a score of 8 to 6."

In 1885, Baltimore finished in last place. Elevated to starting catcher, Bill Traffley's batting average plummeted to .154—among the worst ever for a regular. Traffley had his moments at the plate. He did connect for his only major league home run to go along with his five three-baggers that year. His heavy batting on July 30 and 31 led to five hits (including a trio of triples) and five runs scored in 11-2 and 10-7 beatings of the New York Metropolitans. Bill collected another 3-hit game on August 19.

On defense, ol' Bill made many a marvelous stop, saving runs for his team. He was ranked in the league's top-three for catcher's putouts, assists, and double plays. He also led all Association catchers with a .943 fielding percentage. More dubious in nature were his 104 passed balls allowed that year—the second highest total by a catcher in a season ever. Traffley probably had help in this category. He must have fished a lot of balls out of the dirt while catching the likes of Hardie Henderson (a league-leading 35 losses), Bob Emslie (3–10), and "Shorty" Wetzel (0-2 with an 8.47 ERA in the only two starts of his career). Some fish got away.

The following year, Bill became just a part-time player. One of Traffley's last hurrahs was a fine effort in an 11-7 loss to Brooklyn on June 11, where he went 2-for-4 with 3 stolen bases. By July, he became no player at all as Baltimore let him go and experimented with five other catchers. None of these "catchers du jour" amounted to much.

Another aspect of Bill Traffley's game showed up as scorekeeping and record keeping improved his final year. He swiped eight bases in just 25 games. Traffley's combined 11 triples in 1885 and 1886 were the second highest total of any Association catcher over that span. That indicates Bill Traffley was the 19th century's version of John Wathan— the speedy catcher of many years for the Kansas City Royals.

The 1886 Orioles remained in the cellar at 48–83. They came quite close to being the only ballclub in major league history to bat below the Mendoza Line for the year. Baltimore's miserable .204 BA is the lowest ever for a full season. At .212, Bill Traffley actually hit above the team's average. So, at least for his final year, Traffley remembered to bring his bat. Everyone else forgot.

Bill Traffley ended his professional career catching for the Des Moines Hawkeyes of the Western Association. He must have liked the Iowa city, as he remained there and worked as a saloonkeeper until his passing in 1908. He was 48. Traffley's occupation may provide some insight of why he died from cirrhosis of the liver.

Bill's kid brother, John Traffley, made it into one major league game as an outfielder with Louisville in 1889. It was quite a serendipitous event. John was a 27-year-old semi-pro player from Baltimore. It just happened that the horrid Louisville Colonels were in town in mid-June to play the Baltimore Orioles. With team morale as depressed as their 8–40 record, several players refused to suit-up after owner-manager Mordecai Davidson threatened to fine players $25 for each subsequent loss. Needing bodies in the outfield, John Traffley and a couple of his semi-pro teammates were signed on the spot by Davidson to play for Louisville. Traffley went 1-for-2 in the 4-2 loss to the Orioles, then was released after the striking players settled their dispute. Like his brother, John Traffley also died young, at age 38, as result of a head injury sustained in an accident.

The Louisville Plugger
Tom McLaughlin, SS
1860-1921

Tom McLaughlin and the city of Louisville are forever linked. He was born there, around the advent of the Civil War. He died there, in the summer of 1921. In addition, McLaughlin played his best ball there, back when the Kentucky city claimed a major league team. Tommy was a great defensive infielder. He was also a credible stickman. Generally, he batted over .200 in a given season. Had one wretched year with the bat not been part of his career ledger, McLaughlin would have had a batting average much higher than .192.

Tom McLaughlin remains somewhat of a mystery. The baseball encyclopedias do not list his height, weight, or his batting preference. Even the archives at the Baseball Hall of Fame do not possess a shred of data on McLaughlin. Game accounts referred to him as "little," so he was probably no taller than 5'-7". There is an extremely rare Old Judge Cigarettes baseball card of him, lean of face, moustached, and sporting a spotted tie. The only lasting legacies of the enigmatic McLaughlin are his very interesting set of batting and fielding statistics.

Tommy played his entire career in the American Association. In 1883, he became a mid-season addition for the Louisville Eclipse. Remarkably, the 23-year-old McLaughlin played seven different positions, mostly at shortstop and in the outfield. On September 13, McLaughlin had a spectacular game in a 4–1 victory against the New York Metropolitans. Not only did McLaughlin spark an eighth inning rally with a leadoff hit and run scored; he also fielded so brilliantly that the *New York Times* cited his gloveplay as "the feature of this hotly contested game."

Tommy McLaughlin became the starting shortstop for the renamed Louisville Colonels in 1884. He dazzled with his glove. McLaughlin led league shortstops with 34 double plays and, with an .891 fielding average, was barely beaten out for the lead in that category.

One of Tom's highlights that season occurred on June 22, with the Association-leading Metropolitans visiting Louisville. Ten thousand ball cranks attended—the largest crowd ever to see a game in Kentucky to that date. In the Colonels 10–2 manhandling of the visitors that day, Tom McLaughlin treated the throng of Louisville faithful to a brilliant defensive game at short while hitting a single and scoring a run.

Tom saved Louisville in a late-season game at Brooklyn. Trailing 3–1 in the eighth, McLaughlin hit a 2-run triple to tie the game and scored the winning run off a single by Pete Browning. The *New York Times* mentioned, "the sharp fielding of McLaughlin...prevented [the Brooklynites] from enlarging their base hit column."

With pitcher Guy Hecker's Association record 52 pitching wins, Louisville contended all year and finished 68–40—third of 13 teams. Anchored by the solid middle infield of McLaughlin and John "Move Up Joe" Gerhardt, the Colonels boasted the highest team fielding percentage and most double plays.

Moving over to second base in 1885, Tommy enjoyed a relatively prolific year. In the early part of the season, his play was distinctly spectacular. Yes, there were Tom's typical defensive gems, like the May 24 game against New York where he factored in 16 of the 27 opponent's outs in a 12–6 Louisville win, and his extraordinary 13 assists in a 10-inning win over Brooklyn on June 1. However, of greater interest was Tom's renaissance with the ash lumber.

From May 24 to June 1, McLaughlin went on a six-game hitting streak. During that skein, he totaled 10 hits, 6 runs scored, a double, 3 triples, and at least 4 RBI.[1] It marks one of the best six-game stretches by a below .200 hitter. While America celebrated her independence, McLaughlin batted 2-for-5 and scored three runs in a 13–7 pasting of the Metropolitans. Fresh from that fine performance, Tom hit his first career home run off Jack Lynch—a 37-game winner the year before—the very next day.

As the summer of 1885 marched on, a string of "Oh-for" games caused Tom's fairly credible batting average to evaporate like dew under the hot Louisville sun. Still, he ocassionaly produced worthy moments. With Louisville and the front-running St. Louis Browns locked 2–2 in the sixth inning of an August 30 match, the bases were loaded for Tom McLaughlin. Tommy promptly reversed a Bob Caruthers' fastball into an outfield gap for a bases-clearing triple, which broke the game open.

When the 1885 season was all over, Tom McLaughlin batted .212, scoring 49 runs and blasting nine triples. With 112 games played, he topped the Association, the only below .200 hitter to play every game in a complete season. Despite moving to a new position, McLaughlin still was among the league leaders in putouts and double plays.

In 1886, Tom McLaughlin moved to the New York Metropolitans. But, poor Tommy left his bat in Louisville. Whether it was being unaccustomed to the big city or just plain homesickness, McLaughlin's disastrous campaign with the stick produced an anemic .136 over 250 at bats. His slugging average proved an equally minuscule .156. McLaughlin's paltry batting kept him on the bench for the first half of the season. At least he had company. The New York Mets, who actually played their games in Staten Island, hit poorly and finished next-to-last in the Association with a 53–82 record.

Late in the season, Tom began to play more often, splitting time with Jack Nelson. New York fans were treated to some great defensive work in the middle infield. On August 19, the Mets beat borough-rival Brooklyn by a score of 5–1. On McLaughlin's fielding that game, The *New York Times* stated that McLaughlin's "picking up of difficult ground balls and his throwing to the bases were as pretty as anything seen on the diamond this season. In all, he accepted 13 chances without making an error."

Unfortunately, despite being one of the best defensive infielders in the game, McLaughlin did not play in the majors for the rest of the decade. He did try a comeback of sorts in 1891. In a 14-game appearance with the Washington Statesmen of the American Association, Tom achieved a .268 batting average—a mark he could not touch in his prime. Using dozens of Association-retreads like McLaughlin, the expansion Statesmen finished with a horrible 44–91 cellar-dweller finish in their only season of existence.

Thus ended the brief career of Tommy McLaughlin. The year 1891 also marked the end of the American Association. The Louisville Colonels joined the National League the following year, competing in the league until 1899. At the turn of the century, Louisville

---

[1] A conservative estimate, since RBI was not accurately recorded then.

merged with the Pittsburgh Pirates. McLaughlin returned to Louisville to work as a brass finisher. He died of cancer at age 61, a widower at the time.

Tom McLaughlin possessed a very dependable glove and exceptional versatility as he could play every position outside of the battery. He was also one of the rangiest infielders of the day; twice, he was runner-up in the Association for most fielding chances per game. Contest after contest, McLaughlin handled numerous chances without a miscue. With baseball gloves rudimentary at best and field conditions often deplorable, this was no trivial pursuit. During drought conditions, infields remained rock-hard and made ground balls zip across as if they were hit off modern-day Astroturf. However, 19th century infielders did not get true artificial turf hops. Assorted ruts, rocks, and pebbles were strewn across the dirt and grass of early ball fields. That didn't daunt McLaughlin from making the play.

Tom McLaughlin's batting record hardly qualifies him as a Louisville Slugger. However, for defending the gaps in the middle infield, this man could aptly be called a "Louisville Plugger."

Hammerin' Hank
Henry Easterday, SS
1864-1895

A formidable middle infielder, Henry Easterday's career .180 batting average supports the claim that his offensive numbers were...well, quite offensive. A closer look at Easterday's batting records show Henry was no cream-puff hitter. Easterday's numbers evidence surprising power and speed. In terms of the total package, he was a pint-sized 5'-6" and 145-pound dynamo.

Henry's unusual surname is the English translation of the German Ostertag. Unlike most German names, which refer to the original bearer's occupation or some physical characteristic, Ostertag refers to the sacred Christian holiday. Easterday's descendants emigrated from Germany in the 18th century and settled in Philadelphia.

Signed as a 19-year-old by the newly established Union Association's Philadelphia Keystones, Easterday logged 28 games at shortstop, hitting for decent wood with a .243 batting average. Near the bottom of the Union Association standings at 21–46 when it disbanded in August, the City of Brotherly Love already owned second-division clubs in the National League and American Association. Little affection remained for a third losing ballclub.

Although Henry lacked the requisite games to qualify as a top fielder, Easterday claimed the highest fielding average among Union shortstops with an .875 tally. Making one error every eight chances may not sound so good today, but considering the baseball gloves of Henry's era were about as useful as an oven mitt, it is quite spectacular.

When 1885 rolled around, neither the Union Association, nor Henry Easterday were present. Easterday toiled in the minors until a new opportunity availed itself four years later.

In 1888, the expansion Kansas City Cowboys, of the American Association, needed a new shortstop. Easterday was their man. For a lad from big city Philadelphia, Kansas City must have been a shock to the system. Life in the burgeoning cow town was quite raw in those days. Kansas City had few paved streets or sidewalks. Mud and horse manure caked the ground. As bad as the ballclub was, some cranks might have believed the mud and manure was especially heavy on the Cowboys' bench.

The team employed three managers and finished deep in the cellar at 43–89. The Cowboys were a meager hitting lot with their collective .218 batting average. Only one regular, third baseman Jumbo Davis at .267, batted over .250. Henry Easterday contributed to the hitting malaise by playing in 115 games at shortstop and batting .190. Easterday did manage to somehow hit 3 home runs and steal 23 bases.

As bad as Kansas City stick work was, their dead-last pitching featured suffering Henry Porter, a 37-game loser. Remarkably, Porter also tossed a no-hitter on June 6. The Cowboys also finished next-to-last in fielding. Jumbo Davis committed five miscues in a single game.

Henry Easterday blossomed as a noble flower in a quarry of stone gloves. Finishing statistically as the best defensive shortstop in the majors that year, Easterday's 3.99 assists per game rank as the ninth-best in a season ever. In a July game, Henry threw out ten Brooklyn Bridegrooms' players. Henry's defensive accomplishments that year are more astounding considering Kansas City's ballfield, Exposition Park, had the worst-tended grounds in all of baseball. Perhaps the club couldn't afford a good rake. It didn't matter. Henry Easterday handled the rutty diamond with a cocky nonchalance, making tough plays look routine.

Rookie Herman Long, who later became one of the great shortstops of the 1890s, replaced Easterday in 1889. Kansas City sent Easterday packing to the Columbus Colts, where his batting average plunged to .173 in 95 games. Nevertheless, in that one season, Hank Easterday hit more like Hank Aaron. The impish Easterday socked four home runs to tie for team leader, quite a commendable feat.

Like Kansas City and Philadelphia, Columbus was another losing ballclub. Yet, they had their moments. On June 24, the 19–32 Colts stumbled into Brooklyn to play one of the best teams in the Association. Surprisingly, the Colts upended the Bridegrooms that day. The following day, Easterday's home run off Bob Caruthers, the winningest pitcher of the Association that season, contributed to another startling victory over Brooklyn. After the jubilant Columbus players returned to their hotel, Henry and the rest of the team celebrated to excess and broke out in a raucous Indian war dance ceremony. They must have been a bit overexuberant in their revelries because they lost the final game of the series rather soundly.

Easterday toiled for three different Association teams in 1890. First, he appeared in 58 games for Columbus. With a totally revamped lineup and diluted talent throughout the league, Columbus improved from a losing club to a contender. During his time with the Colts that season, Henry's average slid to .157 with one home run and one arrest. The bust came after the entire Columbus team and the hometown Rochester team violated New York blue laws by playing a Sunday game.

Henry Easterday must have had mixed emotions when sent to the Philadelphia Athletics. Easterday left a fine team for a mediocre one; but he was back home. In 19 games, he added another home run and averaged nearly one run scored per game. Unfortunately, the shoddily-run Athletics fared so poorly at the gate that the team's accountants informed management they had no operating income in mid-September. The team sported a 54–56 record with 22 games still on the schedule. While the team sold many of their better players to other teams to recoup losses, others, like Easterday, were simply released. Rather than close shop, Philadelphia management placed a near sandlot bunch on the field. The "Un-Athletics" managed to lose all 22 of their remaining contests.

Henry's final seven games were with the Louisville Cyclones. After being with several teams straight from Mudville, Henry finally got to play for a winner with the Cyclones.[2] The 1890 Louisville club accomplished the "worst-to-first" turnaround in the talent-starved Association of 1890.

In the 1890 National League vs. American Association "World Series," Louisville tied the Brooklyn Bridegrooms, 3-games-to-3 with one draw. They did not play a tiebreaker. The announced reason: bitterly cold Brooklyn weather. However, truth be known, apathy spelled doom for the Series. Easterday did not appear in the Series, but during an off day made an appearance for the Cyclones in an exhibition game against an outfit of former Louisville ballplayers, which included Tom McLaughlin.

Thus ended the playing career of Henry Easterday; a fascinating odyssey through the American Association's most remote outposts. In four years, he was usually the starting shortstop for his team. Considering that his batting average declined from .243 down to .083, it's amazing he endured. Henry is the only sub-.200 player to score over 40 runs in three consecutive seasons. Finally, he was one of the best defensive infielders of his day—an artist at short.

Henry was barely 30 years old when he died on March 30, 1895. Ironically, Easterday's demise came just 15 days before Easter Day.

Philly Phlash
Charlie Bastian, 2B
1860-1932

Charlie Bastian was a 19th century wizard of the middle infield. Like Tom McLaughlin and Henry Easterday, Charlie Bastian was also diminutive in size (5'-6" and 145 lbs.) and career batting average (.189). While this triad of splendid shrimps is among the most accomplished below .200 batsmen ever, Bastian is the best of the three. While the aforementioned infielders made their mark mostly with also-ran clubs in the American Association, Charlie enjoyed his finest years with winning teams in the National League,

---

[2] The nickname of the Louisville team came after a particularly devastating tornado wracked Louisville.

the premiere league of the day. He is also a veritable Ty Cobb among sub-.200 hitters as he leads them all in runs scored (241), triples (26), and stolen bases (57).

Bastian was born in the city where America declared her independence, and his birth occurred 84 years to the day. His professional baseball saga began in 1883 for a club in Trenton, New Jersey. Charlie stayed closer to home the following year playing for the Wilmington Quicksteps of the Eastern League. The team romped and won the Eastern League pennant on August 15 with a 51–12 record. They quickstepped past the eventual American Association champion, the New York Metropolitans, by a score of 8–6 in an August 4 exhibition game.

A huge contributor to Wilmington's success, second baseman Bastian once played ten consecutive errorless games. Remarkable, considering the primitive state of fielding gloves and inconsistent conditions of 19th century diamonds. He led Eastern League second sackers with a .932 fielding average.

Like something out of a sports fantasy movie, the minor league Quicksteps were invited into the "major leagues" as a replacement for the defunct Philadelphia Keystones of the Union Association. Things looked promising after Wilmington beat Washington 4–3. However, the uplifting tale would soon end for the Quicksteps.

Player defections to the American Association and National League doomed Wilmington. Without an existing reserve clause to bind players to their contracts, the Quicksteps could not outbid clubs offering six-fold increases in salaries. As a reference point, Charlie Bastian earned $175 per month. A "hard working" laborer of the time took home $30 a month. The loss of talent crippled Wilmington, as they stumbled through their next sixteen games with only one win. With average attendance rarely exceeding 500 patrons, the team faltered as badly at the gate as they did on the field.

The Quicksteps' death knell occurred on a cold and overcast September 15, 1884, when they hosted a game against the Kansas City Cowboys. Wilmington manager Joe Simmons looked at the empty stands—as in zero paid attendance empty—and realized the club would not be able to pay the $60 minimum to the visitors.

The players were incensed at the Wilmington *unfaithful*. "This is an outrage," screamed one player. "To hell with these fair weather fans. Disgusting," added Bastian. Simmons gathered the team and announced, "No game today, boys," then summarily pulled his squad off the field and forfeited the game. The team folded just a few days later. Finishing 2–16, Wilmington owns the lowest winning percentage by a major league team (.111) and major league baseball's all-time lowest team batting average (.175 in their partial season).

After Wilmington's demise, the Kansas City Cowboys signed Charlie and took him west with them. Although not much better than Wilmington, going 16–63, at least Kansas City home games were well attended and the team actually realized a profit.

Charlie Bastian's composite record with both teams indicates surprising punch with four doubles, a trio of three-baggers, and three home runs in just 106 at bats. That equates to a high slugging average of .377, nearly double his .198 batting average. A player such as 1980s super-slugger Rob Deer secured comparable numbers. Bastian even pitched one game for Wilmington, ending up with a 3.00 ERA in six innings of work.

In 1999, media "talking heads" pointed out that Sammy Sosa could become the first player to hit as many or more home runs in a season than his team, the Cubs, posted wins.

In fact, Charlie Bastian's two homers with Wilmington matched his team's quantity of wins. Bastian was the only Quickstep to hit a home run.

Bastian's most interesting years were with his hometown Philadelphia Quakers (later known as the Phillies) of the National League from 1885–1888. Highly-touted, Bastian did well in the exhibition season and started the 1885 season as the Quakers' number-three hitter in the lineup. As Charlie's batting average faltered under .150 by early June, he was relegated into the bottom of the batting order.

After disappointing his hometown fans with the bat, Charlie finally solved National League pitching near the close of the season. First came a long RBI double on September 7 in a 3–1 win over the New York Giants. The next day, in Providence, Charlie punched two of just three Quakers' hits, one which helped score the only run of the game. On the 17th of the same month, Charlie cracked a two-run homer that provided Philadelphia insurance runs in a 6-3 defeat of Buffalo. Bastian closed the 1885 season with a 5-for-10 flurry in his final two games.

In his first year with Philadelphia, Charlie hit for a scant .167 batting average, the lowest season average ever for a shortstop (minimum 350 at bats). Bastian often failed to put bat to ball; he struck out a league leading 82 times in 389 at bats. His strikeout frequency is the fifth highest in the entire 19th century. However, Bastian scored 63 runs, the all-time season high for any sub-.200 hitter, and anchored an airtight infield as the everyday shortstop.

Moving to second base in 1886, Bastian delighted hometown fans with improved batting and sensational fielding. Greased lightning on the basepaths, Bastian ran out 11 triples and stole 29 bags. That year, Bastian also batted a personal best .217. With his glove, he led all second basemen with a .945 fielding average. To make Bastian's pinnacle season complete, the Philadelphia club flourished. They finished 71–43.

Playing more of a utility role in 1887, Charlie batted .213 in 60 games. For years, his statistics showed him playing only 59 games. However, research by Clifford S. Kachline uncovered many so-called "phantom ballplayers," defined as names formerly listed in the all-time record who never truly existed. In Bastian's case, a typographical error caused the entry of a "Boylan," playing one game for Philadelphia at second base in 1887. Later corrected on Bastian's behalf, "Boylan" no longer appears in the all-time ledger.

In 1888, a young Irish lad from Cleveland arrived and competed with Charlie for the starting second base job. Though the rookie's stats did not appear much better than Bastian's, the Phils decided by mid-season that Ed Delahanty was worth keeping. With Delahanty's lifetime .345 batting average, fourth best all-time, the Philadelphia ballclub made a rare good assessment in a long history of bad personnel decisions. Charlie did get into 80 games, including several at third base.

Despite a .193 average in 1888, Bastian had many intriguing games. On July 31, he enjoyed a day of what the *New York Times* called, "especially heavy and opportune work with the stick." He had four hits in a 6–5 victory over Boston. From August 8–15, Bastian fine glove work help propel Philadelphia to a 7-game winning streak. The *New York Times* referred to Bastian's fielding as "notably sharp and clean."

Charlie's most controversial game of the 1888 season occurred on August 23 against the eventual champion New York Giants. Bastian looked like a goat when he dropped a fly ball to give New York a 1–0 lead in the fifth inning. In the sixth, with one out, Bastian scorched a liner through the infield for a single. On a hit-and-run, Ed Delahanty foul-tipped the ball back to Giants' captain and Hall of Fame catcher Buck Ewing for the second out. Bastian scrambled madly to get back to first, but Ewing zipped the ball there. It was a close play; however, most observers, especially the Giants, thought the inning was over. Bastian smartly stayed on the bag and brushed the dirt off his trousers as if he beat the throw by three steps.

"Not out," roared Umpire Valentine.

"You're joking," said Ewing.

"No. I'm in earnest," was the reply.

"Then if you are," answered a seething Ewing, "you have made the greatest mistake of your career as an umpire."

The crowd rattled Valentine with their fever-pitched screams of outrage. However, when the umpire saw Charlie Bastian flash a smile back at him, Valentine then knew he had made the wrong call. Philadelphia took advantage of the extra out. After a single put him on second, Bastian came around to score from second when a flustered Ewing dropped a third strike, then threw the ball into right field. The Phillies scored two more in the inning and held on to win 3–2.

Although Bastian was a local favorite, Ed Delahanty made Charlie an expendable commodity on the Phillies' roster. Latching on to Cap Anson's Chicago White Stockings in 1889, Bastian batted an anemic .135 with zero extra-base hits. He literally did not even slug his weight that year. Bastian even suffered the humiliation of batting ninth, *behind* the pitcher. So desperate for a hit one game, Charlie tried to bunt and leg-out a single. Anson, who always considered the bunt a weak and pitiful act, was not pleased. When Bastian returned to the dugout, Anson towered over him, shoved an index finger into his chest, and warned him, "Cut out the baby act or else I'll cut you loose."

However, Anson must have been pleased with Bastian's defensive excellence in a July 25 game at Indianapolis. Playing first base, Anson recorded 10 of his 15 putouts from Bastian's accurate throws at second base. With an additional four putouts, no errors, a single, and run scored in the 10-inning, 7–6 win, Bastian was undoubtedly the star of the game.

In 1890, Charlie found himself in one of baseball's most intriguing episodes of player-management rivalry, the revolt of the Players' Brotherhood League. Important to its financial well being would be the establishment of a successful team in Chicago. Not so easy, considering the huge popularity of the established White Stockings. However, White Stockings' second baseman Fred Pfeffer gained the financial backing of John Addison, a prosperous contractor, to attract a nucleus of the White Stockings players to the new league.

The makeup of the Players' League Chicago Pirates was a veritable who's who of 19th century stars. They included third baseman Ned Williamson, center fielder Jimmy Ryan, right fielder Hugh Duffy, and catcher Duke Farrell. Another Chicago White Stocking to jump ship was Charlie Bastian, who probably just wanted to get away from Anson. Bastian became the team's starting shortstop. The rest of the starting lineup consisted of players from the St. Louis Browns, the American Association pennant-winners from 1885–1888. Prominent players from the Browns were first baseman-manager Charlie Comiskey, third baseman Arlie Latham, left fielder Tip O'Neill, and pitcher Silver King.

The Pirates were hands-down favorites to win the first Players' League pennant. Indeed, Silver King and fellow pitcher Mark Baldwin combined for 64 wins between them and the outfield of Williamson, Ryan, and Duffy all batted over .300. However, other than Farrell and the outfielders, no one else managed to bat over .260. As expected, light-hitting Charlie Bastian produced only 29 RBI and a .191 batting average. Though the Pirates outdrew the White Stockings by 50,000 fans, they failed to live up to their potential and finished a disappointing fourth, 10 games behind the Boston entrant of the Players' League.

After the Players' League disintegrated, before they could play another season, many men scrambled to gain membership back into the two existing leagues. Lost in the shuffle was Charlie Bastian. In 1891, he appeared in just one game with Cincinnati in the American Association's final year of existence. In four at bats, Bastian went hitless. That single game in the American Association makes Bastian one of a select few to play in four different major leagues. Later that year, Bastian made a final curtain call in his hometown, appearing in one game for the Philadelphia Phillies.

A man with such deft hands, as Charlie, would naturally transition into a carpenter following his playing career. Living in Pennsauken, New Jersey, just across the Delaware River from Philadelphia, Bastian worked in this trade right up to his death by heart attack in 1932. He was 71.

After his demise, Bastian's name resurfaced by virtue of a claim by one Daniel M. Casey. A competent southpaw pitcher with the Phillies in the 1880s, Casey purported that he was the subject of Ernest Thayer's poem *Casey at the Bat*. Casey pointed to the fact that the area where the Phils played was known as Mudville. He also cited that the poem's Flynn and Blake, the batters on base when Mighty Casey struck out, were based on Charlie Bastian and Joe Mulvey. Both were light-hitting infielders who preceded Casey in the order. The story earned Casey an appearance on a nationally-aired radio program in 1938. What was never mentioned was that this "mighty" Casey had a career batting average even lower than Bastian's.

As a player, two adjectives often preceded Charlie Bastian's name in the newspapers: "little," and "clever." While Bastian's stature may explain the "little", "clever" was a 19th-century term used to describe particularly alert and cunning ballplayers. It was a high compliment and well-deserved for one of the greatest all-around below .200 hitting players.

"Baseball is the very symbol, the outward and visible expression of the drive and push and rush and struggle of the raging, tearing, booming nineteenth century."

-Mark Twain, 1889

"The pressure never lets up.
Doesn't matter what you did
yesterday. That's history.
It's tomorrow that counts.
So you worry all the time.
It never ends. Lord, baseball
is a worrying thing."

-Stan Coveleski, Hall of Fame pitcher, 1912-1928

Chapter 4
DEAD BATS SWINGING AT DEAD BALLS
1900-1919

Baseball in the early 20th century survived a "best of times/worst of times" phase. Early on in this period, the sport enjoyed a renaissance. The National League pared down from a 12-team structure to an eight-team format in 1900. The Western League moved teams into Washington and Baltimore, cities that the National League vacated in 1900, and attained major league status as the eight-team American League in 1901.

Rather than feud to each other's detriment, the two leagues adopted standardized rules. This culminated in the establishment of the modern World Series in 1903. Many mark this event as the frontier between archaic and "modern" baseball.

Other factors helped to popularize the game. State-of-the-art ballparks, such as Philadelphia's Shibe Park, New York City's Polo Grounds, and Boston's still-extant Fenway Park, were constructed. Team loyalties to their respective burgs solidified. Likewise, a city's prestige correlated to the success of their ball team. Diamond deities like Honus Wagner, Nap Lajoie, and Christy Mathewson were subjects of songs and poems in their host cities. The game was now referred to as "The National Pastime." Through it all, attendance swelled everywhere.

During this period, the style of play seemed exactly as Alexander Cartwright envisioned. The balls of the day were far less resilient than later years, but probably no less "dead" than the balls of the 19th century. With a sphere further deadened by tobacco spit, scuff marks, and excessive use (balls weren't taken out of play until they looked and felt something akin to a rotten eggplant), hitting a home run was not a viable strategy. Playing for one run at a time, bunting, placement hits, and shrewd baserunning were the routes to triumph. Games often were low-scoring affairs. Dominant teams typically possessed great pitching and solid defense.

Other factors decreased overall slugging. A larger home plate meant a larger strike zone. In 1901, the National League adopted the foul ball strike rule (the American League followed suit in 1903). Before then, a player could simply foul balls off with no penalty to the count.

The archetype Dead Ball Era hitter was Ty Cobb of the Detroit Tigers. He is the owner of an untouchable .367 career batting average. As great a player as he was, Ty Cobb lived with the stigma of never playing for a World champion and having such a wretched personality, it makes one wonder if Ty was short for Tyrannosaurus.

Home run production actually increased following the introduction of the cork-centered ball in 1910. A few Dead Ball players could park the ball. In the National League, Gavvy Cravath was a 6-time home run king, hitting as many as 24 for the Philadelphia Phillies in 1915. His numbers have to be tempered with the fact that Cravath took great advantage of the short right field porch of the oddly dimensioned Baker Bowl. There were few American League sluggers of prominence until a pudgy and irascible

Baltimoran named Babe Ruth gave up a probable Hall of Fame pitching career to concentrate on being a full-time outfielder. Ruth's 29 four-baggers in 1919 whet baseball fans' appetite for the home run.

Multiple events doused the American public's enthusiasm with baseball during the close of the Dead Ball Era. A third major league, the Federal League, competed from 1914 to 1915. It saturated the market and diluted the quality of talent in the established leagues. The nation's involvement in World War I put a damper in the nation's interest in leisure activities. That caused many major league teams to lose money and led to the demise of several minor leagues. Even the 1918 influenza pandemic kept away fans wary of catching the dreaded disease in the crowded venue of ballparks.

Damaging to the game's image was the notion of games being fixed. Hal Chase, a talented first baseman, was known to bet on his opponent. Though never formally accused, Chase wore out his welcome everywhere he played. Members of the Cincinnati Reds admitted in court that they deliberately lost games. More damaging was the "Black Sox Scandal," where eight members of the Chicago White Sox, including Shoeless Joe Jackson, were accused of fixing the 1919 World Series. Though eventually acquitted of criminal charges, the eight players would receive lifetime suspensions from baseball.

Ray Chapman's 1920 on-field death by an errant Carl Mays fastball was yet another blow to baseball's public image. Tainted with scandal and mistrust, major league baseball's very survival was in question.

From 1900 to 1909, there were 17 position players, with a minimum of 200 plate appearances, who batted below .200 for their career. That number increased to 27 players the following decade.

The common link through both decades was the dominance of pitchers. Unlike today's major league players, where the best athletes tend to be outfielders, the finest physical specimens in the early 20th century resided on the pitcher's mound. Several pitchers of the Dead Ball Era rank with the greatest of all time. A sampling of these pitching legends includes Cy Young, Walter Johnson, Christy Mathewson, Grover Cleveland Alexander, Eddie Plank, and Three Finger Brown (who actually had four fingers). Illegal pitches, such as the spitter and the scuff ball, were permissible and further tilted the advantage to the pitcher.

In some cases, it was such a mismatch, that pitchers of the Dead Ball Era would actually work the bottom of the order the same way a National League pitcher of today works the opposing pitcher when he comes to bat. Without the threat of the home run, the better pitchers could save their best stuff for the likes of a Ty Cobb or Honus Wagner. This strategy had a profound effect in the high number of complete games pitched during the era.

Another factor was tacit acceptance that certain position players did not have to hit much to hold a job. Catchers functioned largely as defensive specialists. This rationale generally applied, though to a lesser extent, to middle infielders.

Finally, with the advent of a second league (and for two years—a third league) the player pool increased. This introduced lower caliber hitters into the game.

Fritz
Fred Buelow, C
1876-1933

Mike Shatzkin's book, *The Ballplayers*, contains the following on Fritz Buelow: "A dreadful hitter, Berlin-born Buelow was competent enough in the field to share catching duties on three AL teams." For a man who played nine seasons in the majors with nearly 1400 plate appearances, Fritz should have merited a bit more history to the game of baseball.

Born in Germany, Frederick William Alexander Buelow moved to Detroit at an early age. He quickly learned the distinctly American game of baseball, playing on his high school team. After a four-year apprenticeship in the minor leagues, the St. Louis Perfectos of the National League gave Buelow a trial late in the 1899 season.

St. Louis must have initially thought they had the next Honus Wagner. Buelow impressed early by batting an astounding .467 and slugging .733 in seven games. Buelow's heroics included catching a game for the great Cy Young. Fred also secured a 3-hit game in a 10–3 trouncing of the Cleveland Spiders. In another game, Buelow made a great tag at home to preserve a 4–3 triumph over Cleveland. It is no coincidence that a green rookie like Buelow would have some great games against the Cleveland Spiders. At 20–134, they own the worst full-season record of any team in major league history.

Nicknamed "Fritz," a common nickname for players of German ancestry ("Dutch" was the other), Buelow became a victim of the sophomore jinx in 1900. After spending most of the season in the minors, his second cup of coffee was not as sweet as his first; he batted only .235 and fielded poorly in six games.

In 1901, Fritz Buelow jumped to the newly formed American League as a member of the Detroit Tigers. Buelow shared catching duties with Sport McAllister and Al Shaw. In that era, most teams split up the catching assignments, as the result of the pounding on a catcher's lightly-protected body. Of the three, Buelow caught most of the games, starting 69 of the Tigers' 136 contests in their maiden season. Fritz Buelow's finest year produced his first two career home runs, 29 runs batted in, and a .225 batting average. He also fielded his position quite well, as he tied for the league lead in fielding average.

Fritz started in Detroit's first-ever game, one for the ages. Trailing Milwaukee 13–4 going into the bottom of the ninth, the Tigers put on a miracle rally for a stunning 14–13 victory. It remains the greatest opening-day comeback in big league history. Fritz caught a September 15 contest against Cleveland. The Detroits gave their fans plenty to cheer about, leading 21–0 in the seventh inning. The game was mercifully cut short as the Cleveland team had to catch a train to their next scheduled road game. Detroit would finish their debut season 74–61, good enough for third place.

Fritz Buelow's 1902 batting statistics mirrored his 1901 season. On defense, Buelow had a waning year. He fell from leading the American League in fielding average in 1901 to leading American League catchers in errors with 20. The 1902 Tigers also deteriorated to 52–83, finishing seventh out of eight teams.

That same year, Buelow was involved in one of the oddest baserunning plays ever. Catching against the Philadelphia A's, Dave Fultz was on third and Harry Davis was on first. To fool the Tigers, Fultz and Davis attempted a double steal. Davis broke for second, hoping to draw a throw from Buelow, to allow Fultz to run home. However, Buelow did not throw and Davis took second base uncontested. Fultz stayed put. On the next pitch, Davis raced back to *first base*! Baffled and incredulous, Buelow implored the home plate umpire to impart some sanity. However, the umpire's "non-call" indicated his own befuddlement. At the time, nothing in the rules forbid this maneuver.[3] On the next pitch, Davis attempted to steal second again. This time Buelow fired the ball to second base and Fultz scored on the play. The stealing of first would happen two other times, both in 1908. Rule 7.08(i) was later created to prevent such a ploy.

Before the start of the 1903 season, club morale suffered after the suicide of newly-named manager Win Mercer. Despite the loss, Fritz Buelow kept the Tigers' hearts alight during this somber time. Though rarely smiling in pictures, Buelow was a hail-fellow-well-met, a glad-hander, and even a wag. Buelow loved to tell anyone within earshot about his episodes with manager Ed Barrow.

As the story goes, Buelow and Deacon McGuire were the only catchers in spring training camp in Ed Barrow's first year as manager. Barrow, a staid and dignified gentleman, considered his players from a lower caste and avoided any familiar contact with them. Buelow caught on to this and used it to get at "Gentleman Ed's" craw. Fritz would walk right up to Barrow, slap him on the shoulder, and inquire, "How're you today, Ed?" Outraged at this indignation, Barrow chastised the catcher, "That's Mr. Barrow, if you please. Remember it's Mr. Barrow." All the while, Barrow fixed a cold stare at Fred. "Alright, Ed," Buelow replied as he strolled away. This left Ed Barrow seething.

After an afternoon practice, Barrow became concerned when both his catchers were AWOL from the team dinner. The manager ordered his players to comb Shreveport for his missing maskmen. When Barrow retired for the night, there was still no sign of Buelow or McGuire.

The next morning, Barrow continued the search. No sooner did Barrow walk into the hotel bar, that he saw his catcher corps propped up against the bar, singing the hit song of the day, *Always Leave Them Laughing When You Say Goodbye*. As Buelow loved to tell it, Barrow was not laughing. After a verbal diatribe, Barrow was on the verge of saying "good riddance" to his wayward catchers.

"And who will be your catcher, Ed?" Fritz Buelow whimsically asked, knowing Barrow's threats were of the idle variety. The two catchers remained with the team for the entire season. Ed Barrow must have learned a little from Fritz about handling people. He would manage Boston and Babe Ruth to a World Series title in 1918 and later become baseball's first true general manager with the great Yankees' teams of the 1920s and 1930s.

In 1903, Fritz batted .214, the last season he would ever bat over .200. He also stroked six triples. Detroit closed the season with a 65–71 record. Of note that year, Detroit acquired another player who would hit more three-baggers than Fritz. That man was "Wahoo" Sam Crawford—baseball's all-time leader in triples. Crawford and Ty

---

[3] Buelow could have thrown to first and Davis could have been tagged out.

Cobb, who joined the team in 1905, made up the nucleus of Detroit's pennant-winning teams later in the decade.

The descent of Fritz Buelow's batting average began in 1904. For unknown reasons, Fritz's once-modest batting plummeted, making him an All-American out. By the end of July, Buelow sported a microscopic .110 average in 42 games.

Somehow, the Tigers were able to trade Fritz to Cleveland for Charlie "Piano Legs" Hickman. Fritz joined a Cleveland team with talent. Legendary Nap Lajoie played second base. Addie Joss pitched. With Fritz calling some good games, Addie's right arm did the rest enroute to his league leading 1.59 ERA. Buelow hit .176 for Cleveland, which gave him a combined average of .141 for the season. Despite his offensive shortcomings, Buelow fielded well for both clubs.

The 1905 season saw Nap Lajoie named player-manager of the Cleveland club. The citizens of the lakeside town dubbed the team the "Naps," in honor of the great second baseman. Nap took a liking to hard-working Buelow and made him the starting catcher for Cleveland. Again, Fritz did not bat much, .172, but he did hit his sixth and final career home run. On August 23, Buelow caught both ends of a doubleheader against Boston, batted 3-for-7, and smacked in the game-winning run in the bottom of the ninth of the second game.

The Naps made a strong run for the American League pennant in 1906, but would fall five games short of the White Sox. Buelow backed up starting catcher Harry Bemis, meekly batting .163 in 34 games. Fritz finished out his career with the 1907 St. Louis Browns. His arrival made incumbent Browns' backup catcher, Branch Rickey, a marked man. Rickey, who earned management's displeasure by refusing to suit up on Sundays, went to the New York Highlanders the day after Buelow's acquisition. As for Buelow, he ended up not playing many Sundays for the Browns, nor any days for that matter. Before his release, Buelow appeared in 26 games and batted .147. His only RBI came on a July 7 double against Washington.

After a stint in the minors, Fritz managed a club in Bay City. He returned to Detroit and spent many years working as a gateman at the grandstands in Navin Field. He died in 1933, succumbing from a neurological disorder. The disease left him without use of his legs for several years. As Fred Buelow never married, he saw to it that his nephew was bequeathed a trust fund that put him through college and pharmacy school.

When asked to comment about the late Fred Buelow, former pitcher "Wish" Egan, a teammate in 1902, described him as "one of the most graceful catchers in the American League." Egan also added, "There was rhythm in every move. He was the best throwing catcher I ever saw. His only weakness was inability to hit." Frank Navin, Detroit Tigers' president, gave a fitting homage, describing Buelow as "a wonderful help to young fellows coming along. Had he been able to hit, he would have gone down in the records numbered with the best of them."

The King
Bill Bergen, C
1878-1943

.170! Bow to the King! Bill Bergen's batting average is the all-time lowest for any non-pitcher with more than 2500 at bats. The second lowest career batting average is owned by Davey Force, whose .211 batting average is much higher than Bergen's. In his 11-year career, only once did Bergen bat above the Mendoza Line. In fact, Bergen never even cracked above .190 in any other season. In five of his last six seasons, Bergen achieved a very rare Mendoza Line Trifecta: batting average, on-base average, and slugging average *all below .200.* He just missed a career Mendoza Line Trifecta, finishing with a .201 lifetime slugging average.

For Bergen, it can't be claimed, "It's all relative; everyone had a rough time in the Dead Ball Era." Unfortunately, even in relative terms, Bergen's numbers are awful. With a statistic known as on-base plus slugging percentage (OPS), the sum of on-base average and slugging average, Rany Jazayerli of ESPN.com compiled the lowest ratios of an individual OPS divided by the OPS of an entire league over a season. Bill Bergen has the four *lowest* ratios by a regular in history.

It's all in the fine print, but Bill Bergen did have a few positive notes offensively. He hit a surprisingly high number of triples, 21 in all, with four in his rookie year. In the unlikely event Bergen reached base, he also possessed some speed, evidenced by his 23 lifetime stolen bases. Finally, using strikeout data, only available for Bill Bergen's final two seasons, Bergen averaged one strikeout for every 6.5 times he came up to the plate. He managed to keep the ball in play, albeit mainly by way of weak dribblers back to the mound and first base. Bergen was the very definition of a "tapperitis hitter." The canny Bergen was even known to deliberately swing at a wild pitch for the third strike, as rules of the day allowed the batter to run to first.

One need not be Branch Rickey to surmise that Bill Bergen earned his keep with his catcher's mitt. Statistics show Bergen an extremely competent defensive catcher. He ranks with the best fielding backstops ever. Bergen's defensive specialties included a superb ability in getting under and snaring foul balls. Like Johnny Bench and Ivan Rodriguez, Bill also claimed a howitzer of an arm and could get the ball away quickly and accurately to second base while remaining flat-footed. Bill Bergen ranks in the all-time top-twenty for career assists by a catcher. Apparently, Bergen called a good game as well, catching two no-hitters despite usually being on teams with mediocre pitching.

Brothers (and catchers) Marty and William Aloysius Bergen hailed from North Brookfield, Massachusetts. The New England town was also the birthplace of Connie Mack, a catcher in his playing days. Bill Bergen began his professional career in 1899 with various ballclubs in his native New England. Later, he donned the tools of ignorance for Fort Wayne of the Interstate League. In an amazing display of throwing prowess, Bill was behind the plate for Fort Wayne. His team led by just one run while the opposition loaded the bases in the ninth inning with no outs. With three swift tosses, Bergen picked off the runner at third, then repeated the pickoff plays of the remaining baserunners—one after the other—to preserve the win.

While best known in Brooklyn flannels, Bergen played his first three years in Cincinnati. During his 1901 rookie season, Bergen quickly established himself as a suspect hitter by batting .179. But who could imagine that mark would actually be one of his best years? Bergen rapped out eleven extra-base hits, enjoyed a 3-hit game against the New York Giants, and slugged the first of his two career home runs.

One of Bergen's earliest games was an outright fiasco. On June 9, the Giants visited Cincinnati. An overflow crowd of 17,000 packed League Park. By the time of the opening pitch, the throng of spectators spilled out of the stands and along the periphery of the field. Numerous balls, many of which were routine plays, made their way into the crowd resulting in ground-rule doubles. On a couple occasions, the mass of humanity thwarted Bergen's efforts to catch foul pops. The Reds trailed 10–4 when they inserted Amos Rusie in the fourth inning. One of the great fastball pitchers of the 19th century, Rusie was a mere shell of himself and was tattooed for 15 hits and 10 runs in five innings work.

By the ninth inning, the crowd pushed their way within the very boundaries of the diamond. As a result, the Giants—ahead 25–13—were awarded a forfeit. While the official score became 9–0, the statistics of the game counted, yielding a record 49 hits with 13 doubles. Bergen and fellow Red Algernon McBride were the only position players not to secure a hit that day.

Better days remained ahead for Bergen as observers took notice of his solid work behind the plate. In a September 12 match against the Giants, after Reds' third baseman Harry Steinfeldt muffed a perfect pickoff throw from Bergen, the catcher took matters into his own hands and made a pretty over-the-shoulder catch of a foul pop. That catch killed a rally and the Reds went on to win.

In his second season, Bergen batted .180 but drove in a career-high 36 runs. He would never plate more than 22 runs in any other season. In 1903, Bergen enjoyed his landmark .227 season as a backup catcher behind Heinie Peitz.

Sold to the Brooklyn Superbas (later Dodgers) before the 1904 season, Bergen played in the dark ages of the franchise's history. During his eight-year tenure in Brooklyn, the team always finished deep in the bowels of the standings. They owned a wretched 471–745 during that period. While the Giants and even the American League's Highlanders/Yankees were the darlings of New York at the time, the Brooklyn Superbas were the equivalent of a stepchild. Brooklyn exhibited very little civic pride for this ball club. While the other major league teams from New York received extensive newspaper coverage, the Superbas merited little more than a boxscore of their latest loss.

Bergen's initial game with Brooklyn was auspicious enough. He made nine putouts and two assists; three of his putouts came in one inning on high pops hit in foul territory. Another nice effort, on April 22 against Boston, saw Bergen gunning down a baserunner to complete a double play and going 2-for-4 with two RBI. He threw out another four would-be basestealers in a May 7 game against his former Reds. Bergen's biggest batting highlight that year might well have been his sixth inning single on May 28 against the New York Giants' Joe McGinnity, breaking up a no-hitter.

The 1905 Brooklyn Superbas might have been the worst National League team of the Dead Ball Era. They finished with a 49–102 record, Brooklyn's first cellar finish. The team's 3.76 earned run average was the highest in the majors that year. Brooklyn could not hit either. Not one player batted above .300 nor had at least 50 RBI. Finally, Brooklyn had trouble on defense. Their .936 fielding average was by far the worst in baseball. Even Bergen let several slip away. Sharing catcher duties with Lou "Old Dog" Ritter, Bill Bergen finished tied for second in errors by a National League catcher, a category led by Ritter.

By Bergen standards, he improved with the bat in 1905. He reached .190. Bergen also had a few notable outings. He tripled in a run off Wish Egan to help Brooklyn beat St. Louis, 3–1 on May 24. On July 26, Bergen again feasted off Egan for two hits and a run scored in a 6–1 triumph over the Cardinals. In a late-season 10–9 victory over Chicago, Bergen contributed by going 2-for-4 with a pair of runs scored and two runs batted in.

Then there was the April 27 game against archrival New York when Bill Bergen incredibly "threw out" two Giants with one throw. New York's Mike Donlin doubled into center field. So content with himself after his mighty hit, Donlin was unalert when Bergen uncorked a beautiful throw to second baseman Red Owens to pick off Donlin. Firebrand manager John McGraw made such a protracted fuss over umpire Jim Johnstone's call that the arbiter threw McGraw out of the game, making him the second victim of Bergen's pretty play.

In 1906, Bill Bergen reverted to new depths in batting, slumping to .159. While highlights are far and few in between, Bergen's most important at bat of the season occurred on September 8 against rival New York. Despite a mere groundout, the play brought home Jack McCarthy for the only run of the game. Bergen's defensive feat of the year was catching a no-hitter, pitched by Mel Eason.

Bergen only played 51 games in 1907, as Ritter handled most of the catching chores. He equaled his feeble batting mark from the previous year. Bill Bergen did have a credible game against the Giants on July 1; he had a pair of hits (one of which drove in the second run for Brooklyn) and a sacrifice in a 4–0 victory.

Bill Bergen "improved" to .175 in 1908. His "swat for two pillows" brought in the game-winning run in a July 1 game against the Giants. However, nothing that year would match the September 5 doubleheader against Boston. The first game was a defensive jewel. Bergen made four putouts and four assists in a tough-luck 4–3 defeat. In the second game, Brooklyn's Nap Rucker pitched a no-hitter. Bergen's catching helped Rucker fan 14 Boston hitters while walking no one. Three Brooklyn errors denied Rucker the exulted perfect game. Even Bill Bergen's oft-somnolent bat contributed a bases-loaded double to give Rucker more than enough run support.

By 1908, Bergen's combination of vast experience behind the plate and peak in physical skills resulted in a string of sensational years defensively. He set the standard for defensive flawlessness with a stellar .989 fielding percentage. That topped Johnny Kling's .987 set in the previous year. Bergen held the record until 1912. Catching two no-hitters provides evidence that Bergen could direct events on the field. Never afraid of getting into the face of an umpire, Bergen was also ejected from a game that year. Bill

Bergen was, by now, a clubhouse leader with Brooklyn. More, at a stocky 6'-0" and 185 lbs., if anyone was making light of his hitting, they definitely did so outside of Bill's earshot.

Another story that characterized the clever catcher, involving Bill Bergen and Giants' rookie second baseman Larry Doyle, rivals something conjured up by Abbott and Costello:

> Bergen: "What's your name?"
> Doyle: "Doyle, sir."
> Bergen: "Doyle, eh. Do you like it in the big leagues?"
> Doyle: "Yes sir."
> Bergen: "And what do you like to hit?"
> Doyle: "A fastball."
> Bergen: "On the outside?"
> Doyle: "No sir. On the inside."
> Bergen: "High?"
> Doyle: "No sir. Not too high."

You can pretty much guess the rest of the story. Larry Doyle saw nothing but curveballs or high heat on the outside and went hitless in the game. He must have been much more tight-lipped about his hitting preferences after that, as Doyle went on to bat .290 over 14 years.

The 1909 season started off gloriously for Bergen and Brooklyn. Thirty thousand fans crammed the Polo Grounds for the season opener between the Superbas and New York. The game passed into the thirteenth inning with no score. Then, Brooklyn struck. With runners on first and second and a man in, Bergen came to the plate. Here is the *New York Times* account:

> A heavy pall hung over the field, which was intensified when Bergen added another single. ["Red"] Murray [in right field] fielded the ball, and made a good throw to the plate, but ["Admiral"] Schlei let it pass through his legs, and [Tim] Jordan added the second run…when the smoke of the battle cleared away, the Brooklynites had secured a safe [3–0] lead and clinched the game.

There was little else Bergen did with the bat that year. The 1909 season would be Bill Bergen's busiest campaign. In 112 games, he sunk to a .139 average—just 48 hits in 346 at bats with only three extra-base hits. Both Bergen's batting and slugging averages that year are all-time lows for any player with over 300 at bats in a season. One of his rare hits that year yielded a small miracle: his second and final career home run.

Bergen set another record for hitting futility that year. If Joe DiMaggio owns "The Streak," then Bill Bergen has custody of "The Schneid." Through Joe Dittmar's extensive research, he discovered that Billy Bergen holds the record for most consecutive at bats without a hit. The Schneid started after Bergen singled in his first at bat against the Giants on June 29. After that, a hitting drought of 46 straight at bats followed. The two-and-a-half week slump mercifully ended in the second game of a doubleheader against the Chicago Cubs on July 17. In the fourth inning, Bergen beat out an infield grounder to Johnny Evers of "Tinker to Evers to Chance" fame.

On defense, Bill Bergen was Gold Glove caliber in 1909. He led NL catchers with 18 double plays and 202 assists, still the ninth highest season catcher assist total in history. On August 23, the *New York Times* recorded that Bill Bergen gunned down seven would-be base-stealers in a game against the St. Louis Cardinals. Revised accounts show the actual number to be six, still a 20th century record.

Bergen showed some liveliness with the stick early in the 1910 season. Going into May, Bill Bergen was hitting above .200. That did not last long and Bergen plummeted to .161 by season's end. It was another dismal year for Brooklyn; this time they finished 64–90. Interest in the team was so indifferent, that the *New York Times* noted, "The Brooklyn game attracted 400 persons. President Ebbets is the father of the schedule that runs until Oct. 15. By that time not even the players will care to go to his ballyard."

Throughout 1911, the bat of Bill Bergen was little more than an impotent length of wood. He sank to a career-low .132 with just 10 RBI in 227 at bats. Yet, he paced all National League catchers with a .981 fielding average.

In one game that year, nothing went right for Bill. The fiasco happened on June 10; Brooklyn was at Pittsburgh. It started out a scoreless pitcher's duel until the bottom of the sixth inning. Fred Clarke was on third and Bobby Byrne on first for the Pirates when they tried a double steal. While even the consensus of Pittsburgh fans knew Fred Clarke was dead out, plate umpire Bill Klem thought Clarke beat Bill Bergen's tag and called him safe at home. With ball in hand and frustration boiling over, a furious Bill Bergen turned to the legendary arbiter. He emotionally questioned Klem's vision and ancestry. Pitcher Doc Scanlon and Manager Bill Dahlen also joined in the berating of Klem. So overcome with anger, Bergen failed to call time and Bobby Byrne made it to third during the ensuing argument. Klem ejected Dahlen and Scanlon, but let the apoplectic Bill Bergen stay in the game to stew in his own juices.

George Bell, a 27-game loser the previous year, came in to relieve. After Dots Miller walked, the double steal was executed again, with Byrne scoring. By the eighth inning, the Pirates were breezing 8–0 and had the bases loaded when Fred Clarke popped up in front of the plate. On what should have been a routine out, Bergen and third baseman Ed Zimmerman launched into an Alphonse and Gaston routine. That's the skit where Bergen might say, "You catch it, dear Edward," and Zimmerman might reply, "No, kindest William, I insist that you catch it sir." By virtue of a spectacular last-instant catch, Bergen might have averted the shortest hit grand slam in history. To complete his stressful outing, the Pirates scored yet another run on a failed pickoff attempt by Bergen.

Bill Bergen's last hurrah occurred on July 22, when he nearly caught his third no-hitter. Nap Rucker was just one out away when Cincinnati's Bob Bescher hit a soft line drive that just escaped the reach of the Brooklyn second baseman. Of the four Reds to reach base on walks, Bergen threw two out on attempted steals and picked off a third.

Despite still being the top defensive catcher in the game, the clock ran out on the 38-year-old Bill Bergen. For the 1912 season, Brooklyn inserted Otto Miller in as their new catcher. Though Bergen was better defensively, Miller was competent enough and a superior batter. Bill Bergen never played another major league game. Incredibly, from the years 1904 to 1911, the Superbas/Dodgers' collective pitching staff had a higher batting average (.169) than Bergen (.162).

Bill Bergen continued to play minor league ball until 1914. After nearly two decades of enduring catcher's aches and pains, Bergen's 40-year-old body finally gave out. During the war years, he coached and managed minor league clubs in Syracuse and Scranton. By 1920, poor health ended Bergen's days in professional baseball. He remained active in the game, managing semipro clubs in his hometown of Worcester. After a prolonged illness, Bill Bergen died on December 19, 1943. Although married for over 40 years, Bergen had no children.

Bill Bergen may be one of the greatest defensive catchers you never heard about. Extensive research conducted by Charles F. Faber supports Bill Bergen's case as an all-time great defensive catcher. In his *Baseball Ratings*, Faber ranks Bergen as the National League's best fielding catcher from 1908 through 1911.

From an all-time basis, Bill Bergen ranks with the best, according to Faber. Based on his research, Bill Bergen is the National League's third-best-fielding catcher in history. The five best are: 1) Gabby Hartnett; 2) Pop Snyder; 3) Bergen; 4) Johnny Edwards; and 5) Roy Campanella.

Finally, Faber goes as far as to place Bill Bergen as one of the National League's 50 best all-around catchers. He ranks 38th, ahead of quality backstops such as Andy Seminick, Earl Williams, Stan Lopata, and Gene Tenace. And this was even after Bergen actually *lost* points, in Faber's system, by virtue of his poor batting.

Total Baseball also recognizes Bergen's fielding excellence. They rank him the fifth-best defensive catcher of all time. While statistics indicate that Bill Bergen was an outstanding fielder behind the plate, there are other factors to consider. Since Bergen possessed one of the stronger arms of any catcher, he garnered many assists in days when teams bunted more and attempted 50%–60% more steals than they do in the present "homercentric" game. Bergen also toiled for teams with below-average pitching. This, in principle, gave him the opportunity to throw out more baserunners.

Marty Bergen, Bill's older brother, also donned the tools of ignorance as a big league catcher. Marty Bergen started for Boston from 1896 to 1899. Twice, he won National League championships with the Beaneaters. While not as stellar defensively as his brother, Marty was far superior as a hitter, holding a .265 lifetime average. Sadly, Marty Bergen is best remembered for one of baseball's most tragic incidents.

On January 19, 1900, Michael Bergen, Marty and Bill's father, made a horrifying discovery. Within Marty Bergen's Worcester farmhouse, he found Marty Bergen's wife and two children dead from multiple blows from an ax. In another room, Marty Bergen lay dead, nearly decapitated from a slash with a straight razor. The horrific incident was ruled a murder-suicide.

What chain of events could have caused Marty Bergen to snap into such a murderous rage? No one really knows for sure. After the incident, Boston manager Frank Selee told the *Boston Globe,* "[Marty] Bergen's character was above reproach. He was a model man and had no bad habits. Many people had an idea that Bergen was a drinking man, but he was not." There were other references to Marty Bergen's sobriety, even his piety. Bergen's behavior baffled everyone, since he was considered fairly normal by conventional standards. Marty Bergen loved his family, did not drink nor carouse with his teammates, and kept in good shape. At the same time, he was also suspicious, moody, solitary, and aggressive. During his final season, Marty Bergen acted so irrational, that his teammates outright feared him.

Some have contended the reason Bill Bergen stuck around in the majors for years were mostly out of pity over his brother's misfortune. That hypothesis does not seem likely. Baseball is a business and not a charity. More probable is the fact that Bill Bergen played 11 seasons for two losing organizations. The economics of the game made players like Bill Bergen available for meager-budget teams like the Brooklyn Superbas.

Although most pictures of Bill Bergen show him with a beaming countenance, one could wonder about a couple of things. First, how much ridicule did he receive from the press, fans, and teammates over his lack of hitting? Nobody probably said anything directly in Bergen's presence, or else risk getting an eye dotted. Still, there must have been some indirect derision. How did he take it? With that, how much emotional baggage did Bergen carry over his brother's tragedy? Did all these things smolder in his soul?

To conclude, had Bill Bergen possessed the batting ability of brother Marty over his career, he could have enjoyed a Hall of Fame career. Unfortunately, there is no escaping the fact that Bill Bergen's claim to fame will always be baseball's worst-hitting player of all time. Bergen is the undisputed *King* of all below .200 hitters.

The Altoona Swoonah
John Gochnauer, SS
1875-1929

John Gochnauer's saga as a major league shortstop was short and bittersweet. He lasted all of two seasons and change, from 1901 to 1903. If you glance at his career ledger, no home runs, and a .187 batting average, you could infer an uneventful and quite miserable little career. However, if you look *real close* at the numbers, then you find some truly curious statistics.

Gochnauer was a product of the Altoona, Pennsylvania sandlots. As an 8-year-old, he witnessed Altoona's short-lived foray in the Union Association with the Mountain Citys. Inspired by the great play of the Mountain Citys' only bonafide star, shortstop Germany Smith, Gochnauer knew what he wanted to do with his future. He became a crowd-pleaser as an infielder with the local "Jennings" semi-pro team. At the turn of the century, Gochnauer moved to Brockton, Massachusetts and began his baseball career in earnest.

In 1901, John Gochnauer became a late season addition for the Brooklyn Superbas. In his debut game, he had two hits. Gochnauer then played both ends of a season-ending doubleheader against the New York Giants. He shined that day, delivering a 2-run single in an 8–0 rout of the Giants in the first game, then was cited by the *New York Times* for "excellent work" at defense in the nightcap to help Brooklyn sweep their cross-town rivals. For the three games, Gochnauer hit an atypical .364 in 11 at bats and fielded every ball cleanly. It definitely was no indicator of things to come.

As promising a cup of coffee Gochnauer enjoyed, the stark reality was that Brooklyn already had future Hall of Fame shortstop Bill Dahlen. John Gochnauer jumped over to Cleveland, of the American League, to became their starting shortstop.

In his first season with Cleveland, John Gochnauer hit a measly .185. The following year, Cleveland management assumed Gochnauer's batting average could go nowhere but up. They were wrong. Gochnauer matched his 1902 batting record with an identical .185 in 1903.

Gochnauer is baseball's "dualing banjo" hitter of all time. Not only was his batting average produced by the "rusted-gate swing" variety, he is also the player with the most career at bats to both hit below .200 and not connect for a single home run. Sometimes, players and coaches refer to easy-out hitters as a "day at the beach." Gochnauer seems to have been the equivalent of a "week in Tahiti."

Despite Gochnauer's lack of power and a microscopic batting average, John Gochnauer could get a run across. His 48 RBI in 1903 is the *most* by any career below .200 player in a season. Gochnauer's most notable RBI that year occurred in an early-season tilt against Detroit. John Gochnauer came up with a runner on first and the game tied in the late innings. He launched a deep drive towards left field. Sam Crawford was attempting to make the putout; however, Crawford lost track of the ball when it traveled through a billowing cloud of black smoke. The smoke screen emanated from the furnace of a nearby apartment building and drifted over the ballpark the instant Gochnauer hit the ball. Gochnauer's deep fly dropped in to allow the winning run to score. A debate must have ensued over the hero of the game: Gochnauer or the janitor of the apartment building.

A true believer in the adage, "a walk is as good as a hit," Gochnauer's 48 base-on-balls in 1903 was the eighth-leading total in the American League. Rest assured no pitcher was trying to work around this guy either. Gochnauer must have been able to protect the plate well, foul off a string of tough pitches, and coax a well-earned walk.

Unlike a typical below .200 hitter, who compensates lack of prowess with the bat through a dependable glove, John Gochnauer definitely did not fit this mold. Not only was he a buttercup hitter, he was also butterfingers on defense. John Gochnauer owns the single-season record for most errors by a 20th century player. In 1903, Gochnauer dropped, booted, allowed balls to go under his glove, threw over the head of, or into the dirt, a grand total of 98 times. That earned him an .869 fielding average. Therefore, not only did John Gochnauer bat below the Mendoza Line in 1903, he also fielded below the Hobson Line, named after the last infielder to own a fielding average below .900, Butch Hobson in 1978. There were worse. A few players booted over 100 balls in the 19th century and "Piano Legs" Hickman fielded an all-time low .842 as a third baseman in 1900.

Gochnauer owned a career fielding average of .901. He "loses" out to Tom Downey (FA .899) for lowest career fielding average for a shortstop in the 20th century. John Gochnauer's fielding stats makes you wonder how many times he heard, "Hey, Johnny. Get the spring out of your glove," or words to that effect.

In defense of Gochnauer's defense, he was a flashy, yet erratic, shortstop. There are game accounts of the day that specifically cite Gochnauer's spectacular fielding. Of course, there are others where his errors proved costly. He seemed to be the type of player who could make a circus catch, that few others could make, only to boot a routine play from the very next batter. Had he played longer, he most likely would have mastered the mechanics and consistency required of a major league shortstop.

What is truly startling is the composition of Gochnauer's infield mates on the 1903 Cleveland Blues. At third base was Bill Bradley, a 14-year pro with a lifetime .271 average and a four-time leader in fielding average. At second base was the incomparable Napoleon Lajoie, who led the American League with a .355 batting average that year. The first baseman was Piano Legs Hickman, obviously more comfortable at first than third, who batted .295 and drove in 97 runs. The presence of John Gochnauer and his .185 average and 98 errors in this infield seems a bit incongruous. Yet, of the 140 games Cleveland played, Gochnauer started in 134 of them.

The 1903 Blues boasted other great players, Hall of Famers' Elmer Flick in the outfield and Addie Joss as the pitching stopper. That year, Cleveland finished in third place with a 77–63 record. They were just one-half game behind Philadelphia for the runner-up spot, but a good 15 games behind Boston for the pennant and a trip to the first-ever World Series. The question that begs to be asked is whether Cleveland could have finished higher with a shortstop whose numbers were more comparable to his infield mates.

Following the 1903 season, Terry Turner replaced John Gochnauer as Cleveland's shortstop. No other team wanted to bite on a no-hit/no-field player. It still is surprising for a player to appear in 134 games in a single season, then never play again in the majors.

John Gochnauer did continue to play in the Pacific Coast League, with teams in San Francisco and Los Angeles. After the conclusion of his playing career, he became a longtime minor league umpire in several different leagues. He performed those duties right up until his death in 1929.

Irish Jack
John O'Neill, C
1873-1935

When reading of this ancient catcher, imagine the strains of Gaelic music in the background. Jack O'Neill came from County Galway and became one of many immigrants from the "Old Sod" to play America's game around the turn of the 20th century. O'Neill was as good as any catcher of his day defensively.

With brothers Mike, Steve, and Jim, John Joseph O'Neill was the eldest who went on to play major league ball. Only one other baseball family, the Delahanty's, boasted of more brothers to make the majors, with five. The "Fightin' O'Neill's," hailed from Minooka, Pennsylvania (near Scranton-Wilkes Barre).

The most famous of the O'Neill brothers, Steve, played for the Cleveland Indians from 1911 to 1923. In 1918, Steve O'Neill led American League catchers in fielding average. Steve also hit for a .333 clip in the 1920 World Series, won by Cleveland. In 17 years of play, Steve O'Neill amassed 1,259 hits and a .263 batting average. Steve also had a fine managerial career and won a World Series at the helm of the 1945 Tigers.

Jack O'Neill started out as a 29-year-old rookie with the 1902 St. Louis Cardinals, backing up plate blocker Jack Ryan. That year, neither Jack could hit the proverbial "bull in the ass with a shovel," as they combined for no homers and a paltry .163 batting average. Jack O'Neill did involve himself in a bit of baseball history that year as he scored on an inside-the-park Grand Slam by his brother Mike. It was the first pinch-hit slam ever. Pitcher Mike and catcher Jack also made history as the first-ever sibling battery, making them quite famous at the time. And they were quite successful, going undefeated for several consecutive games that year. As a method to keep opposing coaches from stealing their signs, the brothers signaled to each other in Gaelic.

Irish eyes smiled upon Jack in 1903, as he enjoyed the finest season of his career. He became the starting catcher for the Cards and batted .236 with 10 extra-base hits in 75 games, while stealing 11 bases. Superb on defense, rifle-armed Jack O'Neill was particularly tough to steal on that year (135 assists in 74 games—the third highest total in the National League). Unfortunately, the team suffered through a horrid 43–94 season that sent the Redbirds straight to the cellar.

One game that season demonstrated Jack O'Neill's iron resolve. Playing the New York Giants at the Polo Grounds, the O'Neill battery was particularly sharp and the Cardinals pulled ahead 2–1. With Jack at bat in the fourth, pitcher Joe McGinnity threw an errant fastball. A chilling account from the *New York Times* follows:

> The ball struck him [O'Neill] with terrific force on the side of the head and he fell, completely knocked out. McGinnity, who pitched the ball, was at the injured man's side almost instantly, and in a few moments all the players on both sides endeavored what assistance they could on the prostrated player. After vigorous treatment the St. Louis catcher was able to stand up, and he insisted on continuing in the game. When he walked to the base the spectators and players gave him a generous round of cheers. He surprised every one by playing during the remainder of the game in a thorough and lively manner, as though nothing out of the way had occurred to him.

Not only did he show no ill-effects from the beaning, the "very active" work of Jack O'Neill (which included two Giants thrown out attempting to steal) behind the plate was specifically cited. That day, the downtrodden Cardinals prevailed 3–2 in 10 innings.

During the winter, the Cardinals traded O'Neill to the Chicago Cubs for pitcher John Taylor. To sweeten the deal, the Cards added a rookie pitcher with a mediocre 9–13 record. Though the Cubs are often lambasted for their long history of ill-advised transactions, they looked like geniuses when the pitcher, Mordecai "Three Finger" Brown matured into one of baseball's greatest arms.

With the Cubs in 1904 and 1905, Jack O'Neill capably substituted to one of the better catchers of yesteryear, Johnny "Noisy" Kling. These 1904 Cubs of "Tinker-to-Evers-to-Chance" fame, charged out to lead the National League standings, playing just under .700 ball into June. However, they could not match the New York Giants' team of John McGraw and faded into second place.

Enroute to a .214 batting average in 1904, Jack's bat was a bit noisy. O'Neill must have been the first to sing, *I Love New York*, after enjoying a 5-game hitting streak in wins against Brooklyn and the New York Giants. Jack O'Neill had three clutch RBI during this streak, one a game-winning hit over the Giants. O'Neill also smashed his only career home run, a Grand Slam no less. While catching Jake Weimer on August 29, O'Neill and the Cubs literally made short work of the Philadelphia Phillies. The game, won by Chicago, 2–0, was completed in one hour and 13 minutes, the quickest nine-inning game that year. O'Neill singled and scored in that contest.

Though Jack O'Neill batted just .198 in 1905, he had his share of fine outings. On April 26, O'Neill tied the major league record with three double plays in one game by a catcher. Even more remarkable was how each double play transpired: all three were started by center fielder Jack McCarthy, who threw to O'Neill and caught the runner trying to tag-up from third base. He also had a pair of 3-hit games, both contributing to Chicago victories.

O'Neill's most sensational effort of the year, and, perhaps, his career, occurred on August 24. On the road against the Phillies, Cubs' pitcher Ed Ruelbach and Phils hurler Tully Sparks dueled for 12 innings of scoreless baseball. After both teams picked up a run in the thirteenth, the game remained deadlocked until the top of the twentieth inning when the Cubs were able to push a run across and hold on to win, 2–1. The game established the National League record for longest contest ending in a decision. O'Neill played the entire 4-hour marathon, going 2-for-9, calling a brilliant game for Ruelbach.

Picked up off waivers from the Cubs, Jack finished out his career with the dreaded Boston Beaneaters in 1906. They finished last in the National League at 49–102 and, at one point of the season, lost 19 in a row. They, and the Boston team of the previous year, are the only two teams ever to have four pitchers finish as 20-game losers in the same year.

On April 30, Jack O'Neill suffered his worst day as a catcher. Whether a function of being 33 years old, inept Boston pitchers failing to hold the runners, or both, the New York Giants enjoyed a stealfest at Jack O'Neill's expense. The Giants "ran the bases like deer" and racked up 10 stolen bases against O'Neill in an 8–2 cakewalk. Despite that game, Jack played his usual role as a solid defensive backstop. Unfortunately, he experienced a dismal season with the bat, hitting just a buck-eighty.

Jack was also involved in one of baseball's most unusual plays that season. In a September 26 match-up against St. Louis, Boston trotted out rookie outfielder John Cameron, for the starting pitcher assignment. After Cameron gave up an infield singer to leadoff batter Tom O'Hara, the number two batter, Al Burch, hit a screaming line drive that smacked Cameron right on the forehead. The ball then caromed back on a fly to catcher Jack O'Neill to get the out on Burch. O'Neill threw to Fred Tenney at first base to erase O'Hara and complete the 1–2–3 double play. Despite the "heads-up" assist by Cameron, he was too woozy to continue and never pitched in another major league game.

Jack might have played for a few more years if not for an eye injury suffered during the 1904 season. His vision worsened and became blurry enough to prevent him from competing at the major league level. Jack did play in the minors with teams in Nashville and Oklahoma City after the 1906 season.

After leaving the game, Jack settled in Scranton until his death in 1935. He died from pneumonia. The last surviving O'Neill brother was Jim, who passed on in 1976—103 years after the birth of Jack. Despite a career average below .200, Jack O'Neill played in the most lifeless days of the Dead Ball Era. After all, it was defense that earned Jack's keep. Had you asked anyone in his day, Jack O'Neill's exceptional defensive abilities were scourge to opposing baserunners as St. Patrick was to snakes.

Dude! Where's My Bat?
Mike McCormick, 3B
1883-1953

"One-year wonder" Mike McCormick strutted and fretted on the major-league diamond for all of one season. He was gone forever by the next. Mike is also one of the shortest players in the history of baseball, discounting Bill Veeck's ruse of inserting 3'-7" Eddie Gaedel to coax a walk in his only plate appearance. However, no other major league player stood shorter than McCormick, a mere 5'-3" in his spikes.

For years, it was assumed Mike was born in Jersey City in May of 1883. Revised accounts now point his place of birth as Scotland. Unlike fellow Scotsman Bobby Thomson, Mike McCormick did not hit any shots heard 'round the world. In fact, McCormick never even hit a shot heard in Brooklyn; going without a home run in his brief career.

In 1900, Brooklyn captured their second straight National League flag. However, player defections to the American League eroded the club's foundation. By 1903, they were a second division team. This was the state of affairs in Flatbush when they debuted the 20-year-old McCormick at third base in 1904. Fellow players gave him a couple of nicknames. Some called him "Kid." Others dubbed him "Dude." "The Squat Scot" would have also been a perfect sobriquet.

For young McCormick, being part of Opening Day festivities must have been thrilling. Brooklyn hosted their inter-borough rivals, the New York Giants. Despite bitter cold, Brooklyn's enthusiasm over their team resulted in 15,000 jubilant fans jamming into Washington Park. McCormick and the rest of the teammates arrived to the grounds in fancy automobiles. The players then marched across the field, led by the 23rd Regiment Band. The men joined together to help unfurl a huge American flag over the Brooklyn clubhouse.

Unfortunately, reality set in quickly on McCormick. He bobbled the first ball hit to him. Later in the game, he made a second error. New York pitcher Christy Mathewson held McCormick hitless in the 7–1 Giants' rout. McCormick followed that effort up with another error in the next game. He did register his first hit that day, a hard-hit double, and came around to score in a 5–2 loss.

On April 17, Mike McCormick played the first Sunday game in Brooklyn history. Previously banned under the Blue Laws of the time, the Brooklyn front office skirted around the law by not charging admission. The catch: patrons were required to buy a scorecard, at admission ticket prices, to gain access into the grandstand and box seats. McCormick stroked an RBI single (albeit committing two errors), in a 9–0 trouncing of Boston.

On April 21, at Boston, the diminutive McCormick kicked two more batted balls.

After his first six games, McCormick had erred seven times. The *Times* piled on, commenting, "Barring McCormick at third, the Brooklyn fielding was without flaw."

With gossip spreading over replacing McCormick, Mike quelled his critics with several nice plays in the field as Brooklyn beat Boston. He also roped a single and scored that game, driven in by a hit from the illustrious Bill Bergen. McCormick followed that fine effort by factoring in two of the three runs in Brooklyn's 3–2 victory at the expense of the Beaneaters. Again, that game, he defended flawlessly—making three true pegs to first from the hot corner. Following the Boston series, Mike McCormick won a vote of confidence from his manager and teammates.

His bat caught fire in early May. From May 3 to May 11, McCormick hit in seven straight games. That included a 3-hit affair against the Phillies and a pair of 2-hit efforts. Probably, McCormick's most dramatic hit occurred on June 3 against the Pittsburgh Pirates. The defending National League champions clung to a 4–3 lead in the bottom of the ninth. Brooklyn's Charlie Babb stood on second, with two outs and McCormick at the plate. Pitcher Roxy Miller quickly got two strikes on McCormick. After three successive balls out of the strike zone, McCormick lined the next pitch for an opposite field double. The sphere just hugged the first base foul line, scoring Babb. Brooklyn went on to win the game in 13 innings.

After that gallant showing, the hits came with far less frequency for young McCormick. Some lengthy droughts of hitless games defined his summer. McCormick's last hit of the season came on August 31, a fine 2-for-4 effort with a run scored in Brooklyn's 2–0 shutout of Chicago. But it was too little, too late for Mike. Brooklyn's manager, Ned Hanlon, finally lost patience with McCormick's lack of offense. Inserted in his place at third was rookie Emil Batch. Though not as polished defensively as McCormick, Batch could hit. Little did Mike realize, while sitting on the bench all through September, his career had come through the rye.

Mike McCormick played one final game in a major league uniform. On October 1, in the nightcap of a doubleheader against Cincinnati, he started at second base, a position he had not played all season. In his final plate appearance, McCormick recorded a sacrifice bunt. In an ironic twist, manager Ned Hanlon batted McCormick cleanup.

McCormick played 105 games for the Superbas that year, 104 at the hot corner. He compiled just a .184 batting average, but his 22 stolen bases are the most by a below .200 hitter in one season in the 20th century.

Despite a horrible start, Mike McCormick's fielding turned out to be his strong suit. McCormick led the league's third baseman with 21 double plays and a .914 fielding percentage.

His playing career over, Mike McCormick returned to Jersey City and took up work as a maintenance man. He died in 1953 from congestive heart failure. The pint-sized Mike McCormick is worth remembering, and not just for being the shortest actual player in history. Nor should McCormick merely be remembered for leading the National League in double plays. Let us say this Scotsman was one of many who made baseball such a cherished game in the days of *auld lang syne*.

Shipwreck Bill
Bill Shipke, 3B
1882-1940

Bill Shipke's nicknames included "Skipper Bill" and "Muskrat Bill." Batting .199, it's surprising no one came up with the moniker, "Shipwreck Bill." All kidding aside, baseball pundits touted Shipke as a promising player. The April 1909 edition of *Baseball Magazine* stated, "this young man is a ball player, every inch of him." The fact that Shipke only stood 5'-7" and weighed 145 pounds indicates that there was not much ballplayer to go around.

Born in St. Louis, the son of German immigrants, William Shipkenhauer[4] later moved to Colorado. Shipke began his professional career in Missouri, starting with Springfield in 1902. Shipke then played with Fort Scott in 1903, and spent the 1904 season in Omaha.

Drafted by Cleveland, Shipke debuted with the Naps in 1906. Bill played just two games, went hitless, and then was released to the Des Moines Champions. Though back in the bush leagues, Shipke's finest days ensued as his brilliant play spurred Des Moines to the Western League championship. One of his teammates was Ed Cicotte, who later became one of the "eight men out" in the Black Sox scandal.

Cleveland may have regretted letting Shipke go. When starting third baseman Bill Bradley broke an arm and was lost for the season, his replacement, Jap Barbeau, was a .194-hitting error-making machine. Joe Cantillon, Shipke's manager in Washington, declared, "It's my opinion if Cleveland held on to Muskrat Shipke in 1906, the Naps would have won the pennant. They kept Barbeau, though, and he lost enough games by his bad throws to lose Cleveland the pennant. The Cleveland fans would have gone crazy over him [Shipke]."

Sold to the Washington Nationals in 1907, Shipke earned some playing time. In 64 games, he hit .196 and slugged his only home run. His fielding average of .949 at third base was the highest in the league save for Lave Cross, the 21-year veteran Shipke replaced. The Nats finished in last place. However, the debut of legendary hurler Walter Johnson gave the team some hope for better prospects in 1908.

But, Johnson fell ill from an infection before spring training and missed the first third of the season. He finished just 14–14 in his sophomore year. The team only moved up one rung in the standings.

With the 1908 Washington ball club composed of rather ordinary players, Bill Shipke fit right in. Appearing in 111 games, as the regular third sacker, Shipke scored one of the more productive single seasons ever for a career below .200 hitter. Bill garnered 71 hits, scored 40 runs, whacked 8 triples, and stole 15 stolen bases. Unable to consistently produce long drives to the outfield, Shipke became a master of "little ball," totaling 26 sacrifice bunts.

Bill Shipke may have been the first ballplayer to receive help from a sports psychologist. The story involves an astute old gentleman with a profound faith in

---

[4] Baseball encyclopedias identify it as Shipkrethaver.

psychological processes. A particularly ardent Washington fan gained Bill Shipke's confidence and persuaded Bill that he could break him out of his early season slump. He told Bill that he was a conjurer by trade, and proceeded to paste a piece of paper to the handle of Bill Shipke's bat. He convinced Bill that the paper had "magical properties" and that as long as he kept his thumb on the piece of paper, he would be hitting like Ty Cobb within a week. Shipke, either not overblessed with education or plain desperate for base hits, willingly complied.

As crazy as it sounds, Bill went on a tear. For a month or so, Bill hit for .300 and was promoted from number-eight hitter to the top of the batting order. Eventually, enemy pitching overpowered Bill's power of suggestion and he reverted back to a sub-par hitter. As for the old charlatan, he later wrote a book on the psychology of baseball.

The magic truly ran out for Bill when Washington added Bob Unglaub, formerly of Boston, to the team in July. Unglaub, a .308 hitter for Washington that year, supplanted Bill at third base. Shipke spent the remainder of the season gathering splinters on the bench.

Though *Baseball Magazine* stated that "[Washington] manager [Joe] Cantillon swears by him," Bill Shipke could not break into the Washington, nor anyone else's, line-up after that. Shipke made a very brief appearance with Washington in 1909, but in nine games, his .125 batting average was barely visible to the naked eye. He left the majors with more nicknames than career home runs. Shipke remained in baseball as a scout until his death in 1940.

Steady Eddie
Eddie Zimmerman, 3B
1883-1945

The "Z-Man's" name is easy enough to find. It is usually next to the last page in any batting register. Despite having a hole in his bat (.186) for two National League teams bracketed over a six-year period, Zimmerman's third baseman's play was as oiled and slick as his glove.

Like former Brooklyn third baseman Mike McCormick, Edward Desmond Zimmerman grew up in northern New Jersey. Zimmerman played collegiate ball for Manhattan College in 1905. The next year, he was with York (Pennsylvania) of the Tri-State League. The St. Louis Cardinals called him up for a few games near the end of the campaign. Zimmerman hit three singles in 14 times at bats, one of which plated in a run.

"Zimmy," as he was known in his playing days, returned to York the following year and took a tour of Pennsylvania over the next three years, stopping in Harrisburg, Altoona, and then back to Harrisburg. No matter where Zimmerman played in the Tri-State, he was a dependable hitter and fielder.

Midway through the 1909 season, Eddie joined the Newark Indians of the Eastern League. He quickly established himself as the best hot corner-tender in the league, owning a superb .970 fielding average in 46 games. He played in all 156 games for the

Indians in 1910. Though he batted just .243 that year, he crossed the plate 86 times and made good on 32 larcenies. Again, he was the elite at third, leading the loop in fielding.

Throughout his years in Newark, Zimmerman met his share of unique pitching personalities. Some were in the twilight of their careers, like Hall of Famers Joe McGinnity and Rube Waddell. McGinnity, nicknamed "Ironman," would determinedly pitch two complete games in doubleheaders. Free spirit Waddell enjoyed the high life, often taking his meals right in bed, at all hours, much to the dismay of his bunkmate. Another teammate was Al Schacht. Though Schacht had modest success for the Washington Senators, he is best remembered as "The Clown Prince of Baseball," entertaining millions with his ballpark shenanigans for over half a century.

Scouts from all the New York teams crossed the river to see Eddie play. The bird dogs representing the Brooklyn Superbas enthusiastically announced to owner Charley Ebbets, "The player is sure to make good in fast company." Other glowing accounts labeled Zimmerman as, "gingery," and able to drive the ball "for a mile."

While wintering over in York, Eddie received the news he had been awaiting for years. Brooklyn drafted Zimmerman from Newark for the price of $1,000.

Eddie Zimmerman started the 1911 season sensationally. He smashed a triple in the season opener at Boston. Eddie proceeded to hit safely his first four games. His heroics in an April 24 game against Philadelphia, two singles, a run scored, and two runs batted in, broke a six-game losing streak for Brooklyn. By April 26, his batting average reached a lofty .297. On defense, Zimmerman made a pair of spectacular one-handed pick-ups culminating with perfect pegs to first in the Boston series. A sportswriter for The *New York Times* commented: "It's no secret that the Brooklyn team is better than last year. The infield is on the jump all the time, and in [Bert] Tooley at short and Zimmerman at third are two players who hop to everything that tries to slide through the inner defense."

Zimmerman's torrid batting of April reached more tepid proportions as the season wore on. By June 8, his batting average shrunk to .215. On July 4, 1911, the hot corner was hotter than an Independence Day firecracker. On that day, Zimmerman fielded 19 chances flawlessly in a doubleheader—a major league record. He followed that performance with a particularly odd play a few games later. Attempting to catch a St. Louis runner on second, the ball squirted out of Zimmerman's hand and traveled perpendicularly into left field. Too much oil in the glove.

Ed Zimmerman's batting average gradually declined into "Bill Bergen country." He ended the season hitting just .185 in 122 games. Zimmerman is one of only six career sub-.200 hitters to amass more than 400 at bats in a single season. Ed did have a bit of sting in his bat, slamming three home runs and driving in 36 runs. By mid-September Charley Ebbets went with a new third baseman and sold Zimmerman back to Newark. Eddie took his frustrations out on Eastern League pitching, swatting balls at a .366 clip.

Eddie Zimmerman did leave a lasting impression with his defense, leading National League third basemen in fielding average in 1911. "Zimmy" also started 24 double plays, third best in the league.

Over the next three seasons, Eddie became a mainstay for the Newark Tigers of the International League. Named team captain, Zimmerman averaged 150 games a year. In 1912, he hit .283 with 76 runs scored. Zimmy then helped lead the Tigers to the 1913 International League championship.

Zimmerman was a most clever fielder. In one game, a runner was on first. Eddie, manning third, figured the next batter was going to bunt the runner over to second. Charging in with the pitch, Zimmerman guessed correctly and grabbed the bunted ball quickly. Newark was able to pull off a double play—a difficult feat on a sacrifice attempt. In another contest, Newark's pitcher fielded a bunt attempt but was out of position to make a play. Eddie rushed in, snatched the ball out of the pitcher's glove, and whipped it to first with his "steel wing."

Decades before it became vogue in sports, Eddie understood the value of nutrition and off-season conditioning. While working out with the team in Columbus, Georgia in 1914, Eddie wrote an article for the *Newark Evening Star*. It discussed the importance of spring training. Here are Zimmerman's comments:

> I approve of vigorous training methods in the instance where a man reports overweight. He has to take off flesh, but he should do so gradually and by dieting. I have seen many men who have tried to do all of their training on the ball field and never count the dinner table as a necessary adjunct in getting in shape. They figure they have the right to enjoy all the sweets and dainty viands set before them. And then they wonder why they have more and more trouble each season rounding into form, with the ultimate end that they reach their athletic senility much earlier than the fellow who takes good care of himself, particularly in the early stages of the spring training period.

During spring training, Eddie loved to play third base with an unusual amount of "dash and pepper," hustling and jumping around like a caffeinated kangaroo.

"What gives?" asked one of the boys.

"Just trying to scare all of these recruits," replied Ed. "That's how I fool them every spring."

Eddie played another great season with Newark in 1914. He closed out his long stay in the New Jersey town, hitting .268. After the Federal League moved a franchise into Newark in 1915, the Newark Tigers relocated to Harrisburg. In his final season as a professional, Eddie topped .300 for the first time and performed his usual magic at third.

With so many standout seasons at the highest level of the minor leagues, it's odd that Eddie could not get another shot with a big league club—especially with the Federal League in play at the end of his career. Zimmerman never even had the opportunity to manage; quite amazing considering everyone who played with or against him regarded him as a very savvy field lieutenant.

Upon the conclusion of his playing career, Eddie Zimmerman settled in Emmaus, Pennsylvania. He worked as a security guard at a Mack Truck plant. He died one day before VE Day. Eddie Zimmerman's time in major league baseball seemed unjustly short.

Walkin' Tony
Anthony Smith, SS
1884-1964

Tony Smith, a spindly .180 hitter, believed in the adage, "A walk is as good as a hit." With more career bases on balls (95) than hits (90), Smith lived that maxim to the hilt.

The Chicagoan came to Galveston, Texas in 1904 to play for a team aptly dubbed the Sandcrabs. That commenced Tony Smith's odyssey in professional baseball, which would last all the way to 1919. Eight minor league stops ranged from Texas to Toronto.

At age 23, Smith made it to the big leagues. Tony Smith played 51 games at shortstop for the 1907 Washington Nationals, batting a modest but career-best .187. Smith quickly departed to the Cubs' organization from there. With Sioux City in 1909, Smith kept the scorekeepers busy, banging out 183 safe hits, including 45 doubles, 6 triples and 6 home runs. His batting average soared to a lofty .329.

Acquired by Brooklyn in the spring of 1910, Tony won a roster spot and also earned the nod as starting shortstop and leadoff batter. From the outset, Smith proved a cunning player, drawing walks and running the bases smartly. The April 24 *Times* account of one of his trips around the bags relates:

> Tony Smith singled to center, scoring [Art] Erwin, and going to second himself on the throw-in. [Al] Burch bounced a bounder to Bridwell, but just then Smith ran in front of the shortstop, and he foozled the play. Wheat grounded to Doyle, but Smith had a big lead
> off third and beat the throw home.

On April 27, Tony Smith cracked his only major league home run, a ninth-inning blast that saved Brooklyn a shutout by Boston. Smith followed that with another marvelous play. He put the finishing touches on a triple play, applying the tag on a player caught in a run-down between third and home. Bill Bergen assisted on Tony's tag. Also in that game, won handily by Brooklyn, Smith scored a run, dropped down a sacrifice, swiped a base, and helped make a double play on defense.

Unfortunately, Smith's bat rarely made solid contact on the ball. By early May, his batting average slid to .150. Subsequently, he went down to the bottom of the batting order. While Tony Smith improved his average slightly, helped along by an early August doubleheader where he went 3-for-7 with a pair of RBI, it was a classic case of a day late and a dollar short. Dolly Stark took over shortstop chores near the end of the season. Tony collected splinters, watching most of the late-season games from the Brooklyn bench.

For the year, Smith hit just a slim .181 in 106 games. But due to a good eye and knowledge of the strike zone he drew 69 free passes to first. That's the most collected in a season by a career below .200 hitter. Smith also busted out 10 doubles. Smith's defensive prowess placed him first in total chances per game and third among National League shortstops in double plays.

There was one more shot for Tony with Brooklyn, an ephemeral 13-game showing in 1911. He hit just a buck-fifty. Brooklyn management handed Anthony Smith his "walking papers." Following the conclusion of his playing career, Tony returned to Galveston and worked as a hospital security guard for 33 years. He died in 1964, from kidney failure, leaving behind a wife and daughter.

Sticky Wickey
James McAvoy, C
1894-1973

James McAvoy caught fastballs and curves during the best of times/worst of times for Connie Mack's Philadelphia Athletics. A veteran of parts of six seasons during the World War I era, "Wickey" McAvoy handled the slants of legendary hurlers Herb Pennock, Chief Bender, Eddie Plank, and Jack Coombs.

As a youngster, the Rochester-bred McAvoy had one burning ambition: to become a pro baseball player. He quit school in the seventh grade knowing he was not going to be a doctor, or teacher, or lawyer. Instead, McAvoy practiced and played ball in the Rochester sandlots year-round. His diligence paid off. People were talking about McAvoy's fine hitting and superior catching ability.

Wickey McAvoy began his professional baseball career as an 18-year-old when he joined the Baltimore Orioles of the International League in 1913. He caught for Babe Ruth, who was strictly a pitcher then, albeit a good hitting pitcher. When asked about playing with the Bambino, McAvoy stated the obvious when he said "nobody ever hit a ball as high or as far as Babe," but he considered Ruth one of the best pitchers he ever caught also.

Philadelphia became McAvoy's next team, as he received a call-up by Mack in 1913. Having already clinched their third pennant in four years, Wickey made a few harmless appearances at the close of the season. Philadelphia defeated the New York Giants in a five game World Series, avenging a Giants' beating in the 1905 Fall Classic. McAvoy also appeared in a handful of games for the A's in 1914, as they defended their American League pennant. Though heavily favored to repeat as World Champions, this time they lost in a Series sweeping by the broom of the "Miracle" Boston Braves.

Connie Mack managed the Athletics on the field and managed their purse strings as well. As part owner of the club, along with the Shibe family, Mack intently tracked the team's bottom line just as closely as the weekly standings. Despite giving the city of Philadelphia their greatest championship run by a professional sports team ever, fan support was lacking.

As the accounts payable started to pile up, old Cornelius MacGuillicuddy understood the team was mired in debt. With little recourse, he cleaned house in the off-season to drop payroll. Many considered Mack's deliberate gutting of his pitching staff a cost control measure. Chief Bender, Eddie Plank, and Jack Coombs were all placed on waivers. However, an alternate theory exists for the sudden departure of Connie Mack's three star pitchers with little compensation in return. Hushed rumors of a lie-down in the 1914 Series persisted.

Mack's purge continued when he sold Eddie Collins to the White Sox for $50,000. This broke up the A's famed "$100,000 infield." Another of Mack's prized infielders, Frank "Home Run" Baker, refused to accept a drastic pay cut and sat out the entire 1915 season.

By opening day 1915, the Athletics' dynasty was ancient history. At least it bought some more playing time for Wickey McAvoy. With incumbent catcher Wally Schang moved to third base, to fill the chasm left by Baker, McAvoy received a promotion to second-string catcher. While a competent backstop, Wickey did not remind anyone of Roger Bresnahan, batting a mere .190 in 68 games. Of course, McAvoy was not the only one struggling on the Athletics. The defending American League champs plunged from 99–53 in 1914 to 43–109 and last place the following year.

Wickey mercifully missed out playing on the 1916 squad, arguably the worst team of the century. Their 36–117 record proved more pathetic than the 1962 Mets. Back with Philadelphia in 1917, McAvoy played an impressive ten games. He hit .250 (6-for-24) and slugged the only home run of his career.

Before the 1918 season, Connie Mack altered the make-up of his team radically. When all the dealing was over, just Wickey and five others from Mack's 1917 squad remained.

Despite the acquisitions of catchers Chester "Pinch" Thomas and Hick Cady, Connie Mack promoted Wickey the job of starting catcher for the 1918 A's. McAvoy responded with one of the best single seasons of any sub .200 hitter. Buoyed by consecutive two-hit games in late August, Wickey McAvoy owned a quite respectable .255 batting average on August 24. He leveled off a bit in September, finishing at .244. Possessing a powerful throwing arm, Wickey's 123 assists were third best in the American League. He even got to pitch one game, allowing a circuit blast in two-thirds of an inning. In spite of all the turmoil, Philadelphia dramatically improved to 52–76 in the war-shortened season.

Wickey's 1919 season would be his swansong in the majors. He followed his best season with his worst. McAvoy's batting average plunged over one hundred points to .141. McAvoy had company. The entire 1919 Philadelphia ball club resembled a train wreck. Their 36–104 record matched their own 20th century record for fewest wins by a team. After being a part of two pennant winners, Wickey McAvoy played for cellar dwellers in his final four seasons.

During the 1920s, McAvoy played for the Baltimore Orioles, Rochester Tribe and the Buffalo Bisons of the International League. He returned to the winner's circle with the 1922 Baltimore Orioles, one of the great minor league teams in history. McAvoy hit .310 with ten round trippers for a club that went 115-52 and won the Junior World Series, defeating American Association champion St. Paul, five games to 2.

In the opening game of the series, with the score tied 4-4 in the seventh and two men on base, McAvoy homered into the right field bleachers and the Orioles went on to win 9-4. In the second game, it was his single that enabled the Orioles to score their only run in the game. McAvoy's greatest moment as a ballplayer occurred in game four; the Orioles won 7-3 on Wickey's Grand Slam with one out in the bottom of the ninth. The walk-off slam gave Baltimore a 3-games-to-1 lead in the series. Another item of note in that game: McAvoy caught a 22-year-old starter who was quite wild, walking seven in the five innings he worked and giving up all of St. Paul's runs. But McAvoy could later claim Lefty Grove as yet another Hall-of-Fame pitcher he received. In the fifth game, Wickey's third inning triple ignited a five-run rally, all Baltimore needed for a 5-1 series-clinching win.

Had there been an MVP of the series, McAvoy would have been the hands-down choice. During the series he batted .320 (8-for-25), catching all seven games. Wickey's stick, comatose for years during the A's moribund years, came alive to win two games, start a rally that won another, and in the second game kept the Orioles from being shut out.

Following a minor league career, McAvoy continued to play for semipro teams in Rochester until the age of forty-five. Not surprising, considering Wickey was one tough player. McAvoy took delight in showing his badge of courage: gnarled and bent fingers from foul tips and catching too many fastballs from a parade of hurlers.

In his later years, McAvoy remained a great fan of the game. A regular at Rochester Red Wings' games, he made the pilgrimage to Cooperstown every year to see friends and former teammates inducted into the Baseball Hall of Fame. While he enjoyed watching modern baseball, McAvoy felt that today's players are too pampered. McAvoy resented that he never earned more than $5,000 a year in the big leagues. Wickey passed on in 1973. As his days drew to a close, he had the satisfaction of knowing that his beloved Athletics, now in Oakland, once again were World Champions.

Lucky Jake
Oscar Dugey, utility
1887-1966

At 5'-7", little Oscar Dugey packed quite an interesting career into 195 games and a .194 batting average. For starters, he played in a World Series game and was lucky enough to be a member of two different National League pennant winners in consecutive years: the 1914 Boston Braves and the 1915 Philadelphia Phillies. It seemed that Dugey kept a rabbit's foot in his uniform trousers for good luck because he ran like a rabbit himself. Managers summoned the speedy Dugey numerous times as a pinch runner. With 17 career stolen bases, Dugey was a legitimate threat on the basepaths. But Oscar Dugey could also capably play just about every position in the infield and outfield. In addition, he was known as one of the best baseball minds in the game.

Nicknamed "Jake," Dugey is the only major leaguer to hail from Palestine. Palestine, Texas, that is. His mother, the former Mattie Belle Greene, was a descendent of Confederate General Robert E. Lee. Dugey started out his career, as a teenager, with Waco of the Texas League and played with them for five years. He kicked up lots of dirt and dust in the Texas League, leading the circuit in stolen bases both in 1912 (54) and 1913 (69). Drafted by the Boston Braves in 1913, Dugey earned a five-game taste of big league dirt late in the season.

Dugey's first at bat in his debut game versus the Cubs made sparks fly. After leadoff batter and future Hall of Famer Rabbit Maranville induced a walk, Dugey, batting second, stroked a well-placed single. Maranville rounded second and tried to make third, but Joe Tinker tagged him out. The blood pressure of Tinker and Maranville soared and a fight started instantly. Hap Myers of Boston came off the bench to try and break up the fray, and nearly got skulled by Tinker as a baseball thrown at point blank range whizzed past his ear. Dugey and several other players joined the scuffle before the umpires asserted their authority. Myers, Tinker, and Maranville were banished. Dugey finished the game with two hits. According to Dugey, his auspicious debut resulted in manager George Stallings announcing to all the players in the dugout, "I've got myself another Ty Cobb."

For years, the Braves had been the laughingstocks of the National League with eleven straight losing seasons. However, the 1913 Braves team improved to their best record since the advent of the World Series in 1903. They finished 69–82 for a fifth-place finish.

Much of the credit for this turnaround went to their new manager, George Stallings. Stallings, who also managed Fritz Buelow on the Detroit Tigers in 1901, was once such a fierce competitor; he got rid of a player just for whistling a happy tune in the shower after a loss. However, by the time he signed on with Boston, Stallings was a much calmer influence in the dugout. Dugey revered George Stallings, telling *The Sporting News* in a 1964 interview, "Stallings was a kind man, a good man. He never raised his voice and cussed as some managers do. But he never mingled with us. We wouldn't see George outside of the game."

Oscar Dugey stayed with Boston for all of 1914. He played 58 games, batted .193 with one home run (his only one in the majors) and stole 10 bases. Perhaps Dugey's most important function for Stallings was to serve as bench coach. In the lineup, Dugey stole bases. As coach, he stole signs. He would advise batters, with startling precision, of what to expect from the pitcher. When not playing, Dugey either was in the coaching boxes or feeding information to Stallings in the dugout.

George Stallings also assigned Oscar to shoo pigeons away from the dugout by flinging pebbles at them. A fastidious gent, Stallings obsessively policed around the dugout for debris such as gum wrappers and peanut shells. Of all the miscellany around the dugout, Stallings hated pigeons most. Once fans from the opposing teams realized this, they incessantly tossed peanuts towards the Boston dugout to attract the birds, thus doubling the ire of Stallings. Oscar claimed his role as "designated scarecrow" shortened his career because of a sore arm he incurred while pelting pigeons.

From his dugout view, Dugey watched the Braves mired in last-place, 15 games behind the front-running New York Giants, as late as mid-July. Then came the "Miracle of the 1914 Braves." A six-game win streak propelled Boston from eighth to third in the tightly packed National League field. The rush forward continued and by late August, the Braves were vying with the Giants for the pennant. Led by a pair of 26-game winners, spitballer Dick Rudolph and Bill James, the Braves overhauled New York and won the pennant by a $10^1/_2$ game bulge.

Throughout Boston's surge, Dugey played his part. Their turnaround could be marked on July 13—the day of Oscar Dugey's heroic, yet lucky, home run. The Braves and the host Cardinals took a 6–6 deadlock into the twelfth inning. With two outs and a man on first in the top of the inning, Dugey hit a sharp liner into left field that just stayed fair. On what should have been no more than a double, Cozy Dolan misplayed the ball. The sphere scooted all the way to the fence. With Dick Rudolph and Oscar Dugey coming around to score, the benevolent scorekeeper credited Dugey with an inside-the-park home run. Boston held serve and won, 8–7.

Dugey's lively bat continued to make magic in the late stages of Boston's torrid rally. Dugey's pinch single, against Pittsburgh on September 10, contributed to a Boston 7-run inning for yet another victory. The next day the Phillies favored Boston, 5–4, after eight innings. Pinch-hitting again, Dugey led off the ninth with a single, and later scored. With Possum Whitted of Boston perched on third base, he tried to score on a shallow fly ball from the bat of Rabbit Maranville. Incredibly, the perfect throw from the outfield hit a pebble and took a weird hop over the catcher's shoulder, allowing Whitted to score the winning tally.

Oscar Dugey could very well have made a pinch-hit appearance or two in the 1914 World Series against the Philadelphia Athletics. However, Boston never really needed his services. Pitchers Rudolph and James secured two wins apiece in the first-ever World Series sweep. The rout was so absolute, that with the exception of the first inning in game three, Boston never trailed after completing an inning.

On February 2, 1915, the Philadelphia Phillies received the services of Oscar Dugey and outfielder Possum Whitted, completing a transaction that sent 1914 RBI leader Sherry Magee to Boston. This move would later haunt the Braves. Whitted became a starting outfielder. While Dugey did not do much batting that year (.154 BA in 42 games), Philly manager Al Moran employed Oscar in a similar capacity as George Stallings. How else can you explain the Phillies, a pennantless team since the birth of the National League, winning their first title over Boston by seven games? Perhaps, a better explanation for the Phillies' rise to the top is the remarkable home run hitting of Gavvy Cravath and the nearly unhittable pitching of Grover Alexander.

In the 1915 World Series, the Phils beat the Boston Red Sox in game one. Oscar Dugey actually got in some playing time. In game four, he pinch-ran in the eighth and stole second to position Philadelphia for the game-tying run. They left him stranded. In game five, with the score tied at four, Dugey came in again to pinch-run in the eighth inning. On the third pitch to Fred Luderus, Dugey broke for second. This time, a pretty throw to second base appeared to nip Dugey. However, plate umpire Bill Klem ruled Dugey safe, explaining the pitch had grazed off Luderus, giving Oscar a free pass to second. Again, Dugey was left stranded. Boston won the series with a Harry Hooper home run in the ninth inning, completing their fourth straight one-run decision.

For the next two seasons, Dugey would remain a solid bench player for the Phillies. In 1916, he broke .200 for the first and only time, finishing at .220. Add nine bases on balls and Dugey finished 1916 with a .339 on-base percentage, well above the league average.

After hitting .194 for the Phillies in 1917, Dugey went to St. Paul in 1918, where he played and coached. Oscar returned briefly to the Braves in 1920, making five pinch-run appearances and scoring twice. For the first time in his career, Dugey played for a lousy team as the 1920 Braves finished just above the cellar.

Thus ended the playing career of Oscar "Lucky Jake" Dugey. Boston retained Dugey's services as coach for the rest of the 1920 season. Dugey then coached the middle-of-the-pack Chicago Cubs from 1921 to 1924. He was a shrewd and knowledgeable coach, but not too spirited. According to a newspaper account, the Cubs wanted a "live fighting Irishman on the job." Chicago's front office waived Oscar Dugey.

Lucky Jake left the game after that, building a new career as a housepainter in Dallas. In December of 1965, the 77-year-old Dugey took a fall and fractured his hip and femur. While in the hospital, he contracted pneumonia and passed away on New Years Day, 1966. To this day, Dugey remains the only below .200 hitter to be on the postseason rosters for pennant-winning ballclubs of two different teams.

" In order to do the toughest thing there is to do in sports—hit a baseball properly—a man has to devote every ounce of his concentration to it... Baseball is the hardest game to play, takes more skill, more dedication, more determination, more practice, more everything...Here's a baseball player. He has to have good eyesight, good legs, a good arm. He has to hit against a ball that can hurt him. He has to play day and night, travel all over the damn country at crazy hours, and for more months out of the year."

-Ted Williams in *My Turn at Bat*

Chapter 5
FAR AND FEW IN BETWEEN
1920-1962

Between the years 1920 to 1962, cycles of scintillating greatness and moribund mediocrity existed in major league baseball. With so much change from decade to decade, the one common theme, to borrow announcer John Sterling's famous refrain, was "Yankees win! Theeeeeeeee Yankees win!" Of the 43 years comprising this portion of baseball history, the Bronx Bombers appeared in 27 World Series; they never went longer than three seasons without a world championship. Understandably, not a single below .200 player of interest played for the Yankees during their dynasty days. Throughout this period, hitting made headlines. The career below .200 hitter, especially in the 1920s and 1930s, became an infrequent visitor to the game.

The 1920s

Baseball's renaissance in this decade came as a result of three personalities. The first never swung a bat on a major league diamond, but he could wield a ferocious gavel. The owners appointed Judge Kenesaw Mountain Landis as major league baseball's first Commissioner. As a result, the game's integrity experienced renewal. Though the stern judge meted out harsh justice to all alleged perpetrators of the "Black Sox" Scandal, baseball somehow survived this sordid event.

Babe Ruth emerged as the second great figure of the decade. Such a charismatic figure was the Yankees' slugger that he seems almost mythological today. He introduced the baseball fan to the majestic trajectory and "instant-offense" capability of the home run. When experts of the day doubted anyone would ever finish with 40 or even 30 home runs in a season, Ruth simply went out and blasted 54 home runs in 1920. He followed that up with 59 in 1921 and hit the exulted 60-homer mark in 1927. Almost single-handedly, during a period when baseball needed it most, the Babe reinvented the game by feeding the fans' newfound lust for the home run.

The third influence was from John Q. Public. A decade of prosperity, an expanding urban population, declining work hours, and a general increase in leisure time symbolized America's "roaring twenties." The entertainment industry—from movies, to popular music, to spectator sports—flourished. Sports other than baseball also attracted fans by the droves. Football, boxing, golf, and tennis made their mark during this decade. However, all sports and sports heroes took a rumble seat to baseball and Babe Ruth.

The 1920s ushered in a revolution on the field. Teams with power hitters did not have to manufacture runs with Dead Ball Era, "one base at a time" tactics. With slugging averages jumping nearly 20 percent higher than the previous decade, run production reached record levels.

Contributing to this spike in scoring was the general quality of baseballs. They were vastly improved with the introduction of the "rabbit ball." Where entire games in the Dead Ball Era were actually played with a single baseball, new balls were put in use with much greater regularity. The dominance of pitching lost footing, as umpires tightened the reins on illegal pitches, such as the spitball. Pitchers worked harder and threw fewer innings. Relief pitching became more of a fixture. The owners themselves mounted the final assault to the low-scoring affairs of the past. As they witnessed the number of fans, in Yankees' seats, was directly proportional to home runs hit by the Bambino, other owners constructed new ballparks with shorter fences or shortened the fences of existing fields.

Nearly extinct in this decade was the sub-.200 hitter. Position players either hit well or hit in the minors. Of 919 players with 200 or more plate appearances in the 1920s, only two finished with career batting averages below .200. One of them was Louie Guisto. Hailing from the Napa Valley, California, Guisto was a collegiate All-American player at St. Mary's College in 1916. The first sacker did not hit much during his five years with Cleveland (0 HR/59 RBI/.196 BA in 152 games). However, St. Mary's honored him by naming its new ballpark Lou Guisto Field.

The 1930s

It occurred just after the Philadelphia Athletics became world champions in 1929. The nation was in for a sobering lesson on economic cycles. On October 24, 1929, the stock market failed and sent the United States careening into the Great Depression. One-fourth of the American working force became unemployed by the Depression's nadir. By 1932, those holding jobs saw their wages reduced by 35 percent over their 1929 totals.

Like many other industries and institutions, the Great Depression hit baseball hard. The sport faltered in all major economic indicators. Attendance in 1931 was half that of the previous year. For a 3-year period, 1932 to 1934, leagues lost money; they never reached 1930 profit-levels until the late-1940s. For the rest of the decade, player salaries never returned to the 1930 average of $7,500.

Despite all the economic setbacks, the decade witnessed much innovation in the game. They played the first All-Star Game in Chicago in July 1933. Night baseball made its debut in 1935 at Cincinnati's Crosley Field. The Baseball Hall of Fame inducted its first five members in 1936. What seemed more of a science project back then, but would later influence the game tremendously, was the first televised broadcast in August 1939, in Brooklyn.

The only thing that did not decline in baseball was hitting. First, came the prolific batting year of 1930, which saw the entire National League hit for .303 and Hack Wilson set the single-season RBI record with 191. For the remainder of the decade, league batting averages leveled out to the .270 range. Home run totals never came close to the 1,565 hit in 1930. But, for the decade, home run totals reached 36 percent greater compared to the 1920s. Though players thought playing night baseball would be bad for their hitting, nothing in post-1935 statistics supports this claim. Throughout the decade, the likes of Jimmy Foxx, Hank Greenberg, Mel Ott, Lou Gehrig, and Joe DiMaggio compiled some incredible numbers.

As in the 1920s, very few players batted below .200 in this decade. Of 849 players with at least 200 plate appearances in the 1930s, only three would wind-up with a career batting average under .200. That list includes Clarence "Ace" Parker. After blasting a home run in his first major league at bat, Parker took a tailspin to hit just .179 in two seasons with the Philadelphia Athletics. He later starred for the Brooklyn Dodgers. However, these Dodgers played football, as one of the early franchises in the National Football League. Ace Parker is a member of both the College and Pro Football Hall of Fame.

The 1940s

Like a young pitcher getting Babe Ruth out only to face Lou Gehrig, major league baseball had to face more crisis just after getting the Depression years behind them. World War II gripped the nation. As with other measures of austerity at the homefront, the very existence of professional baseball during took great efforts and sacrifice.

With the United States drawn into the war, Franklin Roosevelt had to decide whether to suspend playing baseball altogether. In his "green light" letter, FDR stated, "I honestly think it would be best for the country to keep baseball going."

The first group of players to change from baseball togs to military uniforms included Hank Greenberg and Bob Feller. Ted Williams enlisted in the Navy to become a Marine Corps fighter pilot. Nearly 500 major league players served some time in the military, more than a full season's roster for both leagues. In 1942, an exhibition game featured the American League All-Stars against an All-Star team made up of service players.

So acute was the player shortage that some minor league teams advertised for prospects in *The Sporting News*. Players too young, too old, too short on ability, and even short a limb filled major league rosters during the war. Baseball scouts scoured the continent for talent, resulting in significant numbers of Latino ballplayers signing.

Due to the war, the government requested teams to minimize travel during spring training and conduct training closer to their home cities. The teams complied; for example, the Yankees played their exhibition season in Atlantic City, which is quite cold in March.

Even baseballs became part of the war effort. Since rubber, typically used in the cores of baseballs, was essential to the military, a resin called balata (used to make the coverings of golf balls) was substituted. These balls drew complaints from managers and players for their notable deadness. Frankie Frisch, the great second baseman who went on to manage the Pittsburgh Pirates, made the following comments to John Kiernan of *The New York Times* after the Giants' Johnny Mize hit a particularly deep home run in 1942:

Well that one Mize hit against us certainly looked like a golf ball going away. I guess
they left that one off the ice [alluding to the practice of John McGraw freezing a few
dozen baseballs, to deaden them, when a heavy-hitting team was facing the Giants at the
Polo Grounds]. I'm telling no tales. I'm just saying that Mize really made that one whiz.
But this ball really does seem a little softer than the one we had last year. A lot of good
hitters are down around .260, which doesn't seem reasonable unless it's the ball.

As a result, hitting returned to something more akin to the Dead Ball Era. In 1943, the
American League batting average sunk to .249, the first time a league dropped below
.250 since 1917. Players with as few as 15 home runs in a season made it into the Top-5
for their respective leagues.

From the standpoint of batting statistics, baseball returned to some semblance of pre-
war levels in 1947. That year featured Ralph Kiner and Johnny Mize each socking 51
home runs in the NL, while Ted Williams earned the second of his two triple crowns in
the AL. Of course, the complexion of the game forever changed that year when Jackie
Robinson took the field for the Brooklyn Dodgers. While Branch Rickey gets much
credit for the bold and just decision to sign Robinson, owners for the Pirates and Phillies
wanted to sign Negro League ballplayers during the war. Judge Landis, a staunch
proponent for segregated baseball, thwarted them. The Commissioner's death in 1944
paved the road for integration in baseball.

Eleven players, with 200 plate appearances during the decade, posted career batting
averages below .200. It doubles the total of the 1920s and 1930s combined. The affects of
war, such as the balata ball and cold-weather spring training venues, depressed everyone's batting average. Generally, a dilution of talent increases sub-.200 hitters. The 1940s
also marks the start of a long trend where pitching dominance would drive the number of
Mendoza Line hitters to levels not seen since the Dead Ball Era.

The 1950s

The 1950s featured a Cold War, a hot economy, many babies being born, and a return to
splendor for baseball. The prosperity of the era was a boon for most owners as they
enjoyed record attendance figures and additional revenues from a novel source—
television. That prosperity also resulted in sweeping changes in baseball's near-fifty-year
status quo. They reflected the dynamics in the population base throughout the country.
Whether for better jobs or a better life, many white Americans moved from crowded
cities into either suburbs or the regions now referred to as the Sun Belt. At the same time,
African Americans moved from the rural South into the larger urban centers of the
Northeast and Midwest.

Baseball owners tracked these population trends. Financially suffering franchises in
crumbling urban areas made their moves. Starting with the Boston Braves move to
Milwaukee in 1953, five franchises relocated—four of them going west.

An air of indifference may have defined the departure of the Braves, St. Louis
Browns, and Philadelphia Athletics. However, that could hardly be the case when
outraged fans of the Dodgers and Giants saw their beloved teams depart the boroughs of
New York City to the fertile baseball grounds of California.

The power game returned to baseball in the 1950s. In 1950, major league baseball teams broke the 2,000 home run barrier for the first time. That total crested to 2,294 in 1956. The hit-and-run strategy and stolen bases went largely unused in the decade.

Benefited by the gradual dissolution of Negro League baseball, the assemblage of elite talent in the decade proved as great as any time in the game's history. For starters, sensational hitting outfielders like Williams, Musial, Aaron, Mays, Mantle, and Snider populated the game. Of significance was production from players at positions never known for hitting. Brooklyn, who once had catcher Bill Bergen hit one home run in eight years, now witnessed Roy Campanella become the first catcher to break the 40-home run mark. Eddie Mathews, Bobby Doerr, and Ernie Banks smashed long-held assumptions that infielders outside of first base do not hit home runs.

The wild-swinging batters of the 1950s equated to strikeouts in record levels. From 1949 to 1959, "whiffs" increased 41 percent. Though the prevalent "swing for the fences mentality" contributed to this, an increase in pitcher quality also must be considered.

An outstanding cadre of pitchers hurled throughout the decade. Whitey Ford, Early Wynn, Don Newcombe, Warren Spahn, and Robin Roberts makes up a formidable short list. The relief pitcher truly made an emergence this decade. The 20-save reliever, first accomplished by Joe Page in 1949, was repeated several times in the 1950s—from Jim Konstanty in 1950 to Roy Face in 1958. Improved pitching and defense, as a whole, kept annual league batting averages down into the .250s for most of the decade—the lowest averages since the Dead Ball Era.

Consequently, a slight rise in career below .200 hitters occurred over the previous decade. Of 835 players with 200 or more plate appearances in the 1950s, a dozen wound up with career batting averages under .200.

Another factor might have played a small part in this increase. The talent pool for new baseball players was drying up. Young athletes found other sports to choose from, with leagues such as the National Football League and National Basketball Association offering somewhat viable salaries. The expansion of major league baseball into the West Coast and nationally televised major league games in bush league towns undermined the patronage of minor league ball clubs. Consequently, smaller federations, such as the Piedmont League and the Longhorn League, went under. By 1959, major league teams counted but one-third of the minor league talent available to them, compared to 1950 levels. This became an issue when choosing players to fill a team's 24th and 25th roster spots—allowing some lackluster hitters to get second and third chances in the majors.

1960 to 1962

The turbulence of the decade served as merely a ripple in the first three years of the 1960s. As the "Baby Boom" ended, a new generation of baseball fans came of age. Another factor, network television, fueled baseball's popularity as much as the changes in demographics and population growth. The existing 16-team major league structure could not meet the demand of untapped markets in Minnesota and Texas, as well as the bereft New York market.

For the first time in over 45 years, a rival league was in the formulation stage. The Continental Baseball League planned to place franchises in Houston, Toronto, Denver, Minneapolis-St. Paul, and New York. In an effort to thwart the start-up of the rival league, both existing major leagues expanded from eight to ten teams. The American League expanded in 1961 with teams in Los Angeles and Washington (replacing the original Senators who moved to Minneapolis-St. Paul in 1960). The National League followed suit in 1962 with the New York Mets and Houston Colt .45s.

As a result of expansion, astonishing offensive numbers emerged in the early 1960s. Of course, Roger Maris and Mickey Mantle's home run quest made most of the news in 1961. However, other American League hitters also raked in monster numbers that year. Norm Cash batted .361 and Jim Gentile clouted 46 homers with 141 RBI in 1961. During the expansion of the National League, Willie Mays, Hank Aaron, and Frank Robinson combined for 133 home runs and 405 RBI. More fantastic 1962 numbers came from a pair of Dodgers. Tommy Davis had 230 hits, 153 RBI, and a .346 BA—all league leaders. In addition, speedy Maury Wills stole a record-setting 104 bases. For both leagues, such impressive statistics partly came at the expense of the expansion teams.

On October 16, 1962, Bobby Richardson snared Willie McCovey's screeching liner to give the Yankees their 20th World Series championship. It would be their last for a long interval. As the Yankees dynasty faded, much change would soon be occurring in the game. The world outside baseball also underwent a spasmodic metamorphosis.

The Bloomington Basher
Bill Conroy, C
1915-1997

In 1942, while Ted Williams followed up his .406 season with the first of his two Triple Crowns, Red Sox catcher Bill Conroy enjoyed his career year as well. Boston also gave the New York Yankees a run in the pennant chase before finishing 93–59 that year. One could say 1942 was "Bill and Ted's Excellent Season."

Despite dipping below the Mendoza Line just once in six seasons, Conroy finished his career with a .199 batting average. Despite the low mark, Conroy's numbers reveal that he had above average plate discipline, as evidenced by his knack for drawing walks.

The son of a Bloomington, Indiana railroad engineer, Bill Conroy excelled as a three-sport star in high school, playing baseball, football, and basketball. While playing baseball for Illinois Wesleyan College, Conroy caught the eye of Philadelphia Athletics' scout Phil Haggerty. The 18-year-old pre-law student auditioned his fine maskman skills to Connie Mack while the A's visited Chicago. Mack, once a catcher from baseball's ancient days, was duly impressed with the young prospect and invited Conroy to travel with the team as bullpen backstop.

In a true moment of serendipity, the 1933 Chicago Century of Progress Exposition was in progress that year. As the feature event, the "Battle of the Century" would take place at Comiskey Park, pitting the best ballplayers of the National League against a team of American League All-Stars. The legendary John McGraw managed the National Leaguers; the equally heralded Connie Mack headed the Americans. While the National League players elected to partake in Exposition festivities, Mack ordered his team to Comiskey for pre-game practices. In need of an extra catcher, Mack took Bill Conroy with him to catch batting practice.

What a thrill for teenage Conroy to be alongside the likes of Ruth, Gehrig, and Jimmy Foxx, while working out with the three pitchers of the American League: Lefty Gomez, General Crowder, and the A's own Lefty Grove. Interviewed by several reporters before the game, Bill Brandt asked Conroy to what he attributed his early success. The youthful Conroy calmly replied, "Hard work, good hours, and not watching the clock." To which Brandt wryly commented, "If you didn't watch the clock, how do you know they were good hours?"

Bill Conroy also displayed a bit of mischievous wit when asked to give advice to other young men who aspired to be baseball players. He answered: "I am six feet tall and weigh 175 pounds. My folks always wanted me to play ball. I can tell, because if they wanted me to grow up into an umpire, they would have named me Jesse James."

The American League won the supposed one-time event by a score of 4–2. However, baseball's popularity gave rise to the annual summer rite now known as the All-Star Game. Though he had never played a single professional inning, Bill Conroy was a member of the first-ever American League All-Star team.

Bill quit school and repeated his bullpen catcher duties for the entire 1934 season. Delighted to be part of a major league ballclub, Conroy nonetheless began to grow weary of his warm-up role. During the 1935 Athletics' spring training camp, Conroy told reporters, "I know I have a lot to learn, so I'd like to be placed with some team where I could play regularly." Conroy backed up his veiled ultimatum by showing Mack that he could complement his fine defensive skills by driving the ball as well.

Bill Conroy received his wish and spent his first season in the minor leagues. While batting over .300 for Richmond of the Piedmont League, the ancient finger of Connie Mack summoned Conroy to start a late-season game behind the plate in 1935. Bill smashed a double. After another one-game stay in 1936, Billy Conroy batted .200 in 26 games for the Mackmen in 1937. Defensively, he committed no fielding errors that season.

Released by the Athletics, Conroy traveled west. He spent four seasons with the Oakland Oaks of the Pacific Coast League. A productive player for the Oaks, Conroy batted as high as .291 in 1941. One of Oakland's biggest rivals was the Hollywood Stars. For whatever reason, whenever Oakland visited Hollywood, Harry Ritz, a member of the famed Ritz Brothers comedy trio, loved to heckle Bill unmercifully. These razzings occurred much to the delight of Harry's celebrity friends in the field boxes.

After four years of this incessant verbal abuse by Ritz, Bill Conroy told reporter John Drohan how he turned the tables on Harry Ritz:

> Well, you know I'm a peaceful, law-abiding citizen, but I can only stand so much of that malarkey when I'm going my best. Anyway, things weren't going so good for me and he [Ritz] was giving it to me stronger than ever. Finally, a foul fly went over near [Ritz's] box. I knew it was going to land in the stand, so I thought I would too. I vaulted into the box, but he saw me first and took off. Well, I never did catch up to him, but at least I had the satisfaction of chasing him out of the park.

Had Bill caught him, they could have made a song about of it, entitled *Punching on the Ritz*.

The Boston Red Sox drafted Bill for the 1942 season. While seen as little more than a third-stringer, that changed when Sox's starting catcher Frankie Pytlak entered the military. Then Johnny Peacock, the Sox's newly promoted backstop, caught a severe cold just before the start of the season. Bill Conroy leapfrogged from deep reserve to opening day starting catcher.

An assortment of maladies to Peacock allowed Bill Conroy to start the majority of Red Sox games. There were some good efforts in that mix. On April 16, the Red Sox crushed Conroy's former team, the Athletics, 19–4. On a day that saw Ted Williams go 3-for-4 with a home run, four runs scored, and four RBI, Conroy added a pair of safeties, a run scored, and a run batted in. A compliment came from Connie Mack himself. Mack inquired about Boston's new catcher. When told that Conroy played for him, Mack smiled as he said, "Maybe I sent the wrong boy to the minors." On April 19, Conroy played before over fifty thousand at Yankee Stadium. Unfazed by the rabid Bronx mob, Conroy played solid defense and contributed a sacrifice fly RBI in Boston's 5–2 drubbing of baseball's perennial powerhouse. Conroy also had a great day on June 28 against Cleveland. Bill batted 2-for-3 with an RBI double—then came around to score during an eight-run spree in Boston's half of the fifth inning.

Conroy finished the year with 50 hits in 250 at bats for an even .200 batting average. That may not seem like much when a teammate named Ted Williams doubles that average. Despite this, Bill proved a tough at bat, selective in his pitches and always driving up an opposing hurler's pitch count. Conroy occasionally could knock them deep. He did it four times in 1942. After blasting a pair of home runs in consecutive days, Ted Williams and the boys started calling him "Basher." "Cut it out guys or I won't hit any more," Bill retorted half-sheepishly and half-tongue-in-cheek.

On defense, Conroy was quite competent. He allowed the second fewest total of passed balls (5) of any regular catcher in the league. The ultimate accolade to Bill came from player-manager Joe Cronin. Throughout the season, Cronin told the press, "Conroy's been a lifesaver for us. If we hadn't been lucky enough to have picked him in the draft, I don't know where we would have been."

In 1943, more players went off to war. Ted Williams enlisted in the Marine Corps and became a fighter pilot. Without "Teddy Ballgame," the team dropped from second place to second-from-last. Bill Conroy lost his starting job to rookie Jim Partee. For the season, backup Conroy batted just .180. He had a particularly rough outing on May 9. After Johnny Peacock's ejection for fighting with the Washington Senators' Ellis Clary, Bill Conroy replaced Peacock. Conroy finished the game, but all the boxscore reveals is that he committed an error. Conroy started the second game of the Boston-Washington doubleheader, committed another error early in the game, and then quickly replaced by Jim Partee. The end result for Bill Conroy's punctured twin bill: two games, two errors, and nothing else.

Bill Conroy backed up Partee and Hal Wagner in 1944. After playing 19 games, Conroy dislocated his thumb and was lost for the season. Then his number came up for the draft in 1945. He served in the Navy and even played ball for an all-service team out of Bainbridge, Maryland. After his stint in the service, Conroy returned to play some Triple-A ball until 1948. He never received another opportunity to hike his .199 major league batting average over the Mendoza Line. Bill Conroy died in 1997. He was 82.

No one compares Bill Conroy for catching greatness in the same breath as contemporaries Bill Dickey or Ernie Lombardi. That said, Conroy didn't embarrass himself either. Conroy could be counted on in emergencies or in mop-up roles. The war was a mixed blessing for his baseball career. Though it gave Conroy a second chance in the majors, it also cut short his playing days, at his peak, when he too answered Uncle Sam's call.

The General
Herman Franks, C
1914-

At 1300 S. 700 East Street in Salt Lake City, Utah lies Herman Franks Park. Not many career .199-hitting catchers get much of anything dedicated to them. However, in Franks' second career as a major league manager, he is one of the winningest skippers for both the Chicago Cubs and the San Francisco Giants. Fitting that a man tossed out of so many parks as a manager would have one named after him.

A terrific man behind the plate, Franks fielded the ball impeccably. His career .985 fielding average with only five passed balls are testaments to this. Owning a great arm that few runners dared to run on, Franks was also masterful at calling a game and handling pitchers. Franks caught a Tex Carleton no-hitter on April 30, 1940. He displayed his pit-bullish tenacity when it came to runners heading for home. When Herman got the ball, he blocked the plate with brick wall resolve and would thrust the ball into the runner's ribs with the fury of a Joe Louis left-hook.

In addition to playing baseball at the University of Utah, Herman Franks participated in wrestling. At just 18 years of age, he took his mitt and a train ticket to Los Angeles to play for the Pacific Coast League's Hollywood Stars. Franks spent a seven-year apprenticeship in the minors, highlighted by driving in 84 runs and leading catchers in fielding chances with Jacksonville of the West Dixie League in 1935.

Franks made his major league debut on April 27, 1939 with the St. Louis Cardinals. He came in to relieve starting catcher Mickey Owen in an extra-inning contest with Pittsburgh. In his first career at bat, Franks hit a ground ball to second baseman Pep Young, who bobbled the ball and the winning run came in to score. Franks was 1-for-17 (with 3 RBI) before St. Louis decided he needed more seasoning in the minor league ranks.

Sold to Brooklyn just before the start of the 1940 spring training sessions, Franks enjoyed his best playing days during his two seasons with the Dodgers. He was the team's backup catcher both years.

Brooklyn roared out to win their first nine games of the 1940 season. Win number nine was the Carleton no-hitter over the defending National League Champion Cincinnati Reds. Franks, who scored a run and threw out a baserunner trying to steal, made the game's most hair-raising play. Wally Berger led off the ninth and lifted a pop fly in front of the mound. It looked like the ball might drop in until Franks rushed out and caught it, colliding with Carleton in the process. Herman Franks made the front page of the *New York Times'* sports section that day. Seated with Carleton and manager Leo Durocher in between, the three enjoyed a truly joyous moment.

Though Herman Franks owned a .255 batting average as late as mid-July, he slumped to a .183 mark by season's end. He did have a decent RBI total (14) in only 131 at bats and hit his first of three career home runs. On defense, Franks fielded an impressive .990.

In 1941, the Dodgers took three catchers north: Babe Phelps, Franks, and the newly acquired Mickey Owen. However, Franks soon received a demotion to the minors. By mid-June, Dodgers manager Leo Durocher was doing a slow burn over Babe Phelps. Leo the Lip felt that Phelps was conjuring-up different maladies and ailments that resulted in him missing games. When Phelps failed to show up for a 4-game road swing to St. Louis, citing an irregular heartbeat, Durocher reached the end of his already short fuse. Durocher suspected Phelps of trying to avoid playing and suspended the alleged malingerer from the team. With only one catcher on the roster, Herman Franks returned to the Dodgers.

Franks immediately returned the favor. On June 23, he hit his only home run that season—a game-winning, pinch-hit, three-run shot against the Pirates. It earned Herman another picture on the front page of the sports section. Franks continued his torrid hitting the following day, going 2-for-4 in a shutout of the team from Steeltown. Franks' hot bat made Babe Phelps an expendable commodity. When questioned about Phelps' status, Leo Durocher made his position clear: "If he is reinstated and [GM] Larry MacPhail asks me whether I want him the answer is No. I don't want him on my club." Herman Franks was in Brooklyn to stay.

On June 26, Franks delivered an RBI single and later scored to help Brooklyn rout Boston, 11–2. Through July 2, Herman put together a five-game hitting streak. However, another New Yorker, Joltin' Joe DiMaggio earned all the buzz when it came to hitting streaks, in the midst of his legendary 56-game tear.

Franks was hitting as high as .283 through July. Another late-season fade placed him at .201 for the year. Along the way, Herman contributed, during a pennant race between Brooklyn and the St. Louis Cardinals, which was as exciting as any before or since. Franks caught the July 22 game against Cincinnati. Though Brooklyn lost, the tough catcher made news when his tag of Eddie Joost hit the Reds' shortstop in the jaw and knocked him out. On July 27, home plate umpire Al Barlick ejected Franks in the first inning for not seeing eye-to-eye with the arbiter on balls and strikes. As a bonus, Franks received a wire from National League President Ford Frick informing him he had been fined $25 for "continued use of profanity to Barlick." In an August 10 match, Franks chipped in a hit and crossed the plate twice to help beat Boston, 4–0.

In the end, Brooklyn won the National League pennant on the final weekend of the season. The Dodgers earned the honor of playing the Yankees in the first of seven Subway Series match-ups between the prides of Flatbush and the Bronx Bombers. In his only Series appearance, Herman Franks played in game one as a late inning replacement. His lone World Series at bat dramatically ended the game. Down 3–2 with one out in the bottom of the ninth inning, Ducky Joe Medwick and Pee Wee Reese each hit singles to make things interesting. Franks came up next. Durocher may have opted to pinch-hit for Franks, except for the fact he had no other catchers available. Red Ruffing induced Franks to bounce into a game ending double play. On defense, Herman did throw out Johnny Sturm while attempting to steal.

The Yankees would eventually win the Series in five games. Mickey Owen's infamous passed ball of Tommy Henrich's third strike occurred at a most inopportune time for Brooklyn. The Dodgers led 4–3 with two out and nobody on in the last inning of game four. Franks stated that he was in the bullpen at the time. Could he have caught that pitch? He replied, "I don't know. He [Owen] didn't shift his feet. That was one of his problems." Had Owen held onto the ball, the Dodgers would have squared the series at two games apiece. Instead, the Yankees rallied for four runs to win the game and take a commanding 3-games-to-1 lead in the Series. The Bronx Bombers finished off the devastated Dodgers the following afternoon.

As it had for many players in the 1940s, World War II interrupted Herman Franks' career. Franks received an officer's commission and served four years in the Navy. He played for Armed Forces' teams in Norfolk and in Hawaii, alongside the likes of pitcher Schoolboy Rowe, and outfielders Ted Williams and Joe DiMaggio.

In 1946, Herman Franks joined the Dodgers' Triple-A affiliate Montreal Royals. Normally, that would not be such a memorable event. However, one of Franks' teammates was Jackie Robinson, the first black man to walk on a professional ballfield in nearly 60 years. Franks enjoyed one of his greatest years with Montreal, belting a career-best 14 home runs and batting .280. Of greater importance, Franks became an ally to Jackie Robinson. In an interview with Mr. Franks, he recalled things being as rough for Jackie as they were in the majors the following year:

> He was a great guy. He did a great job for us in Montreal. What a great player. There were a lot of [racial] incidents with him. Players didn't want to play against him. Not all, but a lot of people resented him. We [the Royals] always stood by him. It was the least we could do.

Wherever the Royals and Jackie Robinson traveled, hostile fans followed. Tensions were especially high whenever the team traveled to Baltimore, where anti-Robinson sentiments were vehement. In one game, Montreal led 3–2 going into the bottom on the ninth. With two outs and a runner on first, the batter socked a ball deep into right center field for a hit. A perfect throw, off a relay by infielder Spider Jorgensen, made it to Herman Franks at home well ahead of the runner trying to score from first. When Franks performed his patented hard-tag on the runner to end the game, the irate Oriole went after Herman. With the two wrestling at home, an all-out melee ensued as fans swarmed out onto the field. Many of the fans actually chased after Robinson, taunting him from outside the clubhouse, and forcing him to remain there until morning under protective custody by his teammates.

In 1947, Herman Franks began his career as a manager, starting out in Triple-A with the American Association's St. Paul club. In August, the Philadelphia Athletics needed a back-up catcher after a broken finger sidelined Mike Guerra. Connie Mack summoned Franks' return to big-league baseball. Though not quite as old as Mack, Franks continued the grueling duties of catching in the major leagues after a six-year hiatus.

The year 1948 proved special for both the Philadelphia Athletics and Herman Franks. At the time, Mack was approaching the end of his 50-year reign as manager of the team. The cash-strapped club had languished in the American League second division every year since 1934, often in the cellar. However, the 1948 team would give Mack one final thrill. On top of the American League standings through August, Philadelphia finished in the upper division at 84–70. As for Franks, he hit a productive .224. Against St. Louis on August 7, his solid stick work yielded four hits and a pair of doubles in a 7–1 A's rout. When mentioned that he had a good year with the A's, Herman commented, "Oh not bad. I always enjoyed it there. [Philadelphia]"

In 1949, Leo Durocher, Franks' manager in Brooklyn, moved cross-town and now was skipper of the New York Giants. Durocher, always quite fond of Herman and impressed with his sound acumen of the game, hired him to the Giants so-called "board of strategy."   The Giants played the 1949 season rather flat and a listless defeat in the first game of a doubleheader against Cincinnati did nothing to placate Leo Durocher's sour disposition. Durocher stormed into the clubhouse with a cunning plan. He sought out Herman Franks.

"We gotta do something to shake up this ballclub," Durocher announced to his new coach.

"Yeah, Leo, we better," replied Herman, playing the role of the straight man. "Got any ideas?"

"I got a pip," answered Durocher with a mischievous smile. "What we're gonna do is activate you as a player and have you catch the second game."

"Who—me?" said the startled Franks.

Franks had not caught for nearly a year and added some considerable beef to his midsection since then. Gamely, Herman strapped on the tools for one last time. The result was a gem—two hits in three at bats and a run scored in a Giants victory. Herman Franks' chugging from first to third like a "wheezy steam engine," highlighted the contest. Franks safely made it to third after the ball caromed off his head. Franks, who had exhorted baserunners on first to stretch to third on singles hit to right, truly sacrificed his body to make his point.

The New York Giants employed Herman Franks as a full-time coach throughout the early part of the 1950s. Franks was third-base coach during the Giants' pennant-winning "Miracle of Coogan's Bluff" year of 1951. Some conspiracy theorists claim he stole the sign of the pitch to Bobby Thomson's playoff-winning home run that year. Franks also coached third base when the Giants won their last World Series in 1954.

Herman became Leo Durocher's primary hatchet man. That is, if Leo's throat was a bit hoarse, he would task Herman to holler at a particular player—something Herman could do as well as anybody in the game. "Herman, get on this guy," Leo the Lip would generally say. After a while, Herman Franks made a few enemies among the Giants' players. Franks would complain, "I gotta holler for that big nose so-and-so, then I'm the one that's got to risk my life out there [coaching at third]."

Alvin Dark started at shortstop for the great Giants' teams of the early 1950s. In his autobiography, Dark recalls a game against Brooklyn, at Ebbets Field, where he barreled into Jackie Robinson at third base. After the violent collision, the two exchanged words and threats. Herman Franks, coaching third, quickly attended to Dark, brushing him off and asking how he was. After the game, Herman shadowed Alvin Dark in the clubhouse. Without uttering a word, Herman later escorted Dark into the parking lot and into his car. Upon driving away, Herman looked at Dark, face blood red with fury, and read him the riot act, "You no-good Louisiana Cajun. What'd you do that for? Run into Jackie Robinson in Ebbets Field—are you crazy? Why'd you do a stupid think like that? If you want to have trouble with Robinson or [Don] Newcombe, don't ever do it in Ebbets Field!"

From 1956 to 1960, Herman scouted for the team. He did return briefly to coach the Giants after their move to San Francisco in 1958. Franks later became general manager of their Salt Lake City Pacific Coast League club in 1961.

Herman Franks also skippered teams in the Caribbean winter leagues during the 1950s. One of his clubs, the 1954–55 Santurce Crabbers of Puerto Rico, went 47–25 and won the Caribbean World Series. Franks felt the team was just a pitcher or two shy of being able to win the major league World Series. Herman possessed two great starters in Ruben Gomez and Sam Jones, a 20-game winner in 1959. Franks also had first baseman "Big George" Crowe (an All-Star in 1958), infielder Don Zimmer, and outfielder Bob Thurman (35 major league home runs) providing Santurce plenty of juice in the line-up. If that wasn't enough, Herman Franks also brought Willie Mays down with him and had a very young Roberto Clemente as well.

Herman Franks played an essential role in the development of Clemente. Originally signed with the Brooklyn Dodgers in 1954, Clemente played only sparingly in Brooklyn's minor league system. After coaching Clemente and witnessing his vast ability in winter ball, Franks knew that Roberto was a rare talent. Left unprotected by the Dodgers, Clemente was again eligible for the draft. Since the Giants were World Champions, they had no chance to draft Roberto. Rather than see Clemente languish in the Dodgers' organization, Herman gave Pittsburgh Pirates general manager Branch Rickey a tip on the youngster. The Pirates selected Clemente as the first pick of the 1954 draft.

Alvin Dark took over as Giants manager in 1961. Immediately after taking the reins, he asked Herman Franks to be his coach. However, Franks' commitment with Salt Lake City prevented him from doing so. Herman Franks eventually did join Dark in 1964. At 90–72, the 1964 Giants looked good on paper, but the team was filled with lots of internal strife. Cliques formed in the clubhouse and the players were given to being sullen and temperamental. Though never proven, players alleged that Dark's treatment of minorities was not even-handed. Before season's end, Alvin Dark's position as manager was untenable.

When Giants owner Horace Stoneham made overtures for Herman Franks as the next skipper, Franks treaded cautiously. Displaying loyalty, Franks immediately sought out Dark. "Do you care if I make a pitch for it?" Herman asked Alvin. "Go ahead," said Dark, "I'd rather see you get it than anyone else I know."

Herman Franks became the Giants' manager in 1965. He brought quite a tool bag of managerial skills. "I learned from every manager I ever played for," Herman told *New York Times* columnist Arthur Daley. "From Leo I learned aggressiveness and from Connie Mack I learned patience." However, Franks seemed much more in the Durocher mold. He liked being up close with the players. Though never afraid to get into a players' face when toughness was called for, Franks, like his mentor Durocher, much preferred conning the player into getting the desired result. Atlanta sportswriter Jim Minter described him this way: "I knew I would have a problem with Herman Franks, the Giants' crusty manager. Herman had all the qualifications of a mid-20th century baseball manager. He could cuss, chew tobacco, spit, and scratch." Minter recalls Herman disdainfully launching fusillades of tobacco juice at the sportswriter's feet, narrowly missing his shoes.

Franks' other intangibles helped him win the respect of his players. He spoke fluent Spanish, learned from his days managing Caribbean ball. Franks also enjoyed a well-deserved reputation of taking care of his players. He is credited with straightening out Willie Mays' financial affairs in San Francisco. The mutual friendship between Mays and Franks was obvious to everyone. When asked about the greatest player he ever witnessed, Franks' answers came back quicker than a Randy Johnson fastball: "Willie Mays."

The 1965 San Francisco Giants were a fine team. Willie Mays and Willie McCovey formed a lethal duo, smashing 52 and 39 home runs respectively to finish 1-2 in the National League. On the mound, the great Juan Marichal was at the top of his game. Finishing 22–13, he led the league in shutouts with 10. Batters could only manage a meager .205 batting average against him.

Unfortunately, Marichal was the centerpiece in one of the wildest brawls in baseball history that season. Once again, the Giants and their mortal rivals, the Dodgers, were in the heat of yet another tight pennant race. On August 20, San Francisco hosted the visiting Dodgers. The teams nearly came close to blows over controversial catcher's interference calls. First, the Dodgers' Maury Wills nipped catcher Tom Haller's mitt with his bat intentionally. Next, the Giants' Matty Alou, a fellow Dominican and best friend to Juan Marichal, retaliated by tipping the mask of catcher John Roseboro with his bat. Roseboro threw fire on gasoline as he nearly beaned Alou with his return throw to the mound. Cooler heads prevailed.

Two days later, Juan Marichal faced Sandy Koufax in a Duel of the Titans. However, the game turned ugly early. After Juan Marichal sent Wills and Ron Fairley sprawling on brushback pitches, Roseboro called on Sandy Koufax to give Marichal a taste of his own medicine as he stepped to the plate. Koufax pitched Marichal tight inside and Roseboro winged his throw back to Koufax just past Juan Marichal's ear. Soon, a flurry of words were exchanged between Marichal and Roseboro. Then, Roseboro suddenly ripped off his mask and stood up. Juan Marichal snapped. Marichal clubbed Roseboro across the head with his bat, opening a large gash. Umpires and teammates, including Herman Franks, subdued the enraged pitcher during the ensuing melee. Suspended for nine days over the incident, Marichal missed two starts. The suspension may have cost Franks and the Giants a pennant, as they finished behind the Dodgers by only two games.

Another razor-thin margin pennant race occurred in 1966. Again, Walter Alston's Dodgers eked out a $1\frac{1}{2}$-game margin over Franks' Giants. After Sandy Koufax's ailing left elbow forced him to retire after the 1966 season, the St. Louis Cardinals would inherit the role of spoiler for Herman Franks and the Giants over the next two seasons. By sweeping a pair from the Phillies in a season-ending doubleheader, the Giants clinched their third straight runner-up finish in 1967. Herman Franks observed the finale from the Candlestick Park press box—puffing on a cigar throughout.

One of Franks' former players, Hall of Famer Orlando Cepeda, was a chief catalyst to St. Louis' 1967 pennant. When Cepeda played with the Giants, he and Herman Franks never did see eye-to-eye. Franks questioned Cepeda's mental toughness, while Cepeda accused his manager of deliberately trying to run him out of San Francisco. Though departing on less-than-amicable terms, during Cepeda's later arrest and imprisonment for possession of marijuana, Herman Franks first signed a petition recommending his former slugger's early release.

The Cardinals, led by the unhittable Bob Gibson, left all rivals in the dust to win the 1968 pennant. The Giants positioned themselves for yet another season as the bridesmaid. However, this San Francisco club was losing some of its luster. Most noticeable was the offensive decline of Willie Mays, now in his late thirties. Sportswriter Arthur Daley had the opportunity to meet with Franks and other members of the Giants' brain trust. Daley described Franks alternately as "lovable," "grumpy," "expansive," and "scornful," all within a span of minutes. Reading his fan mail before a game, Franks said to coaches Charlie Fox and Peanuts Lowery, "Listen to this. Some fathead writes: 'Mays, I'm sorry to say, is through. He can't hit anymore.'"

As Franks read on, he became even more angry.

"He wants me to get rid of Mays, [Ron] Hunt, and [Jim] Davenport. What's this clown trying to do—get us into the cellar?"

This prompted Franks to rip the letter into shreds and bellow out in disgust. Charlie Fox, writing out the lineup card for the day, sat at a desk. Lowrey said, "Just a minute, Charlie. Maybe you should leave Mays out of the lineup."

"I already have," said Fox, responded quickly.

But Franks refused to react as expected. He remained calm. "What the hell. I got no imagination. Let's use the same line-up even if we have to bat Mays in the clean-up spot."

Clyde King took over as Giants' manager before the 1969 season. New manager. Same result. The Giants again finished second that year. As Herman was quick to point out, he was not fired by owner Horace Stoneham. Franks resigned from the position after some undisclosed disagreement between himself and Stoneham. In fact, Franks stated that just a few years after his departure, Stoneham confided to Franks that he wished he had Franks back at the helm.

Franks did not really need the job. Before the era of mega-dollar contracts, Ty Cobb and Herman Franks were two of the wealthiest ex-players around. Whereas Cobb made some wise investments, especially in Coca-Cola stock, Franks earned his fortune running supermarkets. His keen business sense enabled him to turn a profit the one season he ran the Salt Lake City club. For years that franchise had been awash in red ink. Herman Franks purportedly attempted to form a group to purchase the Giants in the late 1960s. Had he closed the deal, Franks would have made Willie Mays the first black manager. He also attempted to purchase the New York Yankees in 1972, but lost out to George Steinbrenner.

Before the 1977 season, Chicago Cubs' general manager Bob Kennedy needed a new skipper to guide his failing team, which languished in the National League East's second division for the past four years. He called upon his friend, Herman Franks, to take a hiatus from his lucrative (and less stressful) business career to manage the Cubs. Franks accepted.

Former pitcher Mike Krukow, a 14-year veteran with 124 career wins, recalls his education as a rookie under Herman Franks:

> In 1977, my rookie year with the Chicago Cubs, my manager was Herman Franks. The press that surrounded the Cubs that year were a mixture of characters that had been the covering the game of baseball for what seemed like a thousand years. I really had little experience with the media unless you count the minor leagues. The difference being numbers, in the minor leagues then you had one beat writer that covered the team and did not make road trips. In the big leagues you had about eight beats, that were with the team everyday of the season, and 12 columnists in Chicago alone. So I think it is fair to say that I had no clue as to how to deal with the press.
>
> One day, after a start that did not go particularly well, I was confronted by the writers in front of my lockers. The first question was simple, "What went wrong?" Well the last several weeks I had been watching some of the older players on the team and when they were asked an uncomfortable question they simply said, "No Comment." So, in that I did not want to go into great detail about a stanky outing, I replied "No Comment." Eyebrows immediately were raised.

> The interview went on hold as Jerome Holtzman, an elder statesman and now a Hall of Fame Writer, turned around and walked up to Herman Franks' office. He informed the skipper about how his prized rookie just "no commented" the boys. The next scenario was something to see.
>
> Herman Franks came bouncing down the stairs to the main locker room with nothing on but a pair of white, jockey underwear. He was smoking a huge cigar and he was heading right to my locker. His face was red and the bellows of smoke were emitting from his head. I couldn't tell if the smoke came from the cigar or from out of his ears. He was not happy.
>
> He positioned himself right in front of me and proceeded to give me the "Jimmy Swaggert" about how I should conduct myself in front of the press. In glorious hyperbole, he explained that the press was responsible for putting "asses in the seats" and that I had no "clue of the business formula" that was necessary for the game to survive. He went on and on, which I believe was for the benefit of the press corps, about how I owed it to these hardworking scribes.
>
> He summed it all up by saying that if I ever no commented the writers again during his tenure as manager that he would personally tattoo the words "NO COMMENT" across my forehead. With that, he u-turned it back up to his office and my interview session with the boys started over. I talked for about 45 minutes.
>
> The next day when I got to Wrigley Field, Herman called me into his office. He sat me down and simply said, "Kid, remember one thing about the press. If you are fair with them, then they will be fair with you." It was some of the best advice I ever got.

Franks' take on this amusing story was that it was not his nature to berate a rookie in front of the press, as Krukow claimed, and probably "counseled" the pitcher outside of the scribes' earshot. Franks did confirm that, on occasion, he would roam the Cubs' clubhouse in the comfort of his underwear.

During the 1977 season, Herman Franks found a novel way to get Chicago fannies into Wrigley Field seats: win baseball games. By June 27, Franks' ball club soared to 45–22, atop the National League East standings by a walloping $7^1/_2$ games. Then, like so many other years, the syndrome of playing so many day games in the Wrigley Field sauna took effect. The Cubs' plunge commenced. Chicago's stranglehold on the National League East narrowed down to just three games on July 6. Asked about his slumping team, Herman Franks remained unperturbed, "We're still in first place and we're in good shape." Then he added, "Maybe we'll tighten this thing up and have some real fun." Unfortunately, Franks' predictions came true. The grizzled manager must not have had much fun watching the Cubs fade to an 81–81 record and fourth place.

Herman's high-water season with the Cubs of Chicago occurred in 1978. That year, the Cubbies finally made it back into the upper tier of the NL East, finishing third with a 79-83 record. Near the close of the 1979 season and the team playing above .500 (78–76) at the time, the Social Security-eligible Herman Franks announced that he was no longer a major league manager. Though Bob Kennedy hoped to hire him back, numerous reports speculated Franks would not return for the 1980 season. Interviewed before his final game, Franks said. "I've had it right up to here," putting his right hand to his throat. "Some of these players are actually crazy. They don't want to talk to newspaper people and they want special buses for themselves and the reporters. It's silly things like this that get you fed up. They don't seem to realize that the game of baseball cannot exist without the newspaper people. And they don't seem to know that when the newspaper guys don't want to talk to them, then they're really in trouble."

Franks then brandished a checkbook and showed that he cut a check for $24,000 to join an exclusive country club in Salt Lake City. "You don't think for a minute that I would shell out $24,000 and come back here and manage. Next year I'll be at the country club every day. That's what I'll be doing."

In his final game as manager, Franks watched the Cubs lose 6–0 to Pittsburgh. Joey Amalfitano took over the last week of the season. One of Herman Franks' final statements served a fitting tribute to long-suffering Cubs' fans, "The Chicago Cubs' fans are the greatest fans in baseball. They've got to be."

In his three years with the Cubs (1977-1979), Franks owned a 238–241 record. Compare that to the lusterless 216–270 record the Cubs owned from 1974-1976 and their horrendous 175–252 in the three seasons after Franks' departure.

Herman Franks' innovations helped define his success as manager. While with Chicago, Franks invented the modern-day strategy of the specialist "closer" with relief pitcher Bruce Sutter. Franks also came up with the idea of using a power hitter as leadoff batter, when he inserted San Francisco's Bobby Bonds into the #1 spot in 1968.

Eighty-six-years young, Franks made a showing for the Giants' inaugural game at Pac Bell Park. Despite his advanced age, Herman's mind remains quite sharp; he recalled, in detail, events that occurred 60 years ago. Franks laments the passing of many of his teammates as time unmercifully marches on.

At the close of the century, Herman Franks received yet another accolade. As selected by *Sports Illustrated*, Franks earned praise as one of the state of Utah's 50 greatest athletes. He's done everything a typical red-blooded American male dreams: go to college, serve his country during the war, play/coach/manage major league baseball, and make a fortune in big business—all the while puffing big stogies.

The Pro From Nanty-Glo
Charlie Metro, OF
1918-

Charlie Metro's career in baseball spanned nearly half a century of playing, managing, coaching, and scouting. That included three years and a .193 batting average as a wartime major league ballplayer. His career seems comparable to that of Herman Franks. Despite a weak bat, Metro was one of the best defensive outfielders of his day and a speedy plunderer of bases. A modern-day player best typifying Charlie's brand of play would be Gary Pettis, the exciting outfielder who played for the Angels throughout the 1980s.

Born Charles Moreskonich in the Pennsylvania town of Heilwood over 80 years ago, Charlie later lived in Nanty-Glo, whose distinctive name is Welsh for "Valley of Coal." Metro learned the game on the sandlots of this austere coal-mining community. A high schooler, Metro made the fateful decision to cut class and attend a St. Louis Browns' tryout in nearby Johnstown. He proceeded to hit several balls into the left field screen.

Impressed, the Brownies offered Metro a contract and an escape from the coal mines that swallowed up the majority of the youth in Nanty-Glo.

Over the next six years, Charlie earned his way up the minor leagues. In 1939, Charlie smashed 14 home runs and 75 RBI for Mayfield of the Kitty League. During an interview, Charlie recalled one of his teammates as the great Vern Stephens, the first true slugging shortstop. Stephens still holds the season RBI record for a shortstop with 159. Charlie also contributed a big 1941 season with Texarkana of the Cotton State League, slamming 20 home runs, 96 RBI, and a .287 batting average.

Promoted to Beaumont of the Texas League in 1942, Charlie hit a speed bump in his road to the majors. Managed by Steve O'Neill, who would pilot the Tigers to a world title three years hence, Beaumont boasted an outfield choc-a-block with talent. Metro competed for playing time against Dick Wakefield, Walter "Hoot" Evers, and Johnny Lipon—all of whom went on to accomplished major league careers with Detroit. Metro played sparingly in the outfield and hit just .219. Typically, Charlie came in for Wakefield for late-inning defense. He also bought playing time by experimenting at new positions, such as second base.

Metro recalled a particularly spectacular play while at Beaumont. Playing center field against San Antonio, a San Antonio player was on second when the next batter hit a monstrous fly deep over Metro's head. Charlie raced for the ball and made a beautiful over-the-shoulder catch just in front of the wall in center field. His momentum taking him into the wall, Charlie pushed off, spun around, and launched a 300-foot strike to the third baseman. The baserunner, decoyed perfectly by the third baseman, nonchalantly tagged-up at second and made his way to third base. When the runner saw the third baseman waiting for him with the ball, he appeared stunned and embarrassed. After Beaumont came off the field, O'Neill told Charlie Metro, "That was the greatest play I ever seen in my entire life."

Charlie Metro eventually made the Detroit Tigers roster. Early in the 1943 season, the Tigers brought him up to play the center garden. Charlie recalled his very first game, which he considered one of his most memorable moments as a major league player:

> We were playing the St. Louis Browns. My first at bat was against Al Hollingsworth. He struck me out on three pitches; the bat never left my shoulder. On my next at bat, I got him back when I lined a base hit. That's the game that stands out most in my mind.

Metro became a hero that day with his second hit, coming around to score the deciding run in Detroit's 4–3 conquest. For the year, Charlie appeared in 44 games, mostly as a pinch hitter/runner, and batted an even .200. It could have been much higher, if not for an 0-for-6 marathon against the White Sox.

Metro played another 38 games for the Tigers in 1944. Charlie was excited to be with a pennant contender, as Detroit battled eventual American League champion St. Louis tooth and nail all season. Then, his career with the Tigers took an abrupt and rather acrimonious end in August.

Detroit wanted a roster spot for veteran pitcher Ray Henshaw. Tigers' general manager Jack Zeller originally made a deal to send Metro to Indianapolis, but Metro said, "The hell with this," and refused to go. Zeller asked, sarcastically, "What do you want, your outright release?" "Yes," retorted Charlie, "that's what I want." "Then go get it," he was told. Metro stormed into Zeller's office and obtained a release form. A few minutes later, while cleaning out his locker, Metro met up with veteran outfielder Roger "Doc" Cramer and told him his situation. "Don't do anything until I come back," Cramer told Metro, "I'm going to call Philadelphia." Just then, Zeller came to Charlie and said that he had made another deal. "Oh no you don't," said Metro, "you gave me my release." "Oh, I was just kidding," Zeller replied. "Well, I'm not kidding," Metro answered, waving the signed form in Zeller's face.

Charlie's tactics worked out handsomely. Doc Cramer returned and told Metro, "I just talked to Connie Mack and he wants you in Philadelphia as soon as possible." On August 13, the Philadelphia Athletics obtained Metro from Detroit for the waiver price. He received a contract worth $8,000, 15 percent more than his pay with the Tigers. Though Metro hardly sparkled at the plate for either team, hitting .100 for the Athletics and .161 for the year, Charlie played errorless ball. Connie Mack occasionally spelled his middle infielders with Metro.

For the early part of the 1945 season, Charlie patiently waited his turn. His break came on June 1, when Larry Rosenthal crashed into the Shibe Park left field wall and injured his leg. Suddenly, Metro became a regular in the A's outfield. Metro started strong, knocking four hits in a June 3 doubleheader against St. Louis. Metro repeated that trick three days later against Boston. On June 11, Charlie singled in the only run for the A's in a 3–1 exhibition-game loss to the Philadelphia Phillies. The game, part of a so-called "Sports-Go-Bang Show," raised $5 million in war bonds. The following day, Metro's bat went go-bang. He walloped his first career home run to help Philadelphia beat the Red Sox.

When the Athletics took the coach out of 30th Street Station in mid-June for a 22-game road swing, Connie Mack and the boys didn't realize they were on a train destined for oblivion. The battered Athletics dropped 20 of the 22 road games. Metro played sparingly and hit the same. Metro's three-game hitting streak yielded four RBI in consecutive losses to the White Sox. Upon Philadelphia's return home, they managed to win a few games. On July 24, the Athletics and Tigers battled 24 innings in a 1–1 deadlock called due to curfew. Charlie Metro pinch-hit in the 24th inning and delivered a single, but was left stranded.

For the season, Charlie managed .210 in 65 games. While Philadelphia played terrible baseball, at least Charlie did some slugging for Connie Mack, belting out ten doubles, a triple, and three home runs. Aside from his home run in Boston, Metro's two other blasts came at the expense of the Yankees. Hank Borowy, a 1945 American League All-Star, and Jim Turner were Charlie's victims. However, with many players returning from military service, Metro landed with Casey Stengel's Oakland Oaks of the Pacific Coast League before the year was out.

While in Oakland, Metro made the acquaintance with a cocky teenage infielder that looked up to the seasoned Charlie Metro. "Even then, he told everyone he was going to be a great major league player," Metro said of Billy Martin. The two became longtime friends.

A long tenure in the minor leagues followed. Metro played his entire 1946 season in the Pacific Coast League—first with Oakland, then with the Seattle Rainiers. Jo-Jo

White, a former outfielder on the great Detroit teams of the 1930s, managed Charlie at Seattle. Metro told an amusing tale of a game where he played center field, while manager White played in left. With a steady drizzle falling over Seattle's Sick's Stadium, an opposing batter lofted a two-out fly ball to center field. As the ball sailed towards Charlie, he just stood there motionless, arms to his side, while staring high into the sky. Jo-Jo White nearly became apoplectic while exhorting Charlie to go get the ball. At the last possible instant, the immobile Metro twitched his gloved hand up and caught the ball without seemingly moving another muscle. "Great catch; but don't you ever do that to me again," White told Metro as they made their way to the dugout.

Starting in 1947, Charlie Metro became a player-manager in the low minors. Having learned from the likes of Mack and Stengel, Metro was more than ready to be a skipper. Though competing in remote baseball outposts like Bisbee, Arizona and Twin Falls, Idaho, Charlie achieved no small level of satisfaction as a hitter. With Twin Falls in 1948, Metro blasted .351 with 22 HR and 116 RBI. If that was not enough, Metro managed Twin Falls into the Pioneer League championship. By 1953, he concentrated on being a full-time manager. Successful stints at Triple-A Vancouver and Denver (who won the 1960 American Association Pennant) boosted Charlie into the majors as a coach with the Chicago Cubs in 1962.

Unfortunately, Charlie became one of the "professors" in the Chicago Cubs failed "College of Coaches" experiment. Phil Wrigley, Cubs Owner and "Dean of the College," devised the hare-brained concept in 1961. By alternating the team's coaches as acting managers, Wrigley rationalized the team would learn from the strengths of each coach. As baseball pundits predicted, a lack of continuity ensued. Four coaches "led" the Cubbies to a 64–90 record in 1961.

After Elvin Tappe and Lou Klein got Chicago off to a 16–34 start for the 1962 season, Metro's shot to manage came up. Charlie asked to keep the post for the rest of the year; the other coaches seemed more than happy to oblige. That effectively ended the College of Coaches.

Charlie Metro tried some unconventional tactics to get into the minds of rival managers, like commissioning a handwriting expert to analyze the signatures of Walter Alston, Alvin Dark, Casey Stengel, and the rest of the National League skippers. Presumably, the handwriting analysis would reveal secret strategies. However, the only thing that the handwriting actually revealed was the Cubs' 59–103 won-lost record. The Cubs could thank the woeful 40–120 New York Mets, and Casey Stengel's signature, for keeping them out of the National League cellar.

Over the next few years, Charlie worked as a scout for the St. Louis Cardinals and coached for Al Lopez's Chicago White Sox in 1965. In 1968, the Kansas City Royals hired Charlie as their Director of Player Procurement. The Royals enjoyed much early success through the development of their vanguard farm system. Metro's astute abilities to assess young talent played a large role. Late in the 1969 season, Metro coached for the Royals and the next year took the top field job. In a twist of irony, Cincinnati Reds' General Manager Bob Howsam was about to offer the reins of the "Big Red Machine" to Metro. Howsam's alternate choice, Sparky Anderson, worked out well.

After a 19–33 start in 1970, Bob Lemon took over the Royals. Charlie then became a scout for several teams. He was a "spy-in-the-sky scout" for the Dodgers during the team's glory years in the late-1970s/early-1980s. In 1982, Metro's good friend Billy Martin hired him as a coach for the Oakland A's. The kind gesture by Martin allowed Charlie to qualify for a major league pension after forty-five years in the game. Metro later returned to the Dodgers and continued to work in major league baseball until 1984.

Today, in his eighties, Charlie still raises quarter horses on his ranch near Denver. Though he never won a Gold Glove, Charlie received some recent publicity by having his hands cast in bronze. Artist Raelee Frazier performed the sculpting for her "Hitter's Hands" series. Metro, in a way, served as "manager" of this project, as he recruited and organized 25 Hall of Fame players to get their hands bronzed by Ms. Frazier.

With Ms. Frazier busy bronzing the hands of Sammy Sosa, Charlie made this observation about his own major league career, "I was a great outfielder, and I had a great arm. But I've looked at my hands a lot and thought, 'Why didn't these hands hit as well as they fielded and threw?'"

Charlie passes a rich legacy to the game of baseball. Throughout all his stops as a minor league manager, he influenced and shaped the careers of many players. Eleven of his charges became major league managers. Another thirty-five eventually became coaches in the big leagues. Hall of Famers Steve Carlton, Brooks Robinson, Ernie Banks, Billy Williams, Lou Brock, and Congressman Jim Bunning all were Metro-trained men. Metro's amazing life would make for a great book; and it has in his autobiography, *Safe by a Mile.*

Teddy Ballgame, Jr.
Cramer Beard, Jr. OF
1921-

Though both went by Ted, were lefthanders, and lost several prime years to the war, with a career batting average of .198, no one will ever confuse Ted Beard with Ted Williams. Described as a gamer, Cramer Theodore Beard was dangerous on the basepaths, had surprising power that belied his smallish stature, and played a solid outfield.

Beard grew up in Woodsboro, Maryland. His birthplace is not too far from Burkittsville, the town that gained notoriety as the setting for the low-budget/high-scare movie, *The Blair Witch Project.*

Ted Beard started playing professional baseball in 1942, then served three years in the U.S. Army as a medic. He applied his Military Occupational Specialty extensively during some of the harshest episodes of armed conflict ever witnessed by humankind, during the Pacific Theater in World War II.

After the war, Beard returned as a "lean, mean, hitting machine" and batted .328 with York of the Inter-State League in 1946. In 1948, he enjoyed a spectacular season for Class-AAA Indianapolis. Batting .301 with 85 RBI would be a great year in anybody's book. However, Beard also hit and ran for 17 triples, scored 131 runs, and drew 128 walks—all leading figures in the American Association. A total package, Beard even led outfielders with a remarkable 32 assists. Al Lopez, a nineteen-year major league veteran catcher, skippered the Indianapolis Indians. Lopez would later captain Cleveland and the Chicago White Sox to pennants in the next decade. The 1948 Indians did much to enhance Lopez's resume. They dominated the American Association and finished atop the standings with a 100–54 record. Indianapolis seemed a cinch to win the playoffs.

Immediately after clinching the pennant, the Pittsburgh Pirates announced they were calling up Ted Beard, who had just been voted the Indians' Most Valuable Player. Club President and majority-owner Frank McKinney (crooner Bing Crosby was one of the minority owners) kept a pre-season promise that Pittsburgh would not call up any players until after Indianapolis won the pennant. Now the 1948 Pirates were battling for the National League pennant and McKinney wanted Beard as a late-season addition. Manager Billy Meyer added, "I like his speed; and he's a great defensive player. That's where we can use him. The way the team's going now, it may take a while to break him in, but he'll be playing soon."

Now "Beard-less," cautious optimism about the playoffs prevailed for the Indians. In the opening round, Indianapolis played third-place St. Paul, a club they had no trouble with during the regular season. However, the St. Paul Saints upset the Indians in six games. But Ted Beard's year was anything but over.

When Billy Meyer saw Beard practice in-person, he and the Pirates were convinced. The 27-year-old rookie went right into the starting lineup. In a September 5 doubleheader split with Chicago, Ted Beard knocked two triples and made several spectacular catches in center field. Beard proceeded to hit safely in his first four games.

Cramer Beard wound up playing 25 games that September, hardly as an experimental player. Pittsburgh trailed the front-running Boston Braves by as few as 4 games on September 12. Pirates' management obviously thought Ted Beard had something to offer; otherwise, he would have languished in the dugout. With three triples, five stolen bases, and 15 runs scored in only 81 at bats, Beard savored a most delicious "cup of coffee." Pittsburgh eventually faded to fourth place that year, $8^1/_2$ games behind the Braves. This would be Pittsburgh's only finish in the first division for the next ten seasons.

Bouncing up and down between Pittsburgh and Indianapolis for the next three years, Beard's career year in the majors occurred in 1950. Beard did a little bit of everything that season. The Opening Day leadoff batter, Beard placed safeties in the first six games of the season. During that stretch, against St. Louis, Ted pulled off a "Rickey Henderson," hitting the game's first offering by Howard Pollett for a home run. The resounding blast reached the right field pavilion roof in Sportsman's Park. Beard also singled and scored a second run to earn player of the game honors in the 8–4 Pittsburgh win. Two days later, Beard, Ralph Kiner, Nanny Fernandez, and Wally Westlake each skied home runs in a 9–2 drubbing of Cincinnati. After showing he could hit the long ball, Beard's second home run came by way of speed and guts; it was an inside-the-park shot.

Ted Beard cooled down a bit following his torrid start, but the Pirates stayed hot. On April 28, he singled to light the fuse of a Pittsburgh seventh-inning rally to beat St. Louis 4–3. For an instant in 1950, the Buccaneers ship sailed into first place. Against the Giants on May 5, Beard opened yet another assault with a sixth-inning single, advancing to second when Don Mueller's throw to first glanced off Ted's head. Beard scored twice in that win and was perched among the league's top-5 leaders in runs.

A week later, the Pittsburgh galleon took on water when Ted Beard broke his wrist sliding. They lost their perky leadoff hitter for a month. The Pirates slid in the standings during that period. Beard returned in late June, back in the leadoff spot. He was up to his usual tricks against Philadelphia on June 22. Beard, having already scored once earlier in the game, was on third and Henry Schenz on first. Pirates' outfielder Gus Bell hit to pitcher Bob Miller who threw to Granny Hamner to force Schenz at second and Hamner threw to Eddie Waitkus to double Bell at first. Waitkus' peg to catcher Andy Seminick caught Beard trying to score. Triple play. Philadelphia later won 7–4. Fortune such as this allowed the long downtrodden "other" team from Pennsylvania to win a rare pennant that year.

In a late June weekend affair against the Brooklyn Dodgers, Beard scored three times in a 19–12 losing effort. The following day, Beard tallied four more runs scored with two RBI. His only hit was career home run number three. The *New York Times* described the 16–11 Pirates' win as "a three-hour eleven-minute monstrosity." After the bombardment over two days, Pittsburgh and Brooklyn pitchers may have been allowed to wear WWII-era helmets.

As Pittsburgh sank to the cellar during the sultry days of July, Ted Beard offered a few more interesting efforts. His biggest feat is an accomplishment shared by monster sluggers Babe Ruth, Willie Stargell, Mickey Mantle, Eddie Mathews, and Willie McCovey, among four others. These players are the only ones ever to blast a home run over the 86-foot high right field grandstand wall of Pittsburgh's old Forbes Field.

During a conversation with Ted Beard, just after his 80th birthday, he cited this four-master as the signal event of his major league career. Ted teed his shot against the Boston Braves—off a fastball delivered by Bob Hall. "The first time up," recalled Beard, "I lined out to the second baseman [Roy Hartsfield]. The next time up, I lined out to right field [Willard Marshall]. The third time I got it in the air and hit it over the roof." Beard's bomb was no odd occurrence. Though primarily a line drive hitter, Beard earned a reputation for hitting tape-measure shots.

Beard saved one more top-quality effort that season against the Phillies on July 20. Beard secured a 3-for-5 day and scored twice while the Pirates prevailed 10–8. Whether due to the lingering effects of his May wrist injury or that the last-place Pirates had nothing to lose and wanted to look at some other outfielders, Ted Beard finished the season in his now-all-too-familiar haunts of Indianapolis.

That 1950 season, Beard socked 4 HR, with 12 RBI, and a .232 average. Particularly impressive was the fact that Beard scored 32 runs in only 177 at bats, nearly a 100-run pace through the course of an entire season. Had Ted Beard averted injury, he might have received Rookie of the Year consideration.

After batting a slim .188 with the Pirates in 1951, Ted Beard exited to Hollywood, but not to become a movie star. Beard spent the season with the Hollywood Stars of the Pacific Coast League. This was back in the days when PCL teams played 180-game schedules and the league was a legitimate threat to become a third major league. With the PCL operating as an Open Classification circuit at the time, major league teams could not option roster players to these west coast outfits. However, through a special arrangement, Pittsburgh sent Beard and other players to the Stars for future considerations—just like a trade.

The 1952 Stars may have been one of the finest minor league teams of the decade. However, they may be infamous for their wearing pinstriped shorts, complemented by knee socks and rayon T-shirts. Their manager, Fred Haney (who later managed the Milwaukee Braves to two National League pennants in the late 1950s), thought that the Stars would be speedier with the new uniforms. Haney picked up the idea after observing the attire of a British soccer team. Former Star Gene Handley later recalled, "The nicest thing any of the other teams said to us was, 'Hello, sweetheart.'"

While opposing teams fervently ridiculed the Stars, the shorts-clad team earned the final say on the field. Hollywood won the Pacific Coast League pennant in 1952 with a 109–71 record, outdistancing their only serious challenger, the defending champion Oakland Oaks. Hollywood featured strong pitching and a speedy offense. Ted Beard batted .269 with 11 home runs, 53 RBI, and 24 stolen bases for the Stars.

Beard went from the decade's best minor league team to the decade's worst major league team. Pittsburgh re-signed Beard and he batted .182 in 15 games. Branch Rickey, who masterminded St. Louis and Brooklyn sucessfully as general manager, failed miserably in his youth movement with the Pirates. People in Pittsburgh dubbed them the "Rickeydinks." Other than a fifteen-minute chat with "The Mahatma," when he was first called up to Pittsburgh, Ted had virtually no other contact with Rickey.

The 1952 Pirates finished a dreadful 42–112, the worst season record in Pittsburgh history. Starting catcher Joe Garagiola summed up the Pirates: "We had a lot of triple-threat guys—slip, fumble and fall." Even Ted Beard could not escape the vitriol of the Pittsburgh press. Wrote Dave Ailes, sports editor of the *Pittsburgh Tribune-Review*: "The [1952] Pirates had a fast-stepping young outfielder named Ted Beard. Unfortunately, baseball rules denied Beard the opportunity to steal first base, and that was the only way he could get there."

After suffering the humiliation of playing the summer in short pants, Ted Beard received a new form of indignation with the Pirates' attire: batting helmets. Always the innovator, Branch Rickey made Pittsburgh the first big league team to wear protective headgear. Catcalls, such as "Look at the coal miners," and "Hey, Space Man," rang out of bleachers from Boston to St. Louis. One opposing pitcher wickedly commented, "Who's going to throw at .200 hitters?" Of course, hundreds of batters since have been saved from catastrophic beanings and owe the Pirates for incurring the initial ignominy.

Released outright by the Pirates before the 1953 season, Ted Beard returned west to the Hollywood Stars. With a 106–74 record, Hollywood repeated as Pacific Coast League champions. Beard led the team in batting with.286 average and socked a career-best 17 home runs. In one incredible day, Ted Beard walloped four home runs in *one game* against the San Diego Padres. "I hit four home runs and six RBIs and we won the game 6–5," said Beard of his personal slugfest.

Another memorable incident occurred that year involving Beard, although it seemed more boxing than baseball related. In what many call the wildest brawl in the history of professional baseball, the archrival Los Angeles Angels came to visit the Stars for a doubleheader. In game one, a fracas broke out after Los Angeles' Joe Hatten plunked Hollywood's Frank Kelleher in the back with a bad curveball. Kelleher, a mild-mannered fly chaser who had never been ejected from a game in his 17-year career, dropped his bat, walked out to the pitcher's mound, and punched Hatten. The pitcher returned the favor.

This brought players from both teams out onto the diamond and a half dozen hand-to-hand scuffles ensued. Ted Beard, along with another player, restrained an enraged Hatten from reengaging Kelleher.

After Frank Kelleher's ejection, Beard entered the game as a pinch-runner. Moments later, Beard, while successfully stealing third, unleashed a high slide that spiked Los Angeles' third baseman Murray Franklin on the arm and chest. Franklin, a ball of fury after the intentional spiking, leaped on top the prone Beard and flailed at him. This ignited a second donnybrook, which saw LA's Bud Hardin get his right eye cut and badly swollen. Hollywood's Eddie Malone suffered a spike in the leg, and Angels' first baseman Fred Richards had his pants torn to shreds.

Los Angeles Police Chief William Parker, watching the melee on television, called in every available police unit to Gilmore Field. Fifty police officers swarmed onto the field, into the teeth of the brawl. After half an hour of fighting, order was finally restored. With quasi-martial law installed, the doubleheader was completed with police stationed at each clubhouse.

Ted provided some insight on the Pacific Coast League of the 1950s: "Guys like myself made up the league—well developed players. We didn't have too many youngsters playing." Asked if any celebrities ever showed up to see the Stars play, Ted Beard recalled that William Frawley, television's Fred Mertz on I Love Lucy, never missed a game. Not too surprising, considering Frawley appeared as managers, scouts or other baseball-related characters in several films (e.g., *Alibi Ike*, *The Babe Ruth Story*, and *Rhubarb*). Frawley was also a part owner of the Stars.

Many other celebrities attended Stars' games. Movie actor Frank Lovejoy of *Strategic Air Command*, *House of Wax*, and *The Winning Team*—the movie which starred Ronald Reagan as pitcher Grover Cleveland Alexander, often took in a ballgame. Michael O'Shea, husband of actress Virginia Mayo, was another celebrity-status everyday fan of the Stars. "He [O'Shea] would wear a uniform with my number on it and sit in the dugout," Beard laughed in his recollection. Other well-known celebs known to visit Gilmore Field were George Raft, Gary Cooper, Bing Crosby, Gene Autry, Robert Taylor, George Burns, Gracie Allen, Harry Warner, and Cecil B. DeMille. Autry, Cooper, and Crosby all shared a deep passion for baseball. Gene Autry later owned the California/Anaheim Angels franchise for long years. Gary Cooper portrayed Yankee legend Lou Gehrig in *Pride of the Yankees*. Bing Crosby owned the Pittsburgh Pirates.

Some lovely representatives of the fairer gender also appeared with the Stars. Elizabeth Taylor served as the team's batgirl during her teenage years. The well-endowed Jayne Mansfield became "Miss Hollywood Stars" one year. Mansfield's appearances onto the field released a chorus of moans and howls from the male fans. It was said that no team, even in the major leagues, had as many beautiful women attend games as the Stars. When Beard—single when he played in the league—was asked if he ever dated any starlets, he paused and replied, "No... Not really."

Ted moved up the coast and played with the San Francisco Seals from mid-season in 1954 until 1955. As the Pacific Coast League's prominence waned, Ted returned to Indianapolis in 1956. He hit a respectable .270 that year, but now 35 years of age, Beard's playing in the majors seemed a long shot.

Bet on the long shot. In 1957, Ted Beard imitated Ty Cobb. In just 96 games with the Indianapolis Indians, Beard scored 91 times and posted an extraordinary .347 batting average. The Chicago White Sox gave Ted a couple of shots in 1957 and 1958. Beard scored 15 runs and hit .205 in 37 games for Chicago in 1957, but made only two hits in 19 appearances in 1958. One of his hits was a home run.

Ted continued to play professional ball with Indianapolis until 1963—42 years old at the time of his final game. All told, Beard played an incredible 13 seasons for the same minor league ballclub. He became a player-manager for Indianapolis in 1960, credited with a 35–50 managerial record. Asked if he enjoyed managing, Beard answered: "Yes and no. I wasn't crazy about it."

Despite missing three years of ball playing while serving his country in wartime, Cramer T. Beard's lifetime minor league ledger compares favorably with some of the best players in minor league history—men like Ike Boone, Ox Eckhardt, and Joe Hauser. With his three "lost seasons" Beard missed anywhere from 200 to 400 more runs scored.

Upon conclusion of his playing career, Ted remained in Indianapolis. He worked as an electrical contractor and later worked for the Indiana State Department of Highways. Beard and his wife now reside in Fishers, just north of Indianapolis.

As great a minor league talent that Beard was, he also made an impression in the majors. With 80 runs scored in just 474 major league at bats, his runs scored total would be respectable for a .290 hitter. It is quite amazing for a .198 hitter. Did Beard deserve a longer trial? Ted pensively dismisses the notion, stating, "To compete against [Ralph] Kiner, [Dixie] Walker, and [Gus] Bell in the outfield, you had to stand out, or else."

Gabe
Gair Allie, SS
1931-

Throughout the 1960s and early 1970s, the Pittsburgh Pirates started Gene Alley at shortstop. For a brief time in the 1950s, the Pirates had Gair Allie. Gair's last name was nearly spelled the same as Gene's and he too was a shortstop. One-year wonder Gair Allie should have played more, but the laws of average were never kind to Gair Roosevelt Allie. For any hitter, when the laws of average fail, batting averages are usually not far behind.

Gair Allie grew up in the North Carolina town of Statesboro. In high school, Allie won letters in baseball, football, basketball, and track. The 6'-1", 190-pound right-hander played a year of college ball as a Wake Forest Demon Deacon. Playing summer ball in Nova Scotia, Allie caught the attention of scouts from the Pittsburgh Pirates.

Allie began his pro baseball career in 1952 with the New Orleans Pelicans of the Southern Association. He led the AA-level loop both in games played and walks. With incumbent Dick Groat inducted into the military, Gair Allie's opportunity arose to make the 1953 Pirates' squad. An outstanding spring training made Allie a shoo-in to take over as Pirates' starting shortstop. However, in the first of several misfortunes, just days before the team was to break camp from Havana, Gair lost five months to a broken ankle.

Gair was back on the Pirates' 1954 spring training roster. Every March, sportswriters remark some pabulum about "hope renewing itself at the start of spring training." However, these Pirates may not have believed that canard, certainly not in training camp. Pittsburgh lost an astounding 216 games over the 1952 and 1953 seasons combined. A trio of mediocre shortstops filled in during the previous season. Between Eddie O'Brien, Dick Cole, and Dick Smith (a .134 lifetime hitter), not a single Pirate shortstop knocked a home run in 1953. Gair Allie impressed Pirates' management with spurts of power during the exhibition season. This time, Gair was off to Forbes Field.

Moving Dick Cole over to third base, Gair Allie became the starting shortstop. It only took him nine games to out homer O'Brien, Cole, and Smith. Unfortunately, other than that game, few early-season games left Gair Allie something to cheer about. His batting average plunged below .200 right from the outset. Still, Pirates' manager Fred Haney penciled Allie in the lineup nearly every game.

The late-spring sun heated things up in the land of steel. Gair Allie's bat also sizzled. On June 20, he batted leadoff in a twin-bill against the Milwaukee Braves. In the first game, Allie poked a pair of hits and the game-tying RBI in a tilt eventually won by the Pirates in 10 innings. Allie's three-run long ball in their 8–3 win in the nightcap highlighted the Pirates' eight-run seventh inning. Allie's batting average rose past the freezing point to a balmy .221.

But, that would be Allie's pinnacle. Though he rocked a third home run, like a sine wave, his average worked its way downward again. Eventually, Allie finished the campaign one point shy of .200.

The numbers report Gair had a legitimate chance to strut his stuff. He played 121 games in 1954; 95 at shortstop and 19 at third base. The statistics do not indicate that for the majority of the season, Gair suffered several bouts with a debilitating illness. Gair played through the pain. Most probably, a healthy Allie would have hit much higher. Gair showed flashes of power, hitting six triples and three home runs. However, making consistent contact was a weakness as Gair struck out 84 times, third highest in the National League. Gair did reach first 56 times on bases on balls, boosting his on-base average to .296.

While the Pirates showed slight improvement, they again finished in last place, losing 101 contests. Over the next few years, first baseman Bob Skinner, right fielder Roberto Clemente, and relief ace Roy Face helped turn the club around. Following Dick Groat's return from his military obligation, Gair Allie's days in Pittsburgh were numbered. Groat became the Pirates' shortstop for the next several years and become the National League's Most Valuable Player in 1960.

In 1955, Gair Allie found himself back in New Orleans. Seasoned by a year facing major league pitching, Allie blasted 15 balls deep, knocked in 77, and batted .275 for the Pelicans. Gair really found his swing with Hollywood of the Pacific Coast League in 1956. In the highest level of minor league ball, Gair was batting .292 in 69 games by June. A call-up to Pittsburgh looked inevitable. However, in yet another tough break for Gair, the call-up he received was from Uncle Sam.

As a soldier, Gair's Army experience stationed him at the Brooke Army Medical Center in Sinton, Texas (near Corpus Christi). Though Allie did not play professional ball in 1957, he spent the summer with the Sinton Oilers, an amateur club. With Private

Allie, minor league hitter Matt Sczesny, and Bob Giggie (who later pitched in the majors), the Oilers boasted more ringers than a horseshoe tournament. Indeed, Sinton won the 1957 National Non-Pro Baseball Tournament. Leading the way were Giggie, a sterling 4–0 for the tournament, with Allie and Sczesny both hitting near .400 in the playoffs.

After military duty, Gair Allie lived the life of a baseball nomad playing for various teams in the International League and Southern Association through 1961. Though Gair was a dependable .250s hitter with mid-range power, his door to the majors closed forever.

By the end of the 1961 season, Gair Allie, approaching age 30 and barely breaking .200 with Portsmouth of the Class A Sally League, was through. While Allie was finishing out his string, the once-pathetic Pittsburgh Pirates were the 1960 reigning World Champions. Allie eventually returned to Texas and now lives near San Antonio.

For that one season Gair Allie remains a compelling figure among career below .200 hitters. Not once did Allie have to pack his bags to be sent down to the minors. Nor did Gair ride the pine; he played just about every day. Despite sickness, Allie persevered in his only major league season in Pittsburgh. Additionally, in some areas, Allie was among the best in the league, finishing ninth in the league in walks and tied for eleventh in triples. Allie truly had a "career year" in 1954.

Choo Choo
Clarence Coleman, C
1937-

Hits at the Park is a restaurant located in Norfolk's Harbor Park, home of the New York Mets' Triple-A affiliate Norfolk Tides. For $9.95, their pre-game buffet allows one to feast like a country squire. Team pictures of the Tides adorn the restaurant walls. A close look at the 1969 team photo reveals the somber visage of Clarence "Choo Choo" Coleman. He came out of a two-year hiatus to play with the Tides that year, hitting .256 with 5 home runs, and 32 runs batted in. In many instances, numbers like that by a catcher usually earn a trip to the parent club in September. Unfortunately, that was not the case for Choo Choo. Considering his past, Coleman in a 1969 Mets' uniform would certainly have made for riveting theatre, in the year of the Mets' first title.

Choo Choo's professional career began in 1955 with Orlando of the Florida State League. Coleman played in the Negro Leagues with the Indianapolis Clowns in 1957. Baseball's version of the Harlem Globetrotters, the Clowns garnered fame through their comedic vaudeville routines. Coleman likely played the straight man. However, these Clowns were also a talented team. In 1952, they captured the Negro American League pennant. One contributor was an 18-year-old Hank Aaron, who signed with the Braves' organization shortly after his debut with the Clowns. Coleman's teammates with the Clowns included John Wyatt, a ten-game winning pitcher with the pennant-winning 1967 Red Sox. Paul Casanova, later a Washington Senator, competed with Coleman at catcher.

Following his season at Indianapolis, Coleman returned to Orlando. In 1959, his impressive campaign included 80 runs scored and 80 driven home. In 1960, Coleman caught fastballs and curves with Montreal of the International League, hitting .258 with 5 home runs and 33 knocked in.

Seasoned by six years catching in pro ball, Coleman earned a promotion to the majors. His first club, the 1961 Philadelphia Phillies, could hardly be called competitive. At one point, the Phils lost 23 consecutive games. In 35 games, Coleman contributed an anemic .128 batting average. The Phillies mercifully sent Coleman to Spokane by season's end. Unfortunately, the rest of team stayed in the league.

Choo Choo could not imagine playing for a worse outfit than the Phillies. But, "baseball is a funny game," according to Joe Garagiola in his best-selling book. With the National League expanding from eight to ten teams, senior circuit owners set up a pool of players for the two new expansion teams, the Houston Colt .45s and the New York Metropolitans. Each established ball club submitted 15 draft-eligible players. This pool was a combination of has-beens, never-weres, and never-will-be players. New York and Houston each selected sixteen men from the first pool at $75,000 each. At the end of the draft, they were entitled to two more players at $50,000 each. The final round allowed them to pick four players from the premium list at $125,000 a head. The Mets chose Choo Choo Coleman as their 14th pick in the first pool. Houston general manager Paul Richards summed up the draft by telling the world, "Gentlemen, we've just been f---ed." Mets' management may have been thinking about jumping into the pool's deepest end.

The 1962 Mets played like, well—just like Paul Richards predicted, only worse. Managed by the antediluvian Casey Stengel, his coaches included equally ancient Hall of Famers Red Ruffing and Rogers Hornsby. At his very first press conference, Stengel said, "It's a great honor to be joining the Knickerbockers." Later, Stengel uttered another timeless piece of Stengelese, "Come see my amazin' Mets. I been in this game a hundred years, but I see ways to lose I never knew existed before." With a 40-120 won-lost record, the all-time worst in 20th century major league baseball, the 1962 Mets were best summarized by Stengel's single utterance, "Can't anybody here play this game?"

The Mets sported a few redeeming attributes. After all, they did return National League baseball back to New York. Despite their foibles, nearly a millions fans would meet their lovable Mets at the Polo Grounds in support of their fledgling team. That figure tripled the patronage of the lame-duck Giants of 1957.

Amid a cast of castoff nonentities, some credible individual performances stood out. Frank Thomas belted 34 home runs, a club record that survived until 1975. Hall of Famer Richie Ashburn led the team with a .306 batting average and 12 stolen bases in his final major league campaign. Selected as the team's Most Valuable Player, the pragmatic Ashburn commented, "MVP on the worst team ever. I wonder what they meant by that." As for pitching, durable Roger Craig won ten games, however, that total was against a whopping 24 losses.

Choo Choo Coleman also enjoyed (if that's possible) a very respectable year. He was the first person in a Met uniform ever to hit a home run in a game, which occurred in the second game of the exhibition season. Coleman did not make the team initially and would not rejoin the Mets until July.

After going hitless in his first couple of games, Coleman came alive in a July 27 doubleheader against St. Louis. In the first game he singled, went to second on a sacrifice, then showed how he acquired his nickname. Rod Kanehl bounced a grounder behind second base. When Julio Gotay, the Cardinals' shortstop, kicked the ball away, the Choo Choo express train steamed around third and scored the only run of the game in a blaze of dirt and dust. He tripled and scored again in the second game, prompting Stengel to laud his catcher. "Do you know who my player of the year is? My player of the year is Choo Choo Coleman, and I have had him for only two days. He runs very good."

Coleman posted a memorable pair of games against Cincinnati. On August 2, while pinch-hitting in the seventh inning, Coleman greeted reliever Jim Brosnan's first pitch by driving it over the Polo Grounds' right field stands for a home run. Despite Coleman's heroics, the Reds managed to cling to victory against the Mets, as they had in their seven previous meetings. Confident he could beat the Mets every time, Reds' manager Fred Hutchinson started lesser-light Johnny Klippstein. Hutchinson saved his other stoppers for more respectable opposition. The Mets made Hutchinson pay for his overconfidence. Coleman and the boys piled on six runs in the first, knocking Klippstein out of the box. Stengel's "player of the year" was hardly finished. In the fifth inning, Choo Choo Coleman knocked a Ted Wills' delivery into the right field stands for a two-run homer— his second in two games. Coleman secured three hits that day. Hitting .320 at that point, Coleman's lofty batting average resembled that of his esteemed teammate Richie Ashburn.

Impressed by his hot bat, Coleman made an appearance on the "Kiner's Korner" television show. The ex-slugger deluxe of the Pirates asked Coleman about the origins of his nickname. To which Coleman replied, "I don't know, Bub." Fazed by that response, Kiner then asked Coleman, "What's your wife's name and what is she like?" Choo Choo replied, "My wife's name is Mrs. Coleman and she likes me, Bub." Choo Choo was never invited to Kiner's Korner again!

Coleman had a 1-for-4 game with an RBI in a 9-2 setback against the Cubs on September 22. The losing pitcher Al Jackson dropped to 8-20 and joined Roger Craig as the first pair of 20-game losers on the same team in a generation. The game also marked a changing of the guard. Seventeen-year-old Ed Kranepool replaced first baseman Gil Hodges, who would retire after the 1962 season. Kranepool went on to play seventeen productive seasons with the Mets. Hodges would manage Kranepool and the Mets to an even 100 victories and a World's Championship in 1969.

Another footnote to the game was Richie Ashburn, who played every inning of his illustrious 14-year career in the outfield. He made a just-for-fun appearance at second base. It showed. When Nelson Mathews tried to steal second, Choo Choo Coleman made a good-enough throw to Ashburn. Richie dropped the throw, but fell on Mathews, making further advance impossible. The next batter lined to pitcher Craig Anderson who wheeled and threw to Ashburn for the double-up of Mathews. Ashburn dropped the ball again. After Alex Grammas drove Mathews home with a single, Grammas thought he would have an easy steal of second base. But, a fine throw by Coleman and a splendid tag by Ashburn erased that thought. In the ninth, Ashburn doubled to right, proving his worth at any position.

In the season finale at the Polo Grounds, Choo Choo Coleman scored the last run. To the ten thousand patrons who witnessed the game, there was one great show at the Manhattan pasture. Before the game, a softball exhibition entertained early arrivals. The contest featured local radio announcers and what the *New York Times* described as "tasty pastries from various Broadway shows."

Following softball and pastries, the hardball game commenced. With a 1-1 deadlock entering the bottom of the ninth, Coleman lashed a pitch down the right field line. The ball hit first base and caromed into the outfield for a double. Choo Choo moved to third on a wild pitch and scored on Frank Thomas' line single to left. Game over. With the triumph, the Mets' fans enjoyed a ray of sunshine in an otherwise gloomy season.

In a poignant exhibition, the crowd did not rush towards the exits. Rather, they swayed and sang while the organist reflectively played *'Til We Meet Again*. A microphone was placed on the field and Casey Stengel, still thinking about softball, joked during a post-game interview of getting "eight or six of them girls for my club." Then, out of respect, the crowd watched Stengel make a slow trot across an empty field to the Mets' clubhouse. The strains of *Auld Lang Syne* then filled the ancient stadium that had one season of life left before being torn down for a housing development.

Coleman's campaign proved him as quite a competent backstop. For starters, he played 55 games and batted .250. Of all players with career batting averages below .200, Choo Choo holds the record for the most at bats in a season (152) while batting at least .250. Coleman also displayed some power in his bat that year, as evidenced by his lofty .441 slugging average. While blasting six home runs, Coleman's most memorable shot occurred on August 15 against his old Phillies. In that game, Coleman and Jim Hickman combined to hit a record-tying two pinch-hit homers in the same game. The Mets still lost.

Though described as someone who handled outside curves like a man "fighting bees," Choo Choo did own a handsome .995 fielding average in 1962. Phil Rizzuto also noted that Coleman, while catching, often made it to first base (to back up the play) before the batter arrived.

That runs contrary to other observations about Coleman's defense. While most poor-hitting catchers call good games, that may not have been the case for Coleman. For example, Gene Woodling claimed to have seen Casey Stengel in the dugout with a can of paint. "Choo Choo and I are going to school," Stengel said. Casey painted Coleman's fingers different colors to help him remember the pitching signs. Did the ploy work? Anybody's guess. During one game, the pitcher repeatedly shrugged off Coleman's signs. When the hurler finally nodded in concurrence, Choo Choo was caught looking at his fingers to verify what the pitch would be. In another game, Stengel came out of the dugout to ask Coleman what pitch he selected after a batter hit a home run. "I don't know, Bub," was Coleman's nonchalant reply. "Well," advised Casey, "the next time you give a sign out there, take a peek yourself so you'll know what pitch you were calling." In yet another game, with the bases loaded, two out, and a full count, Coleman allegedly called for a pitchout. When a reporter asked one Mets' pitcher to respond to a question about who is the toughest man to pitch to, "Choo Choo Coleman" became the pitcher's facetious reply.

In all the lore of the 1962 Mets, highlighted in numerous books, Coleman served as the perfect team icon, next to the antics of Marvelous Marv Throneberry. Whether truth, urban legend, or sheer hyperbole, many preposterous Choo Choo Coleman stories began to propagate.

As previously mentioned, Coleman supposedly maintained an unusual habit of calling everyone "Bub." During spring training in 1963, third baseman Charlie Neal struck up a conversation with Choo Choo. Each time Neal would say something, Coleman would either reply, "Yeah, Bub," or "No, Bub." "You don't even know who I am," said an exasperated Charlie Neal. "I was your roommate last season." The taciturn Coleman mulled on that one for a moment and then replied, "I know you all right, Bub. You number four."

Coleman did have some competition for playing time behind the plate and Stengelisms that year. The Mets made Giants' catcher Hobie Landrith their first selection of the regular draft. When questioned about that choice, Stengel replied, "If you don't have a catcher, you're going to have a lot of passed balls." The Mets also drafted another backstop in Chris Cannizaro. Stengel invariably called him Canzoneri, apparently confusing him with 1940s middleweight boxer Tony Canzoneri. On Cannizaro's fielding prowess, Stengel noted, "Canzoneri is the only defensive catcher that can't catch." Then there was Harry "Return to Sender" Chiti. Sold to the Mets from the Cleveland Indians organization, Chiti played 15 games for New York, then was shipped back to Cleveland to complete an earlier transaction. Though not technically correct, people still love to claim that the Mets actually pulled off trading Harry Chiti for Harry Chiti. Throughout 1962, the Mets experimented with nine different players behind the mask. Statistically speaking, Choo Choo Coleman was easily the best of the lot.

In their second season, New York "improved" to 51 wins against 111 defeats. Although he appeared in 106 games, Coleman batted dismally, declining to .178. His three extra-base hits that season were all home runs. In fact, Coleman holds a dubious record for the most at bats in a season without hitting a double. Nearly an automatic out, Coleman's strikeout totals doubled—about his only statistic that went up.

Coleman's greatest moment of the year—perhaps of his career—occurred on May 12th. Playing Cincinnati in a doubleheader and having already lost the first game, the Mets trailed 12-11 entering the bottom of the eighth inning. New York rallied to tie the game and Choo Choo came up with one out and two runners on base. Coleman came through with his third straight hit, a looper to center, to drive in Al Moran with the winning run.

After the game, hundreds of Mets' fans crowded into the center field exit, situated in front of the Mets' clubhouse windows. Known throughout the league for their unruliness, they loudly chanted, "We want Choo Choo! We want Choo Choo!" Finally, their hero stepped out on the landing and waved. The crowd cheered Coleman wildly.

A few years later, Coleman had a short six-game stay with the Mets in 1966. In one of his last games ever, against the San Francisco Giants, Willie Mays was at third. A pitch bounced in front of the plate and Choo Choo got leather on it, knocking the ball just a few feet away. As Coleman recovered, he froze in amazement. Mays, in full flight long before the ball bounced, scored standing up. Giants' manager Herman Franks said after the game he wouldn't even have sent a runner from first to second on the play. "I could see from the trajectory of the ball that it was going to be in the dirt," Mays explained some time later.

After 1966, Choo Choo Coleman retired. However, the game of baseball, once in the blood, can be hard to let go. Three seasons later, Coleman was back, donning catcher's mask, shin guards, chest protector, and glove to stop 98 MPH fastballs and wicked-breaking curves. Starting in 1969 with the Tidewater Tides, Coleman then went south of the border to play several years in Mexico. His 1970 season with the Mexico City Reds ranks as the finest of his career as the ex-Met and Phillie appeared in 142 games with 14 home runs, 75 RBI, and a .294 batting mark. After retiring for the last time in Mexico in 1972, Choo Choo became a butcher in Philadelphia. At last word, he was living in Rochester, New York.

Mets' fans might have thought that the beer companies would have exploited the media potential of Coleman in TV advertising campaigns, especially considering their colorful alumni of Marv Throneberry, Bob Uecker, Boog Powell, and Billy Martin. Characters all. Alas, although his deadpan "Bub" may have been a natural, Coleman never pitched beer on television.

Despite being on the roster of two of the worst baseball teams of the last century, there is much to admire about this gentleman. At 5-feet-9-inches and 165 pounds, Coleman may have been one of the smaller catchers to play the game. Even the mighty Mel Ott, who was about the same stature as Coleman, was moved from catcher to outfield by John McGraw for fear he'd wind up as mincemeat. Coleman also brought some speed and power to his game, thus living up to his sobriquet. Choo Choo Coleman marked a point in baseball history when an African American player could stick around long enough, while batting less than .200 over the course of more than 200 games. In this regard, Choo Choo Coleman was truly amazin'.

"I now will say this for him, whether he can talk for himself or not, I had 15 pitchers who said they couldn't pitch to him, and it turned out they couldn't pitch to nobody."

-Casey Stengel, on Choo Choo Coleman, as quoted in *Sport* Magazine (April, 1966)

"The pitcher has to find out if the hitter is timid. And if the hitter is timid, he has to *remind* the hitter he's timid."

-Don Drysdale, Hall of Fame pitcher

Chapter 6
WHEN PITCHERS RULED THE EARTH
1963-1976

A Tour Of Baseball From 1963 To The Mid-1970s

As the continuum of baseball history goes, the rather short and ill-defined 14-year period from 1963 to 1976 marks an interval when neither the hitters of the National nor American Leagues ever reached a league batting average of at least .260 for any one year. This transient period coincides with events that altered the national landscape forever—a turbulent period of assassinations, a war in Southeast Asia, civil unrest, scientific breakthroughs, and political scandal.

Baseball reflected this social upheaval as the very fabric of the game altered radically. New franchises arose, older ones moved, and the very structuring of the leagues and postseason format changed for the first time in sixty-six years. Even one of the basic rules of the game changed entirely, the batting order, with the heralding of the designated-hitter rule in the American League. In 1965, a ballpark in Texas replaced grass with a plastic playing field.

Of greater impact were the rights of the individual player. Landmark decisions in the cases of Curt Flood and Andy Messersmith resulted in the demise of the reserve clause and allowed players to seek the highest bidder for their services. In the early 1970s, the best players crept above a $100,000 salary. The first mass-market free-agent draft occurred in 1976 with the big winner being Reggie Jackson. He received a five-year contract worth $2.93 million from Yankees' owner George Steinbrenner.

In the very play of the game itself, one common thread permeates this period: the dominance of pitching. Not since the Dead Ball Era and wartime baseball were hitters kept off base with such frequency. Since 1910, eight of the ten lowest organizational (both National and American League) batting averages occurred between the years of 1963 and 1972. The 20th Century's nadir for batting occurred in 1968, when the major league batting average was .237 and the entire American League sank to .230. Runs per game output reached the lowest total since 1907.

Power hitting during that period also suffered. Five of the ten lowest organizational slugging average totals, since 1920, occurred between 1967 and 1976 (and 1976 had the designated hitter in the American League). Only one 50 home run hitter emerged—Willie Mays' 52 in 1965. Moreover, just four years after Roger Maris hit 61 homers, Tony Conigliaro led the American League with 32—barely over half of Maris' 1961 total.

This had nothing to do with the quality of the athlete wielding the bat. Some of the game's greatest hitters played in this era. The proliferation of Black and Hispanic ballplayers onto major league rosters gushed a font of marvelous talent that had otherwise been just a trickle even after Jackie Robinson. There were no "Bergen-like" easy outs in any major league line-up. As former Reds' pitcher Tom Carroll (a career 8–4 record with the 1974 and 1975 Cincinnati Reds) commented, "I would always get excited about playing the Pittsburgh Pirates, as that was near my hometown. I would really get worked up facing Willie Stargell and put everything into getting him out. I did well against him. But guys like [Mario] Mendoza would give me trouble if I didn't come at them with the same level of intensity."

There were four major underlying factors to the relative dominance of the pitcher:

1. **Expanded Strike Zone** - A 1963 rule expanded the strike zone from the batter's knees to the top of his shoulders when assuming his natural stance. Formerly, the top of the knees to the armpits marked the strike zone. After the "bataclysmic" 1968 season, the strike zone again reverted to its pre-1963 dimensions. Additionally, the height of the pitcher's mound was lowered from 15 inches to 10 inches before the start of the 1969 season.

2. **Relief Pitchers** - Improved coaching techniques, better quality fielding gloves, and newly-placed emphasis on defensive strategies were crucial for success in this new era of "small ball." The most significant defensive strategy was the deployment of specialized relief pitchers. The use of the fireman remains an integral part of today's game.

3. **Pitching Excellence** - Not since the Dead Ball Era did a more splendid crop of pitchers make their emergence. Sliders exploded from Steve Carlton; Nolan Ryan and Tom Seaver brought hard heat; Bob Gibson, peering into his catcher, scared batters nearly to death; Sandy Koufax broke wicked curveballs; Phil & Joe Niekro and Wilbur Wood tossed baffling knuckleballs; and Juan Marichal, could throw just about all of these pitchers with equal devastation. There were many, many more. Some were spectacular for a short time like Dean Chance, Denny McLain, Andy Messersmith, and Mark Fidrych. Others were solidly consistent for a long spell like Don Sutton, Don Drysdale, and Catfish Hunter. In the unlikely event any of these pitchers could not throw a complete game, sensational relievers like Mike Marshall, Rollie Fingers, and Sparky Lyle made the game's outcome academic.

4. **Fewer Minor League Teams** - While serving as hitting coach for the Oakland A's in 1968, Joe DiMaggio offered his thoughts on the hitting lag: "There [are] 168 fewer minor league teams today. That's got to be the reason. Pitchers can be taught to throw hard and low, and they can do it in the big leagues. But hitters can't be taught to respond quickly enough to hit hard-and-low pitching—not without years of practice in the minors. If you could master hitting by thinking or by simply learning the technique, you'd have a lot of 50-year-old .300 hitters still around."

Of the 1,287 batters who had at least 200 plate appearances between the years of 1963 and 1976, 32 players had career batting averages below .200. As you would expect, the book is well represented by players in this period of depressed hitting.

A Guide To Japanese League Baseball

Usually following failed major league careers, a few American baseball players took their bats and gloves to the Land of the Rising Sun. It may be appropriate to be familiar with the fundamentals and nuances of Japanese major league baseball. While it is not the intention to provide a thesis on this topic, here are a few things worth knowing.

The Japanese first played *Yakyu* (field ball) or the Anglicized *beisuboru* in the 1870s. Before that, with the exception of *sumo,* the concept of athletic competition did not exist in the isolated nation. The first professional league was born in 1936. Today, it is by far the most popular sport in Japan.

There are two leagues, the Central League and the Pacific League. Each league is comprised of six teams. The majority of the Central League teams play in the Tokyo-Yokohama metropolitan area while the Pacific League is concentrated in the Osaka-Kobe-Kyoto center. Like our major leagues, the Pacific League employs the designated-hitter rule while the Central League does not. The Japanese regular season lasts all of 130 games. Pennant winners from each league play in the Japan World Series in October.

Unlike our baseball clubs, nearly all teams are corporate-owned. For example, the Yakult Swallows do not represent the city of Yakult for there is no such city of Yakult. The Swallows are from Tokyo and are owned by the Yakult Corporation, a health food manufacturer. A popular liquid yogurt drink they produce is called the Yakult Swallow. The Lotte Orions are owned by a food and department store chain. The Nippon Ham Fighters are owned by—you guessed it—a pork production company.

The Yomiuri (Tokyo) Giants are "Japan's Team." Combining the legacies of the New York Yankees, Green Bay Packers, Boston Celtics, and Montreal Canadiens, one gets a flavor of how the country reveres this team. As former Japanese League ballplayer Dan Briggs said, "The entire Japanese league structure exists primarily to provide competition for the Giants." For many years, the Giants refused to allow foreigners on their team, which endeared them with the more hard-line Japanese fans.

Japan's most famous player was Sadaharu Oh (retired 1982), who with 868 home runs owns the most home runs of *any* professional baseball player. Oh's combination of samurai swordsmanship skills, stinging wrists, and a batting eye compared to Ted Williams led to six Triple Crowns and nine Most Valuable Player awards. No Top-100 list of greatest baseball players can be complete without Sadaharu Oh. However, even Oh lost some of his luster after an unsuccessful stint as manager of the Giants. Recently, he led the Pacific League's Fukuoka Daiei Hawks to the Japan Series championship in 1999.

The quality of Japanese professional players can be described this way: the A-List starting Japanese ball tossers are on a near par with the best American players. Ichiro Suzuki proves that tenet, garnering many *besu hitto* with the Seattle Mariners. Lesser talents may be Triple-A. However, bench players may be only Double-A caliber. Most of the better Japanese teams would be also-ran teams in the majors. Fastball pitchers, like

Hideo Nomo, are the exception and not the rule in Japanese ball. Most of the native pitchers cannot throw *sutoraiku* above 90 MPH. and mostly rely on a steady diet of breaking stuff and change-ups.

Japanese coaches employ training regimens more suitable for Navy SEALS than baseball players. Training camp starts as early as February. A typical day may entail up to 12 hours on the field. Pre-game warm-ups become so grueling that players begin to wear out by mid-season. The Japanese take Willie Stargell's favorite quote, "You play baseball, not work baseball," and do exactly the opposite. Managers and coaches tend to be strict taskmasters. As Charlie Manuel noted, "I've never experienced anything like it in all my years in baseball. The coaches even told me when to change my socks."

Tie games are possible in Japanese baseball. Fifteen-inning marathons cannot occur as games have an extra-inning limit and a time limit as well. In fact, with a culture so absorbed in not "losing face," ties are a quite desirable outcome, as neither team is humiliated. On the down side, there have been a few instances of teams missing the playoffs because of reduced winning percentage points from ties.

While not totally excluded, participation by foreign players, or *gaijin*, in the Japanese major leagues is strictly quota controlled. Until recently, teams were restricted to signing no more than two foreign-born players. That is now up to four. While every now and then a foreign player plays *beisuboru* in Japan in their prime, like Bob Horner or Cecil Fielder, most of the American players are either third stringers or players on the wane as major leaguers. Still, the pressure on *gaijin* to perform is immensely intense, for they are paid much more than native talents. Although wonderful stories of American ballplayers being worshipped by the Japanese people exist (brothers Leron and Leon Lee are textbook examples), more often than not, American ballplayers leave Japan after a year or two. Language and cultural barriers remain contributing factors to their departure.

Dodger Doug
Doug Camilli, C
1936-

Extreme pressure faces any young man following in the footsteps of a famous father. That pressure amplifies when the profession involves playing baseball in front of thousands of people. With a career .199 batting average, catcher Doug Camilli would never quite match the solid lumber of his dad, the great Dolph Camilli. Doug, who played nine years in the majors as a back-up catcher for the Los Angeles Dodgers and Washington Senators in the 1960s, is one of five players whose fathers won the Most Valuable Player award. Dale Berra, Eddie Collins, Jr., Dave Sisler, and Bump Wills are the others.

No biography of Doug Camilli would be complete without a discussion of his famous sire. Adolph (nicknamed Dolph) Camilli starred as a graceful fielding first baseman with long ball power. The elder Camilli wore the threads of the Chicago Cubs, Philadelphia, Phillies, Brooklyn Dodgers, and Boston Red Sox. In a twelve-year career that spanned from 1933 to 1945, Camilli slugged 239 home runs, with 950 batted in, and a .277 batting average.

In 1936, with the Phillies, Camilli started a seven-year streak of bashing at least 23 home runs per season. That same year, Doug was born. In 1937, Dolph not only knew how to get on base, leading the National League with a .446 percentage, he was equally adept at keeping people off the bases, as led led all first basemen with a .994 fielding percentage.

When Dolph first joined Brooklyn in 1938, the Dodgers played the role of perennial second-division also-rans. Named team captain, the calm, yet steadfast Camilli perfectly complemented high-strung manager Leo Durocher. For starters, he was no one to trifle with. As a former prizefighter, whose brother Frank[5] died in the ring fighting World Heavyweight Champion Max Baer, Dolph Camilli quelled clubhouse frays with little more than a quiet word and meaningful look. He also dissuaded veterans from hazing Dodger rookies Pee Wee Reese and Pete Reiser.

Dolph Camilli won the National League's Most Valuable Player award in 1941, after leading Brooklyn to their first pennant in 21 years. He paced all batters with 34 home runs. Dolph also drove in 120 runs. At the tender age of four-years-old, Doug Camilli also had some face time in the news that year. A popular picture circulated around the nation's newspapers showing young Doug, in a miniature baseball uniform, taking a rather healthy cut at a ball in Ebbets Field. Young Doug Camilli worked out with the team when they were in Brooklyn. Much diamond wisdom, from the likes of his father, Reese, and maybe even Herman Franks, must have been imparted into the formative mind of this young baseball brat.

As a man who truly bled Dodger blue, Dolph Camilli refused to report to the hated New York Giants after being traded to them in 1943. Later, Dolph Camilli served in the

---

[5] Frank Camilli fought under the name Frankie Campbell.

Army and finished out his career in Boston. Dolph Camilli died in 1997 at age ninety. He fathered seven children, four of whom became professional ballplayers. Only Doug made it to the majors.

One of the many major leaguers to play college ball at Stanford (Class of 1958), Doug Camilli originally started out as an infielder-outfielder. He moved to catcher as he worked his way up the Dodgers' farm system. Doug Camilli tore the horsehide off the ball in his second year of playing for pay. With Great Falls of the Pioneer League, just out of college, Camilli blasted 18 HR, with 95 RBI, and a .314 average. After another fine campaign with Class AA Atlanta, Doug Camilli first joined the Dodgers late in the 1960 season. Like father. Like son.

As a dependable back-up to incumbent Dodger catcher John Roseboro, during the Sandy Koufax/Don Drysdale era, Camilli typically played 45-50 games a year. His 1962 season is one of the best batting performances by any career below .200 hitter. In 88 at bats, Doug lambasted the ball for a .284 average, hit four homers, and plated in 22. On defense, Camilli's .983 fielding average matched Roseboro. But, Doug Camilli would rather forget one particular defensive play that season. On an attempted steal by the Cardinals' Julian Javier, Camilli's throw to second nicked pitcher Drysdale on his elbow, not the most efficient way to throw out a base stealer.

Several of Camilli's best performances occurred down the stretch, with the Dodgers and Giants in a September death struggle for the pennant. It was also an exciting time for fans as they tracked Camilli's fleet-of-feet teammate Maury Wills' run to the stolen base record. On September 8th, Los Angeles held a slim half-game lead over San Francisco when Dodgers' manager Walt Alston asked Camilli to start against Pittsburgh, in place of the battle-weary Roseboro. Camilli responded brilliantly, spearheading a second-inning attack with an RBI triple and later scoring on Andy Carey's double. That day, Camilli reached safely on all four plate appearances and scored a second run in the Dodgers' 6-1 scuttling of the Pirates.

Pleased with Camilli's performance, Alston rewarded him the next start. Again, Camilli responded, delivering a double to drive home Frank Howard with the game-winning run. Another start for Camilli yielded a new form of heroics. He made a sensational tag on Houston's Hal Smith at home to preserve a 1-0 victory over the Colts. Camilli also had several other starts during the stretch drive.

The Dodgers' built some breathing room over the Giants in the standings, but faltered late, allowing San Francisco to force a season-ending tie and the fourth-ever playoff in National League history. At the time, the tiebreaker meant a best-of-three match.

Game one of the playoff was played in San Francisco. The Giants jumped on Sandy Koufax early and cruised to an 8-0 rout. Doug Camilli pinch-hit a double to deep left-center that went for nought. The bitter rivals traveled to Los Angeles to play game two. By the Dodgers' half of the sixth inning, they were already trailing 5-0. By then, the gloom in the Chavez Ravine stands was thicker than the Los Angeles smog. But, in the sixth, the Dodgers made a dramatic turnaround. First, Junior Gilliam walked. Giants' skipper Alvin Dark assumed starter Jack Sanford was tiring (despite only two hits allowed). In came Stu Miller. The ancient warrior, Duke Snider, greeted Miller with a double. A sacrifice fly drove Gilliam home with the first Dodger run in 36 innings. A Wally Moon walk and a Frank Howard single later, a second run scored. Dark yanked

Stu Miller and put Billy O'Dell on the mound. The Dodgers subbed for John Roseboro, 0-for-2 in the game, with Doug Camilli.

Camilli's playoff magic continued with a sharply-hit single to right field to load the bases. O'Dell then proceeded to hit Andy Carey with a pitch, forcing in Moon with the third run of the inning. Next, Lee Walls belted a double to clear the bases and give the Dodgers a 6-5 lead. Los Angeles added another run that inning. Camilli stayed in to catch. The Giants' rallied in the eighth to knot the game at seven. But, with a Dodgers' run in the ninth, they prevailed 8-7. At 4 hours and 18 minutes, this was the longest nine-inning game on record at the time.

Doug Camilli did not play the deciding game of the playoff in Los Angeles. Maybe he should have. With the Dodgers leading 4-2 going into the ninth inning, Camilli must have been reveling at the thought of meeting the Yankees in the World Series. But, the Coogan's Bluff ghost took a train to the coast. San Francisco victimized the normally solid Ed Roebuck (only one loss in his previous 80 games) for four runs. The stunned crowd watched the Dodgers' meekly go out, one-two-three, in their half of the ninth. For the second time in eleven years, the Giants wrested the pennant out of the Dodgers' seemingly firm grasp. Even the game's winning pitcher, Don Larsen, was yet another apparition of Dodgers' failures past.

After his solid 1962 season, Doug Camilli's batting average plummeted. In 1963, Camilli batted a weak .162. However, he still seemed to contribute every time he played that year. Camilli worked behind the plate for several shutout games of Koufax and Drysdale. On June 16, 22-year-old rookie Nick Wilhite would pitch his first game in the majors against Chicago. Wilhite nervously observed the Cubs' thrash Los Angeles in game one of the doubleheader, 8-3, in front of 54 thousand Dodger fans. Doug caught Willhite's debut and quickly settled the young pitcher down by calling the right pitches at the right time. Willhite scattered five hits enroute to a 2-0 complete game shutout. Willhite could also thank Camilli for his fourth-inning run-scoring single.

Nick Willhite's only other victory that year came three weeks later. Again, the rookie's catcher was Doug Camilli. Not only did Camilli direct the 3-1 victory over the Reds, he walloped his first home run of the year to produce two runs. Camilli blasted another long ball five days later for Sandy Koufax. That drove in two of the Dodgers' six runs against the Mets. Befuddling the New Yorkers with 25 shutout innings in three previous starts, Koufax did the same this day with a 3-hitter and 13 strikeouts. Camilli added a third home run later that season.

The Dodgers' left all National League rivals in the dust to capture the 1963 pennant. Doug's Dodgers also avenged his father's 1941 World Series defeat against the Yankees. A picture of Doug Camilli was prominently featured on the back cover of the *New York Daily News*, flanked by his father (whom at 55 still looked like he could play) and Leo Durocher, a coach for the Dodgers. Although Roseboro caught every inning of the Los Angeles sweep of New York in the Fall Classic, Doug received his well-deserved ring.

In 1964, Doug's batting average remained mired in the league's lower rungs. With only a .179 slate, zero home runs, and one run scored in 131 plate appearances, Camilli's offense hardly resembled his hard-hitting father. Camilli's solitary run is a dubious record in a season by a non-pitcher with over 100 plate appearances. Despite his failure with the stick, Camilli's catching skills did not suffer. In 46 games, he owned an impeccable .990 fielding percentage.

Doug's career highlight occurred as the result of his glove and brain, catching Sandy Koufax's third of his four no-hitters. In a 3-0 whitewashing of the Phillies, Koufax's wicked curveball foiled the Phils as the lefthander struck out 12 and barely missed becoming the only pitcher to hurl two perfect games. Koufax's only blemish was issuing a walk to Richie Allen on a 3-and-2 count in the fourth inning. Many observers felt that plate umpire Ed Vargo missed the call. Allen was subsequently thrown out stealing by Camilli; thus Koufax faced the absolute minimum of 27 batters in the contest.

The defending champions couldn't come close to contending in 1964. Even the Los Angeles Angels finished with a better record than the Dodgers. With Walter Alston's club in need of retooling, Camilli was part of the big 1965 trade with Washington that also sent mighty slugger Frank Howard to the Senators. In exchange, the Dodgers received another lively arm named Claude Osteen, to augment Koufax and Drysdale.

Although the Senators hardly shared the success of the Dodgers during the 1960s, often residing in the American League basement, at least Doug Camilli received some more playing time. On April 18, Camilli had three hits with a run scored to help beat the Chicago White Sox. Later that month, Camilli and Frank Howard blasted home runs off Baltimore's Robin Roberts. Roberts wasn't so gracious with the rest of the Senators, winning a complete game by the score of 5-3. In his first season with the Senators, Camilli kept busy with career highs in games (75), at bats (193), hits (37), and total bases (54).

For the next two campaigns, Camilli saw increasingly less playing time, yielding to Paul Casanova. But, Camilli could still knock balls over the fence, hitting a pair of homers in each of those years. Pinch-hitting, with Washington trailing by two runs in a game against Detroit in July, 1967, Camilli singled to center and was later brought home by Frank Howard with the tying run. Tim Cullen also scored to give Washington a come-from-behind victory. This perpetuated a very rare Senators' six-game winning streak.

Camilli could still call a great game. The squatting maestro, who caught so many gems for the Dodgers, nearly called his second no-hitter with Pete Richert on June 18, 1966. Other than a second-inning safety by Brooks Robinson, Richert and Ron Kline combined to hold the Orioles to one hit.

On September 24, 1967, Doug Camilli made his final appearance as an active player. Pinch-hitting for Bob Humphreys in the bottom of the ninth, Washington had runners on first and second, two out, and trailed Detroit 4-3. The Tigers desperately needed the game to remain in the wild pennant chase. The odds seemed to be in the Tigers' favor with Camilli batting only .173. Detroit reliever John Hiller quickly got two strikes on him. But, Camilli started fouling off pitches and worked the count to 3-and-2. Then he fouled away several more before lining a clean single to right field. The game was tied at 4-4. The next batter, Fred Valentine, sent a deep drive out of left fielder Jim Northrup's reach and Paul Casanova trotted home with the winning run. The satisfying performance for Camilli effectively ended his days as a player.

Staring in 1968, Doug launched into a new career as a coach for the Washington Senators. For two campaigns, Camilli coached in the District of Columbia, one season for Ted Williams in 1969 (a rare Senators' winning season). That season, activated briefly as a player, Camilli managed to strap on the mask once again for one game. He hit a single in three trips. Doug Camilli moved on to Boston. From 1970-1973, Camilli coached for the Red Sox squad, who included a rising star named Carlton Fisk. A long time member of the Boston organization, Camilli managed in Greensboro of the Sally League and Winter Haven of the Florida State League during the 1980s. Camilli[6] also fathered a son, Kevin, who played in the Red Sox organization.

In five years with Los Angeles, Doug Camilli made his mark. Although a backup backstop for the solid John Roseboro, Camilli was always willing to give the Dodgers good glove work. As the son of Dolph Camilli, he took opposing pitches deep with surprising frequency. Surely, Camilli could have been a regular and more productive catcher in a different organization. However, for the boy who took batting practice with his father in Ebbets Field, being a Dodger always seemed in the stars for Doug Camilli.

Omaha Ernie
Ernie Fazio, 2B
1942-

While Ernie Fazio's big league career may not seem like much, his amateur days were the stuff of legend. In 1959, representing Oakland, California, 17-year-old Ernie Fazio bashed the first-ever Grand Slam in a Connie Mack League World Series game. Still a teenager, Fazio spent the summer of 1961 playing for the Western Canada Baseball League's Saskatoon Commodores. Fazio hit .306 and led the league with 28 stolen bases to guide his team to the league title. However, Fazio's most scintillating days came in 1962. That season, Ernie, who stood just 5-feet-7 in his stocking feet, led a band of hustling Davids that challenged the very Goliaths of college baseball.

Ernie Fazio played ball for Santa Clara College, a small Jesuit school in California. Although the Santa Clara Broncos team finished last the year before, their 1962 turnaround could be directly tied to their talented lineup. No less than six players went on to become major leaguers. Catcher John Boccabella, infielder Tim Cullen, and pitchers Nelson Briles, Bob Garibaldi, and Pete Magrini joined junior shortstop Ernie Fazio. The Broncos surged to a 39-8 record, winning the conference title and NCAA District 8. Along the way they defeated interstate rival powerhouses Stanford and USC. Pitcher Bob Garibaldi tossed a no-hitter against the Southern Cal Trojans. Santa Clara enjoyed the number one ranking in the country.

After losing their first College World Series game to Florida State, the Broncos fought their way through the loser's bracket. Santa Clara defeated, in succession, Missouri, Holy Cross, Florida State, and Texas to face the Michigan Wolverines in the Series' finale. In the longest College World Series game ever played, tiny Santa Clara played Michigan to a standstill for 15 innings before bowing by a score of 5-4. To cap off his memorable year, Ernie was named First team College All-American.

---

[6] Lou Camilli, a late 1960s/early 1970s infielder for Cleveland, is no relation to Doug Camilli. Lou Camilli's career average showed .146, making him an honorary member of the Mendoza Line family.

Though eligible for one more year of college ball, for the princely sum of $100,000, the expansion Houston Colt .45s signed Ernie Fazio. One month later, the San Francisco Giants lured Bob Garibaldi, just a sophomore, away from college. The exodus of young talent from Santa Clara infuriated the Reverend James Sweeters, the school's athletic moderator, who blasted professional baseball scouts as "ruthless, persistent competitors" in their recruitment tactics. Rev. Sweeters later sent a terse letter to Commissioner Ford Frick, admonishing that baseball should prohibit signing underclassmen as professional football and basketball did at the time. Perhaps, the Reverend's letter had an impact. Major League Baseball eliminated the "bonus baby" system and instituted a draft in 1965.

Houston projected young Fazio as their second baseman for years to come. Just a month after his signing, Ernie Fazio found himself in the majors...briefly. Appearing as a pinch runner in his first big league game, Fazio was asked by the first baseman to step off the bag so the fielder could dust it. When the courteous rookie obliged, the first baseman brandished the ball, which he had hidden behind his back, and tagged Fazio out. With just one hit in a dozen games, and several miscues at shortstop, soon Fazio found himself in the minors. It didn't help that Fazio played during a stretch when Houston lost 20 of 23 games.

Renowned sportswriter Mickey Herskowitz, covered the Colts for the *Houston Post*. During the season, he penned a series of satirical articles, entitled "Letters from Lefty." The format was taken from the old Ring Lardner series, *You Know Me, Al* in which a rookie ballplayer writes home to a friend. In a July "letter" Herskowitz lampooned the tough travails of young Ernie Fazio, writing that Fazio "had some terrific fights with the ball" at second base and that he switched from a 32-ounce bat to a 29-oz. bat because "the lighter bat is easier to carry back to the dugout."

Known as "Midge," Ernie kept busy in 1963, playing in 102 games for the Colts. Unfortunately, his .184 batting average and five RBI in 228 at bats were more .22 caliber than Colt .45. For much of the campaign, Fazio's name lined the bottom of the National League batting list. On Ernie's behalf, he contributed decent totals in runs scored (31) and extra base hits (15), including his only two home runs. Fazio's low RBI total can be attributed to the fact that he usually batted leadoff and few players in the Houston lineup made it to base with any regularity. Seven Colts' regulars were batting .217 or less entering late July.

Fazio had few efforts of interest that season. On June 9th, 1963, he stroked a single in the first-ever major league Sunday night game. The game resulted in a 3-0 Houston victory over the San Francisco Giants. The catalyst for this novel scheduling was to avert Houston's dreadfully oppressive daytime heat in the pre-Astrodome era. However, that just caused players to be eaten alive by mosquitoes, as opposed to daytime flying insects. Colts' Stadium seemed more pasture (or swamp) than ballpark.

Two days later the Colts and Cubs were knotted at 2-apiece going into the bottom of the tenth. Houston had a runner on first with Fazio at bat. Manager Harry Craft gave Fazio the bunt sign. He executed the play perfectly, getting Cubs' reliever Lindy McDaniel to throw wildly to first for a two-base error. After an intentional walk to load the bases. Bob Aspromonte electrified the crowd with a walk-off Grand Slam.

On June 26, Ernie Fazio placed three hits, adding a run and an RBI in Houston's extra-inning win over Milwaukee. He must have liked Braves' pitching. Ten days later, Fazio had three more safeties against them during the span of a doubleheader. He also crushed his first home run that day to account for Houston's only run of the twin bill.

Realizing that Fazio needed more seasoning, Houston management sent Fazio to Class AAA Oklahoma City. Nellie Fox took over as starting second baseman for Houston in 1964. Unfortunately for Fazio, injuries contributed to a sub-par year, postponing his plans for a return to the big club. Meanwhile, a young infielder in the Colts Double-A affiliate in San Antonio was tearing up the Texas League. His name was Joe Morgan.

In 1965, the Houston ball club changed their name to the Astros. Ernie Fazio competed with veteran Nellie Fox and Morgan for the right to be the starting second baseman in the "Eighth Wonder of the World," the Houston Astrodome. Joe Morgan beat the older two players out in spring training. Ernie Fazio returned to Oklahoma City.

Fazio discovered some of his old college magic while playing with the Oklahoma City 89ers in 1965. The always-hustling pint-sized infielder belted 23 home runs and made the Triple-A All-Star team. To top it off, the 89ers beat Portland for the Pacific Coast League championship. Despite Fazio's efforts, the Astros dealt him to the Kansas City Athletics as the "player to be named later" in an earlier deal that sent Jim Gentile to Houston in June.

A mid-season call-up in 1966, Fazio batted .206 in 27 games for Kansas City. After such an inauspicious display of fielding four years prior, Ernie Fazio's defense had improved to the point where he finished the season playing errorless ball.

Kansas City owner Charles Finley enlisted the help of Fazio in a unique capacity. When Finley moved the team to Oakland in the winter of 1967, he used Ernie Fazio, who resided there and had local connections, to be an advance public relations man. When a church organization of say, 100 people, wanted to hear about the Oakland A's, Ernie would give a sermon and sign autographs.

Ernie Fazio would never wear an Oakland uniform. Just before the start of spring training, Finley sold him outright to Vancouver of the Pacific Coast league. One reason for the sale was another up-and-coming Italian-American second baseman in the Oakland organization. Like Fazio, this player came to the majors early, spent a long stint in the minors, and followed that with a brief return to the majors. His name was Tony La Russa.

Ernie Fazio's early entry into the majors may have been his undoing. Had a more established ball club signed him, he could probably have gained valuable experience and been brought along slowly. Then, Fazio probably would have entered the majors with his confidence intact. In hindsight, the Houston front office probably realized they rushed Fazio into an overwhelming situation. However, this ragged expansion club lacked the luxury of developing talent in their farm system, which was non-existent in the beginning. The ledger closed for Fazio with a .182 career average in the big leagues. Fazio's most curious statistic was having twice as many career extra base hits (16) as runs batted in (8).

After his playing days, Fazio returned to his Oakland roots and settled in San Leandro. He presently runs a rental service in the Bay Area. Old baseball teammates from Santa Clara meet annually for golf and reminiscing. Three have since passed away, as did their legendary coach, Paddy Cottrell. With the exception of Nelson Briles, a career 129-game winner and owner of two World Series rings, none of the Santa Clara players achieved great success as major leaguers. Bob Garibaldi and Pete Magrini never won a game in their injury-riddled careers. Tim Cullen and John Boccabella batted .220 and .219 respectively.

Despite a less-than-stellar career in big league ball, Ernie Fazio was still a winner, having proved as much with amateur, college, and professional ball clubs in Oakland, Saskatoon, Santa Clara, and Oklahoma City. As former Yankees' infielder Tony Kubek once said, "No matter how many errors you make, no matter how many times you strike out, keep hustling. That way you'll at least look like a ballplayer."

Mr. Baseball
Bob Uecker, C
1935-

Why would Bob Uecker be here in the first place? After all, the Baseball Encyclopedias list Uecker's career batting average at .200—perched exactly on the Mendoza Line. However, dividing Mr. Baseball's 146 lifetime hits by his 731 at bats yields a career batting average of .1997. Since batting averages, by convention, are rounded off to three decimal points, Uecker gets the .200. Nevertheless, from a purely mathematical standpoint, however slight, Bob ended his playing days below .200 That gets this truly lovable and laughable character on the rolls of Mendoza's Heroes.

Bob Uecker wasn't the first to make much ado of an ordinary career to become an announcer, author, a TV personality, and baseball funnyman. Joe Garagiola, another catcher, did it first. Maybe the backbreaking, high pain threshold breeds characters like Ossee Schreckengost (the Dead Ball Era zany who ordered Connie Mack to put a clause in Rube Waddell's contract barring him from eating crackers in bed), Moe Berg, Yogi Berra, Choo Choo Coleman, and Tim McCarver. While Garagiola was undoubtedly the better player, Uecker seems to have outdone him when comparing second careers. Consequently, Uecker has become a ubiquitous mass-media figure. In print, on radio, in television, and even at the Cineplex, Bob Uecker continues to make an impact.

A common and powerful bond exists between Bob Uecker and the city of Milwaukee. For starters, he was born in the "Beer City" in 1935 and he grew up there. He originally started out as a pitcher. Though scouted, Bob went undrafted after high school. At age 19, Uecker joined the Army and was stationed at Fort Leonard Wood, Missouri. While trying out for the baseball team, the coach asked Bob about his previous baseball experience. "I played baseball at Marquette College." Uecker fibbed just a little. Not only did Marquette not have a varsity baseball team, Uecker never attended the school. Otherwise, Uecker's comments were completely truthful.

Uecker impressed everyone as the team's catcher and received second looks by the scouts. This time, his hometown team signed him. "I signed with the Milwaukee Braves for $3,000," noted Bob in one of his more famous quotes. "That bothered my dad at the time because he didn't have that kind of dough. But he eventually scraped it up." His other version of the same event is, "The Braves officials took us to one of the city's swankiest restaurants. My dad was so nervous he rolled down the window and the hamburgers fell off the tray."

However, baseball's king of comedy was nothing to laugh at as a minor leaguer. On three occasions, Uecker batted over .300 in the minors, with a high of .332 and 21 homers for Boise back in 1958. Uecker also established his reputation as a solid defensive catcher with a tremendous throwing arm. In 1961, playing for Louisville in the old American Association, Uecker led all catchers in fielding and batted .309.

In 1962, after toiling several seasons in the "little show," Uecker got the chance to play for his hometown Braves, the first denizen of Milwaukee ever to do so. Appearing over parts of two seasons, Bob Uecker played alongside Braves' legends Hank Aaron and Eddie Mathews. During his brief tour with Milwaukee, he batted robust enough, going .250 with 20 hits in 80 at bats. Uecker would later joke that he was named "Minor League Player of the Year, in coincidentally, his first year in the majors.

Just before the start of the 1964 season, the Braves traded Uecker to the St. Louis Cardinals. While Uecker was disappointed to leave his beloved Milwaukee, he was probably happy to be on a major league roster for an entire season. The chirpy 1964 Cardinals were full of future announcers with Uecker, Tim McCarver, Bill White, and Mike Shannon.

As the backup receiver for McCarver, Uecker batted .198 over 40 games. His memorable moment that season occurred on September 1, when his ninth inning single brought home a run to beat his old Braves 5-4. Uecker also hit his only home run of the season in the fourth inning. The win vaulted St. Louis into third place and initiated the Cardinals' incredible late-season rally (and equally incredible Philadelphia Phillies' collapse) to take the National League pennant.

In the World Series, the Cardinals went on to defeat the Yankees in seven games with heroes Bob Gibson, Ken Boyer, and Lou Brock. This Fall Classic also marked the end of the Ruth-to-Gehrig-to-DiMaggio-to-Mantle Yankees dynasty, as New Yorkers would wait over a decade for their next Series' appearance. Bob did raise an eyebrow or two during pre-game warm-ups in the first game of the World Series, as he "borrowed" an unattended tuba and proceeded to shag fly balls with the instrument.

Amidst the jubilation in the victorious Cardinals' clubhouse, after their hard-fought triumph, emotions flowed as freely as iced bottles of champagne. While outfielder Curt Flood bordered on tears describing his feelings to Maury Allen of the *New York Post*, Bob Uecker presented a different perspective: "I'm on a damn championship team, man, do you know what that is? I'm going out tonight and throw up in every bar in St. Louis." Uecker, whom Allen described as a "catcher who never catches because Tim McCarver never rests," then rubbed his face with shaving cream, threw champagne over his head, and beat his chest while yelling, "I am the greatest."

While with the Cardinals, Bob Uecker may not have frequented the diamond on a regular basis, but he made his earliest showings of his now-famous wit and humor. One of his earliest routines was doing an impression of legendary broadcaster Harry Caray, with the Cardinals at the time. "For awhile, I had him down pretty good," Uecker said. "I did him every day. We got a kick out of it. I did it in front of Harry. I did it on the team bus. When people imitate you, you've got to be somebody. They don't imitate people who aren't anybody."

After two seasons, the Cardinals, perhaps weary of Uecker's bat work or banter or both, traded the funny bone backstop to Philadelphia. Uecker claimed, "I knew my career was over. In 1965, my baseball card came out with no picture." In 1966, Uecker enjoyed his most productive season in the majors. He probably must have felt comfortable with eccentrics like Richie Allen, whom Uecker described in his autobiography *Catcher in the Wry*, as someone "who liked everything about a ballpark except getting there." There was also Bo Belinsky, a "flamboyant left-hander who thought he had been Rudolph Valentino in a prior life." Relief pitcher John Boozer's idea of fun was to eat bugs and worms and watch people gag. And, only on the Phillies would John Boozer have a teammate named Bobby Wine.

Brought to Philadelphia to back up left-handed veteran Clay Dalrymple, who struggled to hit .213 the year before, Bob Uecker would get a chance to start against left-hand pitching. On opening day 1966, Uecker caught Chris Short and drove in a run with a single as Philadelphia beat Cincinnati 3-1. He hit home runs on consecutive days at the end of April. In his first six games, Uecker had produced four hits and driven in six runs.

The first time the Phillies met the Cardinals, Bob exacted some revenge on his former team. He singled to open the winning rally and scored the tie-breaking run on a bases-loaded walk to Dick Groat. On June 3, Uecker slugged his fourth homer of the year. By the All-Star break, Uecker was hitting in the .270s and had raised his home run total to six. Uecker even received votes for All-Star Game consideration.

On July 17, Uecker tagged his seventh home run in a fifteen-inning win over the San Francisco Giants. Third on the club in long balls, Uecker later commented, "I had no personal goals in mind, which was just as well, because I did not hit another homer during the rest of the season."

For whatever reason, Uecker's once-lofty batting average slid to .208 by season's end. Still, he did finish in the Phillies' top-five in circuit blasts and drove in 30 runs. The Phils ended up in fourth place that year—going 87-75. It would be their highest finish until 1975.

Uecker came out of the gate slow in 1967. As he would later aptly remark, "I had slumps that lasted into the winter." And the spring. Riding the bench mostly, Uecker was batting just .171 for the Phillies when they traded him back to the Braves (now in Atlanta) for infielder Gene Oliver. Summing up his experiences in the City of Brotherly Love, Uecker said, "I didn't get a lot of awards as a player, but they did have a Bob Uecker Day Off for me once in Philly." In Atlanta, he served as Joe Torre's backup behind the plate. Filling in for Torre after an injury, Bob Uecker produced a monster day at the bat on June 21. Collecting five runs batted in with a Grand Slam and a double, Uecker provided more than enough offense for the Braves to beat the Giants 9-2. Bob Uecker played down his homer by saying, "I hit a Grand Slam off Ron Herbel and when Herman Franks came out to get him, he was bringing Herbel's suitcase."

Though he blasted two more homers that year, his last season in the majors proved quite disastrous. He batted a microscopic .137 for the Braves and a composite .150 for the year. However, Uecker's solid defense was good enough to earn him a personal best eighty games played. About his career, Uecker crowed, "Anybody with ability can play in the big leagues. But to be able to trick people year in and year out the way I did, I think that was a much greater feat."

In the final analysis, Bob Uecker sells himself short. With a bat in his hands, Uecker could be dangerous. Two of his fourteen career home runs came against the slants of Sandy Koufax. His superb defensive skills likely kept him in the game. When Milwaukee Brewers' announcer Merle Harmon would tell the audience that, "He was a fine catcher, with a strong throwing arm, and a good handler of pitchers," Bob Uecker would reply, "You're killing my reputation."

Bob Uecker will never be confused with Cardinals' speedster Lou Brock. Not once in his career did he earn a triple or a stolen base. Yet Uecker maintains he presented the illusion of a fast runner by "always knocking off my helmet so it looked like I was really moving."

Bob Uecker's big break in broadcasting came as the fortuitous result of Allen "Bud" Selig's 1970 purchase of the bankrupt Seattle Pilots. Upon moving the team to Milwaukee, Selig hired Uecker to be part of the Brewers' broadcasting team alongside Merle Harmon. In no time Harmon and Uecker became a popular duo. Harmon played the straight man. One routine had Merle telling the listening audience, during the pre-game show, that Bob had just returned from some fictitious speaking appearance in another part of the country. Though each intro was unbeknownst to Bob, he would ad-lib a story based on the bogus visit. In Harmon's book *Merle Harmon Stories*, he recounts a Uecker tall tale about a journey to Boyertown, Pennsylvania for the National Casket Manufacturing Association Convention. Although Boyertown is the casket-making capital of the United States, the town never actually held a Soapbox Derby-style race. Nor was Uecker the race's announcer.

> They put wheels on these caskets and line 'em up at the top of the hill on Main Street. Then they cut 'em loose and they roll down to the finish line. Since no power is allowed, the skill of the driver is very important, Of course, someone always has to cheat and this one guy put an 80-horsepower motor in his casket. Naturally, he quickly roared out in front of the others. By the time he passed Fourth Street he was clocking 60 miles per hour and raised up out of the casket to see where he was. Just then the town drunk staggered out of a bar. When the drunk saw the driver and the speeding casket zoom by...well, the guy has never taken another drink. Now, let's get to the lineups.

For the next year-and-a-half, this Harmon-Uecker routine continued as a pre-game tradition. Non-baseball fans joined in the silliness, tuning in only to listen to comedy and not the ballgame. Fans sent in mail by the bucket load, including written scripts, and suggested Uecker's next monologue and location.

Following Merle Harmon's retirement, Bob Uecker assumed the role of lead announcer. Though he never played in a World Series game (employing tubas as oversize gloves doesn't count), Uecker did get his first opportunity to broadcast a Series when the Brewers faced-off with the St. Louis Cardinals in the "Suds Series" of 1982. As an announcer, Uecker's name has become as synonymous with Milwaukee baseball as Henry Aaron and Robin Yount. As the celebrated "Voice of the Brewers," Uecker has logged an impressive 30+ seasons at the microphone broadcasting major league baseball in his hometown. Five times, the highly-respected Uecker has won Wisconsin Sportscaster of the Year. On the national baseball front, Uecker gained new legions of fans as the play-by-play announcer for ABC Sports' Monday Night Baseball, the League

Championship Series, and the World Series. Certainly, Uecker's popularity stems from his mirthful look at baseball and life in general. To hear him comment, "The wind took that baby," with a straight face, after a Brewer outfielder misplays a fly ball, is priceless.

Despite recent heart surgery and chronic back pain, Bob Uecker continues to broadcast a full docket of Brewers' games. Uecker probably never dreamed of entering the Baseball Hall of Fame without a ticket, but may someday find a place in the Cooperstown Shrine. The Ford Frick Award honors broadcasters among the Hall's enshrinees.

The multi-talented Uecker also made his mark in the entertainment industry. His acting career received an impetus after a 1969 visit with trumpeter Al Hirt. "Al Hirt is really the person responsible for my first appearance on the Tonight Show," Uecker explained. "He had opened up a small night club in Atlanta and he had asked me to come up on stage."

Hirt and the crowd roared with laughter as Uecker used his self-deprecating humor to bash himself on his playing ability. Or lack thereof. Quite impressed, Hirt used his well-extended connections to arrange an appearance for Bob on the Tonight Show, starring Johnny Carson. Uecker quickly became one of Carson's favorite guests, making 100 or so appearances.

Perhaps the Uecker legacy will live on. As he explained on several occasions,

> The biggest thrill a ballplayer can have is when your son takes after you. That happened when my Bobby was in his championship Little League game. He really showed me something. Struck out three times. Made an error that lost the game. Parents were throwing things at our car and swearing at us as we drove off. Gosh, I was proud.

On his way to becoming a national celebrity, Uecker has visited Mike Douglas, David Frost, Merv Griffin, and David Letterman. He even made appearances on offbeat shows such as The Superstars, The Midnight Special, and WWF Wrestling. On the latter show, Minnesota Governor Jesse Ventura, then a wrestling announcer, made light of Bob's .200 batting average. Bob Uecker attained the epitome of pop icon status when he hosted NBC's Saturday Night Live.

As one of the most popular ex-jocks to appear in a Miller Lite beer advertisement, Bob Uecker's spot shows him at Yankee Stadium with ticket in hand crowing to an usher, "I must be in the front row." After a quick film cut, Uecker sits with no one else but pigeons in the uppermost reaches of the bleachers. A piece of baseball jargon resulted from that commercial. The "front row" phrase endures in stadiums across the country and "Uecker seats" are what fans refer to as the highest altitude seats in a ballpark.

Always the class clown, Uecker caused an uproar at one of the Lite "alumni" gatherings. During one filming, pitchmen from earlier commercials were brought together to film a new spot. Set in the desert with the "talent" dressed in Western garb, Uecker complained that he didn't know how to wear cowboy clothing. When he appeared during production wearing his chaps, sans jeans, he proved his point. On the set, Uecker "mooned" his cohorts.

Uecker's television resume goes beyond guest appearances, commercials, and play-by-play. He hosted two syndicated television shows, Bob Uecker's Wacky World of

Sports and War of the Stars. In 1985, Bob starred in ABC's situation comedy Mr. Belvedere, which ran for six seasons. Uecker portrayed George Owens, a former athlete, employed as a sportscaster for a Pittsburgh television station. While the show was not the comic equivalent of Seinfeld, Belvedere managed to air for over 100 episodes.

With his growing popularity, Hollywood beckoned in 1988. Bob Uecker made his motion picture debut in *Major League*, a comedy starring Charlie Sheen and Tom Berenger. Uecker portrayed oft-inebriated play-by-play announcer Harry Doyle. At the time, the movie seemed more fantastical than *Star Wars*, with the premise of the Cleveland Indians contending for the pennant. With the success of the Cleveland team throughout the 1990s, truth can be stranger than fiction.

Major League spawned the sequels *Major League II* and *Major League III-Back to the Minors*. The latter film is so bad that Uecker commented, "I finished filming and got on the airplane the next day, and it was playing on the airplane." Artistically speaking, the trilogy certainly pales in comparison to diamond classics like *Field of Dreams, Bull Durham*, and *The Natural*.

Though Bob Uecker owns as many Oscars and Emmys as he does Most Valuable Player awards, he did earn an accolade for his acting. In 1993, he was inducted into the Wisconsin Performing Artists Hall of Fame.

Bob Uecker can say all he wants about his on-the-field foibles. And, he usually does. "Baseball hasn't forgotten me," he says. "I go to a lot of old-timers' games and I haven't lost a thing. I sit in the bullpen and let people throw things at me. Just like old times."

However, with six years of major league service, a World Series ring, and even All-Star consideration, Uecker's career was not all that bad. That aside, he most likely would be relegated to relative obscurity, if not for his self-deprecating wit and vibrant personality that have earned him star-quality recognition since his retirement from the game.

In a comment that's as much a criticism of baseball economics than his lack of ability, Uecker says, "If I were playing today, I'd be a million-dollar player. Is that scary, or what?"

Maestro
Tony La Russa, 2B
1944-

Tony La Russa may become the first member of *Mendoza's Heroes* to be inducted into the Baseball Hall of Fame. However, La Russa would not be the first position player to hit below .200 and honored in Cooperstown. Longtime Dodgers' manager Walter Alston struck out in his only major league plate appearance.

Before becoming one of baseball's finest managers, infielder Tony La Russa interspersed 132 major league games into 16 seasons of professional ball. He batted just .199 without slugging a single home run nor stealing a single base. From a longevity perspective, La Russa's playing career is quite noteworthy. He started playing right at the time John Glenn became the first American to orbit the earth. By the time La Russa finished, Project Apollo was in the history books and Skylab was in space.

Tony La Russa was born and raised in Tampa, Florida. With a climate conducive to year-round play, many ballplayers hail from this Gulf Coast city. Just on La Russa's American Legion team alone were major leaguers Ken Suarez and Lou Piniella.

As soon as he graduated from Jefferson High School, 17-year-old Tony La Russa signed with the Kansas City Athletics for somewhere between fifty to a hundred thousand dollars. Just 18 on opening day, young Tony spent the 1963 season on the Kansas City A's roster. While one of only three players to start at shortstop as an eighteen-year-old[7], La Russa rode the bench most of the time. In Ron Luciano's *Baseball Lite*, La Russa once confessed: "I was overmatched in those days. I was praying I wouldn't be used. I was always very honest with myself. I knew I couldn't play in this league."

While most teens would brood due to inactivity, Tony La Russa used this time to observe and understand the game. When he earned a rare appearance, La Russa played rather well. He batted .250—11 hits in 44 at bats—and fielded decently.

Unfortunately, La Russa incurred a severe shoulder injury while making a throw during a softball game. His arm never fully healed. With the bad shoulder, Tony La Russa did not fit into Kansas City's immediate plans. Languishing in their farm system, La Russa would not return to the major for five years, and then just for five games. La Russa managed a single in three at bats in the Athletics debut game in Oakland. Merritt Clifton recalled, "Tony La Russa distinguished himself during his brief stint with Oakland in 1968 by arriving early for games and playing pepper in his street clothes for a few minutes with those of us who hung around the player's parking lot."

La Russa's major league apex, as a player, occurred in 1970. He backed up second baseman Dick Green in 44 games and pinch hit in eight others. Of his seven career runs batted in, six came in this season. He also secured a three-hit ballgame against Minnesota on August 10 that included a leadoff double in the eighth inning to ignite a game-winning rally. Though La Russa only batted .198, he managed to outhit Green that season.

---

[7] Robin Yount and Alex Rodriguez also started at shortstop at age 18.

The Oakland ball club was a scintillating team to watch. Owner-innovator Charlie Finley introduced everything from orange-colored baseballs to gold-colored bases, to college sprinters on the rosters solely as pinch runners during the decade, much to the bemusement of the staid rules committee. The nucleus of the A's dynasty in the early half of the 1970s also formed that year. Outfielder Reggie Jackson, third baseman Sal Bando, and shortstop Bert Campaneris all were regulars on the field. Reserve outfielder Joe Rudi and catcher Dave Duncan became starters by the time Oakland won the first of their three consecutive World Championships in 1972. On the mound, rookie Vida Blue joined ace Catfish Hunter. Blue would pitch a no-hit game in only his second major league start.

La Russa began the 1971 season with Oakland's Triple-A affiliate in Iowa. Called up to Oakland, Tony went hitless in 23 games and eight at bats before Oakland sold him to the Atlanta Braves on August 14. La Russa punched a couple of hits in a Braves' uniform over seven at bats.

One of La Russa's finest seasons as a professional player was in 1972 with the Richmond Braves of the International League. La Russa hit .308 with a career high 10 home runs. But that performance did not even earn La Russa a quick look with Atlanta. Following the season, Atlanta shipped Tony La Russa to the Chicago Cubs in exchange for pitcher Tom Phoebus.

With Wichita of the now-defunct American Association, Tony La Russa scored 82 runs with career bests in RBI (75) and batting average (.314). That earned him a single pinch-run appearance with the Cubs and he scored in his last major league game.

But, Tony clung to the hope of one more shot in the big leagues. Like a hired mercenary, he played one year each in the Triple-A affiliates of the Pittsburgh Pirates, Montreal Expos, and Chicago White Sox from 1974 to 1976. La Russa batted well every year. In fact, with Denver in 1975, he posted career bests in runs scored (87) and doubles (23). In the highest echelons of the minor leagues, there is always a niche for players like Tony La Russa. They add stability to rosters in constant flux due to experimenting with green talent and rehabilitation assignments for established major leaguers.

In 1977, the Cardinals organization employed La Russa's services for their Triple-A New Orleans ball club. Incredibly, this would be La Russa's seventh major league organization in as many years. Now 32 years old and struggling with a .188 batting average, Tony La Russa's playing days ended. In George Will's *Men at Work*, Tony admitted he should have quit when he was 24 because his skills were regressing. When asked by the club to stay on as coach, La Russa agreed and began a new phase of his baseball career.

La Russa's modest big league totals included 35 base hits in 176 career at bats. On defense, he was a versatile and credible fielder. In the minors, he tallied an impressive 1,172 hits and a .266 batting average. Understanding his limitations early on, Tony La Russa had the foresight to work on his college degree in the off-season. La Russa earned a bachelor's degree in Industrial Management from Southern Florida University and also graduated from the Florida State University School of Law in 1978. Tony passed his bar exam in December 1979 to become a licensed attorney. By then, new career opportunities were coming his way.

La Russa's experience of playing and observing baseball for nearly two decades and his rigorous study of law makes for a very focused field manager. History shows this vividly. Of five major league managers with law degrees (John Montgomery Ward, Hughie Jennings, Miller Huggins, Branch Rickey, and Herold "Muddy" Ruel), the first four players are enshrined in the Baseball Hall of Fame. Even Ruel, a 19-year catcher, possessed numbers that placed him on Hall of Fame ballots for several years.

In 1978, the Chicago White Sox hired La Russa to manage their Class AA affiliate in Knoxville. By mid-season, he moved up to the White Sox as a coach. La Russa replaced Don Kessinger as the ChiSox manager on August 12, 1979. Completing his quick rise as manager, La Russa was just 34 years of age, becoming one of the youngest ever full-time skippers. Though the White Sox were marginal at best when La Russa took over the team, he gradually rebuilt the ball club. First he shored up the pitching with LaMarr Hoyt and Britt Burns and middle-infield defense. Next, Tony acquired an array of potent-hitting outfielders and designated hitters like Ron Kittle and Harold Baines. Tony's acumen for identifying talent established him quickly as one of the game's top managers.

After third-place finishes in 1981 and 1982, La Russa led the White Sox to the American League West title in 1983 with 99 victories, the most in the majors. Though the Baltimore Orioles prevailed in the American League Championship Series, La Russa won the first of his three Manager of the Year awards. In 1984, La Russa's Chicago squad were tied for first at the All-Star break before stumbling to a fifth place finish. The following season, the ChiSox rebounded to finish third at 85-77. However, after a 26-38 start in 1986, La Russa was out of Chicago.

Only unemployed for 18 days, La Russa returned to Oakland to assume their managerial role. He immediately turned around a team that had not been a contender for years. After leading the Athletics to a pair of third place finishes, he built the ultimate wrecking crew in the 1988 Athletics. One of baseball's most formidable teams ever, that squad blitzed to a 104-58 finish, earning La Russa his second Manager of the Year accolade. The club featured the "Bash Brothers" in the person of Mark McGwire and Jose Canseco. With 42 home runs and 40 steals, Canseco became baseball's first 40-40 man and won the American League's Most Valuable Player award. With respect to pitching, La Russa featured an excellent starting rotation, anchored by Dave Stewart and Bob Welch. Essential to Tony's pitching strategy was his penchant for quickly going to his bullpen. La Russa's masterstroke was converting aging starter Dennis Eckersley to a "school's out" caliber closer.

After sweeping through Boston in the American League Championship Series, La Russa's Oakland club were heavy favorites to knock out the Los Angeles Dodgers in the World Series. However, Kirk Gibson's hobbling, Hobbsian homer, with two out in the ninth inning of game one, dealt Eckersley and the Athletics a mortal blow. Then, pitcher Orel Hershiser wiped the swagger out of Oakland's fearsome batting order with his two complete game victories, including the clincher in game five.

In 1989, with the return of Rickey Henderson and the addition of pitcher Mike Moore, La Russa and the A's swept the San Francisco Giants in the earthquake-marred "Bay Series." The 1990 team again romped through the American League competition, but this time received a World Series sweeping at the hands of the Cincinnati Reds. The 1990 World Series was the only time in history that two American Legion teammates, La Russa and Reds' manager Lou Piniella, squared off against each other as managers.

After falling out of first place in 1991, La Russa's 1992 club wrapped up the division title with a 96-66 record. With yet another popping of champagne bottles in the clubhouse, Tony had now managed five American League West champions in ten seasons. He earned his third Manager of the Year award for the effort. This time, however, the Toronto Blue Jays ended Oakland's season early in a well-played and dramatic Championship Series.

As all good things must come to an end, the pitching arms of Oakland finally broke down and the front office, consumed with debt, sold off its remaining stars. Dave Stewart, the staff ace, went to Toronto. La Russa's 1993 charges finished in last place at 68-94, earning a dubious honor of becoming the second "first to worst" team in history. The 1915 Philadelphia Athletics, led by Connie Mack, were the first. Tony La Russa's normally calm and collective demeanor gave way to episodes of fury as the losses kept mounting. Unable to obtain quality stars from his ineffective pitching staff, La Russa experimented by having his three best pitchers go out each day for three innings each.

Somehow, La Russa made the most of a weakened Oakland squad and had his charges contending, a single game behind the Texas Rangers in the American League West lead in 1994. Entering the final two months, one could place smart money that La Russa would have managed and willed Oakland to another divisional flag. However, the game's power mavens, driven by greed and stupidity, forced a cancellation of the rest of the season. Like the speedometer of some wrecked car indelibly frozen on 95 MPH, the infamous Strike of 1994 resulted in the Athletics (and all other ball clubs) stuck in a non-linear time warp.

After another disappointing last-place finish in 1995, La Russa had done all he could with Oakland and resigned. While venerable Connie Mack will forever hold the A's franchise managerial records, Tony finished as Oakland's all-time leader in games managed (1,471), victories (798), and division titles (4).

The St. Louis Cardinals hired La Russa in the off-season to be their manager. After 17 seasons in the American League, this was La Russa's first managerial post in the Senior Circuit. One of La Russa's first moves was recruiting some of the stars from his Oakland teams to the Cardinals. With the help of Athletics' alumni Mike Gallego, and pitchers Rick Honeycutt and Dennis Eckersley, La Russa led the Redbirds to the 1996 National League Central crown. Because of his shrewd wheeling and dealing, the Cardinals barely missed playing in another World Series. The 1997 Cardinals finished with a disap-pointing 73 wins, but Tony and slugger Mark McGwire reunited. While St. Louis of the late 1990s did not play up to La Russa's standards, St. Louis fans seemed content with watching Mark McGwire obliterate home run records with his mighty blasts. McGwire's powerful stroke resulted in balls hit so far they needed flight attendants on them.

Tony La Russa's Cardinals returned to the winner's circle in the 2000 season, running away with their division, and sweeping through the Atlanta Braves. They made the vaunted Braves club look as if they'd never experienced post-season play. Only the Mets' five game Championship Series triumph doused an otherwise fine season for St. Louis.

At the close of the 2001 season, La Russa's had logged 22 seasons at the major league helm. He leads active managers in career victories and ranks 11th all-time. No stranger to the post-season, La Russa's White Sox, Athletics, and Cardinals have won eight division titles and one World Series in 1989. One of the keys to his success is his principal objective to take individual players and form them into a tightly knit confederation. Conformity to team standards and the summary unloading of malcontents is La Russa's Law. When Jose Canseco was a rookie, he failed to run out a ground ball. Upon his return to the dugout, La Russa told the gigantic mass-of-muscle, "Do that again, I'll knock you on your ass." On another occasion, Tony La Russa caught Mark McGwire wearing shorts at the ballpark. La Russa told McGwire, "You can go inside and put fifty dollars on my desk." When McGwire asked why, La Russa explained, "Anybody who has legs like that can't wear shorts around here."

A staunch conformist, La Russa remains quite visionary in his on-field strategy and tactics. Not only did he tinker with pitching rotations with three innings a man, he has, on occasion, batted his pitcher in the eighth spot to create a pre-leadoff hitter and give Mark McGwire more RBI opportunities.

Tony La Russa is also actively involved in several animal rights activities. In 1991, Tony and his wife Elaine founded the Tony La Russa's Animal Rescue Foundation (ARF) in Walnut Creek, California. A lost cat started it all. In 1990, with the New York Yankees at the Oakland Coliseum, a stray feline wandered onto the field. With play halted, the frightened animal scampered around the infield and outfield before Tony coaxed the cat into the Oakland dugout. The next day he brought the cat—who he named "Evie"—to a shelter near his home. Upon learning that the shelter would euthenize the animal within a week due to overcrowding, La Russa personally placed the cat with a new owner. In the wake of that experience, La Russa made the establishment of a no-kill shelter his personal project.

Today, the ARF is one of the nation's most idealistic animal protection agencies. Not only do they aid abandoned and homeless animals, but promote the concept that strengthening the bonds between humans and animals enriches people's lives. With these goals, La Russa's foundation designed progressive animal outreach programs for terminally ill children, the elderly, victims of domestic violence, and others who can benefit from the healing companionship of animals.

A lifelong vegetarian, La Russa also takes a strong anti-hunting stance. Just remember to leave your full-length mink coat at home if you ever plan to visit the La Russa's. That's something star outfielder Dave Parker found out the hard way upon first meeting Elaine La Russa.

A generality of baseball is that great players do not necessarily make for successful managers. Legendary performers like Ty Cobb, Walter Johnson, and Pete Rose never took their teams into the World Series. History shows that typically the best managers completed marginal careers. Successful skippers like Connie Mack, Sparky Anderson, and Gene Mauch all batted below .250 in the majors. Tommy Lasorda, a pitcher, lost all four of his decisions. One surmises that the men with fewer physical gifts compensate for these shortfalls with a keen mental understanding of baseball's nuances. For Tony La Russa, a maestro of the green chessboard, that attribute seems most appropriate.

Catcher In The Ryan
Mike Ryan, C
1941-

Several major league catchers like Bill Bergen, Choo Choo Coleman, and Bob Uecker have managed to hang around for relatively long and productive careers despite possessing batting averages below .200. Other than a rare Johnny Bench, Mike Piazza, or Ivan Rodriguez, the grueling regimen of squatting in unnatural positions for extended periods tends to depress hitting. Mike Ryan's career is the most prodigious of these good field-not so good hit backstops. Though he failed to bat over .200 in seven of his eleven campaigns, Mike Ryan endured by virtue of his outstanding defensive skills.

The oldest of six children, Mike Ryan first established his baseball prowess on the sandlots of Haverhill, Massachusetts. He grew to be a mountain of a young man at 6'-2" and 215 pounds. Though he never played high school ball (the small Catholic school he attended did not have a team), Ryan played in numerous amateur leagues. He was selected for the Hearst national baseball team, in its day the equivalent of a U.S. Olympic team. During a regional tryout at Fenway Park, Ryan impressed Red Sox scouts with his size and top-flight skills as a receiver. They later signed him to a contract.

Despite failing to ever hit above .248 in the minors, Mike Ryan's all-around play secured a rapid rise through the Red Sox's farm system. In 1962, while at Waterloo (Iowa), Mike led Midwest League's receivers in putouts and assists. With Reading (Pennsylvania) two years later, he paced Eastern League backstops with a fine .990 fielding average and 12 double plays.

After the season with Reading concluded, Mike Ryan returned home to Massachusetts. On October 2, 1964, Ryan had just returned from an evening out with his friends. Greeting him at the door, his father told him the Red Sox called and told him to report the next day. During the drive to Fenway Park, Mike Ryan wondered if he was traded or waived. Upon his arrival, Ryan was told that he would be starting catcher for Bill Monbouquette. Ryan's surprising debut game exceeded expectations. He smashed a single, drove in two runs, and earned a base on balls.

Though Ryan hit just .159 over 33 games in 1965 backing up Bob Tillman, Mike clouted three home runs—including a pair in a single game against Detroit. The next season, he started at catcher for the BoSox, played in 116 games, batted .214, and drove in 32 runs. His first of two homers that year cleared the famous Fenway Park "Green Monster," landing into a screen atop the thirty-seven-foot wall. That blast ignited a Boston rally against the Yankees, from 2-down, for an eventual 5–3 win.

A member of the "Impossible Dream," 1967 pennant-winning Red Sox, Mike split catching duties with Bob Tillman and Russ Gibson. That squad included leftfielder Carl Yastrzemski, shortstop Rico Petrocelli, first baseman George Scott, and centerfielder Reggie Smith. In one of many dramatic moments that year, Ryan helped carry outfielder Tony Conigliaro off the field after he was nearly killed by a Jack Hamilton fastball that beaned his head.

With 27 RBI in 226 at bats, Mike Ryan definitely contributed to the Dream. On May 31, Mike delivered a deftly placed suicide squeeze bunt to score the winning run in a 3–2 triumph over the California Angels. He drove in three runs in a game to help Boston beat Kansas City on July 1. Another Boston win, against Kansas City the next day, saw Ryan tie the game up with an RBI single (just one of three hits for Boston facing a young Catfish Hunter). On July 16, Mike Ryan went 2-for-3 with two runs scored to help Boston rout Detroit, 9–5. The biggest home run of his career came in the nightcap of an August 1 doubleheader with the Kansas City Athletics. Ryan bombed a game-busting 3-run homer to give Boston a split of the twin bill.

As the incredible 1967 American League pennant race tightened, Boston wanted a battle-tested catcher for the stretch drive. They acquired Elston Howard from the Yankees on August 3. Though used less frequently, Mike Ryan still managed clutch performances. Ryan's September 10 bases-loaded triple off Jim Bouton of the Yankees broke open the game and kept Boston within a half game of first place. A few days later, Ryan made several front pages when he was photographed blocking the plate and literally knocking Bert Campaneris out of the sky to complete a double play. Taking a spike in the arm from Campaneris, Ryan required eight stitches to close the wound.

In one of the weirdest pennant races ever, not decided until the final pitch of the season, Boston edged out Minnesota, Chicago, and Detroit. At .568, the Red Sox had the lowest winning percentage of an American League pennant winner in the era before divisional play (pre-1969). In the end, it looked as if none of the four teams wanted the pennant. Their combined won-lost record in the final week of the season was 6–14.

In the 1967 World Series, Ellie Howard received the nod as Boston's starting catcher. Ryan did get into game four, going 0-for-2 against the Cardinals' Bob Gibson in his lone appearance. Gibson pitched a 6-0 shutout that day. On defense, Ryan made four putouts. The Red Sox eventually lost the Fall Classic to the St. Louis Cardinals in seven games, thus perpetuating the Babe Ruth curse.

In 1968, the Red Sox traded Mike Ryan with cash to Philadelphia for pitcher Dick Ellsworth and catcher Gene Oliver. At first, the transaction looked one-sided in favor of Boston. Ellsworth pitched to a 16–7 slate while Ryan skidded to one of his worst seasons, batting a punchless .179. However, Mike Ryan would soon turn things around.

Mike Ryan's pinnacle year in the majors occurred in 1969. He hit the long ball with some regularity early in the season. In a 6–1 beating of the San Diego Padres, Ryan tallied a homer and double. By June 21, Ryan had clouted eight home runs—as many as Willie Mays at that time. Though his production tailed off, Ryan played in 133 games, earning career highs in almost every offensive category. With 91 hits that season, Ryan is the all-time single-season hit leader for below .200 hitters. Ryan also homered on 12 occasions. On defense, Ryan led all National League backstops—Johnny Bench included—with 79 assists, catching Phillie hurlers Rick Wise, Grant Jackson, and Woody Fryman.

Giving way to Tim McCarver as the Phillies' starting catcher in 1970, it looked as though Ryan would get his job back on May 2, after McCarver broke his right hand on a Willie Mays foul tip. As "Phils' fate" would have it, in the very same inning, Ryan broke his left hand while tagging out Willie McCovey at home plate.

With both catchers shelved for nearly 200 games between them, Philadelphia was forced into summoning a string of career minor league catchers to don the tools of ignorance. Mike Compton, Del Bates, and Jim Hutto all had their "15 games of fame," dove below .200, and were scarcely heard from again. Even bullpen coach Doc Edwards, an ex-Marines' medic, received a battlefield (or should we say, ball field) commission and caught 35 games.

Despite being on the disabled list three different times due to the hand injury, Ryan still managed to salvage the season. He led the Phillies in games caught with 46. Twice that year, he played the role of iron man, catching both ends of a doubleheader. Ryan was behind the plate for 20 innings in an August 1 sweep of the Giants. Eight days later, he performed the same feat in a split against the Cubs; "Mighty Mike" also hit a home run and scored two runs in the nightcap.

Over the next three seasons, Mike Ryan served as understudy for three different catchers. Each year yielded the same result: Phillies in last place. In 1971, Ryan backed-up Tim McCarver. One legendary Ryan moment occurred at the 1971 grand opening of Veterans Stadium. The ceremonial first ball was to be dropped from a helicopter, hovering hundreds of feet above the stadium. Given the honor of catching the air-dropped sphere, Mike Ryan wryly commented, "Last year they had four catchers hurt and now they are going to bomb one."

The aloft ball was released into a swirling wind caused by the whirling helicopter blades. Ryan, starting at second base, chased the drifting ball into center field, unfamiliar territory for a catcher. Mike bobbled the ball momentarily but miraculously held on amidst a chorus of cheers. That started a tradition of unique deliveries of the baseball on opening day at Veterans Stadium. The ceremonies included parachutists and the legendary "Kiteman" who figuratively "crashed and burned" his ramp-launched hang glider in center field during the 1972 home opener. That bobbled catch by Ryan was the closest he came all year to committing an error, as he fielded his position flawlessly in 43 games.

The 1972 edition of the Phillies finished an awful 59–97. Tim McCarver started the season as catcher, then was traded to Montreal for John Bateman. While Ryan batted .179 for the third time in five years, he had the thrill of catching several games for Steve Carlton during his unbelievable Cy Young Award winning 27–10 season.

Mainly responsible for breaking in a young Bob Boone, Ryan's final season with Philadelphia occurred in 1973. Boone would later become the all-time leader in games caught—a record eventually eclipsed by his contemporary Carlton Fisk. Mike Ryan would hit for a career-best .232 including a 3-for-3 game (with two runs scored and two RBI) in a 9-6 April 17 win.

Ryan finished out his playing career in 1974 with the Pittsburgh Pirates. On opening day in St. Louis, in the bottom of the tenth inning, the bases were loaded with Redbirds with the dangerous Lou Brock at bat. Brock hit a soft liner to right. Pittsburgh outfielder Gene Clines rushed in to make the catch, but the ball was ruled trapped by first base umpire Lee Weyer. Clines fired home to Ryan, forcing out Jim Dwyer. Ryan then threw to third base to erase Tim McCarver. The stunned base runners did not move because it looked like the ball was going to be caught. The outfield single turned into an odd 9–2–5 double play.

After coaching and managing in the Philadelphia organization, Mike Ryan was promoted to bullpen coach for the parent club in 1980. He earned a World Series ring as a member of the Phillies' only world championship team. For the next 16 years and through two more World Series appearances, Ryan mentored backstops from Boone to Bo Diaz to Ossie Virgil to Lance Parrish to Darren Daulton, finally retiring in 1995. Ryan currently lives in New Hampshire and collects antiques.

Mike Ryan is related to Jack Ryan, also a catcher. While this Jack Ryan did not rescue *The Cardinal of the Kremlin*, he did play three years with the St. Louis Cardinals. With a career spanning over four decades (1889–1913), the elder Ryan's career register showed 4 home runs, 154 RBI, and a .214 batting average.

Despite a .193 career batting average, Mike Ryan's stellar defense and fair-to-middling power were good enough to allow him to be the everyday catcher for two different teams. His lifetime .991 fielding percentage ranks him in the Top-10, only .002 behind all-time leaders, Bill Freehan, Jim Sundberg, and Elston Howard.

Oil Can
Ray Oyler, SS
1938-1981

Ray Oyler's lifetime batting average of .175 is low even by pitcher's standards. In fact, of all non-battery players with over 1,000 at bats, Ray Oyler owns the lowest career batting average. His biggest weakness at the plate was failure to make contact with the ball, incurring nearly one strikeout for every $3^1/_2$ at bats, worse than all-time strikeout leader Reggie Jackson. On occasion, a mere foul ball by Oyler caused mocked cheering in the dugouts and among spectators. Oyler even led the International League with 130 strikeouts in 1963.

Oyler became so intense about getting a base hit that he exhibited frenetic mannerisms in the batter's box. Once, in spring training, a very young Nolan Ryan fooled Ray so badly on a curveball, that Oyler swung straight down on the ball, like some frustrated woodchopper. It also did not help his confidence much, while at bat with two outs, to see the batter in the on-deck circle with his baseball glove.

Gratuitous lambasting concluded, Ray Oyler possessed some very positive ball playing attributes. Occasional power on offense with a combination of sure hands and great range on defense were Oyler's tickets out of the bushes and into a fairly productive six-year major league career.

Quite an athlete in high school, Raymond Francis Oyler hailed from Indianapolis. As a prep star, Ray lettered in football and basketball in addition to baseball. Ray did not play pro baseball until he was over 20 years of age because of a four-year hitch the United States Marine Corps.

He started his professional career with Duluth-Superior in 1960, hitting .261 with 90 runs scored. Along the way up the Detroit Tigers' farm system, Oyler fielded splendidly. He led the Sally League in putouts at Knoxville in 1962. With Syracuse of the International League in 1963 and 1964, Ray earned honors as the league's top-rated shortstop. Though he owned a modest .236 batting average for his minor league career,

Ray soaked the ball for 19 home runs in 1964. That completed his apprenticeship to becoming a major league shortstop.

A relatively senior rookie at age 26, his first season with the Detroit Tigers in 1965 was an auspicious one. Playing at least one game at every infield position, Oyler whacked five home runs and batted .186 in barely under 200 at bats.

The 1966 season depicted classic pattern Oyler: great fielding and sub-.200 batting, although there were some valiant efforts. A fourth-inning double by Oyler on May 21 put Detroit ahead to stay in a win against the eventual champions of 1966, the Baltimore Orioles. He followed up that effort with two walks and two runs scored to help the Tigers again knock off the Orioles by the score of 3–2. On June 18, Oyler made a sensational diving catch on a Mickey Mantle liner to help preserve a tenuous 4–3 lead over the Yankees. Earlier in the game, Oyler took a Pedro Ramos fastball square on the helmet, but showed no ill effects from the beaning. Long-time fans may have been reminded of the old sports section headline describing Dizzy Dean, "Dean hit in head. X-Rays reveal nothing."

To get Ray's glove onto the infield in 1967, Detroit moved Dick McAuliffe from shortstop to second base. The tactic paid instant dividends for the Bengals. Oyler became a mainstay in the Tigers' lineup that year as he enjoyed his finest season. He appeared in 148 games, all at shortstop. It was the only year he batted over .200 (.207) with 33 runs scored and 29 RBI, all career highs. Oyler's lone home run that year was a three-run blast off Jim Hardin of the Orioles. It won the ballgame for Detroit.

The 1967 Tigers' wild ride reflected the volatility of the Sixties. Engulfed in civil strife, race riots struck the city of Detroit, severe enough to cancel two of the Tigers' home games in July. The American League pennant race was equally compelling. Four teams—Boston, Chicago, Detroit, and Minnesota—battled wire-to-wire. On the final day of the season, the Tigers had the opportunity to tie Boston for first place and force a playoff. First, they had to sweep the California Angels in a doubleheader. To get more stick in the lineup, Dick Tracewski, a .280-hitting utililityman started at shortstop ahead of Oyler. Detroit won the opener, 6–4. However, the Bengals' fell short in the second game by a score of 8–5, sending eight pitchers to the mound in the process.

The fact that 1968 was "The Year of the Pitcher" became clearly obvious to Ray Oyler. Nearly every batter in the junior circuit suffered through blazing fastballs, biting curves, cutting sliders, and fluttering knuckleballs. Pitching stars Denny McLain, Luis Tiant, Sam McDowell, Dave McNally, and Wilbur Wood seemingly didn't let anyone get on base. Carl Yastrzemski hit .301. The second best batter, Danny Cater, stroked .290. In that climate, Ray Oyler batted a microscope .135. No player in baseball history, seeing action in 100 or more games played, ever secured a lower batting average in a single season. Not even relief pitcher Mike Marshall in 1974, who batted .235 in 106 games. Oyler actually went hitless the entire *months* of August and September.

Oyler's year of historic bat futility began immediately. A 1-for-16 start iced his average down to .063. His biggest hit in April wasn't even with the ball. Against Cleveland, on April 25, Oyler chased a shallow fly ball to left field. Willie Horton, the lumbering left fielder, never saw him coming. In a skull-jarring collision, Horton (who outweighed Oyler by 50 pounds) was knocked unconscious and carried off by stretcher to the local hospital. Oyler stayed in the contest, quite chagrined that he allowed the opposing pitcher (Steve Hargan) to get a triple.

During the month of May, Ray Oyler experienced a slight improvement. His batting average actually surged back to .200 before plummeting again. Oyler also punched his only home run of the year, a solo shot off Baltimore's Dave McNally that factored in Detroit's 4–0 whitewashing of the Orioles.

In one game, Cleveland Indians' infielder Larry Brown recalled Ray getting a hit, off a change-up, from flame-throwing Sam McDowell. Brown lamented, "Ray 'Cotton Pickin' Oyler couldn't hit the ball if Sam ran it across home plate. But Sam had to throw him slow stuff."

Yet, there was Mr. Oyler, starting at shortstop for the front-running 1968 Tigers. He made inning-saving defensive plays on a regular basis to the benefit of Denny McLain, Mickey Lolich, and the rest of the Tigers' ballclub. Ray Oyler ranked third among American League shortstops with a .977 fielding average.

That year, McLain became the last pitcher to win 30 games (31–6) in a season. Taking up the slack for Oyler in the batting order were Hall of Fame outfielder Al Kaline, first baseman Norm Cash, catcher Bill Freehan, and other complementary players such as Jim Northrup, Willie Horton, and Gates Brown (who hit .370 as a pinch-hitter deluxe). In the final year of non-divisional league play, Detroit rolled to a 103–59 record, 12 games ahead of the runner-up Orioles. The 1968 Tigers succeeded despite having the left side of their infield at or below the Mendoza Line: Oyler and third baseman Don Wert, a .200 hitter.

In the 1968 World Series, against the St. Louis Cardinals, Detroit manager Mayo Smith made a tough decision. Having an archetype "good field-no hit" player in the lineup, like Ray Oyler, was suicidal in a short series. Reserve infielders Tom Matchick (.203), and Dick Tracewski (.156), were not hitting any better. Smith took a great risk in handing starting shortstop duties to center fielder Mickey Stanley for the final week of the regular season and for the World Seies. Many baseball experts claim this to be one of the greatest gambles by a World Series manager. Yet, the move enabled Al Kaline, injured for part of the season and platooned between the outfield and first base, to be an everyday starter in right field.

The strategy paid off handsomely. During the World Series, the outfield of Horton, Kaline and Northrup smashed a combined 5 home runs, 19 RBI, and a .312 average. Stanley played a competent shortstop and contributed four runs scored. Whenever Detroit was ahead in the late innings, Oyler was inserted into the game for defensive purposes. He made four appearances and recorded two putouts. Ray Oyler was on the field in the ninth inning of game seven, as Mickey Lolich pitched a complete game 4–1 victory. Detroit rallied from a 3-games-to-1 deficit to defeat Bob Gibson, Lou Brock, Orlando Cepeda, and the Cardinals.

Despite Oyler's tailspin with the Tigers, more adventures followed with the ill-fated 1969 Seattle Pilots, who would exist all of one season. With enough debt and front office problems to fill a Boeing 747, the team moved to Milwaukee to become the Brewers. The story of the Pilots is a curious one. Perhaps, the single best reference on the history of the Seattle Pilots resides in Jim Bouton's exposé, *Ball Four*.

Unlike the Kansas City Royals, who emphasized youth in their expansion draft, Seattle's strategy involved a "future is now" approach. Ten of the first 15 picks were aged 27 years or older. The Pilots' initial draft selections, first baseman Don Mincher, speedster Tommy Harper, and Ray Oyler reflected the build-up of experienced ballplayers. The general consensus was that Seattle had the makings of a competitive major league team.

Of all the Pilots, the city of Seattle took an immediate shine to Ray Oyler. Much of this had to do with the work of radio disc jockey Bob Hardwick. He figured that after his previous season, Oyler was the player deemed most in need of a fan club. The Ray Oyler Fan Club quickly boasted a membership of over 5,000. The members even chipped in to put Ray in an apartment with his own car. In Seattle's home opener, horns bellowed, confetti went aloft, and signs fluttered to commemorate Oyler's first at bat as a Pilot. On opening day in Detroit the year before, Tigers' fans booed Oyler as he was introduced in the starting lineup. Later, in that same series, Ray reciprocated the fan club's appreciation by knocking a home run in the bottom of the ninth to beat the White Sox.

Typically, the Ray Oyler Fan Club incorporated the following hijinks, as recalled by a member: "I was a 14-year-old and a freshman at Hazen High School in Renton in 1969. I still have my Ray Oyler Fan Club card. We used to sit in the left field bleachers and on certain fan club nights, a radio announcer would be out there and punch a hole in your card if Ray struck out swinging. I also remember Jim Bouton sending kids up to give notes to attractive women watching the game...then reading about it in his book, *Ball Four*."

Of all the Seattle players, Oyler was truly the team's "fighter Pilot." First, in a May 12 game against the Yankees, Seattle welcomed the Bombers to the Pacific Northwest with a 7-run barrage in the first inning. With the Yankees trailing, 7–3, Bobby Murcer came up for the Yankees in the third. Having already hit a home run off Marty Pattin in the first inning, Pattin wanted to give Murcer a token of his appreciation. Pattin threw a fastball at the direction of Murcer's head, sending him sprawling. Murcer did not charge the mound. Instead, he looped the next into pitch right field for a single—and kept right on going to second. Ray Oyler took the throw well ahead of Murcer. But Murcer didn't care; he was looking for something to hit hard and barreled directly into Oyler, nearly sending the Pilot airborne.

The ex-Marine retaliated. Oyler and Murcer traded punches for several moments before the usual teammates to the rescue arrived. During the ensuing melee, Oyler and Murcer were pinned in the bottom of this pile of humanity, literally face to face. According to Bouton, the following dialogue took place:

"Ray, I'm sorry," Murcer said. "I lost my head."

"That's okay," Ray replied. "Now how about getting off of me. You're crushing my leg."

"I would," Murcer said. "But I can't move."

In another altercation, Ray Oyler Fan Club members were appalled to see their hero get pummeled by Jim Campanis in a game against the Royals. In this "Battle of the below .200 hitters," the .147-career-hitting Campanis outweighed Oyler by thirty pounds and got the best of the Seattle shortstop. Bob Hardwick flashed a telegram to the Royals' front office, to express the fan club's outrage. "Five thousand members of the Ray Oyler

Fan Club protest the slugging of our beloved leader. Please do not misinterpret our club motto, 'Sock it to Ray Oyler,' as this is an expression of encouragement," the telegram said.

Early on, the Pilots were indeed nobody's pushovers. By late May, Seattle was barely below .500 and sitting in third place. Going into the all-star break, they clung to fourth place out of six teams in the American League West. Ray Oyler contributed to their success. Not just with defense. Oyler launched homers with alarming frequency. He hit most of them at home, over the short porch left field corner at Sick's Stadium.

The team nicknamed Oyler, "Oil Can Harry," because, as Bouton put it, Oyler always looked as if he just changed a set of piston rings. In an 8–1 win over Baltimore on May 27, Ray hit a home run at Sick's Stadium that traveled all of 305 feet and barely cleared the fence. "As soon as I hit it, I knew it was out," Oyler told Bouton with a wry touch of temerity. Bouton remarked, "They have named the spot [the left field corner] after Greenberg's Gardens. They're calling it Oil Can's Corner." Oyler also went deep the next day against Baltimore. The Pilots might have won that game had they not forfeited a pair of runs in the embarrassment of batting out of order. Orioles' manager Earl Weaver noticed the gaffe. On June 21, Oyler's two-run shot in the sixth inning broke a 3–3 tie for a victory over the Royals. It was already his sixth home run of the year. Could Ray Oyler hit 10? 20?

However, as the dog days of August wore on, Oyler and the Seattle Pilots began to implode. Ray Oyler stopped hitting home runs. Then on August 7, Ray Oyler committed a crucial, rare error against Boston, allowing the BoSox to rally from a 4–2 deficit in the ninth to win 5–4. Bouton writes:

> Ray...spent a long time after the game facing his locker, drinking beer, and playing genuine sorrow. The clubhouse was routine morgue and four sportswriters were trying to ask Oyler about the error—in hushed tones, of course. Newspapermen are required to play the sorrow game too, although why they should care, I can't imagine.
>
> [John] O'Donoghue, surveying the scene said, "Goddam vultures. Hanging around waiting for the meat to dry." And Tommy Harper said, "What the hell do you need quotes for? They all saw the play." And Don Mincher said, "Miserable bastards."

Injuries to key players, such as Tommy Davis and Mike Hegan, coupled with faltering pitching, resulted in a mid-August mark of 48–66. By then, the Pilots were 20 games in arrears to the front-running Minnesota Twins.

Of greater concern than what was transpiring on the diamond were the problems in the front office. For starters, the sheer absurdity of trying to use a 1930s vintage minor league ballpark as a major league venue tried everyone's patience. With little over 30,000 overpriced seats (many situated behind steel girders) and unreliable plumbing, the Pilots might have been better off playing in the Space Needle. The franchise averaged less than 8,500 in per-game attendance. As for corporate support, Boeing Aircraft, the city's biggest employer in the BC (before coffee) era, purchased just six season tickets. The team was hemorrhaging money.

On October 2, 1969, just over five thousand Pilots' fans came to see Seattle lose 3–1 to the Oakland A's. The Ray Oyler Fan Club experienced a mild thrill in seeing their icon get a single that day. Little did anyone realize, they were witnessing the last-ever Pilots' game. Seattle finished the year in the American League West basement at 64–98 and 33 games out of first.

Ray Oyler fulfilled his role as underdog to the pleasure of his fan club. He batted .165 as their regular shortstop; however, Oyler did hit a career-high seven home runs. As always, he fielded beautifully. Oyler will forever hold Seattle Pilots' single-game records for most double plays by a shortstop (4), most double plays started by a shortstop (3), most putouts by a shortstop (5), and most assists by a shortstop (8).

In Bouton's *Ball Four*, a "warts and all" tell-all, very few people come out of it unscathed. He depicts Oyler as kind of a wag. What Bouton has to say about Ray Oyler is not always particularly flattering. While in the clubhouse during a rain delay, Ray Oyler pondered the irony of being an expansion teammate of pitcher Gary Bell, after incessantly heckling him on the field on his "sexual preference" for years. Gary Bell did not take this stuff lying down, telling the married Ray Oyler, "Ray, when you come to the ballpark tomorrow, will you bring my socks. I left them under your bed."

Bouton also tells the time Ray was catching sinkerball pitcher Bob Locker while warming up. Oyler missed the ball and took one right in the groin. He proceeded to crawl back to the dugout on his hands and knees, then threw up. Bouton recalled, "The boys were hysterical. We were getting beat in a ballgame and we were laughing. Joe Schultz laughed so hard he had to take off his glasses, dry his eyes and hide his head in a warm-up jacket."

One of Seattle's last front-office moves was trading Ray Oyler to Oakland. He did not stay with Oakland, but did latch on with the California Angels, hitting just .083 in 24 late-season games. One of his pair of hits that year helped mount a late rally to beat Minnesota on August 5. That ended Oyler's major league career. For the next two seasons, Oyler played ball in the Pacific Coast League, even serving as a player-coach for Hawaii in 1973, before hanging up his spikes and glove for good.

After his playing days, Ray Oyler moved back to his adopted hometown of Seattle. He was a salesman for a while, then worked for the Safeway supermarket chain. Later, he managed a bowling alley in Bellevue before finding employment with the Boeing Company. Sadly, he was only 42 years of age when he passed away in 1981 of a heart attack. Hard luck befell other members of the 1968 Tigers. Pitchers Don McMahon and Joe Sparma also died of heart attacks. Norm Cash drowned in 1986 after falling out of a fishing boat. And perhaps the most dismal story of them all: Denny McLain, who had a ticket to Cooperstown at age 24, squandered it through gambling, drugs, and embezzlement. Today, McLain spends his days behind bars in a Michigan prison.

Dick McAuliffe, the player who begrudgingly moved from shortstop to second base in 1967 to make room for Ray Oyler, put it best. He simply said, "Oyler...was the best shortstop I ever played with."

"I have always maintained that the best remedy for a batting slump is two wads of cotton. One for each ear."

-Bill Veeck

Senator Stumpy
Jim French, C
1941-

How many people can say they had a horse named after them? Jim French can. As the story goes, legendary horse breeder and owner of Darby Dan Farms, John W. Galbreath, took a shine to the young catcher and fellow Ohioan. He helped Jim get a baseball scholarship at Ohio University, of which Galbreath was an alum. French's equine namesake was quite the thoroughbred as a 3-year-old. A descendent of Triple Crown winner Man o' War, the four-legged version of Jim French finished second in the 1971 Kentucky Derby and Belmont Stakes, and showed in the Preakness. Jim French, the horse, also won other major derbies, such as the Santa Anita Derby, then went on to a successful career as a stud.

With only three stolen bases in nine attempts over his career, baseball's Jim French may not have run like a thoroughbred. Yet, the Washington Senators always had room in their stable for this backup catcher, whose fine batting eye and A-1 arm earned him seven years in "The Show."

In Merritt Clifton's 1986 essay, *Pardon My French*, Clifton states that French may be the most underrated catcher of all time. Clifton also relates that French may have been one of the top all-around catchers during the late-1960s/early-1970s era. That's pretty bold talk when examined against some of his contemporaries: Johnny Bench, Manny Sanguillen, Tim McCarver, Jerry Grote, Bill Freehan, and John Roseboro.

Clifton cited the following to support his assertions. On offense, despite his sub-.200 career batting average, Jim's lifetime on-base percentage of .331 is better than most of the catchers of his time and not too far behind some leadoff hitters (compare to Hall of Famer Lou Brock's career .344 OBP). French is one of the rare players with more career bases on balls (121) than hits (119). Clifton writes:

> French's abilities went almost totally unrecognized by both fans and baseball people. He played his whole time for a basement ball club, an expansion team nobody watched, and piled up impressive stats in categories not even listed in *The Sporting News*. Truth is, the importance of assists-to-games ratio and on-base average was scarcely recognized at all during French's career, when scientific statistical analysis was still in its infancy.

Asking him whether he was familiar with Merritt Clifton's research, Jim commented, "I wish I had this information back when I was negotiating [a new contract]. It didn't matter back then anyway. They gave you what they were going to give you and the hell with you."

French rose through the minors in adequate fashion. In his second year of professional ball, with Rocky Mount of the Class A Carolina League, French batted .270 with 86 runs scored. He also led the league in sacrifices. With his rifle arm, Jim paced Carolina League backstops in assists.

During spring training 1965, Jim recalled one of his most humorous moments on the field. As he was catching Dave Stenhouse in an exhibition game, Stenhouse proceded to work himself into some trouble. Washington manager Gil Hodges, a very stoic field boss, came out to the mound to talk with Stenhouse. The Senators' pitchers generally dreaded a visit by Hodges, especially Stenhouse, whom Jim described as being somewhat anxious. During the ensuing pitcher's mound conference, Jim recalls watching Dave Stenhouse pick up the rosin bag and flip it up and down in his right hand. Hodges asked the sweating Stenhouse how he was feeling. To which the pitcher replied, "Alright." Then, Stenhouse started to pat his face with the rosin bag like it was a powder puff. Upon seeing that, Hodges said, "I don't think you're okay," and called in for a reliever.

Though French did not make the 1965 opening day roster, Jim impressed scouts after hitting .256 with York (Penn.) against tough Eastern League pitching. Following the September roster expansion. French broke in like gangbusters. In his very first game, against California Angels' fireballer Dean Chance, Jim secured two hits, two walks, two runs batted in, and a stolen base. French also scored a run that day, coming home ahead of fellow rookie Brant Alyea, whose debut wowed Washingtonians. Alyea jumped on the first pitch he saw in the major leagues for a pinch-hit, 3-run homer. The next day, French went 2-for-3 and drove home another run.

All told, Jim French finished that season with lots of promise. He batted .297 with a home run and 7 RBI in a 13-game appearance. Unfortunately, a 1966 leg injury, the acquisition of Doug Camilli, and the unexpected emergence of Paul Casanova curtailed French's playing time with the Senators over the next couple of years.

In 1968, Jim French became Washington's second-string catcher. The tandem of Casanova and French combined for a meager 5 HR/35 RBI/.195 BA for the sad-sack cellar-dwelling Nats. However, in French's 53 catcher appearances, he got enough mustard on his throws for an extraordinary 42 assists.

The Senators' collective fortunes took a major upswing when they hired the sainted Ted Williams as their manager in 1969. Jim once stated that the single highlight of his career was playing under perhaps baseball's purist batter ever. With Williams at the helm, the team batting average soared from .224 in 1968, second worst in the American League, to .251, which ranked Washington third. Williams guided the Senators to their only winning season in the history of the short-lived franchise, going 86–76—a 21-win increase over the previous year. Ted Williams' efforts netted him yet another accolade in his illustrious life: 1969 American League Manager of the Year.

Jim said the following about Williams:

> He was the most charismatic person I ever met. You probably had the experience of being in a big room and somebody like him would walk in. Immediately, the room becomes quiet as you knew somebody important just entered. But he was also a very mercurial man. One day, he can be the nicest guy to you and the next day not even talk— not even hello. That was his personality. It wasn't that he was trying to single you out or something. That's the way he was. That, especially at the time, and even today, put

everybody on edge. Well maybe not everybody, but someone like myself, who was no established star by any stretch of the imagination.

From a handling of people viewpoint, he was of the old school. He was the boss; "This is the way that it is done." There's nothing wrong with that. But he wasn't even open to discussion to speak of. He might discuss it, but there was always one conclusion—his way. Which is okay; he's not alone there. So, I think he would have trouble today.

As far as knowledge of pitching and knowledge of hitting, I don't think anyone comes close to him, ever! He came in and he did a hell of a job for us. He got the most out of us that anyone could the first year and the second year. But I think he lost interest after awhile.

Jim French's offensive numbers peaked during Ted Williams' tenure. Perhaps the most significant change, which can be attributed to Ted Williams' tutelage, are his walk totals. French's 1969 totals in bases on balls more than double those of his previous season. He managed that feat with almost the same number of plate appearances. Williams, a batter who seldom chased a bad pitch out of the strike zone, obviously imparted his wisdom on pitch selectivity to French.

In 1969, French slammed out 11 extra-base hits and enjoyed his best defensive year. In 63 games, French collected 44 assists. In both 1968 and 1969, French owned the highest catcher's assists-to-games ratio in either major league by a substantial margin.

The following year, while the Senators made yet another descent to the American League East cellar, French played the most games of his career (69) and put up a .211 batting average. Against Detroit, on September 5, Jim's 14th-inning single drove home the winning tally in the bottom of the ninth.

In the late 1960s, Batman was one of television's most popular shows. In baseball, Jim French and pitcher Jim Hannan were a real-life "Dynamic Duo." Teammates since 1965, in the last two years of the 1960s, the battery of Hannan and French combined for 10 wins against just two losses. The heartbreaking defeats were by scores of 1–0 and 2–1. While Jim did not feel any particular tangible synergy between Hannan and himself, like most of the Senators' hurlers, Hannan trusted French's judgment regarding pitch selection and rarely shook him off.

Jim French's roommate on the road was Frank Howard, the game's premiere slugger during the late 1960s. The two seemed like a true odd couple with the 6-foot-7 Howard towering a foot taller. While Jim earned a number of nicknames—most not appropriate for polite company, according to French—Frank Howard always called him "Stumpy." According to Jim French, "When he [Howard] was irritated with me, he would tell me to go play handball against the curb."

In 1971, Jim played the final game in the tortured history of the Washington Senators. Even this swan song turned into a fiasco. Ahead 7-5 at home over the Yankees on the strength of a Frank Howard home run, Senators' pitcher Joe Grzenda pitched to his backstop Jim French in the ninth inning. Suddenly, with two outs, knowing the team was headed for Texas the next season, hundreds of fans poured onto the field, preventing the game from continuing. The scoreboard numbers were removed. Dirt and grass found their way into fans' pockets. Home plate was dug up by the angry mob. Radio announcers Shelby Whitfield and Ron Menchine couldn't hide their disappointment. The umpires ruled the game a forfeit. The Senators lost 9–0.

In the post-mortem of the Washington Senators, owner Bob Short pointed to the competition for fans with the highly successful Baltimore Orioles. Washington denizens could see champion-caliber baseball within a half-hour's drive. Less publicized was Short's blunt observation that the District's white population were simply afraid to travel to RFK Stadium due to the rampant crime rate. The African American citizens living in the district were generally not in an economic footing to support a major league baseball team.

By 1972, Jim French was gone and so were the Washington Senators. Bob Short moved the franchise to Arlington to become the Texas Rangers. After the move, the break-up of the former Senators began. Jim French and Paul Casanova went to Atlanta before the season even started. French spent his final year of professional ball with Triple-A Richmond. Frank Howard became a Detroit Tiger by mid-season. Even the Splendid Splinter Ted Williams was out as manager after a miserable 100-loss season. By then, he was just plain "bored," according to Jim.

Jim French later earned his Master's Degree in economics, then went to California to became a commodities trader. French now lives in Chicago, works full-time, and is working towards his law degree from the John Marshall Law School. When asked if any of his classmates remember him when he played, his reply was, "Hell, they're so young, half of them never even heard of the Senators."

Why did such an unusually gifted player like Jim not succeed in the big leagues? Would things have worked out better if Jim French played for someone else? Jim offers that he hit between .260 and .290 in minor league ball, but his lack of playing time greatly curtailed his major league opportunities to excel. "I would get pinch hit for by the fifth inning," French lamented. "Not everybody is a Smoky Burgess." French readily admits that he was an above-average handler of pitchers. "I had a great arm and was quick to get rid of the ball, and I knew when guys were running." French also added to this innate ability by keeping on his pitchers, "They're going to run. They're going to run," he'd say.

Other factors contributed to French's less-than-spectacular big league life. During the mid-to-late 1960s weight training and nutrition were unheard of, and the old tradition of "running until you couldn't walk" held sway. "So, your aerobics were good, but you weren't playing basketball." On nutrition, French claims that he now eats far better and healthier than in his playing days. Today, weight training and modern exercise physiology are taken very seriously by ballplayers.

Despite it all, Jim French sums up his career this way: "I'm damn proud to say that I played in the major leagues and batted .196."

The Bull
Frank Fernandez, C
1943-

Meet the Babe Ruth of *Mendoza's Heroes*. With 39 circuit clouts, Frank Fernandez, by far, has the most career home runs of any player to bat below .200 in major league baseball history. Had Frank played 120–140 games a season, he might have posted Mickey Tettleton-type numbers—20–25 homers and a .220–.250 batting average each season. Unfortunately, as a back-up backstop his entire big league career, Frank Fernandez never played in more than 94 games in any year during his six seasons in the majors. Occasionally, managers played him in the outfield in order to get his potent bat in the lineup.

The Staten Island native attended Villanova University, where he played both baseball and basketball. Signed by the New York Yankees organization, Fernandez led Florida State League catchers with 739 putouts and 66 assists in 1962. In 1966, playing for Toledo of the International League, Frank blasted 23 home runs and was an International League All-Star.

Frank Fernandez began his major league career in 1967 wearing Yankee pinstripes. A September call-up, Frank stroked a base hit in his first at bat. On September 29, each of his two doubles drove in a run and helped the Yankees beat Kansas City, 4–3. Fernandez walloped his first home run in the final game ever played by the Kansas City Athletics. The seventh-inning solo shot off Jim Hunter proved to be the difference in the Yankees' 4–3 win. Frank Fernandez finished the year with a modest .214 average in nine games.

In 1968, Fernandez headed north as the Yankees' team broke from spring training. On opening day that year, the strong, big-boned Fernandez enjoyed a glorious outing. First, as starting catcher Fernandez had the honor of receiving the ceremonial first pitch. But the honorary tosser wasn't a typical hoary politician, an ex-ballplayer, or even a male for that matter. Marianne Moore, a Pulitzer Prize winning poetess, earned the privilege. The eighty-year-old threw a knee-high strike to Fernandez, who tactfully edged forward a couple of steps towards Moore before the pitch. In a gallant gesture, the handsome bachelor later leaned over the box-seat railing and kissed the poetess on the cheek.

In the second inning, Fernandez kissed a George Brunet fastball over the fence for a home run. Only "poetic justice" can explain that the solo shot would stand as New York edged the California Angels, 1–0. Fernandez crowned his great day by calling a superb game for Mel Stottlemyre, who held the Angels to only four hits. After the game, Fernandez received yet another accolade. The *New York Times* featured a photo of Fernandez hitting his home run below another picture of Mickey Mantle (in his final opening day), stroking a single. The caption for the photographs read: "Yankee Sluggers Display Their Abilities."

As the season wore on, Fernandez became another victim of the "Year of the Pitcher," hitting just a buck-seventy. Though posting a low batting average, Frank Fernandez made his hits count. Of his 23 safeties, 14 were for extra-bases. His 30 RBI yielded an incredible 1.3 RBI per hit. Four tallies came with a single swing off Dick Ellsworth of the Red Sox—Frank Fernandez's first of three Grand Slams. His seven home runs in 135 at bats equated to a home run every 19 at bats, equal to Athletics' slugger Reggie Jackson, who finished fourth in the league in homers. Yet, like most long ball sluggers, Fernandez would all-too-often shrug his powerful shoulders as the home plate umpire bellowed "Strike Three!"

For the next two seasons, despite limited playing time, Frank Fernandez would be one of the more respected home run hitters in the American League. He showed his raw power, by hitting tape-measure drives into the left-field upper deck of Yankee Stadium, some 450 feet away. In 1969, his final season with the Yankees, Fernandez hit .223 (a career high) and connected for an even dozen home runs. On April 11, Fernandez torched the Washington Senators for two home runs, including a Grand Slam off Jim Hannan. Using a selective eye, Fernandez coaxed 65 bases on balls, earning an excellent .401 on-base percentage.

However, once the Yanks brought up a talented young catcher from Columbus named Thurman Munson, Fernandez's days in New York were numbered. The Yankees dealt Frank Fernandez and veteran pitcher Al Downing (he of Hank Aaron's record-setting 715th home run fame) to Oakland for Danny Cater and Ossie Chavarria.

For the 1970 A's, Frank Fernandez reveled in a splendid power year. While splitting catching duties with Dave Duncan, Fernandez crushed the long ball 15 times, a record for the most home runs in a season by a career sub-.200 hitter. Frank also drove in 44 runs, another career best. Over the span of two games, on August 11 and 12 against Cleveland, Fernandez chalked up seven RBI. Projected over a full season of 500 at bats, Fernandez would have been on-pace to blast 30 home runs and drive in about 90 runs.

Truly startling about "Home Run" Fernandez was the timeliness of his round-trippers: seven of them were game winners. Three came as a pinch hitter off the bench. Another shot went for a Grand Slam off Mickey Lolich. Oakland owner Charlie Finley was so delighted with Frank Fernandez, after he delivered a game-winning pinch-hit three-run homer with two outs in the bottom of the ninth, that Finley cut Fernandez a $2,000 bonus check right after the game.

Frank Fernandez played baseball hard. In a 1970 game at Baltimore, Fernandez reached first on what he deemed an obvious base hit. Fernandez became upset when he saw "E" flashed on the scoreboard lights. Distraught over the scorer's ruling, Fernandez fired his batting helmet toward the press box. It landed halfway up the screen. The esteemed broadcaster Harry Caray, who called games for Oakland just before his legendary stint with the Cubs, chastised Fernandez's poor sportsmanship. On the air, Harry commented, "All Fernandez is making all the fuss about is whether he bats .200 or .198 this season."

After years of struggling in Philadelphia and Kansas City, the Oakland Athletics were, at last, a competitive franchise. Oakland finished 89–73 in 1970 to take second place in the American League West. Frank Fernandez played his part. The great Oakland dynasty was about to begin. Unfortunately, Fernandez would not be there.

Starting in 1971, Frank Fernandez's bat suffered an inexplicable meltdown. He hardly had time to unpack his suitcase when Oakland dealt Fernandez, Don Mincher, and Paul

Lindblad to the Washington Senators for Mike Epstein and reliever Darold Knowles in early May. Ted Williams and the Senators saw enough after Fernandez had a 3-for-30 drought and quickly sold him back to Oakland. After bouncing between Oakland and their Triple-A affiliate in Iowa, the A's sent Fernandez packing again—to the Chicago Cubs.

With the Cubs, Frank Fernandez had a momentary wake-up call. Though he only batted .171 in 18 games and 41 at bats, Fernandez hit four home runs. The ivy-covered left field wall and bleachers must have seemed inviting. One of his homers helped beat the Mets in an encore visit for the one-time New York Yankees' catcher. Fernandez's final career home run was off Rick Wise of the Phillies. The second-inning solo shot staked the Cubs to a 3–1 lead. That wasn't particularly noteworthy. However, Wise then proceeded to retire the next 32 Cubs' batters in a row and singled in the winning run in the 12th inning to edge Chicago 4–3.

Frank Fernandez sipped a "cup of coffee" for the Cubs in 1972, going hitless in three at bats before vanishing from the major league scene. After his playing days, Fernandez returned to New York City and became a manager of a shipping terminal in Staten Island.

In the final analysis, Frank Fernandez offers some stunning and historical baseball figures; a statistician's treasure chest. Unfortunately, he lacked the requisite number of at bats necessary to qualify. Yet, Fernandez compares favorably to the titans of the game. His career home run percentage bests Johnny Bench, Hank Aaron, and Stan Musial. He ranks sixth all-time in base on balls percentage. On the flip side, Fernandez's strikeout percentage is higher than baseball history leader Reggie Jackson.

More than just a slugger, Frank Fernandez earned accolades for his superb fielding as well. He retired with an outstanding .992 fielding average. In his career, Fernandez handled the outstanding pitching arms of Mel Stottlemyre, Fritz Peterson, Catfish Hunter, Vida Blue, and Rollie Fingers. Fernandez also possessed a rifle-arm like arm behind the plate. His catcher's assist totals were low because few runners dared challenging him.

While most south of the Mendoza Line dwellers counted on a sure glove or mitt to stay alive in the majors, Frank Fernandez had the unique distinction of being both a damage-inflicting hitter and competent fielder. It's remarkable that Frank could finish batting below the Mendoza Line, yet rank highly against the legends of Cooperstown.

Smokey
Adrian Garrett, 1B
1943-

Garrett Morris was probably one of the more obscure members of the original *Saturday Night Live* cast. However, he did appear as one of the show's funniest characters, Cuban ballplayer Chico Escuela, whose catch phrase was "Baseball been bery, bery good to me." With 40 years in the game, baseball has also been "bery" good to Adrian Garrett. Nicknamed "Pat," after the sheriff made famous for taking down Billy the Kid, Henry Adrian Garrett was also called "Smokey," purportedly for being a dead-ringer for the old-time Red Sox pitcher, Smokey Joe Wood.

For a man with four minor league home run titles, untouchable hitting records in Venezuela and Japan, and one of the most flawless left-handed swings this side of Don Mattingly, Adrian Garrett would be an unlikely candidate for *Mendoza's Heroes*. Yet his balance sheet reads a paltry major league batting average of .185. How possible? Anybody intimately associated with baseball knew Garrett swung a lethal bat.

During his boyhood in Sarasota, Adrian would catch glimpses of the great Ted Williams during the Red Sox's spring training camp each year. So enrapt with the Splendid Splinter's artful swing, young Garrett devoted hours in his backyard patterning after the master's left-handed stroke. Garrett's efforts paid off. As a student in junior high school, Garrett was handpicked to be in a commercial with the great Williams himself. "He was a real gentleman," Garrett recalled in an interview. "He gave me a signed bat, glove and ball. I don't have them anymore. I wore them out playing with them."

Garrett signed with the Milwaukee Braves' organization in 1961, earning his stripes in the bushes. In 1965, Garrett slugged three homers in one game during Atlanta's last season as a minor league franchise. The homers accounted for all of Atlanta's runs as they beat Toledo, 3–2, in 10 innings.

He played his first major league game with the Braves in 1966 and had another short stint with the Chicago Cubs in 1970. Adrian batted a composite 0-for-6 in those two very brief trials. But in the minors, Garrett was a formidable slugger. While spending several seasons in the Texas League during the late-1960s and 1970, Adrian seldom hit Texas League singles. Or doubles. He did wallop several Texas League homers, as he led the Double-A circuit with 27 in 1967 and 29 in 1970.

Garrett took his big bat to Tacoma next. Pacific Coast League hurlers cringed. Garrett socked 43 balls into the seats, setting club records for home runs, RBI (119), and total bases (272). Expecting a promotion to Chicago in September, Adrian Garrett instead got a surprise. The Cubs traded Adrian to the Oakland Athletics for slugger Frank Fernandez and outfielder Bill McNulty. With the division winning A's that year, Smokey got his first major league hit and career homer number one—a two-run souvenir to help Oakland upend the Milwaukee Brewers. Garrett's 44 homers in a single year of American professional baseball lead all below .200 hitters.

After going hitless in 11 at bats for Oakland in 1972, Adrian Garrett returned to the Chicago Cubs in 1973. In 36 games with Chicago, in the midst of an incredible 4-team division race in the National League East, Garrett hit three more home runs and broke .200 for the first time in a season with 12-for-54 (.222) hitting. In a September 19 pinch-hitting appearance against the Expos, with Chicago trailing by four runs, Garrett ignited a rally by singling in Randy Hundley, then scoring himself on a Rick Monday home run. The Cubs went on to an 8–6 victory.

Although Garrett had another hitless major league season in 1974, this time he went 0-for-8 for the Cubs, he did add his fourth minor league home run crown. With Wichita, Garrett paced the American Association with 26 blasts.

The California Angels obtained Adrian Garrett from the Cubs late in the 1975 season. The Angels may not have been contenders, but they gave Adrian some legitimate playing time. Manager Dick Williams played Garrett everywhere: at first base, in the outfield, DH, and even at catcher to get his potent bat on the field. "I would go to the ballpark knowing I would have a good chance of being in the lineup," Garrett related. "All the other times, I would go to the ballpark knowing I had a good chance of *not* being in the lineup."

At last, major league players and fans caught a glimpse of Garrett, who for so many years terrorized minor league pitching. In the only season over 100 at bats, Garrett hit a respectable .262 with 6 homers and 18 RBI. Smokey also led the team in slugging average (.477). Granted, Garrett did not play a full season for the Angels, but it affirms his assertion. If a major league team would have put Garrett in the lineup and left him alone for a full season, he could have produced some startling offensive statistics.

One of Adrian's homers that year was a game-winning 3-run shot off Goose Gossage, then with the White Sox, to break a 16-inning scoreless tie. In another game against the Yankees, Garrett did his best Rod Carew impersonation, hitting 3-for-3 with a double, two runs scored, and a RBI in an Angels' 8–1 rout.

Smokey Garrett became the center of controversy in an August 21 tilt with the Yankees. Naturally, Billy Martin played the part of instigator. The game was scoreless until the Angels' half of the fourth. Garrett singled off Catfish Hunter to score Mickey Rivers. After Garrett's hit, the Yankees' skipper charged plate umpire George Maloney with allegations that Garrett was using excessive pine tar on his bat. If Martin was correct, Garrett would be ruled out and Rivers would have to return to second. Maloney inspected Garrett's stick and deemed it legal. Martin announced he was playing the game under protest. Maloney shrugged.

The Yankees rallied to beat California, 5–2. Martin withdrew the protest after the game. However, what if California had won and Martin had wanted to bring the protest to a head? "Nothing probably," he said following the game. When Garrett came up again, the bat had been cleaned up nicely. There went the evidence.

Eight years later, Martin used the same ploy on George Brett after the Kansas City star knocked a game-winning homer. This time, the "Pine Tar Incident" became a memorable chapter in baseball history in which Brett, Martin, and the rulebook were placed center stage.

Adrian Garrett could not sustain this success in 1976, and after 29 games and .125 hitting, his major league career washed out. In parcels of eight big league seasons, Garrett played 163 games, just one game more than a single season's worth. His career slugging average was a respectable .333.

"I always thought if I had the chance to play, I could have done a lot better," Garrett mentioned. "But I was in a situation where a lot of times I was behind guys that were pretty good players." Garrett's misfortune was vying with experienced veterans for playing time, like Felipe Alou and Rico Carty in Atlanta, Billy Williams in Chicago, Mike Epstein in Oakland, or Bruce Bochte and Tommy Davis in California. The designated-hitter rule may have been his godsend, had Garrett played in the American League earlier. With 400 plus at bats per season, under DH conditions, Garrett could have given some American League pitchers the same misery he extended to his minor league brethren.

Following his major league days, Adrian Garrett spent three seasons in Japan with the Hiroshima Toyo Carp from 1977 to 1979 (the 1979 Carp won the Japan Series). He was a good *gaijin*, hitting 102 home runs in that span. Garrett still holds the Japanese records for the most home runs (15) in the month of April and the most home runs (3) in an All-Star Game. Even today, Japanese reporters come to the States to interview Adrian. He also played several years of Caribbean ball and owns the Venezuelan League consecutive-game hitting streak record of 28, which he set in 1975.

Garrett began his long coaching career in 1982 with the Chicago White Sox organization. For a time, Adrian managed the Pale Hose's Triple-A club in Denver. Garrett joined the Kansas City Royals' coaching staff in 1988 as their third base coach. He served as the team's hitting coach from 1991 until 1992 and got the chance to mentor an outstanding hitter in George Brett. About the man whom many credit with coming up with the term Mendoza Line, Adrian said:

> George is the best hitter I've ever had. I didn't teach him anything. He probably taught me more than I taught him. George Brett could do anything with a bat. And, it didn't matter how he was hitting; he never got too high or too low. I just let him hit. Hey, if it ain't broke, don't fix it.

From 1993 to 2001, Adrian Garrett served the Florida Marlins' organization. He started as the hitting coach for the Marlins' Triple-A affiliates in Charlotte and Edmonton. In 1999, Adrian became the Marlins' roving minor league hitting instructor. Garrett was instrumental in the resurrection of the Florida Marlins, as the team built the right way—with farm-grown talent and not through the quick fix of free agency. Rising stars Cliff Floyd and Preston Wilson are a couple of success stories that Garrett helped in their development. On the Zen of hitting, Adrian Garrett has this to say:

> Confidence creates relaxation and relaxation creates results. A .300 hitter has a 70 per cent failure rate, so you don't want to beat them down further. You've got to be thinking as a hitter, but not over-thinking. If you're in the batter's box thinking where your feet and hands should be, your head gets clouded. You can't think a runner from third base. You just execute.

Former Florida Marlins' manager John Boles says about Garrett: "He's the best. I don't think I've ever met a better man than Adrian Garrett. He's a great organizational guy, a terrific instructor. He just doesn't have a selfish bone in his body. If you had to say who you'd like your sons to grow up to be like, it'd be Adrian Garrett. That's the absolute highest compliment I can pay."

Adrian's kid brother, Wayne Garrett played 10 seasons in the majors for the New York Mets, Montreal Expos, and St. Louis Cardinals. Wayne Garrett starred as the Mets' regular season starting third baseman during their first two World Series seasons in 1969 and 1973. For his career, Wayne crashed 61 home runs—50 more than his brother—and batted .239. Wayne also hit three home runs in the post-season, including two in the 1973 World Series. One of Adrian's favorite moments in the majors was in 1973, as a Cub, when he hit a home run against Wayne's Mets at Wrigley Field. As Adrian rounded third, he approached his brother and offered him a fraternal wink. Jason Garrett, Adrian's son, played professional baseball in the Marlins' organization until injuries ended his career in 1998.

Of all career professional ballplayers with below .200 batting averages in the major leagues, Adrian Garrett is the home run king of them all. Garrett's potent stick accounted for 11 major league blasts, 102 *sayonaras* in Japan, and 280 bashed potatoes in the minors. Grand total: 393. If you count his inestimable Caribbean League totals, Adrian likely crushed more than 400 baseballs over the fence.

Sweet Fancy Leather
Rich Morales, IF
1943-

"This game is better than all of us. Pass it on," Rich Morales once told a group of young players competing in the lowest level of minor league ball.

Although Rich Morales could be speaking about his lack of success in the major leagues with a bat, his sagacious advice is really intended for young players learning the game. The meaning of Morales' words are philosophical rather than autobiographical. Baseball, Morales intends, should be played with respect and honor to the game's traditions and history. Furthermore, part of that reverence should be cross-generational. The wisdom and experience imparted from veteran to neophyte make baseball strong and lasting.

Only a handful of major league players, save catchers and pitchers, batted below the Mendoza Line with over one thousand at bats. Rich Morales, the sure-handed infielder who played nearly five hundred games for the Chicago White Sox and San Diego Padres, is one of them. With a less than formidable batting average, one can debate if Morales possessed a decent hitting stroke. However, no one questions Morales' ability to get a throw off to first base quicker.

Rich Morales' genes apparently foretold athletic greatness. How could he miss when his father was a pro boxer and his maternal grandfather was a pro soccer player from Scotland? While playing high school ball in the talent-rich leagues of San Francisco,

Rich batted .442 and .391 in his final two years. Morales earned Player of the Year honors in 1961 and was a member of the All-Peninsula team in 1961 and 1962.

Signed by the Chicago White Sox following high school, Morales immediately showed his expertise with the glove by leading Midwest League (as a member of the Clinton, Iowa team) shortstops in putouts and double plays in 1963. He also was productive as a hitter that year, socking 3 home runs, driving in 69 runs, and scoring 75 times. When Rich Morales' son was born in 1964, he was on a road swing with Portsmouth of the Carolina League. Unable to be present at the delivery, Morales did the next best thing for his progeny by blasting a home run. While playing for Lynchburg of the AA Southern League in 1965, Morales led the league's shortstops in fielding.

Rich Morales' travails as a big leaguer began in August 1967 with the White Sox. He earned a brief eight-game look, went hitless in 10 at bats, then went back down to the minors. During his best season of professional ball, with Hawaii of the Pacific Coast League in 1968, Rich's offensive numbers looked like he borrowed them from Ozzie Smith: no homers, 58 RBI, and a .264 average. On defense, he led Pacific Coast League shortstops in putouts and assists. That earned him a September call-up with the parent club. Morales stroked his first major league hit and wound up batting .172.

In 1969, Morales earned a chunk of playing time, backing up two of the American League's best defensive infielders of the day—second baseman Bobby Knoop and shortstop Luis Aparicio. That year, Rich batted .215 in 55 games. At 68–94, the 1969 White Sox did not hit or pitch particularly well. However, Chicago could boast of fine defense. The Sox made the second-fewest errors in the league and ended fourth in double plays.

Once known as the "Go-Go Sox" during Chicago's pennant-winning year of 1959, at 56–106, the 1970 edition of the team could be the "Oh-No Sox." Like many of his fellow teammates, Rich Morales struggled at the plate. He batted a faint .161 with a solitary home run and only two RBI in 112 at bats.

Over the next two years, Rich Morales' batting improved markedly. In 1971, Morales hit a career-best .243 and even slugged .319, by virtue of 8 doubles and 2 HRs.

Rich Morales stayed busy the next season. Sharing the shortstop duties equally with Luis Alvarado, Morales appeared in 110 games. That year, he was the only American League infielder to play at least ten games at three different positions. While his batting average slipped to .206 that year, Morales enjoyed career highs in runs, hits, and RBI.

The 1972 White Sox were quite an interesting team. Under manager Chuck Tanner, the White Sox used a three-man pitching rotation with workhorse knuckleballer Wilbur Wood (24–17 record in $376^2/_3$ innings of work), Stan Bahnsen, and Tom Bradley. Carlos May stabilized the outfield. They also made a nice acquisition in picking up Dick Allen, who led the American League in home runs (37) and RBI (113). As a result, the Pale Hose finished 87–67, good for 2nd place in the American League West—quite a change from their disastrous 1970 season.

The ball playing profession can be difficult on families. Rich Morales, Jr., the son for whom dad hit a minor league home run, remembers living in the Delprado Hotel in Chicago. Deprived of a stable home life with his parents constantly arguing, the younger Morales was expected by his father to take the lead in his own baseball career. The senior Morales prodded his son's athletic endeavors, saying: "Don't expect me to come into your room on Saturday morning at nine and take you to the field and throw batting practice to you, because I'm not going to do that. But if you come into my room at nine in the morning and ask me to throw batting practice for you, I'll do it."

In his final two years, Rich Morales' hitting regressed dramatically. Perhaps, he never became used to National League pitching. Early in the 1973 season, the White Sox traded Morales to the San Diego Padres. With the Padres, Morales gained immediate employment, becoming a first-stringer at second base. Though Rich may have been an easy out with the Padres (.164 average in 244 at bats), he was simply spectacular on defense. Despite playing a position, second base, with which he was not normally accustomed, Morales gloved a near-flawless .988 with more than enough range to make the right side of the infield impenetrable.

The year 1974 would be Rich's final major league season. He backed up shortstop and frequent Mendoza Line-traipser Enzo Hernandez. Morales actually outslugged Hernandez, .295 to .285, and beat Enzo in the season home run derby 1–0. During Morales' two-year stay in San Diego, the Padres finished dead last in the National League West with back-to-back 60–102 seasons.

Following his playing days, Rich Morales taught the game he grew up with and loved. He managed in the Cubs and A's minor league organizations. Afterwards, Morales scouted for the White Sox. Morales made a short return to the majors as bullpen coach for the Atlanta Braves in 1986 and 1987. Morales also managed the 1989 Calgary Cannons, the Triple-A affiliate of the Seattle Mariners, to a 70–72 record and a post-season appearance. Out of baseball, Morales lives in Pacifica, California, and enjoys gardening.

Rich Morales' son briefly made it up to AAA-level ball as a catcher. He also gained some notoriety, in author Brett H. Mandel's study of the lowest depths of minor league ball in *Minor Players, Major Dreams*. Mandel, a municipal employee from Philadelphia, cajoles his way onto a roster spot with the 1994 Ogden Raptors, an independent team of the rookie-level Pioneer League. Mandel writes of his Plimptonesque experiences. Rich Morales, Jr. was an assistant coach for the Raptors at the time. Incredibly, Mandel did manage five at bats that year. Though hitless, he did get an RBI on a groundout and singled in an exhibition game against the all-woman Colorado Silver Bullets. At the time of writing, the younger Morales now coaches in the Milwaukee Brewers organization.

Gentlemen like Rich Morales, Cesar Guitierrez, Enzo Hernandez, Marty Martinez, and, of course, Mario Mendoza played in a different era of baseball. They preceded the notion that "five-tool" players (those that can beat you with batting power, hitting consistency, speed, defense, and throwing arm) would ever play shortstop. Players like Alex Rodriguez, Nomar Garciaparra, and Derek Jeter would probably have been outfielders in the 1960s and early 1970s. In Rich Morales' day, shortstops were, primarily, defensive specialists. Hitting? That was a bonus—kind of like a dancer who can belt out a tune.

Plum
Bill Plummer, C
1947-

During his playing days, catcher Bill Plummer made his name being a small cog in the powerful Big Red Machine. Though he did not necessarily sow all the seeds, Plummer's contributions earned him the fruits of performing for three World Series teams and garnering two World Championship rings. In his second career, Plummer skippered dugouts from the low minors right up to "The Show." The man has seen a lot of tobacco juice expectorated in his thirty-five plus years in professional baseball.

Throughout Plummer's long professional baseball career, he was always regarded as a vanguard defensive catcher. Plummer led his respective minor league in putouts three times, assists twice, and led the American Association with a .994 fielding percentage in 1970. Former Reds' pitcher Tom Carroll, a teammate of "Plum" during the 1974 and 1975 season, described him as "an active and lively catcher, who always called a good game. He was very alert and talked to the pitcher when the need arose."

An Oakland native, Bill Plummer comes from a lineage of accomplished ballplayers. His dad was a minor league pitcher in the 1920s and his uncle, "Red" Baldwin, caught in the minors from 1915–1931. Plummer attended Shasta Junior College before signing with the St. Louis Cardinals as an eighteen-year-old in 1965. Acquired by the Chicago Cubs in 1967, he appeared in a couple of games for the Cubs in 1968. Plummer then went to the Cincinnati Reds in a package deal that brought submariner Ted Abernathy to Chicago. Plummer had a pair of short stints with Cincinnati in 1970 and 1971. At one juncture early in his career, Plummer's major league batting average was as low as .034.

After an impressive year of Triple-A ball in 1971, slugging 17 home runs for Indianapolis, Bill Plummer joined the Reds to stay. As the longtime understudy behind the plate to the great Johnny Bench, Plummer gave Bench's knees a rest for 20 to 40 games a season. Even Pete Rose felt that Bill Plummer would have hit well if he had constant playing time. Rose was right. When Bench broke a finger during the 1972 season, Plummer stepped in as starting catcher for three weeks and hit .233 during that stretch.

While Plummer hit above .200 in only three of his ten seasons, he had some power, as evidenced by slugging at least five extra-base hits and one home run every year from 1972 through 1978. On July 16, 1973, Plummer poked a double off Ken Brett of the Phillies, then came around to score on a Pete Rose two-bagger for the only run for either squad. Later that month, he crashed a 3-run homer against the Braves to win another game for the Reds. Bill Plummer also hit a pair of homers off Steve Carlton in a 1974 contest.

In 1975, Plummer contributed to the Reds' championship season. Plummer earned four game-winning RBIs, quite impressive considering his total of 19 RBI for the entire campaign. A 1975 game typified Plum's gritty style of play. On the final contest of the season, the Reds were comfortably atop the Dodgers in the National League West standings. Sparky Anderson filled his lineup with second-stringers and gave Plummer a rare start. In the bottom of the ninth, with the game tied, Bill made it to first on an error. A passed ball got him to second. He then took third on a fielder's choice. Plummer made it home by beating out a high-chopper from the bat of Cesar Geronimo. The end result: the not-so-speedy Bill Plummer made it around the bases, to score the game-winning run, without the benefit of a single hit.

His best year in the bigs was his 1976 campaign. That year, Plummer actually hit for a higher batting average than Bench (.248 to .234) and had career highs in home runs and RBI. Against St. Louis, on June 5, Bill Plummer hit like Johnny Bench, knocking a single, triple, and homer and driving in seven runs in a single game. Had teammate George Foster not been picked off just before Bill's home run blast, the clout would have been a Grand Slam. After the game, for once, reporters wanted a quote from Plummer. Here's what he had to say of his rarefied performance:

> It was a dream day for an extra man. I can't remember having a day like this, unless it was in the Little League. I'm not going to hit .300 [his batting average was parked at .305 after the game], but I'm not going to embarrass myself either. Confidence is a big thing.

The icing on the cake for Plummer that year was being a member of one of the greatest teams in baseball history. The Reds swept the Phillies and Yankees enroute to their second straight World championship. Bill Plummer received rings and earned handsome rewards from his World Series shares. His 1976 share alone was $500 more than his entire salary of $26,000 that season. Many tremendous players, including Ernie Banks, Carl Yastrzemski, and Barry Bonds, never won a World Series. However, there is a dark side to all this. For many years Bill Plummer played second fiddle to Johnny Bench. Serviceable seasons all, yet they still took their toll on the psyche of this competitive athlete. Johnny Bench, in his autobiography, explains:

> Don't think I'm not affected by the guys in back of me. Athletics is full of careers spent in reserve, guys who were there only to fill in.
> I'm not saying that second string makes a guy suicidal, but it does eat away at you. Bill Plummer played behind me for seven years and I know it affected him. He played tennis almost every day just to break up the monotony of not playing baseball. And then he had to face the reporter in every city who sooner or later asked how it felt to play behind me. It didn't feel that great.

Plummer's plight was a feature story in *Sports Illustrated* magazine. The story clearly showed Plummer had the mental toughness to endure this role year-in and year-out. "He's a man," commented Sparky Anderson. "He doesn't like what he does. Nobody would like being a caddie. But he handles it," added the Reds manager.

Despite his lack of playing time, Plummer was never treated like a scrub. He actually exacted a large degree of respect from teammates and rival players. Being a 6'-1" and 210-pound mass of muscle aided in that perception. A fanatical fitness buff and cattle rancher in the off-season, Plummer symbolized one tough hombre. The *Sports Illustrated* story mentions Bill Plummer's visit to a nightclub, while the Reds were visiting San Diego. Bill came to the aid of teammate Clay Carroll, who was having a disagreement with a trio of over-inebriated and over-zealous Padres fans. Plummer landed a right on the chin of one member of this rowdy trey, whose momentum proceeded to topple over the remaining pair like so many dominoes.

As the Big Red Machine started to show its wear and tear, some of its components were replaced. The Reds and Bill Plummer parted company in the spring of 1978. He played his final big league year in a reserve role for the Seattle Mariners. Plummer actually had one of his better hitting years (a .215 batting average and a .333 slugging average), but now in his thirties, time had run out.

Almost as soon as he hung up his mitt and mask, Plummer began coaching and managing. Starting in 1979 with the Instructional League for Seattle, Bill Plummer worked his way up the Mariners' hierarchy. From 1982 to 1983, he coached Seattle's bullpen. From 1988 to 1991, Plummer served as the team's third-base coach.

Bill Plummer ultimately reached the pinnacle as manager of the Seattle Mariners in 1992. Unfortunately, very little went right for Plummer that year. One could trace a March exhibition game, where Plummer's lineup card contained two first basemen and no designated hitter, as a harbinger of the season to come. Not all the bad luck was under Plummer's control. Beset by injuries, a bullpen populated with "interchangeable disasters," and an assortment of other personnel shortfalls all season, the 1992 Mariners finished dead last with a 64–98 record. Some accounts state Bill Plummer's once-great rapport with many of the Mariners, during their development in the minors, became a detriment to him when forced to wear the "black hat" as a manager in the majors.

Lou Piniella replaced Bill Plummer as the Mariners' manager, a position he still holds entering the 2002 season. As for Plummer, he moved on to coach the Colorado Rockies through 1994. From there, Plummer spent two seasons as manager for the Class AA Jacksonville Suns of the Detroit Tigers organization. He led the Suns to a first-half title in 1996. With the Suns, Plummer allowed Pamela Davis to come into a game and pitch a scoreless fifth inning against the Australian Olympic team. In the 7–2 Jacksonville win, Davis became the first woman to win a ballgame for a minor league affiliate of a major league team. "She should be real happy with herself," said Bill Plummer. "It was nice to see her get the win. She probably wanted to go more, but everything worked out really well."

From 1997 to 1999, Plummer skippered the Western League's Chico Heat. Though years and tiers separated his days with the Reds, Bill Plummer returned to the winner's circle as he led his team to the 1997 Western Baseball League Championship. While residing in Chico, Plummer also earned his Bachelor of Arts degree from Chico State University. He presently manages the Yuma Bullfrogs of the Western League.

Bill Plummer truly personifies the term, a "baseball man." While Plum accumulated a lot of bench time—because of Johnny Bench, one surmises that he also learned a lot about the game watching the likes of Bench, Pete Rose, Tony Perez, and Joe Morgan for years. His ability to pass these observations to his charges, from kids fresh out of high school to greats like Ken Griffey, Jr., may be Bill Plummer's lasting legacy to the game of baseball.

Perhaps, if Plummer played for lesser-caliber teams, he probably would not have been shortchanged the playing needed to punch his average above .200. But would he be wearing those two big rings?

Grinder
Charlie Manuel, OF
1944-

In over 1,800 professional baseball games, Charlie Manuel walloped a grand total of 310 home runs. Yet, his career batting average in the major leagues shows a paltry .198. So, how does a man who could barely hit in the big leagues play six seasons with the Minnesota Twins and Los Angeles Dodgers? And, a better question, how does a man with these credentials become a long-time batting instructor and manager? Simple. Charlie Manuel knows the game and he knows hitting.

The son of a Pentecostal minister, Charlie Manuel was born in West Virginia, but moved to Buena Vista, Virginia (near Roanoke) in his youth. The big redheaded country boy was a local hero after a distinguished high school career. Charlie Manuel lettered in baseball, football, basketball, and track in high school. Not only did young Charlie captain the baseball and basketball teams, he was also an All-Star basketball selection three years, MVP in basketball twice, and MVP in baseball once. The Minnesota Twins drafted him in 1963.

Nicknamed "The Grinder," Charlie's minor league stock rose greatly after nearly winning the 1967 Midwest League Triple Crown. He led the league in batting average with a .313 clip, tied for the lead in runs batted in with 70, and was runner-up in homers with 15. Buoyed by a strong 1968 with Class AA Charlotte, Chuck received an invite to the Twins spring training camp the next season. Though he hadn't played Class AAA ball yet, Manuel literally forced manager Billy Martin to find a spot for him on the roster after tearing up the Grapefruit League. Quite confident of himself, Manuel, during one exhibition game, actually emulated Babe Ruth by pointing towards the outfield fences while at the plate. Manuel then summarily slugged the ball near the spot he pointed to. Several baseball managers, such as Whitey Herzog, thought Chuck could average 20 home runs and bat .300 in the majors.

Charlie Manuel's rookie year with the 1969 Twins seemed auspicious enough. Off to a sensational start, Manuel missed a large portion of the season after breaking his ankle. One of his biggest games of the year came on July 13. Trailing the Seattle Pilots 4–0 going into the bottom of the eighth inning, Charlie Manuel took matters in his own hands. First, he smashed a two-run double to launch a comeback. Then, in the bottom of the ninth, with the bases loaded, Manuel's single drove home the winning run.

By July 20, the day astronaut Neil Armstrong made his historic moon walk, Manuel owned a respectable .266 average with a couple of home runs. Inexplicably, Chuck would not earn another safety in August and September, 36 hitless at bats to finish with a .207 average. "I hope I don't have to wait for them to walk on the moon again to get another hit," Manuel was heard saying in frustration. The 1969 Twins won the first-ever American League West title, but the Baltimore Orioles took them out in a 3-game sweep. Charlie Manuel drew a walk in his lone American League Championship Series plate appearance that year.

Manuel played 59 games, 52 as a pinch hitter, for the 1970 Twins and hit .188. The Twins was loaded with flycatchers: Tony Oliva, Bobby Allison, Cesar Tovar, Rich Reese, Ted Uhlaender, and Jim Nettles. Manuel knocked a lone home run. Though Minnesota repeated as American League West champions, they incurred another sweep at the hands of the Orioles. In one pinch-hit appearance, during the series, Manuel struck out.

Over the next two years, Manuel managed to hit only .196 in a combined 81 games for the Twins, including the last of four career home runs. After spending the entire 1973 season in the minors, the Twins traded Charlie Manuel to the Los Angeles Dodgers for outfielder Jim Fairey. In 1974, while with the Albuquerque Dukes of the Pacific Coast League, Manuel crushed the ball to the tune of 30 homers, 102 RBI, and a .329 batting average. That earned him brief stays with Los Angeles in 1974 and 1975, but only as a pinch hitter. With his four pinch-hit appearances for the Dodgers in 1974, Manuel could boast of playing for three division champions in his short career. Cashing out with a below .200 batting average, Manuel hardly reached the potential that many observers expected from him.

After his release from the Dodgers, Charlie Manuel continued his playing career in Japan. Manuel played his first three years with the Yakult Swallows, owned by a health food/beverage conglomerate. Before Manuel's arrival, the Swallows gulped down defeats so often they were Japan's version of the Washington Senators. Joining the team in 1976, Manuel only hit .243 in his first year, mostly due to injuries and the adjustments Americans must go through to cope with the Japanese strike zone. This strike zone seemingly grew larger for foreign players.

A year later and fully adjusted, Manuel destroyed Japanese pitching to the tune of 42 *houmu rans* with 97 RBI and a .316 batting average. This helped lowly Yakult reach second-place for the first time in franchise history. It took several years and thousands of miles, but at last, Manuel had re-discovered a consistent long-ball stroke.

By 1978, with his well-known reputation as both a fun-loving guy and a heavy-hitting outfielder, fans must have thought Charlie Manuel the reincarnation of Babe Ruth. Incredible tales circulated throughout Japan of Big Chuck living it up in Tokyo's notorious Ginza district. His escapades allegedly started early in the evening and concluded right up to the pre-game warm-ups for an afternoon game. Manuel would then proceed to hit a couple of home runs, while catching a few winks in the dugout when his team was at bat. The little-known player in America achieved superstardom in Japan. The

Japanese looked at Charlie as if he were Godzilla in cleats. He was even featured as an action hero in Japanese comic books, battling giant snakes with his baseball bat.

In 1978, Manuel again paced the Swallows with 39 home runs and 103 RBI. He also owned a .312 batting average. Single-handedly, Charlie Manuel carried the long-suffering franchise to triumph with their first Central League pennant and Japan Series Championship. Manuel's home run in game seven of the series clinched the title. Now, the Swallows gulped down their opponents like Gatorade.

One would have thought Yakult management would deify Manuel as much as the populace. However, a clash of idealism between Charlie and manager Tatsuro Hirooka caused tension between the two. Hirooka, known as the "Iron Shogun," was a harsh disciplinarian. Despite literally carrying the team on his back, Hirooka rode his star *pureya* Manuel hard over everything from his fondness for fast food to failing to shine his baseball spikes. It was enough to make Manuel angrily retort, "I'm 34 years old and I figure I'm old enough to decide what to eat and whether or not I should shine my shoes for a baseball game."

More often than not, Luigi Nakajima, the half-Italian/half Japanese team translator, served as killed messenger in the war between Manuel and his despotic manager. Manuel even nicknamed Luigi the "Sandwich Man" for always being in the middle of these frays. When Hirooka, through Nakajima, ordered Charlie to run ten additional wind sprints, Manuel replied emphatically to Nakajima, "F--- you, I ain't." This left Nakajima in a real quandary trying to relay *that* message back to Hirooka. Once, when Nakajima chastised Manuel about arriving to practice late, the big American lifted Nakajima up by his lapels and asked him to repeat what he said.

What really got the Yakult coaches in an uproar was when the bucolic Charlie Manuel would greet them by their first name. One coach in particular, Kanji Maruyama, focused his rage on Nakajima each time Manuel greeted him with, "Hi Kanji," in his deep Southern drawl. Maruyama believed insistently that Manuel was deliberately undermining his authority. No matter how emphatically Luigi implored Charlie Manuel to properly address his superiors, Manuel would not relent. Eventually, Maruyama gave up on making this an issue and became good friends with Manuel.

During a nationally televised game, Hirooka pulled Charlie Manuel out of the game for dropping a fly ball. The long smoldering feud between Manuel and his manager reached critical mass. After Hirooka muttered something at his mercurial outfielder as he returned to the dugout, Manuel's anger boiled over. Although said in native Japanese, Hirooka's intonation seemed universal enough to Charlie. Manuel collared Luigi Nakajima, demanding to know what his manager had said to him. Coaches and teammates intervened in time to prevent the resumption of World War II. Under the pretense of "quality control measures," the Yakult front office sent the slugger to the Kintetsu (Osaka) Buffaloes in 1979.

In his two years with Kintetsu, Chuck Manuel would earn even greater fame in the Land of the Rising Sun. Since Kintetsu played in the Japanese Pacific League, Manuel fortuitously benefited playing under the designated-hitter rule. For the first two months of the 1979 season, he crushed the ball for 24 home runs, leading perennial also-ran Kintetsu into first place. Japanese sportswriters dubbed Manuel *Akaoni*, which translates as "The Red Devil." Then disaster struck Manuel in the form of a 90-mph fastball from one Soroku Yagisawa. The errant pitch, which may or may not have been a deliberate beaning, literally destroyed Manuel's face. He suffered a broken jaw, a broken nose, and lost ten teeth. To repair the damage, Manuel underwent a five-hour surgery.

This is Charlie Manuel's account of the incident. Told in Robert Whiting's *You Gotta Have Wa,* Manuel squarely blames Yagisawa:

> I stand way away from the plate. I'm tall and I stand erect in the batter's box. The ball didn't slip. Yagisawa is a veteran pitcher and his control is too good. When he hit me in the jaw, he didn't come off the mound. I couldn't breathe and he just turned away and started playing catch with one of the infielders like it was no big thing. When I left the field, I turned and pointed to him and said, "I'll get you." He just grinned at me and tipped his cap.
>
> The Japanese don't throw at each other that much. But they watch U.S. baseball on TV and they see beanballs and they think it's the American way, that it's okay to throw at a *gaijin.* What they don't understand is that it is part of our code of behavior for the batter to retaliate.

The Japanese press, flagrantly disdainful in their bias against foreign ballplayers, dismissed the beaning as "an unfortunate accident" which warranted little more than a small byline in the back pages. However, a Japanese sportswriter named Morse Saito did not agree with that perspective. Disgusted with the attitude of his own press as he was with Yagisawa's brutal and craven act, Saito wrote an article condemning Japanese baseball tactics as "bush league." Saito went on to explain that the NHK television sportscaster did not mention the Japanese pitcher by name. Saito cited evidence of Japanese pitchers trying to protect their own baseball league records by deliberately walking Manuel as he approached the home run record for a month. "The psychologically more mature Japanese are shocked and regret that pitch."

Despite literally eating his food with a straw, Charlie Manuel returned to the Kintetsu lineup by early August. He finished the season with 37 home runs to pace the Pacific League and led the Buffaloes to the league pennant. The Japanese sportswriters, impressed by Manuel's *Samurai* spirit and partly out of guilt over their treatment of him after his beaning, selected him as Pacific League Most Valuable Player. Manuel became the first foreigner to collect the honor since 1964 and the first American MVP ever.

Healthy for the entire 1980 campaign, Charles Manuel nearly won the Triple Crown, blasting a league-leading 48 home runs[8] and 129 RBI. Again, Manuel's monstrous slugging paved the way for the Buffaloes to capture a second Pacific League pennant. In both years, Kintetsu narrowly lost the Japan Series to the Hiroshima Carp, 4-games-to-3. But all was not well with the Buffaloes and Manuel.

Again, Japanese sensitivities worked against Charlie. Despite his extraordinary 1980 season, he actually lost favor with management, writers, and fans after leaving the team in mid-season to attend his son's high school graduation back in the States. Though Manuel carried the team on his back to another pennant, Kintetsu management accused him of deserting the team while they were in a tight race for the first half title—which

---

[8] At the time, Manuel's 48 home runs were the most ever hit by an American player.

they eventually lost. When contract negotiations soured, Charlie Manuel saw another team release him while at the top of his game.

Manuel returned to the Yakult Swallows in 1981 for one final hurrah. The coast was now clear after the departure of manager and adversary Hirooka. Playing in his late thirties, Chuck Manuel's career in Japanese baseball faded quickly. In his final year as a professional player, Manuel's once-lofty home run totals declined to just 12.

During his six seasons in Japan, Manuel's career totals equated to a .303 batting average with 189 home runs and 491 RBI. On three occasions, he was a "Best Nine," Japan's equivalent of a top player. Along the way, Manuel earned many friends with his Ruthian clouts and playboy lifestyle. Yet, Manuel's combativeness and refusal to adhere to Japanese traditions, made him more than his share of enemies.

Manuel returned to America in 1982. He took a position as a scout for the Minnesota Twins. Although he dropped from a $250K a year player in Japan to scraping by on just $20,000 as a bird-dog, Manuel candidly stated, "You know what, there's a lot less problems at $20,000."

Also serving as a roving hitting instructor, one of Charlie's earliest successes was with Kirby Puckett, then playing Rookie League ball in Elizabethton, Tennessee. In a 1996 interview with Scott Miller of *The Pioneer Press*, Charlie Manuel stated that Puckett would approach him and, with a twinkle in his eye and a smile on his face, ask:

"How do I get to the big leagues?"

"By getting hits," Manuel would reply.

"I can do that," Puckett would answer back, looking Manuel square in the eye, grinning.

"One time he [Puckett] said, 'Charlie, don't you like black guys? You never work with me on my hitting,'" Manuel said, smiling at the memory. "And I told him, 'You can hit. I don't want to work with you. I'll just mess you up.'"

This launched a new dimension in Charlie Manuel's baseball career. Manuel became a hitting guru. He had managed at every tier of the Twins' farm system. Twins' fans can thank Manuel because he helped develop many of the players that won Minnesota their two World Championships in 1987 and 1991.

Charlie moved on to the Cleveland Indians to become the team's batting instructor in 1988 and 1989. Next, Manuel managed the Colorado Springs Sky Sox from 1990–1992. Under Manuel, the Sox made three consecutive playoff appearances, culminating with their first Pacific Coast League Championship in 1992. Charlie earned 1992 Pacific Coast League Manager of the Year honors. Later, Manuel was inducted into the Sky Sox Hall of Fame. His colorful style of leadership and exciting brand of big inning offense, known as "Charlie Ball," enamored him with the Sky Sox's faithful fans. Manuel's famous exhortation to his players in a tight game was, "Go to the mountain, son." Quite apropos with Pikes Peak looming in the Colorado Springs background.

Colorado sportswriter Marty Grantz observed, "The fans, player, and media choice for all-time Sky Sox manager, Charlie's Virginia drawl often reminded listeners of the cartoon character Foghorn Leghorn. His eccentric exchanges almost always ended with the word 'son.' Fitting because Charlie had the familiarity of everyone's grandpa, or at least their favorite uncle."

After the Colorado Rockies took over the Colorado Springs franchise, the Indians moved their Triple-A team to Charlotte in 1993. Charlie Manuel led the Charlotte Knights to an International League crown and managed the International League All-Star Team.

Following the 1993 season, Manuel returned to Cleveland as their hitting instructor. Though not the household name amongst hitting experts, one usually thinks of Charlie Lau or Walt Hriniak, the Indians improved from a poor hitting team to a powerhouse outfit. Just ask Jim Thome, the Tribe's all-time best slugger. He credits much of his success to Manuel, who mentored Thome since his earliest days in professional baseball. In fact, of the great Cleveland hitters of the 1990s, such as Albert Belle, Manny Ramirez, Kenny Lofton, and Thome, all have one thing in common: they were Charlie Manuel-trained men. Even the surly Albert Belle knew the man with the deep southern drawl could teach ballplayers the discipline of hitting.

In the summer of 1998, Charlie Manuel was having problems. His weight climbed to almost 260 lbs. Then, in the matter of weeks, he lost 40 pounds and complained of fatigue. While golfing just before the 1998 All-Star break, Manuel suffered a mild heart attack, his second within the decade. Further testing revealed a serious coronary artery blockage. Manuel required a quadruple coronary bypass, a demanding and risky surgery. While in the hospital, before the operation, Charlie Manuel stayed focused on the essence of his entire adult life: baseball. In between prods and pokes by doctors and nurses, Manuel had numerous calls and visitors from the likes of Eddie Murray and Manny Ramirez, who brought Manuel to tears. Jim Thome even stopped by for some hitting advice. It must have been good advice, since Thome homered and tripled to beat the Yankees the following day. Terry Pluto, the *Akron Beacon-Journal* columnist wrote:

> The night before his quadruple bypass, Charlie Manuel thought of everything for which to give thanks. "But I didn't think about dying," he said. "I just didn't believe it was my time. Now, I won't kid you. I was scared. But I just knew deep inside, it would be all right."

Charlie Manuel underwent a harrowing operation that sawed his chest cavity open to replace artery blockage with veins from his legs. The surgery a success, the old warhorse astounded doctors by donning an Indians' uniform and working the dugout just five weeks after surgery. Recovery times are normally measured in months, not weeks.

After Cleveland's 1999 season fell short of expectations, Charlie Manuel replaced Mike Hargrove as the new manager of the Cleveland Indians. That ended Manuel's second tour as the Tribe's hitting coach. From 1994-99, the once-meager hitting Indians paced the American League in runs scored three times and led the league in homers twice, setting a franchise record by knocking 220 balls over the fence in 1997.

In the 2000 season, Charlie Manuel made lots of news. Manuel again underwent emergency surgery, this time for a ruptured colon in spring training. He was also ejected from two of his first three games. In an episode that actually endeared him with fans tired of the jaded behavior of today's ballplayers, Manuel "punished" his underachieving Indians by taking away the clubhouse Ping-Pong table and banning card playing.

Manuel's charges eventually played better ball. Barely above .500 in August, the Indians finished 90–72. But, the Indians just missed out on an American League wildcard berth. Interestingly enough, in the year 2000, two managers in the American League Central division owned the last name of Manuel; Charlie and the Chicago White Sox's Jerry Manuel. Coincidentally, both batted below .200 for their big league careers.

In 2001, Charlie Manuel returned Cleveland to top dog and a position Manuel was quite familiar with throughout most of his baseball life. The Tribe battled back from a slow start to their sixth American League Central title in seven years.

Had the breaks gone right, perhaps Manuel would have had the success in the major leagues that he had in minor league ball and in Japan. It seems incredible that Manuel, who could only hit four home runs in six seasons in the big leagues, could equal that total in two Japanese ballgames. Still, not too many players can lay claim to each jewel of the Triple Crown during their professional careers. The final word on Manuel's long and distinguished career as a player, manager, batting coach, reveals his affiliation with no less than 19 playoff baseball teams. Certainly, Charlie Manuel has followed the advice that he's given to youngsters; he's been to the baseball mountain.

Pancho
Frank Baker, SS
1946-

While short a baker's dozen, three different players named Frank Baker have appeared in the majors since 1900. Most everyone schooled in baseball history knows of Hall of Fame third baseman John Franklin (Frank) Baker by his well-known sobriquet "Home Run." A Dead Ball Era slugger, he led the American League in home runs four straight years and hit some dramatic round-trippers in the 1910 World Series. The other two Frank Bakers were contemporaries during the early Seventies. The Cleveland Indians owned an outfielder named Frank "no middle name" Baker (4 HR/38/RBI/.232 batting average). The player of this focus is Yankees/Orioles shortstop Frank Watts Baker.

The tall and rangy man nicknamed "Pancho" graduated from Southern Mississippi University. Though he never hit above .261 in any one season of his professional career, Pancho's defense showed panache. Possessing a full shortstop's toolbox: good speed, arm, range, hands, and quickness, everyone considered Baker a top-notch fielder. The Yankees kept Baker on their 15-man "protected list" in 1968, barring any expansion team from drafting him. While with Syracuse in 1970, Baker led International League shortstops with a .965 fielding percentage.

Frank Baker's best year may have been his rookie campaign of 1970. Busy in Syracuse, Baker and the Chiefs battled for the International League pennant. Frank Baker's wife also stayed busy, giving birth to twins in June. After placing Ron Hansen on the disabled list, the Yankees recalled Baker on August 9th.

Baker began well enough, securing five hits in his first ten at bats. He reached base ten times in his first four games. On August 14, in only his fifth major league game, Baker's two-out double in the eighth inning snapped a deadlock to defeat the Chicago White Sox. When asked about his early success, Baker replied, "I'm surprised, all right. At Syracuse this year, we were fighting for the pennant and I didn't think they'd take anybody from the club right now."

Staying on with the team as the backup shortstop for Gene "The Stick" Michael, Baker actually out hit Michael (.231 to .214). The 1970 Yankees had a resurrection of sorts that year, finishing in second place—the Bronx Bombers' highest standing since their World Series appearance in 1964.

After struggling through a hole-in-the-bat .139 season in 1971, Baker spent the next year in the Yankees' farm system. He was dealt to the Baltimore Orioles just before the start of the 1973 season. Primarily a defensive replacement, handy Frank appeared in 44 games, playing every infield position. Though all he could cash in with the bat was a dollar-ninety, on September 28, Dr. Longball made a rare call on Frank Baker. His only major league home run, a Grand Slam against the Indians, helped in a Yankees' 18-4 uprising. Baker also delivered a two-run single that day.

Baker also tasted the sweetness of victory that year, as the Orioles won the 1973 American League East division title. In the 1973 Championship Series, won by the Oakland Athletics 3-games-to-2, Frank Baker appeared in two games as a late-inning replacement.

In his final season, in 1974, Frank Baker again made Baltimore's postseason roster. Again, Baker played in two games without a plate appearance (He did commit one error in the field). And again, the Orioles lost to Oakland.

Frank's older brother, John Baker, played linebacker in the American Football League from 1963 to 1967. For Frank "One Home Run" Baker, batting might have been a chore. However, playing shortstop was a "piece of cake." For a manager, Baker was a good asset to have in the hip pocket.

Vuke
John Vukovich, 3B
1947-

John Vukovich holds a dubious record; the lowest batting average (.161) for any non-pitcher with at least ten years in the majors. Clearly, Vukovich was not a player you might want on your rotisserie league team. However, his sterling defensive talents allowed him to complete a relatively long career. The archetypal "Hoover," not only was John a third baseman with great range, but also adept enough to play all four infield positions.

A Sacramento native, John Christopher Vukovich displayed a deft glove as early as high school. During four years at Amador County High School, in Sutter Creek, California, he led his district in fielding every season. A multi-sport athlete, Vukovich also earned the 1964 California High School Football Player of the Year honors. His ascent through the Phillies' farm system included a Sally League championship with Spartanburg in 1967. In 1969, Vukovich won the Eastern League third baseman fielding title with Reading – one of four fielding crowns at the hot corner John accrued as a minor leaguer.

Denny Weiner, a former minor league prospect for the Phillies, has fond memories of Vuke: "In 1969, I was drafted by the Phillies on the second round in the winter draft. When I arrived at spring training in Clearwater, I was given a locker next to Vuke. He, being the veteran, kind of took me under his wing and made me feel quite comfortable and at ease. I learned a lot about character and being a professional."

Vukovich enjoyed a memorable 1970 season with Eugene (Oregon) of the Pacific Coast League. That year, he slugged 22 home runs, drove in 96, and batted .275. He also paced league third sackers in all fielding categories. With the help of Vukovich, Eugene won the league championship. On these merits, John Vukovich received a late-season promotion to Philadelphia. He went 1-for-8 in a three game trial with the Phils during their final season in old Connie Mack Stadium.

As a rookie, John Vukovich became the Phillies starting third baseman in 1971. Batting just .166, with no home runs in 74 games, Vukovich went hitless game after game. Yet, Vukovich's superb defense kept him in the lineup. During Rick Wise's no-hitter over Cincinnati that year, Vukovich made numerous heart-stopping, hit-robbing plays at the hot corner to preserve the no-hit effort. With two outs in the bottom of the ninth, Pete Rose slapped a sharp liner down the third base line. For an instant, Wise's heart sunk, Then suddenly, Vukovich speared the ball out of the air for the last out of Wise's no-no.

After spending a year in the minors to work on his hitting, the Phils decided that John Vukovich would not be part of their plans. Shipped off in a seven-player trade at the end of the 1972 season, Vukovich departed Philadelphia with starting third baseman Don Money. The Phillies ended up starting a rookie at the hot corner in 1973. This rookie suffered throughout the season, batting just .196 and striking out a whopping 136 times. Not exactly a star in the making. Yet, that rookie became one of baseball's all-time great third baseman—Mike Schmidt.

John Vukovich played two seasons in Milwaukee, averaging one strikeout for every four at bats. Yet, five of his six career home runs came in Milwaukee flannels. On occasion, Vukovich hit in the clutch. as displayed in a July 28, 1973 game against the Yankees, when his single up the middle brought home the winning run.

In 1974, his career year with the stick, John crashed three homers and 11 RBI in just 80 at bats. He also had a personal-best .313 slugging average that season. Though Schmidt could hit three four-baggers in a single doubleheader in any park, including Yellowstone, John Vukovich's modest bat did have some sting in the junior circuit.

Traded to the Cincinnati Reds in 1975, Vukovich beat out several candidates to become the Reds' starting third basemen. But his tenure with Cincinnati and Sparky Anderson was volatile at times, as evidenced in this excerpt from *The Big Red Dynasty*:

> ...In the third game of the LA series, with the bases loaded in the second inning and Vukovich due up, Anderson pinch-hit Driessen.
>
> Vukovich, whose parents were in the stands, exploded. All the way from the dugout runway to the clubhouse, his rage carried him from light bulb to light bulb like a giant firefly in a horror flick. He burst every bulb—and wanted more. Pop! . . . Pop! . . . Pop! . . . Pop!
>
> After the game, Anderson made his case.
>
> "Simple," said Sparky. "Who's my better hitter—Vukovich or Driessen?" Anderson had said in spring training that his priority for third base was defense.

Though John hit his high-water mark in season batting average with a .211 clip over 31 games, Pete Rose would permanently move from the outfield to third base in early May. John Vukovich would not be around to see the Big Red Machine win their first World Series in 35 years, as the Reds traded him (for Dave Schneck) back to the Phillies.

In his second stint with the Phillies, John played parts of five seasons, from 1976 through 1981. The Philadelphia ball club, vastly improved their club from the bottom feeders when Vukovich played there the first time around. From 1976 to 1983, the Phillies made six postseason appearances—twice as many in all their other years combined. With a fundamentally solid infield, Vukovich had few opportunities to ply his trade and witnessed most of the Phillies' conquests from a dugout view.

After playing a scant 16 games over a span of four years, John Vukovich finally earned a chance to play in 1980. He made the final roster after spring training in an unusual way. Vukovich had practiced playing catcher and stuck with the team as their third-string backstop. Though Vukovich never caught a game, he capably backed up infielders Mike Schmidt, Larry Bowa, Manny Trillo, and Pete Rose over his 49 games as a reliable late-inning defensive replacement. During one mid-season juncture, a hamstring pull felled Mike Schmidt for two weeks. John Vukovich filled in competently, as the Phillies won seven of eleven during that period.

After over a century of failure, the 1980 Phillies finally won baseball's big prize, capturing their only World Series ever. Though John Vukovich was on the postseason roster, he became the lone Phillie not to appear in either the National League Championship Series nor the World Series. Yet he played his role, as a positive clubhouse influence to both veteran and young players. He helped liven the Philadelphia bench, especially during their crucial late-season drive and dramatic post-season.

As soon as his playing days ended in 1981, Vukovich began a long incumbency within the coach's box. For six campaigns, Vukovich coached the Chicago Cubs from 1982 through 1987. He also served as a one-day interim manager after the Cubs fired Jim Frey in 1986. He piloted the team to a 1–1 record before Gene Michael's permanent appointment. Writer Russ Lake recalled: "I wondered—'Has he ever had that many media members around him before?'"

In 1988, Vukovich rejoined the Phillies for a third time. Manager Lee Elia had known Vukovich since his days at Eugene and knew he would be a good addition to his coaching staff. Maybe too good. On September 23, 1988, the California Angels fired Cookie Rojas while the Phillies dismissed Lee Elia. The Phils were heading to a last place season, depths they had not seen since 1973. Moose Stubing and John Vukovich would manage their respective ball clubs for the remainder of the season. John Vukovich fared well, winning five of nine games. Stubing, however, lost all eight games for the Angels thereby suffering the ignominy of being the only man in major league baseball history to go both hitless as a major league player (0-for-5) and winless as a manager.

Vukovich remains on the Phillies coaching staff at present, variously serving as first base coach, dugout assistant, spring training coordinator, and finally third base coach for four Philadelphia managers. Though the Phillies have posted only two winning seasons in this period, the triumphant campaign in 1993 was most memorable to John Vukovich and the Phils. In that year, Philadelphia led the division wire-to-wire, upset the Atlanta Braves in the National League Championship Series, and came oh-so-close to defeating

Toronto in the 1993 World Series. That World Series featured the famous 15-14 game. Everybody hit in a game that resembled batting practice. Vukovich probably wished he could have participated.

Though seriously considered for the job of Phillies manager at the end of 2000, the club picked Larry Bowa, who retained Vukovich as third base coach. They were former Phillies' teammates and boyhood friends growing up in Sacramento. In spring training, Vukovich complained of severe headaches. The cause of the headaches was soon determined—a brain tumor—and Vukovich underwent surgery to remove the cancer in May, 2001. So far, so good. Unfortunately, one dullard of a television announcer poked fun of Vukovich's hairstyle during a highlights show, not realizing Vukovich was losing his hair due to radiation treatments.

Like father. Like son. Philadelphia took Vince Vukovich, John Vukovich's son, in the 20th round of the 2001 amateur draft. The younger Vukovich, an outfielder, helped lead the University of Delaware Blue Hens to the NCAA tournament. Father Vukovich served as chief advisor for the signing. But this was not going to be another J. D. Drew fiasco, as negotiations were completed in less than five minutes.

No mere footnote, John Vukovich[9] has dedicated nearly 30 years, over half his life, to the success of the Philadelphia Phillies' ballclub. He has been with them in their best times and in the club's darkest days. The John Vukovich legacy in baseball as a player, coach, and more importantly as a positive role model and teacher of young ballplayers, remains secure.

Schneck In The Grass
Dave Schneck, OF
1949-

In an interview, Dave Schneck claims his manager, Yogi Berra, really did utter the classic pizzeria Yogiism. There's a million variations, but the gist of the story goes like this: When asked if he wanted his whole pizza cut into four or eight slices, Yogi said, "Better make it four. I'm on a diet." But no matter how you slice it, Dave Schneck, a stocky, 5-foot-9-inch flycatcher, had an interesting 3-year ride with the New York Mets.

Originally a pitcher, Schneck sported an impressive 20–2 record at Whitehall (Pennsylvania) High School. The school won the Lehigh Valley League title all three years Dave Schneck played for them. However, scouts became more impressed with his powerful lefty swing and his .362 batting average in 1967, his senior year.

The New York Mets drafted Schneck in the 17th round. His first year as a pro was full of bad luck. For starters, he broke his collarbone in spring training. Once healed, Schneck initially tried to make it as a pitcher; first, with Raleigh-Durham of the Carolina League, then to Florida when the rookie league season began. Schneck pitched well, but decided he wanted to move to the outfield. Whitey Herzog, a Mets' farm director, approved the move and sent Schneck to Marion (Virginia) of the Appalachian League to be their

[9] John Vukovich is no relation to George Vukovich, who played a similar reserve role for the 1980 Phillies in the outfield (or the Brewers' pitcher of the same timeframe, Pete Vuckovich).

starting center fielder. More bad karma followed; Schneck took a pitch on the arm and broke his wrist. When he recovered, Schneck was as surprised as anyone when he went straight to Double-A ball. Dave hit .164 with two homers.

After the season, Schneck, only 19, traveled back to Allentown to marry his high school sweetheart. However, his budding baseball career soon took a two-year hiatus. "The day we got home from our honeymoon," Schneck recalled during an interview in the *Allentown Morning Call*, "I got my draft notice." For Dave Schneck, this would not be two years of playing baseball exhibitions in Germany for the U.S. Army. Schneck spent 14 months in Vietnam, in-country at the height of the war. He fought bravely amidst deadly conflict. While the Mets were marching to their first World Series, Schneck's platoon faced heavy opposition during one fierce firefight. Incurring heavy losses, only half of the platoon survived. Dave Schneck was fortunate.

The Mets thought enough of Schneck to keep him on their 40-man roster while in Vietnam. His military obligation honorably completed in 1971, Dave Schneck went from the killing fields of Vietnam to his field of dreams—the Mets' spring training camp. Schneck didn't make the parent ballclub, but instead made his mark in Visalia and Memphis, belting a combined 34 home runs in a single season. Once, a photographer, after taking a snapshot of Schneck batting, was so duly impressed with his swing, that he remarked, "Kid, you keep swinging like that and you'll be in the majors for a long time."

In 1972, Schneck started the season with Memphis. Tearing up Texas League pitching for 24 home runs, 76 RBI, and a .304 average, the Mets called him up in mid-July to fill a spot in their injury-decimated outfield. San Diego was hosting the Mets. Upon joining the team, Schneck realized he left his bats in Texas. Johnny Antonelli, Dave Schneck's manager in Memphis, wanted to surprise his star by packing Schneck's bag and then breaking the news about his promotion. The only trouble was Antonelli forgot to pack the bats. Dave Schneck ended up borrowing a club from Ted Martinez.

Dave Schneck was also devoid of a decent set of clothes. Brent Strom, a San Diegan and one of Schneck's Memphis' teammates, sent him to his mother's house to get some laundry done. As for a jacket, Schneck went to see Lou Niss, the Mets' traveling secretary, for a clothing allowance.

"When I knocked on the door," Dave recalled, "a black guy answered. I was so nervous; I didn't recognize him. So I asked, 'Are you Lou Niss?' He said, 'What are you talking about, man?' It was Willie [Mays]. I eventually found Lou Niss. He gave me a couple hundred dollars. I bought a coat, some slacks, a shirt, and a tie. I think I wore them for two weeks."

When Schneck arrived at the ballpark that night, he saw the lineup card and nearly went into shock. "I'm batting fourth, between Mays and [Rusty] Staub," he recalled during an interview. When the youngster took his swings in the sixth inning with one on, two outs, and the Mets trailing 2–1, Steve Arlin quickly worked two strikes on Schneck. But on the third pitch, Schneck clouted the ball 400 feet over the right-field wall to win the game.

"He was dancing halfway to home," said Sheriff Robinson, the first-base coach.

"I never saw a guy run around the bases so fast," Mets' Manager Yogi Berra commented.

"He was smiling from ear to ear; he was flying," Eddie Yost, the third-base coach, added.

"Some guy brought me the ball," Schneck said. "I took it to Tom Seaver and asked him to sign it for me. He said, 'What are you talking about, kid? You won the game for me. I should be thanking you.'"

The next day, Schneck made a running one-handed grab of Jerry Morales' drive to deep right center to preserve another victory. The following game, Schneck slugged his second homer, plus a double and single in four times at bat. Sportswriters were quickly comparing him to one of his teammates, the legendary Willie Mays. Schneck cooled down considerably and the next Willie Mays found himself back in the minors by August.

In 1973, Schneck started out with Triple-A Tidewater (Norfolk). After a decent season Schneck found himself back in a Mets' uniform as a September call-up. He delivered some hits and played solid outfield as the Mets won their second National League pennant. Though ineligible for the postseason roster, Dave Schneck still got to dress, sit on the bench, and pitch batting practice every day.

Inheriting the center field position from the retired Mays in 1974, Schneck, who had yet to crack .200 in a season, was hitting everything and anything. After feasting on a four-hit game against the Phillies, Dave Schneck was hitting .545 by mid-April and second in the National League in batting average. People were seeking out Dave Schneck, as much as Tom Seaver or Rusty Staub, for autographs.

Dave endeared himself to the Mets' fans through his outfield play. As one ardent admirer recalled, "Schneck was fearless when going after a deep fly and had some spectacular crashes—at full speed—into the Shea Stadium wall." After war in Vietnam, Schneck probably harbored little fear of outfield fences. In an outer garden mishap, Dave Schneck suffered a horrific collision with George "Stork" Theodore. Fans at Shea Stadium claim they could hear the sounds of bones crunching upon impact.

One can surmise the progress of Schneck's season. Long bouts of inconsistency drained Schneck's Cobb-like average down to .205 by year's end. "What happened? I have no idea. I just lost it, totally. It was brutal. I told [beat writer] Red Foley, 'I feel like I'm in a bottomless pit.' The next day, everyone read that in the papers. Whatever happened, I never found it again. I got sent down, and I never made it back up again."

In that up and down year of 1974, Dave Schneck blasted five home runs, drove in 25, and tied a major league record for most at bats in a single game on September 11. In the longest major league game not to end in a tie, a 25-inning, seven-hour marathon, Schneck stroked two doubles in eleven at bats. The Mets lost the game to the St. Louis Cardinals by a score of 4–3 with the winning run scored by Bake McBride, who made it all the way from first to home on an errant pickoff throw. Many records were set in the game, but the most remarkable one was the use of 180 baseballs.

Just three years after being touted as baseball's next star, Schneck was out of the major leagues. As baseball researcher and Mets' fan Bill Deane pragmatically observed, "Schneck was one of many 1970's Mets (Benny Ayala, Mike Vail, Steve Henderson, et al.), who raised eyebrows early, only to disappoint."

After the 1974 season, Schneck was part of a multi-player deal with the Philadelphia Phillies that landed them eventual World Series hero Tug McGraw. Dave also toiled in the minor leagues in the Cincinnati Reds and the Chicago Cubs' organizations.

"My last pro year was 1977," Dave Schneck told reporter Ted Mexiell. "I was at Triple-A Wichita, in the Cubs' chain. Denver was the Expos' Triple-A team. I went 3-for-5 my last game. The hit in my last at bat was off a lefty named Terry Enyard."

"When the game was over," Schneck continued, "I went back to my locker stall and cried my eyes out for a half hour. Not one guy left; every guy on the team waited to shake hands and say goodbye. It was my choice to retire. I was 27. I'd been in the majors, but had been kicking around in the minors the last three seasons. I knew that was it." Schneck has no regrets. "I played for the fun of it," he admits and claims he never even paid attention to the Mets' place in the National League East standings.

Dave Schneck returned home and became owner of a waterproofing business. Since 1991, he has been the proprietor of *The Hitter's Edge* batting cages and amusement center in Whitehall Township, near Allentown, Pennsylvania. In 1999, at age 49, Dave made a comeback of sorts. Playing alongside his son, Cory, for the ICC Pirates of the Tri-County adult baseball league, Dave went to the plate for the first time in 22 years. The result? Schneck crushed a line drive over the right-center field fence for a home run. Afterward, he tearfully embraced his son back in the dugout.

Instead of spending $50 for a Willie Mays autographed baseball, for the same amount of cash, one can have a one-hour batting lesson from the man once hailed as the next Willie Mays. Schneck offers this advice to youngsters: To perfect a batting swing, it takes at least *20,000 strokes* in the cage over a six-month period. Astute guidance from a man who owned a pretty sweet swing himself.

The Big Slug
Jim Fuller, OF
1950-

During the 1970s, actor Robert Fuller starred on the NBC Saturday night schlock fest known as *Emergency*. In the same decade, baseball's Jim Fuller patrolled the outfields for Baltimore and Houston. Had a pitcher taken a liner up the box from this heavy slugging powerhouse, he would need a paramedic. At a burly 6'-3" and 220 pounds, Jim Fuller offered an imposing figure at the plate. Invariably, Fuller came to bat with one thought on his mind—to send the baseball into orbit. One of the few things thicker on Jim's body than his powerful arms might have been his distinctive mutton-chop sideburns.

Born in Bethesda, Maryland, the Baltimore Orioles drafted Fuller. Jim started out in 1970 with the Florida State League Marlins of Miami. Fuller launched 9 home runs, 64 RBI, and batted .247 for the eventual league champions that year.

Renamed the Miami Orioles in 1971, they were often referred as the "Baby O's" by the local press. With Fuller and most of the previous season's roster intact, Miami rolled to a 94–47 record to win their third straight league flag. Jim Fuller blasted 33 home runs to tie the all-time Florida State League home run record. Hitting .326, he also set franchise records for runs scored (105) and runs batted in (110). Easily, Fuller won the league Most Valuable Player honors.

Fuller split the next season between Double-A Asheville and the Orioles' long-standing Triple-A affiliate in Rochester. He crushed another 34 home runs for both teams combined.

Jim achieved cult-status for Rochester in 1973. The International League's home run and RBI champion with 39 and 108 respectively, Fuller also possessed a rifle arm, the strongest in the Orioles' chain. That combination earned him his second Most Valuable Player award. Unfortunately, his biggest weakness was strikeouts. Fuller heard the umpires punch him out an astonishing 197 times that year, which included five in a single game. Even if the contest was out of hand, Rochester fans would stick around just to see what mighty Jim would do in his final at bat. Often, there were only two outcomes.

Fuller punched his ticket to Baltimore that year and singled in his first big league at bat. With two home runs in nine games for the Orioles, Fuller smashed 41 balls over the wall. Jim saw lots of action with the eventual 1974 American League East champions, with 11 doubles and 7 home runs. Fuller earned a relatively lofty .392 slugging average. In a May 12 tilt against Cleveland, Fuller unloaded two home runs. The Orioles could have used him on the postseason roster as they were held to one run or less three times in their Championship Series setback to the Oakland A's.

Unfortunately for Jim Fuller, the talented Orioles outfield featured Al Bumbry, Paul Blair, Rich Coggins, Don Baylor, and Ken Singleton—all ahead of Fuller in Earl Weaver's flycatcher depth charts. Thus, Jim spent the next two campaigns toiling in Rochester. In 1976, Fuller seemed poised for another chance in the bigs. By early July, in a Rochester uniform, Fuller had 18 homers and 53 RBI. Then, a broken thumb sidelined him for a month. That break was bad enough, but Fuller's next ignominy was his replacement—Eddie Murray.

Fuller resurfaced briefly with the Houston Astros in 1977. He added another two long balls to make his career total 11. However, his .160 batting average and preponderance for striking out doomed any further opportunities. In the final analysis, when Jim Fuller connected, the ball invariably traveled long distances. Unfortunately, connecting with the ball was always a dicey proposition. Of his 254 at bats that resulted in outs, over half (130) occurred via a strikeout. Jim Fuller may have been born 25 years too soon. He played in an era of pitching dominance when strike zones were not yet the length and breadth of a shoebox. Fuller's lofty home run totals support the claim that he would be more of a desirable commodity today.

"It looks easy. When you see ballplayers at the stadium or on television, catching a fly ball, it seems—'This is what we did when we were kids. We could be down there. There isn't that much separating me from Bo Jackson or George Brett. I could do that.' Baseball fosters illusions. Baseball fosters hopes. Baseball inflates us. Baseball lies to us seductively and we know we're being seduced and we don't complain."

-John Thorn, baseball author

Chapter 7
OF STRIKES AND STRIKEOUTS
1977–2000

A Tour Of Baseball From 1977 To 2000

Historically speaking, baseball has undergone massive changes during this time. Most notably are the new perceptions and notoriety of our professional athletes. After a glimpse of this in *Ball Four* (1970), an increased presence and ultimate omnipresence of the media now reveal that our sports heroes harbor unsavory personaility traits. These traits are fully reported in newspapers, on ESPN, and the Internet. How much do we really want to know about Howard Spira, Margo Adams, and the athletes unfortunately tangled up with them? Do the sports pages need to resemble police blotters? Moreover, how surprised should we be that our athletic idols and Hollywood heartthrobs have the same human frailties when our elected officials exhibit same?

Great growth and great turmoil occurred in major league baseball, mirroring America's (and Canada's) obsession for major league sports. Baseball owners earned unfathomable revenues from ever-increasing live attendance, ticket prices, and television earnings. The players also enjoyed a share of this revenue, as salaries increased to high six-figures even for utility players. At the same time, however, an emboldened and unified player's union and avaricious agents put players and owners (now operating without the aegis of the reserve clause) into a series of disputes on the labor front.

The first debacle occurred in 1981, with the failure of owners and players to ink a new contract. That triggered a baseball strike that wiped out up to 62 regular season games for some teams and forced baseball into the untenable proposition of crowning split-season champions.

There were work-stoppage close calls in 1985 (a two-day walkout by players over salary caps) and 1990 (an owner's lockout over the players demand for collusion protection). However, despite the best efforts by owners, players, and agents to undermine the game, attendance figures kept climbing and climbing. Increased revenues led to new ballparks. Some parks sported the "doomsdome" look (Minneapolis and Toronto) while others smartly built in the retro-ballpark look (Cleveland, Arlington, and Baltimore).

With new cities demanding franchises of their own, three sessions of expansion upped the number of franchises from 24 in 1976 to 30 in 1998, the highest number of teams in major league baseball since 1884. Only one-quarter century after both leagues split into two divisions, each major league realigned into three divisions—East, Central, and West. In each league, the three-division alignment added another division champion and a "wild card" team into the playoff fold. The thought of a team finishing second in a five-team division and eventually winning the World Series frosted the blood of many old-school purists.[10]

With baseball attendance in 1994 at record levels, owners contended that player salaries were driving them (particularly the so-called "small market" teams) into bankruptcy. Baseball owners wanted revenue sharing and a player salary cap in the negotiation of the next basic agreement. However, any discussion of a salary cap met with adamant refusal by the iron-solid player's union. Both parties were at an impasse. On August 12, players went on a strike that was baseball's equivalent of Armageddon. The strike of 1994-95 canceled a World Series for the first time since 1904 and nearly saw the 1995 season open with replacement players. As such, a curtailed 144-game schedule was employed in 1995.

Nationwide dissatisfaction, by the fan base, as a result of the strike, eroded attendance and TV ratings in 1995. What might have aided baseball's recovery in 1996 was the same prescription that came to the rescue in 1920: the home run. Master blasters like Mark McGwire, Juan Gonzalez, and Junior Griffey made assaults on Roger Maris' exulted 61 home runs. McGwire not only eclipsed Maris in 1998—he shattered it with 70. Sammy Sosa's 66 round-trippers that same year further proved that no home run record is ever going to be safe in the upcoming years. And, Barry Bonds further added to pitcher's woes and upped the ante with a staggering 73 circuit clouts in 2001.

The period's popularity among fans and ability to overcome scandal, strike, dissatisfaction with jaded players, and even economic recession can be credited to the exciting big-bang style of offense.

The effects of lowered pitcher mounds, narrower strike zones, and a newly-introduced cowhide covered ball, finally pushed the advantage to the batters starting in the 1977 season. The National League saw home run productivity jump from 1,113 in 1976 to 1,631 the following year. Leading the onslaught was the Reds' George Foster and his 52 blasts. With the additional factors of the DH-rule and another round of expansion in 1977, the American League hammered out a major league record 2,013 homers.

League home run records were again set in 1987, when a monstrous 2,634 homers were struck in the American League. National League sluggers also contributed 1,824 homers that year to break their 1970 record. But, that was merely a harbinger. In 1996, homers flew at a record total of 4,962. The fallout also saw a new seasonal record (257 by the Orioles) and a record 82 players who hit 20 or more with 14 individuals who hit 40 or more. In 2000, the National League broke the 3,000 HR barrier with 3,005. The organizational all-time record for home runs was also set in 2000 with 5,693.

While home runs were being hit in unheard of numbers, the stolen base also achieved a renaissance. Rickey Henderson set all-time (1,370 and counting) and single season (130) stolen base records. Vince Coleman of the Cardinals set a rookie record with 110 steals and became the first player ever to purloin 100 or more bases in three consecutive seasons. Otis Nixon, Marquis Grissom, and Kenny Lofton are other prominent base thiefs of this era.

---

[10] The wild-card Florida Marlins won the World Series in 1997.

Batting averages have also climbed steadily. Since 1998, organizational batting averages have topped .270. Twice, with George Brett's .390 in 1980 and Tony Gwynn's .394 in 1994, did players make runs at the elusive .400 batting average.

With all the offensive pyrotechnics, one must wonder what happened to pitching. Indeed, seasonal earned run averages skyrocketed in both leagues. With the advantage back to the hitters, many theories abound. I offer the following compilation:

1. **Watered Down Pitching** - This is not surprising, since the media seems to have embraced this conclusion, but it is generally accompanied by a lack of evidence. There are more runs, so the pitchers must be lousy. Subconsciously, this relates to the old notion that "Pitching is 90 percent of baseball." When the Baby Boomers and older generations pine about the game of late-1960s/early-1970s [when a run was a run], you rarely hear it mentioned that the hitters were lousy. Using the assumption that pitching is watered-down, we would still expect the best pitchers in the game today to stack up well against the best of recent years. Mark Amour analyzed this hypothesis by comparing ERA's of the 15th-ranked pitcher over the past 30 years:

YR	AL PITCHER	TEAM	ERA	NL PITCHER	TEAM	ERA
1969	Nagy	BOS	3.11	Jenkins	CHI	3.21
1979	Comer	TEX	3.68	Shirley	SD	3.38
1989	K. Brown	TEX	3.35	M. Maddux	CHI	2.95
1999	Finley	ANA	4.43	Bottenfield	STL	3.97

This table indicates trends that even the upper-shelf pitchers are giving up more runs. The 15th best pitcher in each league in 1999 gave up nearly 1/3 more earned runs than his counterpart did 30 years earlier. Moreover, 1969 was an expansion year. Other than a Pedro Martinez or Randy "Big Unit" Johnson, it seems that hitters are feeding off all pitchers—good, bad, and ugly.

Add to the mix the fact that some of the best pitchers are relegated to closer roles as set-up men or closers. That is the modern-day strategy, after all. Managers are taking quality innings away from moundsmen, well-suited to tossing 200 or so innings as the team's #2 starters, as they are throwing just 80 innings a year as the ace reliever.

2. **Smaller Ballparks** - Three ballparks (Astros Field, Pac Bell Park, and Camden Yards) have outfield fences less than the major league rulebook minimum specification of 325 feet. Yes, there are Comericas and Safecos in the mix, but future ballparks will be getting smaller, not bigger. Big hitters in small parks equates to the crowd-pleasing, ESPN-appeasing home runs

3. **Smaller Strike Zone** - If the umpires called the strike zone in the rulebook, offense would decrease. The knee-high and letter-high strikes are just not called anymore. It seems as if today's strike zone is from the mid-thigh to just above the belly button. This causes pitchers to get behind in the count and have no recourse but to throw one into the batter's wheelhouse.

4. **Larger Players** - Athletes in all sports are getting larger, but baseball is different in that increased strength and power favors the hitter. Yes, more pitchers throw in the high-90s these days and strikeouts are more prevalent. However, arm mechanics and physical limitations of the elbow and shoulder joints pretty much precludes that we will ever have a 110-MPH pitcher without his arm flying off. Hitters do not face these potential injuries, allowing the ball to be hit harder and further. Hitters work out with weights nearly year-round. As Jim French explained, neither he (nor anyone on the Senators) ever lifted a weight since no one knew of the benefits.

5. **Decreased Premium on Defensive Skill** - This is both real (defensive skill is easier to find) and perceived (managers consider defense less when making personnel decisions). Throughout baseball history, the importance of tangible defense skills has continually decreased. Gloves are bigger, fields are more symmetrical, and balls are perfect. Defense is easier to play, and therefore there is less premium on defensive skill. Do you think a career .175 hitter like Ray Oyler would be a starter today?

    Even at the skill positions, managers have more freedom. Hank Aaron, Mickey Mantle, Willie Mays, and Carl Yastrzemski all played middle infield in the minor leagues. Were they to come up today, some of them might have continued to play the infield. Conversely, if Alex Rodriguez (who is larger than the above players) would have begun his career in the 1950s, wouldn't he have been an outfielder?

6. **Harder Baseballs** - One player interviewed thought today's balls are hard as rocks compared to the balls he swung at in the 1980s. While scientists claim the compression tests are inconclusive, the Costa Rican ball of today is probably wound tighter than the Haitian ball of previous years.

The great Dodgers' and Washington Senators' slugger Frank Howard blasted 172 home runs from 1967-1970, an era of dominant pitching. When asked if he could hit 70-80 long balls today, he flatly states he didn't think so. Howard credits today's hitters as being physically superior and in better condition than players of his time. He admitted that the modern game's team pitching staffs are definitely thin. However, Howard does feel that the economic windfall, through job opportunities for more players and organizational personnel, is good for the game.

Surprisingly, with all the hitting going on in this period, there were a number of players who hit below .200 for their career. Between the years 1977 to 1995, 32 of 1,979 players, with 200 plate appearances, hit below .200 lifetime. The majority were catchers; but there are a sampling from all positions.

"Hitting is an art, but not an exact science."

-Rod Carew

Snake Man
Bob Davis, C
1952-

Once asked above his favorite hobbies, Bob Davis did not hesitate and listed snake hunting. Bob probably had an easier time with rattlers than with curveballs, as judged by his career .197 batting average. Perhaps, the snakes didn't bite as hard as some of the breaking pitches. A catcher, who polished benches throughout most of his career, Davis played with three expansion teams but lacked a solid bat to be an everyday player.

A sixth-round draft pick of the San Diego Padres in 1970, Robert John Eugene Davis was a veritable Mickey Cochrane in the low minors. With Tri-Cities in 1971, Davis tore up Northwest League pitching, batting a stellar .328 and leading the league with 14 home runs and 83 runs batted in (in just 296 at bats).

Despite reporting into training camp without Triple-A experience, Bob Davis became the Padres' starting catcher for opening day, 1973. His elation was short lived, as Davis was back in the minors after just five games and an .091 batting average.

That same year, for the fifth straight season since their inception, the Padres finished in last place. Unable to draw fans, owner C. Arnholt Smith had all but closed the deal to sell the team to a buyer who would eventually move them to Washington, D.C. The move seemed so inevitable that the club packed everything for shipping. The Topps Card Group printed the Padres' 1974 baseball cards with the team name, "Washington." In the eleventh hour, however, McDonald's magnate Ray Kroc stepped in to purchase the team and kept it in San Diego. Kroc also brought his unorthodox style of management to the team. During the 1974 home opener, the Padres were getting shellacked by the Houston Astros, 9–2. Commandeering the ballpark's public-address system in the eighth inning, the "Burger King" began to berate the team as if they were a bunch of fry cooks. Kroc's tirade went like this:

> Ladies and gentleman, I suffer with you [a streaker runs out on the field]. Get that streaker out of here! Throw him in jail! [Moments after security hauled off the streaker, the crowd cheering wildly]…I have some good news and some bad news. The good news is you loyal fans of San Diego have outstripped Los Angeles. They had 31,000 on opening night. We have almost 40,000. God Bless you! The bad news is that I've never seen such stupid ball playing in all my life!

Lucky for Bob Davis who missed out on the public humiliation, as he was playing in the minors. Ray Kroc did spend some of his burger billions to build the team. Dave Winfield started in 1973. Later, Hall of Famers Willie McCovey, Rollie Fingers, and Gaylord Perry joined the team. Consequently, home attendance improved and so did the Padres.

In 1975, Bob Davis had an outstanding year with Hawaii of the Pacific Coast League. By mid-July, Davis was batting .329 with 69 RBI before being called up for the rest of the campaign by the Padres. He was a member of the Pacific Coast League and Topps' Triple-A All-Star teams.

From 1975 to 1977, Bob Davis backed up Freddie Kendall behind the plate. The Oklahoman had a decent year in 1975, batting a career-high .234 in 43 games. In an August 22 match-up against the Phillies, Davis produced a 3-hit game. The Padres, as a team, also had something to celebrate about that year. For the first time in their existence, the Padres lost last place, finishing in 4th with a 71–91 record.

In 1976, Bob Davis had the honor of again being the starting catcher on the rite of opening day. Aside from scoring a run and delivering an RBI, Davis caught a gem of a game from Randy Jones. Jones tossed a no-hitter through five innings before settling for an 8–2 knockout of Atlanta. Davis caught several of Jones' fine efforts during his 22–14, Cy Young Award-winning season. Bob Davis' stick work yielded .205 over 51 games.

For the 1977 season, Bob decided that a new hairstyle might help his batting. Going with a frizzed coiffure, he immediately caught the attention of Padres' announcer and malaprop king Jerry Coleman. During a game, Coleman noted, "Bob Davis is wearing his hair different this year, short and with curls, like Randy Jones wears. I think you call it a Frisbee." Davis' pie-pan flying disk frizz hairstyle didn't help. He batted just .181 in 1977. Nevertheless, on May 15, Davis was Samson for a day against the Phillies, hitting his first big league home run off Steve Carlton.

The year 1978 would be Bob Davis' final season with San Diego. At 84–78, the team had their first-ever winning record. Davis played in 19 games for the Padres. He got the chance to catch a few of Gaylord Perry's moistened deliveries. Perry went on to win 21 games and cop the second Cy Young Award for San Diego in three years.

Before the start of the 1979 season, Bob Davis became a supplemental draft pick of the Toronto Blue Jays. That year, he backed up Rick Cerone, the team's catcher since their inception in 1977. Davis must have had trouble adjusting to junior circuit pitching; he batted just a buck-twenty-four in 34 games. The only thing more atrocious than Bob Davis' batting average that year was the Blue Jays themselves; they finished 53–109. Fortunately, the Blue Jays weren't berated by their team owner on the public address system. However, the Blue Jays' record certainly qualified as "stupid ball playing." To make things worse for suffering Toronto fans, they couldn't even drown their sorrows at the ballpark. Old Exhibition (nicknamed "Prohibition") Stadium did not allow alcohol.

In 1980, Davis split catching duties with Ernie Whitt and appeared in 91 games for Toronto. He hit .216 with 4 home runs and 19 RBI. He also amassed 11 doubles enroute to a decent .321 slugging average. Though the Jays finished, again, in last place, their record improved by fourteen games.

For 1981, the Blue Jays decided on Ernie Whitt as their catcher of the future. They also signed cagey veteran Buck Martinez to be the second-string backstop. Bob Davis, the odd man out, was quietly shipped to the California Angels. Davis played just one game with the Halos—going 0-for-2, his last game in the majors.

Given enough playing time, Bob Davis could have improved his hitting and he apparently had some mileage left, based on his relatively solid 1980 performance. Unfortunately, Davis toiled for San Diego and Toronto, two fledging teams undergoing growing pains. Still, anybody who is an eight-year veteran by the age of 29 has accomplished something.

Dangerous Dan
Dan Briggs, 1B-OF
1952-

Serious fans of the television series Mission Impossible recall that before Jim Phelps, Dan Briggs was the original leader of the IMF team. With a career batting average of .195, each at bat for first baseman/outfielder Dan Briggs could have been considered a "mission impossible." In actuality, however, this ballplayer achieved degrees of success in the minors, majors, and even in international baseball.

The Danny Briggs story begins in the wine country of northern California. A heralded pitcher and first baseman out of Sonoma High School, Dan garnered honors as 1970 Topps' High School All-American. He was also the 1970 San Francisco Bay Area Player of the Year. The California Angels selected Briggs in the second round of the 1970 major league draft.

Though he pitched well after a brief stint in the minors (2–0 with a 1.29 ERA in 1970), through the urging of his coaches, Briggs gave up the pitcher's mound to concentrate on being a position player. Dan progressed well through the Angels' farm system, batting over .300 at every level. In 1975, after batting .323 with the Halos' Pacific Coast League affiliate in Salt Lake City, he was called up to Anaheim for the final month of the 1975 season. Dan Briggs batted .226, his major league best, in 13 games that year. His first home run was a two-run shot off Steve Busby of the Kansas City Royals.

In 1976, Dan Briggs split his time between first base and the outfield. That year, he counted a career best 53 base hits while batting .214 with one homer and 14 RBI. Briggs recalled a memorable moment with his throwing arm that season. While playing the outfield for one of the first times in his major league career, Dan gunned down Carlton Fisk at home plate while trying to tag-up from third on a fly ball. Legendary announcer Dick Enberg, then a broadcaster for the Angels, was forced to eat his words after announcing, "this will score Carlton Fisk," on the assumed sacrifice fly.

During a game near the end of the 1976 season, the Angels were being beaten rather handily. To avoid using up any more pitchers, manager Norm Sherry summoned Dan Briggs out of the dugout and into the bullpen to start warming up for mop-up duty. Enthralled with this once-in-a-lifetime chance, Briggs sprang into action, adrenaline pumping, fastballs crackling in his catcher's mitt, curveballs breaking sharply. Dan flashed back to his glory days at Sonoma High while tossing in the bullpen. As cruel fate would have it, the Angels scored several runs, but not enough to take the lead. Norm Sherry changed his mind about pitching Dan Briggs, much to the latter's great disappointment. Briggs' major league pitching career ended where it had started—in the bullpen.

The following season, Briggs batted an anemic .162 in his final stint with the Angels. However, he did accomplish an extraordinary fielding feat at first base when he made two unassisted double plays in a single game. This rare double-double play has only happened twice since: Dave Kingman in 1982 while with the Mets and by the White Sox's Dave Martinez in 1997.

When Briggs played for the Angels, they were largely an unsuccessful team. Despite their failings, pitcher Nolan Ryan dominating the opposition with his blazing fastball and unhittable curves. A plague of Ryanitis befell the American League during those years, as numerous opposing batters inexplicably fell ill on the days when Ryan pitched. In one game, Dan Briggs recalls catcher Andy Etchebarren getting an intentional walk signal from manager Dick Williams. When Etchebarren approached the mound, to tell Ryan to issue a free pass, Nolan gave the veteran backstop such a cold stare that Etchebarren returned to his squat without a word ever said. Nolan Ryan proceeded to strike out the batter.

In a story Dan told to author Mike Shannon, Briggs recounted a visit to 1600 Pennsylvania Avenue, resulting from being a teammate of a luminary such as Nolan Ryan. Due to many baseball fans on President Jimmy Carter's staff, including Press Secretary Jody Powell, they all wanted to meet Nolan Ryan. As it turned out, Ryan became ill, but second baseman Jerry Remy, Briggs, and several others went anyway. Surprised by their easy entry into the White House, the Angels' troupe wandered around, and saw the president hunt for a pencil, before eventually entering the Cabinet Room. Remy, a voracious reader of President Nixon's Watergate affair, stood at the podium, imitating Nixon speaking. Later, the group foraged through trashcans. "When one of the secretaries asked what we were doing, we said we were looking for the missing tapes that exonerated Nixon." The silliness continued when the group sat in on a press conference concerning the Panama Canal. Briggs actually raised his hand, but wasn't called on. The ballplayer was prepared to ask, "We don't need it anyway, do we, since all our ships won't fit through there?"

Dan Briggs mentions fabled manager Dick Williams as one of his great early influences in the big leagues. Briggs learned early on that you could gain Williams' favor, "if you played the game the way he wanted it played. He loved players who could execute fundamentals." When Briggs won a spring training game with a nicely placed suicide squeeze bunt, Dick Williams ran out of the dugout and hugged Dan as if he just won game seven of the World Series with a Grand Slam. Likewise, Briggs recalls the discomfort of making a gaffe with Williams in observance. In a game against the Red Sox, big George Scott hit a bouncing grounder to Briggs at first, who let it carom off his chest for an error. When the inning was over, Dick Williams had a word with Dan that went something like this:

> Williams: "Dan, would you have made that play [fielded the ball] in Idaho Falls [Briggs' Rookie League team]?"
> Briggs: "Yes Skip."
> Williams: "And would you have made that play in El Paso [his AA team]?"
> Briggs: "Yes Skip."
> Williams: "How about Salt Lake City [his AAA team]? Bet you would have made that play in Salt Lake City."

Briggs: "Yes Skip."
Williams: "Well miss another like that and you'll be back there."

In 1978, playing with the Triple-A Portland Beavers in the Cleveland Indians organization, Dan tore up the Pacific Coast League with 20 homers, 42 doubles, 109 RBI, 286 total bases, and a .330 batting average. Portland was loaded with talent that year. Former Indians and A's catcher Ron Hassey and oft-traveled reliever Larry Andersen were Briggs' teammates. According to Dan, Andersen may have been one of the greatest practical jokers ever. While at a crowded airport terminal and wanting a seat, Larry Andersen sneaked the public address system away from airport employees and announced to the passengers that their flight had moved to another gate. A typical prank for a man quoted to say, "You can only be young for just a short time, but you can be immature all your life."

Dan Briggs received a late-season cup o' coffee with Cleveland in 1978. The Boston Red Sox were struggling to stay ahead of the resurgent New York Yankees in the American League East. Both teams had late-season series with the Tribe. Briggs and the Indians reveled in playing the role of the spoilers. Against the BoSox on September 13, Dan Briggs hit a triple off Dennis Eckersley, later scoring the game-winning run in the 2–1 Indians triumph. In the very same game, he made a spectacular diving catch in the outfield, still featured in some baseball highlight videos.

In the Yankees' series, Briggs swatted a late-inning homer on September 22 to give Cleveland an 8–7 victory. In the next game, a 10–1 Indians' rout, Briggs made a heads-up play. Standing on third base, Dan deliberately let a Thurman Munson pickoff throw hit him on the hip. The ball rolled away and he came in to score. On his next at bat, the fiercely competitive Munson called for nothing but curveballs from Dick Tidrow. Briggs recalls, "Each one of those curves must have broken 30 feet, and every time I swung and missed, Munson shook his fist in the air and screamed, 'Yeah!' like the Yankees had just won the World Series."

Briggs takes great delight in claiming had he not helped defeat Boston with his triple, the Sox may have won that game. As a result, Boston would have captured the American League East flag by one game. No famous one-game playoff with the Yankees. No Bucky Dent nor Brian Doyle post-season heroics.

Dan Briggs enjoyed his finest major league season with the 1979 San Diego Padres. That season, the mustachioed lefty appeared in 104 games, scoring 34 times, bashing eight home runs, and driving in 30, all more than his other six seasons combined. Briggs supplied most of the dynamite in an 11–3 demolition of Chicago on June 4, accounting for a pair of runs and three RBI, including a home run.

Briggs' biggest thrill that year was hitting a game-tying home run against the Los Angeles Dodgers. Especially satisfying was the fact that Dodger skipper Tommy Lasorda managed Briggs while playing winter ball in the Dominican Republic. "He has a style you could take or leave," Briggs said about Lasorda, "but his understanding of the game, especially the moves and decisions he made in the 1981 World Series, are pure genius." Perhaps not as personally satisfying, but still quite amusing to Dan that year was witnessing the antics of the famous San Diego Chicken mascot.

During the 1980s, Dan Briggs hardly had time to set his cap and glove down. First, it was off to Montreal with infielder Billy Almon in an exchange for Dave Cash. In nearly any other year in the tortured history of the Expos, Dan would have seen lots of playing time. Unfortunately for Briggs, the Expos played good ball in the early 1980s and boasted Andre Dawson and Warren Cromartie in the outfield. Dan spent the entire 1980 season with the powerhouse Triple-A Denver Bears.

Briggs had an attention-grabbing year with the 1980 Bears. Not only did Dan hit .316, but he played on probably one of the best assemblages of minor league talent in the last 30 years. The 92–44 squad featured five eventual major leaguers: speedster Tim Raines; and sluggers Tim Wallach, Dave Hostetler, and Randy Bass. Bobby Ramos rounded out the group.

His 1981 campaign in mile-high Denver was even better. Briggs hit .314 and belted 22 home runs. Furthermore, he led the American Association with 110 RBI. Finally earning a trip to Canada, Dan rejoined Dick Williams for a short stay with the Montreal Expos. It was the only postseason for the Expos and the only time Dan Briggs played for a winning major league ballclub. Dan offered one observation about the fans of Montreal that may explain their present-day problems. "All the time I was there, I never saw a fan catch a foul ball."

Briggs' final major league stop was to the Chicago Cubs in 1982. Briggs developed sort of a cult following as the last man on the bench. But the 48-game trial with the Cubs, mostly as a pinch-hitter, ended with a thud—just six hits in 48 at bats. The Wrigley Field faithful could only sigh.

His major league career concluded, Dan Briggs' playing days were far from over. His career then shifted to Japan, where he played with the Yakult (Tokyo) Swallows of the Central League for two seasons. His Japanese League career statistics, respectable enough, as quite modest according to Briggs. Yet, he still found his time there one of the greatest experiences of his life. Unlike most *gaijin* (foreigners), whom Japanese teammates and fans generally treat with scorn, Briggs found his experiences quite positive. It helped that the Yakult team was far more acclimated to American culture than the other Japanese teams. In fact, they held spring training in Yuma, Arizona each year. One interesting item in Briggs' 1983 statistics: nine times he made it to first the hard way—hit by a pitch. A high total in the Japanese Central League that year; it also supports Chuck Manuel's theory that the native Japanese find it tacitly acceptable to throw at *gaijin*. Upon his arrival in Japan, Briggs was quickly taken aback by the long grueling workouts that the Japanese coaches levied upon the players. "The Japanese believed in working the players to death during practice," Briggs said. "But for most of the players, it was really fake work, otherwise you would burn out early. Even before a game, they wanted you to take a hundred swings at batting practice. You ever try going to bat in a game after a hundred swings? Your arms get pretty tired."

Dan's *gaijin* teammate with Yakult was a Latino outfielder named Bobby Marcano, who died of cancer a few years ago. Though Bobby never played major league ball, he is one of Japan's all-time batting leaders with a career .287 batting average in eleven years. Briggs recalls being Marcano's neighbor in a Tokyo apartment. Marcano's English was marginal, so Dan spoke to Bobby in Spanish, which he learned while playing winter ball in the Dominican Republic. To complete this modern day Tower of Babel, Bobby Marcano's children, having been born in Japan, spoke mostly Japanese.

Bobby Marcano and Dan Briggs were once special guests at a Las Vegas-style nightclub that sat a thousand people. Both players were to sing karaoke to the packed club. Briggs remembers Bobby Marcano having a beautiful voice. The club went wild after Marcano offered perfect renditions of several Julio Iglesias' songs. Now it was Dan's turn. He sang *When the Saints Go Marching In*. According to Dan, both the saints and the audience were holding their ears as his singing career lasted all of one song.

During his baseball tour of Japan, Dan's father visited him. The elder Briggs, a Navy veteran, went to nearby Yokusuka Naval Base, curious to ascertain the whereabouts of some locals he met when his ship arrived there during the Korean War. Incredibly, some of the same men were still working at the shipyard 33 years later.

After his two-year hitch in Japan, Dan Briggs returned to the States with the New York Yankees' organization. The Yankees had recently cleaned house of veteran ballplayers in their Triple-A ranks, so Briggs was an ideal fit to their decimated farm system. Though he played with the Bronx Bombers during spring training, Briggs saw no vacancies at first base with Don Mattingly on the squad. Dan did become an International League All-Star first baseman for the Columbus Clippers in 1984 and 1985, his final season of professional ball. Dan Briggs' 15 HR, 71 RBI, and .285 average led the way to a 1984 pennant for the Clippers.

Though never actually playing a game for the Yankees, Dan Briggs did the next best thing. When the Yankees visited Columbus to play their annual exhibition game early in the 1985 season, New York had just lost their first three games of the year to the Red Sox. Thanks to Dan Briggs, the Clippers did nothing to salve the Yankees' losing ways. In the exhibition, Dan Briggs drove in four runs with a double and a home run as Columbus pounded New York 14–5. The game must have been a wake-up call for the Yankees, who ended up finishing the season 97–64.

Following his playing days, Briggs became a teacher for baseball clubs around the globe. A natural for the position, Briggs had played ball all over the United States, Canada, the Dominican Republic, and Japan. As a baseball coach and consultant for Major League Baseball International, Inc., Dan has worked with the national baseball teams of Australia, New Zealand, Slovenia, Austria, Germany, Finland, Norway, and Russia. Dan Briggs and other "baseball missionaries" earn the position based on their reputations as people vice their batting averages. According to Steve Baker, vice president of market development for Major League Baseball International, "We look for guys who, of course, played in the majors, but were also known as ambassadors of sports." Baker adds, "We want former players that can represent themselves and major league baseball in the best possible way…we just look for good people."

In that capacity, a unique demonstration of baseball diplomacy occurred in 1996. A team of former major leaguers matched-up against an All-German baseball team in Bonn. Retired players, such as Briggs, Ron Pruitt, Vance Law, Wayne Gross, Ron Leflore, George Vukovich, Mick Mahler, Len Barker and John Stuper were members of the U.S. team. A crowd of over 4,000 watched the Germans defeat the Americans by a score of 7–4.

In addition to his international work, Briggs frequently uses his expertise as a clinic instructor for amateur and professional clients. Briggs also runs the Big League Baseball School, near Columbus, Ohio, along with ex-pitcher John Pacella. Pacella, who holds a career pitching record of 4–10 over six major league seasons, mostly with the Mets, is probably best known for his ball cap falling off every time he threw a pitch.

Dan Briggs, a California Berkeley attendee, served as head baseball coach at Ohio's Denison University from 1990 to 1999. A Division III school, highly regarded for its academics, Briggs forged a fairly successful nine at Denison. His 1993 team, at 20–18, was the finest team in the school's history. Still, not too many were going to confuse them with Arizona State. "We don't have too much [major league caliber] talent at this level. But the kids are a great bunch and they play hard," Briggs said. "I have some situations that your higher-level coaches don't have to worry about. Like, what are you going to do when your starting shortstop tells you he has to miss practice to attend a poetry class."

Recalling his education as a baseball mentor, Briggs comments:

> My approach to the fundamentals, strategies, and discipline embodies those skills I learned during my professional playing career. I can count at least 15 current and former major league managers for whom I've been fortunate to play. [These include] Tommy Lasorda, Jeff Torborg, Dick Williams, Dave Garcia and Jimy Williams, to name a few. I've seen the whole spectrum of communication levels, coaching strategies, and disciplinary systems.

Although he has accomplished many things in professional baseball, Dan Briggs remains pragmatic about his career in the major leagues. "At that [major league] level, bat discipline is so important. I would go through a season trying out four different stances. You can't do that against major league pitching. It didn't help when I would sit on the bench for weeks at a time. You need the at bats to get into a rhythm."

Dan Briggs remarked on what could have been when discussing his pitching: "I think I could have made my real mark in the majors had I stayed a pitcher. I could throw in the 90s. Of course, who knows what would have happened? I could have blown my arm out."

Some players, such as outfielder J. R. Phillips have been described as Four-A hitters. Their loud batting dominated Triple-A pitching yet oddly become silent at the major league level. Dan Briggs, with his excellent minor league career totals—147 home runs, 848 runs batted in, and an outstanding .294 batting average, never quite duplicated these figures in "The Show."

Most sub-Mendoza Line first basemen and outfielders have careers lasting as long as a Hollywood marriage. Dan Briggs, however, combined many intangibles to scratch out seven years of major league existence. With decent power, a cannon for an arm, and lots of hustle, his career hardly self-destructed in five seconds. And, Dan Briggs' contributions as a teacher, mentor, and baseball ambassador cannot be measured.

The Thief
Larry Murray, OF
1953-

The first base runner intently studies every nuance in a pitcher's delivery—his hands at the set, his leg kick, the pitcher's eyes spying him across a shoulder (or nearly staring straight at him from lefthanded hurlers). Keenly aware of the count on the batter, the opposing catcher's arm strength, and his own coach's signal, the runner deliberately takes a lead off his base. Confident, daring baserunners stray out further, exercising bold, springly steps. Then, with his mind believing in his own success, instinct takes over—the runner dashes to second.

A Chicago native, born on April Fool's Day in 1953, Larry "Slick" Murray took great delight in fooling opposing catchers in the minors, stealing as many as 62 bases in the Florida State League in 1974. Larry also lead the Eastern League with 92 runs scored at West Haven in 1976, helping the club to a first place finish and a sweep of Trois Rivieres.

Outfielder Larry Murray played in the majors from 1974 to 1979, parts of three years each with the New York Yankees and the Oakland Athletics. While not too many people confuse Larry Murray with Eddie Murray, they both had something in common other than identical surnames. Both were switch-hitters. However, unlike Eddie Murray who hit well enough to be a Hall of Fame shoe-in, Larry Murray owned a paltry .177 career batting average. Yet, Murray's 20 career stolen bases are the most by any below .200 hitter over the last 90 years.

In 1974, the speedster earned a very brief look from the New York Yankees. In his first two call-ups, Murray played in a dozen ball games, but batted only twice and scored two runs. Larry logged some time with the 1976 Bronx Bombers in their first pennant-winning season since 1974.

Halfway through his major league career, Murray became part of a big trade early in the 1977 season. The Yankees sent Murray, pitcher Dock Ellis, and infielder Marty Perez to the Oakland Athletics for hurler Mike Torrez. The trade was a crucial move for the Yanks as Torrez became a linchpin in the Yankees' back-to-back championships in 1977-1978. While Oakland owner Charles Finley apparently got hornswaggled in the deal, the change of scenery worked out fine for Larry Murray. He caught a break and played 90 games that season for the moribund Athletics. While a .179 batting average prevented Murray from getting on base all that often, he was quite effective when he did. In 14 attempted steals, Murray made good a dozen times. He also enjoyed a splendid season as a flycatcher, making just a single error.

How bad were the 1977 Athletics? Last place bad. Finley had dismantled the team that won three straight World Series titles from 1972-1974 and five consecutive division championships. This resulted in Oakland's free fall. The club even finished behind the expansion Seattle Mariners, whom were playing in their inaugural season.

Larry Murray's swan song in the majors would be his busiest. Murray scored personal highs in every batting category, including two of his three career home runs and 20 of 31 RBI. Yet, his lowly .186 average made him most expendable. Rare for a team to sport a right fielder with such a weak stick, the stark reality of the Athletics talent-poor ball club meant a 54-108 finish in 1979. For Oakland, the A in A's meant "Awfuls" and not Athletics. So penurious was Finley, the team did not even have television or radio coverage. When the commissioner's office ordered Finley to support radio coverage of the team, he complied by broadcasting the games over a tiny AM station in Berkeley. The transmitted pumped out a radiated signal of just ten watts. No matter, not many fans listened anyway to this shell of a team.

Despite the disastrous campaign of 1979, the A's starting left fielder was a rookie hailing from Murray's hometown of Chicago. That first year player led the Athletics with 33 stolen bases. A few years later, he would practically redefine the stolen base as an offensive weapon, swipe 130 sacks in a season, and garner over 3,000 hits. Eventually, this rookie would play with Oakland, New York, Toronto, San Diego, and lead the universe in stolen bases. His name was Rickey Henderson.

Because of Henderson, and an inability to hit much, Larry Murray never surfaced again in a major league uniform. Too bad. Beginning in 1980, Oakland began a resurgence. Just two years after their 1979 debacle, Oakland recaptured the American League West.

Magic Mitt
Luis Pujols, C
1955-

The Dominican Republic shares the Caribbean island of Hispaniola with politically volatile Haiti. Her chief exports to the U.S. include ferronickel, sugar, gold, coffee, cocoa, and major league baseball players. One can assemble quite an impressive All-Dominican team with the likes of pitchers Juan Marichal, Mario Soto, and Joaquin Andujar; outfielders George Bell and the Alou Brothers Felipe, Matty, and Jesus; infielders Tony
Fernandez, Pedro Guerrero, and Julio Franco; and catcher Tony Pena. Three of today's greatest players, slugging outfielders Sammy Sosa and Vladimir Guerrero, and pitcher deluxe Pedro Martinez also hail from the Dominican Republic. The below .200 team features another native from that part of the world. He is Luis Pujols.

A member of the Houston Astros (1977-1983), Kansas City Royals (1984), and Texas Rangers (1985), Pujols was a splendid defensive receiver with a howitzer for a throwing arm. In seven of his nine years in the big leagues, Pujols fielded .990 or better. With the bat, unfortunately, Pujols propped up the old baseball phase, "He can't hit his own weight." Pujols weighed 195 pounds. Even in the minors, Pujols wasn't much of a stickman, batting just .242.

Born and raised in Santo Domingo, the capital of the Dominican Republic, Luis Pujols starred in high school when he caught the eye of big league scouts. He signed his first professional contract with the Astros in 1973 at the age of seventeen. That same year, Pujols established himself as a top-notch defensive catcher, as he led Appalachian Leaguers with three double plays. Pujols' rise through the bushes included also leading this league in putouts and assists in 1974. The next season, Pujols earned selection as a Midwest League All-Star.

Pujols made it to the majors in 1977 as a late-season call-up. In 1978, Houston played musical catchers all season long with Bruce Bochy, Joe Ferguson, Reggie Baldwin, and Ed Herrmann. Yet, Pujols ended up leading the Astros in games caught with 56, quite surprising since he spent nearly half his time with Triple-A Charleston. Although Pujols suffered through a silent .131 batting average, he did slam his first major league home run off Hal Dues of the Montreal Expos.

For the next five seasons, Pujols backed up Alan Ashby from 1979 to 1983. His 1980 season was a watershed in many ways. Although he batted only .199, Pujols earned career highs in games played (78), at bats (221), runs (15), hits (44), and runs batted in (20). Two of his RBI won ballgames for Houston. Near the end of the season, Luis became married right at his worksite. For the marriage, Luis donned a suit and stood upright, a bit unlike his normal working position. Pujols' marriage ceremony took place at home plate of the Houston Astrodome on September 28.

Best of all, Pujols played on one of the most memorable teams in Astros' history. Close to their first-ever first place finish, Houston appeared shattered after an end-of-season sweep at the hands of the Los Angeles Dodgers. Houston's losses forced a tie in the National League West. However, the Astros regrouped to defeat Los Angeles in a one game playoff. Luis had a role in what many baseball experts call the greatest league championship ever played: the Philadelphia vs. Houston war of 1980. This tension-filled, five-game classic featured late-inning dramatics, controversial calls, and terrific pitching duels. Showing a knack to hit Philadelphia pitching, Pujols earned the starting nod in the series' opener.

Pujols walked once in four trips to the plate in game one, won by Philadelphia 3-1. The game would be the only one played in the regulation nine innings. Alan Ashby caught game two, when the Astros evened the series by breaking a 3-3 tie with four runs in the tenth inning.

Luis Pujols caught every inning of game three, in which the Astros' pitcher Joe Niekro twirled ten scoreless knuckleball innings. Reliever Dave Smith continued the shutout and took the win as Joe Morgan's triple and Denny Walling's sacrifice fly off Tug McGraw scored the game's only run in the bottom of the eleventh. Houston was within one nail-biting win of their first ever World Series. Philadelphia, conversely, teetered on the brink of their fourth National League Championship Series loss in five seasons.

In game four, Pujols connected for a triple off Steve Carlton in the fifth inning and scored Houston's second run. His sixth inning fly ball seemingly scored Gary Woods from third to give the Astros a commanding 3-0 lead. However, on an appeal by the Phillies, Woods was called out for leaving the base too early, thus nullifying Pujols' RBI. After a painful foul tip on the ankle, Luis Pujols left the game in the eighth inning. His replacement, Bruce Bochy, was playing in his very first game of the series. In many ways, the inning proved to be a tough frame for the Astros. Philadelphia scored three tallies to take the lead. However, the Astros fought back to tie the game in the ninth inning. In the top of the tenth, the Phillies pushed across two runs—the first one by virtue of Pete Rose barreling into Bochy in a bruising home plate collision. Philadelphia prevailed 5-3.

In the final game, Pujols again squatted behind home plate. Drawing a base on balls, Pujols headed home after a double by Craig Reynolds, but was nailed on a perfect relay throw by Manny Trillo. Midway through the game, Alan Ashby replaced the banged-up Pujols. The Phillies appeared dead and buried—trailing 5-2 in the top of the eighth inning and with Astros superman Nolan Ryan on the mound. But, Philadelphia clawed their way back to send the miraculous game into extra innings. In the tenth, after Del Unser scored on Gary Maddox's tenth-inning double, Dick Ruthven held off Houston for an 8-7 decision. For the Astros, the end could not have been more bitter. For jubilant Philadelphia, winning their first pennant in thirty years, the finish equated to an unbridled celebration. The Phillies went on to win their only World Series in their 120 plus years of existence. Houston still waits their first World Series berth.

In the strike-shortened 1981 campaign, Pujols put up career bests in both batting average (.239) and fielding average (.995). He appeared in two games of the divisional playoff series against the Dodgers, going 0-for-6 in another dramatic series that went the distance. Again, Houston fell short as Los Angeles prevailed in five games. ·

Despite hitting another buck-ninety-nine batting average in 1982, Luis Pujols discovered a power surge. He blasted four of his six career homer runs that season and owned a fairly respectable .324 slugging percentage. However, Pujols did lead the National League in a dubious category: passed balls. The miscues weren't all his fault. Flutterballer Joe Niekro used Pujols as his personal catcher.

Indeed, Pujols caught some terrific pitchers with the Astros in his tenure: Niekro, J. R. Richard, Bob Knepper, and Don Sutton. All tossed baseballs in the multicolored uniforms of the Houston Astros. But the one that would stand out in Pujols' mind (and stinging palm) was the engineer of the Von Ryan Express, the remarkable Nolan Ryan. On July 16, 1982, against Pittsburgh in the Astrodome, Pujols caught Ryan as the latter proceeded to strikeout eleven. Ryan utterly dominated the hot-hitting Pirates that day. However, Ryan's finish left even his teammates in disbelief. Ryan's last four pitches were clocked at an astonishing 94 MPH. "He broke the webbing of my glove on a third strike to Dave Parker," Pujols said.

In 1983, Pujols again hit south of the Mendoza Line, but still showed a knack for the timely blow. Pujols delivered two game-winning runs batted in. By 1984, however, Pujols was back in the minors. Exchanged to Kansas City late in the 1984 season, Pujols played a scant four games in royal blue. Signed as a free agent by the Texas Rangers in 1985, Pujols caught only one game. A serious shoulder injury derailed his major league career.

Luis Pujols finished out his ball playing career in 1987 with Indianapolis, then a Triple-A outfit of the Montreal Expos. The Expos later appointed him a player-coach. In 1988, Pujols began a five-year stint as the Expos' roving catching instructor. In 1993, he made it to the parent club as an *instructeur* (Quebecois for coach) at first base. Pujols' *instructuer* days lasted eight years. From 1999 until his dismissal during the 2000 season, Pujols served as Montreal bench coach. Owner Jeffrey Loria fired Pujols against the strong wishes of manager Felipe Alou, who looked to Pujols as his right-hand man. In less than a year after Pujols' canning, Loria saw that Alou shared a similar fate.

A well-respected and versatile coach, Pujols filled in for Alou in the dugout after an ejection. Pujols taught young Chris Widger proper footwork behind the plate, and served as an interpreter for Montreal's continuing pipeline of young Latino ball playing talent.

When current pitching sensation Pedro Martinez was starting out in Montreal, the talented pitcher often had trouble with his command. Martinez would mentally self-destruct to the detriment of the team. Coach Pujols took the youngster aside and told him, "You are your own worst enemy." The pitcher took the message to heart and decided to keep a lid on his own simmering emotions. "I was always angry at myself," Martinez said. "I was trying to blow fastballs by everybody. Be a power guy. I'd miss on the inside part of the plate, hit people, get warned [by umpires], get mad. It had to stop."

Luis Pujols also managed in the Dominican Winter league. He was skipper of the Leones del Escogido (Chosen Lions) Baseball Club of Santo Domingo. Pujols led his club to a 28-20 mark in 1994 and a 23-25 mark in 1995. Starting in 2001, Pujols received another chance to manage. The Detroit Tigers hired him to be skipper of the Class Double-A Erie Seawolves of the Eastern League. Pujols guided the team to an outstanding 84-58 record and the Northern-Division regular season title. Currently living in Florida's Boynton Beach, the multi-talented Pujols is a licensed pilot as well as an avid fisherman. His regular fishing partner is none other than Felipe Alou.

With over a quarter of a century of professional baseball experience, Luis Pujols understands the minute details that helps teams win. Twice, cruel fate denied Pujols the chance of earning the biggest prize in baseball. First, as a player with Houston, and then as a coach of the 1994 Expos, favored to win the World Series in the Strike-marred 1994 season. Perhaps, someday, Pujols will get that prize.

Mr. October, Jr.
Brian Doyle, 2B
1955-

During the near century of World Series play, several very ordinary mortals have come up large in these championship games. A short list of unlikely heroes throughout the history of the Fall Classic includes Al Gionfriddo (1947), Dusty Rhodes (1954), Chuck Hiller (1962), Al Weis (1969), Rick Dempsey (1983), and Craig Counsell (1997, 2001). Perhaps, the unlikeliest of all is career .161 hitter Brian Doyle. Anytime a .220 hitter drives in a couple of runs in a World Series game, odds are that journalists will make reference to Brian Doyle—guaranteed. Brian admits that he receives "more calls that I can ever get back to," each autumn.

Nearly twenty-five years ago, Brian Doyle replaced the injured Willie Randolph at second base. In the process, Doyle became a Yankees' postseason legend. By hitting .438

with four runs scored and two batted in, Doyle helped the Yankees defeat their arch-rivals, the Los Angeles Dodgers in the 1978 World Series. Overnight, Doyle went from obscurity to sensation in the news capital of planet earth.

Brothers Denny (16 HR/237 RBI/.250 average in eight seasons with Phillies, Angels, and Red Sox), Brian, and his twin brother Blake Doyle learned the game of baseball on the lush bluegrass fields of Kentucky. While most associate Brian with the Yankees, he actually toiled for five seasons in the Texas Rangers' organization.

In 1972, Brian played his first year of professional ball with Geneva, New York of the NY-PENN League. There he hit .256 with four home runs. Doyle also led league shortstops with twenty double plays. That year, Doyle became part of baseball history by participating in the first game ever umpired by a woman. Her name was Bernice Gera. After years of emotional and volatile legal wrangling, the courts cleared the way for Gera to be an umpire. On June 24, her initial assignment would be as arbiter on the bases at Geneva's Shuron Park for a season-opening doubleheader against the Auburn Phillies.

The first three innings of Gera's debut game were uneventful, always a good sign for an umpire. However, in the fateful fourth inning, Brian Doyle inadvertently initiated a chain of events that would turn Mrs. Gera's historic game into a debacle. With Auburn's Terry Ford on second base, Geneva second baseman Jim Pascarella speared a line drive off the bat of John Dawkins for one out. Pascarella quickly pegged the ball to shortstop Brian Doyle, covering second. Doyle routinely stepped on the bag before Ford could scramble back, completing the double play. However, inexplicably, Gera outstretched her arms to signal Ford safe. Within seconds, she corrected herself (no tag was necessary because a force out was in effect) and changed her call to out. Auburn manager Nolan Campbell sprinted out from the dugout in a rage. Like a locked-on Sidewinder missile, Campbell went straight for Gera.

"He kept yelling at me and spitting the tobacco he was chewing," she recalled in an interview. "I told him I made a mistake and he said it was the second I hade made. The first was putting on my uniform." Campbell then suggested that Gera should have "stayed in the kitchen, peeling potatoes." Soon thereafter, came another first. Fed up with his antics, Bernice Gera tossed Nolan Campbell from the game, making him the first manager ever thrown out of a game by a female umpire. However, the damage to Gera's psyche was irreparable. After the 4-1 Geneva win, Bernice Gera marched into the office of the Geneva general manager Joe McDonough. "I've just resigned from baseball." She left the stadium in tears, never to umpire another game. Gera, who died of cancer in 1992, today holds a place of honor in the Baseball Hall of Fame, where her photograph, pink whiskbroom, and the uniform she wore are on display.

Brian Doyle came to the Yankees organization in 1977 (with infielder Greg Pryor and cash) in a trade for Sandy Alomar. Brian's 1978 rookie season with New York consisted of 39 games and a measly .192 average in 52 trips. Unfortunately, Doyle did not register even one extra base hit nor draw a solitary base on balls. And, he drove in zero runs. With just three strikeouts, Doyle apparently had no problem making contact. But, his contact meant that he hit the baseball right at somebody. Despite a weak bat, Doyle's defensive play at all three infield positions did not suffer. That's why he was in Yankee pinstripes in the first place. Even that was a most tenuous position. Doyle may hold some sort of frequent-flyer mileage record for a ballplayer in a single season. While shuttling back and forth between the minors and the majors, Doyle went from New York to Tacoma, Washington no less than *five times* in 1978.

After settling into New York pinstripes and getting to know all the guys, Brian Doyle unwittingly pulled off a prank against the Yankees' brain trust. The real mover and shaker behind the ruse was Yankees' center fielder Roy White and Blake Doyle. Brian Doyle told the story:

> Blake, my twin brother, broke his arm running over a catcher while playing Triple-A ball. My daughter had just been born in New York and we [The Yankees] were going out on a West Coast road trip. He had called to congratulate me and I didn't know how he had broken his arm the night before. So he and his wife came and visited. I asked him to stay with my wife and 3-year-old son, because nobody was around to stay with them. When we came back, Roy White talked Blake into coming into the [Yankee] stadium and playing me. So Blake went into the clubhouse and first went to [trainer] Gene Monahan, who asked, "Brian, what happened?" Blake said, "Well, I was carrying groceries up the steps this morning. I tripped and fell. I went to catch myself and broke my arm." So Gene said, not knowing it was my twin brother, "Well we got to go tell Billy [manager Billy Martin]." We were scheduled to play in the Game of the Week—and I was playing.
>
> So Blake, with Gene and Roy walked into Billy's office. Billy was eating a *World's Finest* Chocolate Bar. When Blake walked in with a cast all the way up to his shoulder, Billy bit down on the chocolate bar so hard, he broke his [dental] bridge. Billy said a few expletives and asked Blake what had happened to him. Again, Blake told the story of breaking his arm carrying groceries up the steps. Billy picked up the phone and called Al Rosen, who was general manager, and said, "Al! Get down here right now." In just a few minutes, Al comes walking in and Blake goes through the whole story again. And Billy goes, "Now what are we going to do? Who are we going to call up?" I walked in and said, "Yeah, but Skip, I can still play today."
>
> What was even funnier was Yogi [Berra] sitting on the couch in Billy's office and saying, "Oh, I knew it was Blake all along."

Doyle played with New York at the height of their "Bronx Zoo" era. And 1978 would prove to be their zaniest year. The Yankees owned the back pages of the *New York Post*. In July, the Boston Red Sox appeared to be in cruise control, owning a 14-game cushion over the defending World Champs by July 19. Around that time, the powder keg mixture of owner George Steinbrenner, manager Billy Martin, and outspoken slugger Reggie Jackson detonated. After Martin suspended Jackson for bunting against orders, Martin flatly went on record stating Jackson was a *born liar* and Steinbrenner was a *convicted liar*. Martin's Steinbrenner comment was a reference to the owner's illegal Presidential contributions to Richard Nixon in 1972. The term "Billy Ball," once known as a crowd-pleasing style of play on the field, now became synonymous with controversy and dissension. That was the last straw for Steinbrenner, as Martin resigned just before his inevitable firing. Bob Lemon, who had just been summarily dismissed from the White Sox, replaced Billy Martin.

Did the soft-spoken youngster Doyle feel out of place playing with some of the most controversial and outspoken assemblages of ballplayers ever? Not really. He explained: "I was the young kid. I just stayed out of the way, watched, and kept my mouth shut. It wasn't like I was a green rookie. My brother [Denny] played for nine years; he was in the big leagues when I was in the seventh grade." But, despite his attitude to stay out of the fray, Brian did try to play "enforcer" once. When Cliff Johnson and Goose Gossage traded fisticuffs in the Yankees' clubhouse, Doyle attempted to pry the combatants apart. However, as Gossage put it, Brian was quickly tossed aside like a rag doll. Doyle smartly sought for help.

After Martin's resignation, the Yankees sizzled under new helmsman Bob Lemon. Meanwhile, in Beantown, the accursed Red Sox did a major meltdown in August. Spurred by a remarkable September four-game series sweep of the Red Sox in Boston, known by suffering BoSox fans as "The Boston Massacre," New York rallied ahead of Boston. With two weeks left in the season, however, New York began their own tailspin. The Sox caught the Yankees on the final day of the regular season, forcing the first-ever divisional playoff at Fenway Park. Yankee shortstop Bucky Dent, who hit only four homers all season, lofted a fly ball that barely cleared the Green Monster for a three-run homer in the seventh inning. The Yankees, trailing 3-2 at the time, held on to win 5-4. The excruciating last out for Boston was made by Carl Yastrzemski, who popped up to Graig Nettles with runners on first and third base. Thus ended Boston's utterly tortuous season.

Brian Doyle's remarkable tale never would have transpired had Gold Glove second baseman Willie Randolph not pulled a hamstring on the penultimate day of the 1978 season. Bob Lemon wanted a platoon strategy with the lefthander Doyle and switch-hitter Fred Stanley, a .219 bat during the regular season. In an effort from being the "out man" in the lineup, Doyle worked diligently to hit the ball to the opposite field. "My strength was hitting the inside pitch, but I tried to use an inside-out swing and hit the ball to left field," Doyle explained to Ron Fimrite of *Sports Illustrated* magazine. "I got a few hits and hit .280 in the League Championship Series [against Kansas City] but basically gave myself up. The other teams figured, 'Here's this kid choking up on the bat four inches and trying to hit to the opposite field, let's bust him inside.' Then they started pitching to my strengths."

Actually, Doyle stroked .286 in the Championship Series, 2-for-7 with one RBI. Game one saw Doyle get two hits, one of which knocked in Reggie Jackson in the 5th inning. The Yankees cruised 7-1 and eventually finished off the Royals in four games.

As tumultuous as the collective personalities of the 1978 Yankees were, this 100-63 team ranks high with the greatest teams in baseball history. Standouts included outfielders Reggie Jackson, Roy White, and Mickey Rivers. Chris Chambliss played first. Graig Nettles manned third and the aforementioned Willie Randolph stood his ground at second base. Catcher Thurman Munson caught Cy Young winner Ron Guidry, who won 25 of 28 decisions with a microscopic 1.74 earned run average. Catfish Hunter and Jim Beattie both responded with one Series victory apiece and bullpen ace Goose Gossage led the league with 27 saves.

However, the true Series' busters resided in the bottom of the order in Mssrs. Doyle and Dent. Expecting not much more than solid defense from the pair, instead, the New York fans were treated to a reprise of the Maris & Mantle boys. Dent hit .417, drove in seven runs, and was proclaimed Most Valuable Player. As for Brian Doyle, he earned seven hits in 16 at bats for a .438 batting average, leading all players. Between the two, their incessant jabs led to a knockout of the Dodgers.

With the Series all square after four games, Dent and Doyle bashed three hits apiece in game five, won by the Yanks 12-2. Doyle's eighth inning single equated to the Bombers

16th single of the game, a Series record. The "Killer D's" repeated their demolition of the Dodgers in the deciding sixth affair. With the Yankees trailing 1-0 in the second inning, Brian Doyle faced Don Sutton with two runners on base. Graig Nettles resided at second and Jim Spencer stood on first base. Doyle lofted a floater just over the outstretched arm of left fielder Dusty Baker for a Nettles-scoring double. The two bagger was Doyle's first major league extra base hit. Dent singled up the middle to send Spencer and Doyle home. In the bottom of the third inning, Doyle provided defensive heroics. With a run in and two Dodgers on base, Reggie Smith ripped a grounder up the middle. Doyle backhanded the ball and flipped awkwardly, but on target, to Dent, initiating an inning-ending double play. In the sixth, Doyle provided a soft liner to center to score Lou Piniella. Dodger center fielder Rick Monday threw a bullet to the plate, but Dodger catcher Joe Ferguson fumbled the chance. With New York now ahead 4-2, Tommy Lasorda came out to yank Sutton. Bucky Dent greeted Bob Welch with a single to score Doyle. For good measure, Reggie Jackson concluded the scoring with a patented home run that Jackson admired as it left the ballpark. In the eighth, Doyle saved a run with a stop of Vic Davalillo's bouncer up the middle. With the 7-2 victory, the Yankees again were the World Champions of baseball.

At one point in the Series, Doyle stroked five straight hits and enjoyed back-to-back three hit games. Playing error-free defense as well, the media swarmed after Doyle and not Jackson. Of the crush of reporters, Doyle said, "I couldn't really move." Added Mr. October himself, "We couldn't have won it without them [Dent and Doyle]." Considering Doyle's seldom seen rookie status, it's most commendable the way he fielded his position, yet not too surprising. However, Doyle's hitting at .391 over the post-season, raised many eyebrows. Not only did Doyle account for himself well in the high-pressure stakes of post-season baseball, a venue where so many "legends" often vanish, Doyle thrived in an environment where butterflies in the belly feel more like pterodactyls.

Doyle told Ron Fimrite:

> Everybody kept asking me if I felt pressure, and when I said no, no one could believe it. The reason was because I had a wife and child across the country and had been up and down from the minor leagues five times that year. The pressure for me was meeting my monthly bills and being away from my family. When I was put on the postseason roster, I knew I was going to make more money in a month than I did in the previous five years.

Indeed, Doyle previously spent his off-seasons as a salesman at a haberdashery in Bowling Green, Kentucky. Though Doyle must have heard a million different versions of the same question, he considered a "keen focus," "preparation," and "relaxation" key elements to his successful World Series.

The remainder of Brian Doyle's major league career went by surprisingly uneventful. Unable to usurp Willie Randolph at second base, Doyle continued to play the middle infield role for two more seasons wearing Yankee pinstripes, relegated to long stretches in the dugout, as well as trips to the minors. World Series legends aren't often sent down to the bush leagues. Nor do they ride the bench often. Yet, for the realist Doyle, he kept his success in perspective and took it all in stride.

One of the funniest things Brian recalls occurred during the 1979 season. The hijinks were supplied by Rogers "Bobby" Brown, a player Brian described as having "all the tools, except the ability to hit a curveball." Eager to impress, young Brown, a switch-hitter, had already struck out three times in the game, swinging feebly on breaking pitches. In his next go around, Brown had two strikes. Easily understanding Brown's weakness, the pitcher tossed another curve. Brown swung so violently that the bat ended up hitting him solidly on the head. The unfortunate Brown had whacked himself with his own war club in the helmet so hard, that everyone in cavernous Yankee Stadium could hear the reverberation. With Brown stumbling around dazed near home plate, the Yankee dugout roared in laughter for over an hour. Pitcher Rudy May guffawed so loud, that teammates had to carry him back to the clubhouse. May had given himself a bad case of abdominal cramps.

In 1980, Brian Doyle hit his only major league home run. It was not a curveball. Len Barker of the Cleveland Indians, a flamethrower, delivered the offering. Brian pointed out that the hard-throwing Barker "supplied most of the power." Brian remembered that as he rounded second, the scoreboard lit up to announce the Yankees' 100th home run of the year. "I was digging for a triple," Brian mirthfully added. Oddly enough, Brian Doyle muscled up and hit his only double of the year the night before against Boston. "I hit the ball right off the '8' of the '385' mark on the right-center field wall. I thought that it was going out, but it wound up being a double."

Traded with Fred Stanley for pitcher Mike Morgan, Brian Doyle sported Oakland A's threads in 1981. On April 10, he pulled off the rare hidden ball trick to tag out a greatly chagrinned Glenn Adams of the Minnesota Twins. During a game against Toronto, big Otto Velez, on first, barreled into second in an attempt to break-up an apparent double-play ball. Doyle, instead of avoiding contact with the beefy Velez, tried to make the throw. The ensuing collision flipped Doyle over, and he landed headfirst, separating his shoulder. Doyle was batting .125 in 17 games at the time of the injury, without a single error in the field. Unable to gain full strength in his arm, Doyle retired in 1982 after a couple of aborted comebacks.

Today, Brian and the rest of the Doyle brothers operate a very successful baseball academy in Winter Haven, Florida, aptly known as the Doyle Baseball School. After Denny retired in 1975, the three brothers spent a couple of years planning the school. Originally envisioned as a part-time business venture, the locale was also to be a warm-weather location for the brothers to play golf in the off-season. Scheduled to open in the winter of 1978, Doyle's spectacular postseason could not have occurred with more fortuitous timing. Broadcaster Tony Kubek kept telling the nation that the positive ethic Doyle brothers were poised to open up a baseball school. "You couldn't have paid for better advertising," said Brian. "We were jammed in our very first week and by the second week, the school became a full-time job for the brothers Doyle." Now, after 24 years in operation, the school continues to do well. Most recently, the school has run classes on the grounds of the Walt Disney Sports Complex.

Brian Doyle's numbers in four big league seasons are as modest as the man. Doyle did offer that he hit .280 during the intervals in which he started two games in a row. He also hit reasonably well in the minors at .254. At every level of his professional career, Doyle put the ball in play, almost never striking out. "I never had a problem with defense.

That's for sure. That was my strength," Doyle had said on many occasions. With more chances, Doyle could have done better in the majors. His 1978 World Series wasn't some "out of body" experience as some people have claimed.

Regardless of debating the merits of Doyle's career, baseball's eternal charm truly smiled upon an unlikely lad named Brian Doyle in the fall of 1978. For a few short weeks, with the world as his witness, Doyle scooped up every grounder and made his every throw perfect. And, once at bat, pitches appeared as big as balloons. For a lifetime, Yankees' fans everywhere can relish Doyle's heroic World Series. It could not have happened to a nicer person.

Throwin' Owen
Larry Owen, C
1955-

Like Mickey Owen of 1941 World Series' infamy, Larry Owen also played catcher. Larry lasted six years and 171 games with the Atlanta Braves and Kansas City Royals. One of Larry's former coaches summarized Larry Owen this way, "Not much of a hitter, but one hell of a catcher." Indeed, Larry earned his keep being a defensive specialist behind the plate. Owen could come up with pitches in the dirt, block the plate, and possessed a bazooka for an arm. Excellent at understanding his hurlers, Owen routinely called entire games without ever having the pitcher shake off his sign.

The Clevelander enjoyed a fine college baseball career at Bowling Green University. He ranks third all-time for the Falcons in runs batted in with 132, which ties him with Jeff Groth—who went on to play football with the National Football League's New Orleans Saints. Other Bowling Green alumni to make it to the majors are Kip Young, Doug Bair, Roger McDowell (of *Seinfeld* fame), and the great Orel Hershiser.

After college, Larry became a 17th round draft pick of the Atlanta Braves in 1977. The following year, while playing Double-A ball in Savannah, Larry caught Jim Bouton, attempting to make one of his comebacks. Bouton's fastball no longer carried the zip of his Yankees' days. However, Bouton developed a knuckleball that fluttered to homeplate and made his fastball appear "sneaky-quick" and tough to hit. Bouton, no stranger to clowning, loved to pull practical jokes. With another pitcher, Roger Alexander, Jim set up an elaborate booby trap of fireworks and smoke bombs in the visitors' dugout. They lit the fuse just before the playing of the National Anthem. As soon as the visiting Nashville team, managed by Stump Merrill, returned to the dugout, it looked as if commandos ambushed them. "Merrill was so mad, he was ready to kill someone," Owen said while laughing.

Larry enjoyed some fine years defensively in the minors. In 1978, he led the Southern League in catcher putouts and assists. He repeated the feat in 1979, while in the International League.

Shortly after the settlement of the 2-month long baseball strike of 1981, Owen received a call-up to Atlanta. Thrilled to be in the majors, Owen quickly did a "Pascual Perez," the pitcher immortalized when he missed his first start because he arrived late to

Fulton County Stadium. Once Owen finally made it to Atlanta, he too had trouble negotiating the snarled gridlock and extensive road construction on the city's freeways. "It took me five years to get to Atlanta and once I got there I wondered if I was ever going to make it to the ballpark." Unfortunately, Owen's bat might have been stuck on Interstate 75. He went 0-for-16 as a rookie.

Two of Larry's minor league teammates also joined him that year, the courageous Brett Butler, who later played ball while battling cancer, and Steve Bedrosian. Owen and "Bedrock" Bedrosian formed a battery together, playing winter ball in the Dominican Republic. As pitcher and catcher, they became good friends. Larry was at Steve Bedrosian's bedside at a Dominican hospital after Bedrosian was involved in a car accident overseas.

While fine-tuning his game playing winter ball, money was literally no object to Larry Owen. Not paid terribly much to begin with, Owen earned a mixture of U.S. dollars and Dominican pesos. Like some modern day Pied Piper, Larry often tossed the pesos to the Dominican children.

After a couple of brief stays in Atlanta during the 1982 and 1983 seasons, Larry Owen owned an anemic .083 career average. But in 1985, he busted loose with his first two homers, 12 RBI, and a .239 batting average. His best game of the season was a 3-for-4 effort when he factored in four of the ten runs Atlanta scored while routing the Dodgers.

Signed as a free agent by the Royals in November 1986, Larry saw lots of action in the 1987 season. He made 76 appearances that year, primarily as a defensive replacement for starting catcher Jamie Quirk. Owen also was Charlie Leibrandt's catcher of choice. Just like Tim McCarver for Steve Carlton, Larry Owen usually caught whenever Leibrandt started. Working extensively with one of the best finesse pitchers of his time meant a lot to Larry, who regularly could get Charlie to throw his "A-Game" in this synergistic relationship.

Another Royals' teammate Larry held in the highest esteem was the Hall of Famer George Brett. Larry Owen offered an insightful look at the difference in the treatment between a .300 hitter and a .190 hitter. Even something as basic as the wood used for their baseball bats varied greatly. When the shipment of Louisville Sluggers arrived, Brett's bats would have a grain composition of 12–13 grains. A low granularity bat makes them the highest quality Hillerich & Bradsby manufactures. Brett's script signature was boldly engraved into the wood of his Sluggers. As for Larry, his bats had a grain composition of as much as 60 grains across the barrel of the bat—maybe better than particle board at Home Depot, but not by much. In lieu of a script signature, Larry's bats were simply stamped "OWEN."

Desperate for a decent-quality bat, Owen rummaged through the Royals' equipment room for a good piece of lumber. Going through George Brett's stockpile, Larry grabbed one covered in the sticky black substance, pine tar. Was it "The Pine Tar Incident" bat? At that moment, George Brett confronted Owen. George informed Larry that while the bat was once his favorite game stick, it was not the famous bat used when he hit the home run later disallowed upon the protest of Billy Martin in 1983.

Larry still owns the bat to this day. Remarkably, although the bat is black as coal from top to bottom, it contains a swath of wood, 3" in length and around $1\frac{1}{2}$" in width, that is clean, shiny, virginal-looking ash. This surface is right at the sweet spot of the bat, the handiwork of a disciplined and accomplished hitter.

Whatever club Larry used in 1987, he did some damage with it, hitting five of his eight career home runs that season. Owen and the Royals participated in a dramatic pennant race with the Minnesota Twins and Oakland Athletics for the American League West crown. One of Larry's biggest thrills was gunning down speedy Alfredo Griffin, while trying to steal second, to end the game in a Royals' victory over the A's in a key late-season match-up. The Twins prevailed by just two games over Kansas City and went on to win the World Series.

Larry Owen's final year in the big leagues came with the Royals in 1988. He did reasonably well, batting .210 and fielding a career best .989.

After his retirement from the game, Larry returned to Ohio and took a job with Franklin International, the maker of adhesives on non-lick stamps. No stranger to this firm, when not playing winter ball, Owen worked in the company's labs during his off-seasons. In today's baseball, salary structures have exploded, making off-season employment moot, and off-season conditioning vital. Larry worked his way up to corporate management of this large company. And, Larry also does television color commentary for the Ohio State University baseball team.

For Larry Owen, baseball was all about knowing your limitations and perfecting the skills that got you in there. Larry realistically realized that as a batter, he would not be another Mickey Cochrane. But, Owen understood his position and worked to be the best defensive receiver in the game. He devoted the majority of his time in perfecting his catching craft, blocking balls in the dirt, practicing proper footwork, and charging bunts. Owen always spent more time with pitchers than other players. If the pitchers were shagging fly balls, so was Larry. If a pitcher wanted to work on tossing a split-finger fastball, Larry would selflessly forego his own batting practice and catch him. Whatever the pitchers were doing, Larry stayed within earshot, learning.

The diligence paid off. Larry owns an extraordinary defensive record. His 38 assists in 1987 was the seventh-best for catchers in the American League—and he only played part time. Behind the numbers are the facts that everyone associated with the game knew—Owen could catch. During a nationally televised Braves game against the Dodgers, baseball announcer and former catcher Joe Garagiola told the viewing audience that Larry's skills behind the plate were truly worth watching closely. It takes one to know one.

Mighty Martin
Marty Castillo, utility
1957-

Marty Castillo joins Brian Doyle as regular season toads with princely performances in the World Series. Marty played his entire big league career with the Detroit Tigers. A versatile fielder, Castillo manned third base, catcher, and the outfield. Occasionally, the Tigers even penciled him in the lineup as a designated hitter. The "Castle" had some juice in his lumber, hitting eight fence-clearing flies in 352 regular season at bats. Castillo is also the only position player, with a career batting average below .200, ever to blast a home run in a World Series game.

Both the Minnesota Twins and California Angels expressed interest in the Long Beach, California native while Castillo attended Chapman College. Castillo also starred on the diamond and found time to be a vocalist for a popular college band. Playing guitar was Tim Flannery, who also made it to the majors.

The Detroit Tigers made Castillo their fifth selection in 1978. Marty posted decent numbers in the minors, knocking as many as 17 homers with Triple-A Evansville in 1980. On defense, he led 1982 American Association catchers in assists and base runners caught stealing. He also played several games at third base, first base, and the outfield.

Castillo first sipped a couple of cups of coffee in the Motor City in 1981 and 1982. During spring training, in Lakeland, Florida, Castillo gained attention in his unusual habit of carefully surveying the infield at Joker Marchant Stadium before walking on the turf. Eventually, the reason for Castillo's obsession was revealed. Marty had acridiphobia: the fear of grasshoppers.

In 1983, Marty Castillo received an early promotion to Detroit after clouting 12 homers in just 54 games for Triple-A Evansville. That year, Castillo walloped his first major league home run, a dramatic ninth inning Ballantine blast to beat the Brewers 5-4. Castillo also earned a three-hit game against the Angels. On defense, Castillo fielded his positions well, at third base and flawlessly at catcher.

The 1984 campaign was Castillo's best by far. Castillo backed up Lance Parrish behind the plate and shared the third base duties with Tom Brookens, Dave Bergman, and Howard Johnson. Marty hit .234 with four home runs and seventeen RBI in 70 ballgames.

The 1984 Tigers boasted one of the dominant teams of the decade. Managed by Sparky Anderson, the club roared off to 35 wins in their first 40 games, and then cruised to a 104-win season. The Bengals became the first team since the 1955 Brooklyn Dodgers to spend the entire season in first place. While Detroit possessed the long-standing nucleus of pitchers Jack Morris and Dan Petry, outfielder Kirk Gibson, and the middle infield duo of Alan Trammel and Lou Whitaker, the squad also had a wonderful complement of role players. Along with Castillo, guys like Doug Bair, Dave Bergman,

Tom Brookens, Barbaro Garbey, John Grubb, and Rusty Kuntz all wore the "Auld English D" that year. Sparky Anderson said it best: "This was a great year, but not necessarily a great team."

In the American League Championship Series against the Kansas City Royals, the prohibitive favorite Tigers swept the table. Game one was a fourteen-hit, three home, 8-1 romp. Batting eighth and starting at third base, Marty Castillo contributed two hits and a run batted in.

The remainder of the Series proved far more competitive. In the second game, after Detroit built a 3-0 lead over the first three innings, Royals' rookie starter Bret Saberhagen settled down and blanked the Tigers over the next five innings. Meanwhile, Kansas City inched back to tie the game with single runs in the fourth, seventh, and eighth innings. Through the ninth and tenth innings, Tigers' reliever Aurelio "*Senor Smoke*" Lopez and the Royals' bullpen ace Dan Quisenberry exchanged goose eggs. In the top of the eleventh, Johnny Grubb doubled home Lance Parrish and Ruppert Jones for two Tigers' runs. Lopez held the Royals scoreless in the last of the eleventh for the win. In the game, Castillo appeared as a substitute and went hitless in one at bat.

In game three, the Royals' Charlie Leibrandt and the Tigers' Milt Wilcox (with help from American League Most Valuable Player Guillermo Hernandez) tossed matching three-hitters. The Tigers scored in the second inning, courtesy of Marty Castillo. With Chet Lemon on third, Darrell Evans on first and one out, Marty Castillo came to the plate. It looked like disaster when Castillo hit a two-hop grounder right at Royals' shortstop Onix Concepcion. Though not the speediest runner around, Castillo legged out Frank White's off-balance relay throw to first. Lemon scored on the play. Marty Castillo then stole second base. The *New York Times'* feature picture shows Castillo sliding under a leaping Frank White at second base.

Castillo also played a wonderful defense that game, making three putouts and three assists at third base. In the seventh inning, Castillo made a backhanded stop of a smoking liner off the bat of Darryl Motley for the out at first. In the ninth inning, Castillo caught the last out at third for the 1-0 final score. The Tigers were American League Champs. For the Series, Castillo went 2-for-8 with two driven in. Trammel and Parrish led the team with three RBI apiece.

Pundits refer to the 1984 World Series as the "Fast Food Fall Classic." This title resulted by virtue of Ray Kroc of McDonald's restaurant fame owning the San Diego Padres, while Domino's Pizza magnate Tom Monaghan owned the Tigers. The Series also featured the rematch of managers Dick Williams and Sparky Anderson, who were rivals in the 1972 World Series. In that previous meeting, the Hairs (the mustachioed Oakland A's) defeated the Squares (the clean-shaven Cincinnati team). Williams' A's won out over Anderson's Reds.

Game one was played on the west coast. The Tigers drew first blood in the Series with a 3-2 victory. Larry Herndon's two-run blast in the fifth inning provided the edge. Marty Castillo started the game at third and went 0-for-2; however, he did make a crucial defensive play before being lifted for a pinch-hitter. San Diego pinch-hitter Kurt Bevacqua slashed a double into the right field corner. While attempting to stretch the hit for three bases, Bevacqua stumbled rounding second. That gave right fielder Kirk Gibson the split second needed to gun the ball to relay man Lou Whitaker. Castillo received a perfect throw from his second baseman and applied the tag to Bevacqua, quelling any further San Diego rallies.

The Padres rebounded in game two. Bevacqua, who finished the regular season on the Mendoza Line, gained a measure of revenge. Bevacqua's three-run home run off Dan Petry in the fifth inning proved to be the deciding blow in San Diego's come-from-behind 5-3 victory.

The Tigers won the third game by a 5-2 margin. The game was historic, if not boring, for several reasons. First off, twenty-four men were left on base stranded by the two ball clubs, a World Series record. The Padres also tied a record for most base on balls surrendered in a Series' game with eleven. Because of this, some people have commented that this particular game, all three hours and eleven minutes of it, proved sheer torture to watch. Another significant item about the game was the home run by Marty Castillo. Batting ninth and facing Tim Lollar in the second inning, Castillo's blast came with Chet Lemon on base. Lollar threw a blunder—a fastball right into the heart of the plate. Castillo deposited the pitch into the upper deck in left field at Tiger Stadium. The blast staked Detroit to a 2-0 lead. "I wanted to do a couple of cartwheels, a backflip, and a roundoff," said Castillo. He knew better, as the stoic Anderson would never tolerate such tomfoolery. "We're a '50s team playing in '80s," Castillo commented. *Newsweek* magazine wrote, "Fittingly, it was good-field-no-hit Castillo who got one of the night's few fat pitches—a high fastball."

Marty Castillo watched game four from the dugout as Darrell Evans manned the hot corner. This time, Alan Trammel provided the bat with a pair of two-run homers. Tigers' pitcher Jack Morris scattered five hits as Detroit prevailed 4-2 to take a 3-1 series lead.

In the fifth game, Marty Castillo earned the start at third. As they had done all season, Detroit jumped out to a 3-0 lead. Kirk Gibson's two-run first inning blast began the scoring. However, San Diego chipped away at the lead and tied the game 3-3 after four innings. Detroit reclaimed the lead, 5-3, with runs in the fifth and seventh. Kurt Bevacqua, the other unlikely hero, brought San Diego within a run with his second long blast in the eighth inning. With the ballgame in the balance, catalyst Castillo led off with a single. Later in the inning, with Castillo on third and Lou Whitaker on second, Kirk Gibson sent the Motor City into a frenzy with a monstrous three-run shot. The Tigers' season ended just as it started—gloriously. They were 7-1 in the postseason. With the victory, manager Sparky Anderson became the first baseball skipper to earn World Series titles in both leagues. For Marty Castillo, it was the culmination of a career year. Castillo ended his dream postseason with a .294 average, a home run, four batted in, and zero errors.

As reward, Castillo made the national magazines. In the October 22, 1984 issue, *Sports Illustrated* called Castillo "an outgoing practical joker, one of the more popular Tigers. He's so nice that Tom Monaghan, owner of the club and Domino's Pizza, doesn't object to Castillo's endorsing Little Caesar's Pizza. When asked if the home run might open the door to more commercial opportunities, Castillo said, 'I'm not going to worry about it. But my new phone number is…'"

Unfortunately, as all good things must come to an end, Castillo's fairy tale ended all too soon. Even as Castillo and the Tigers were celebrating their game three victory, Sparky Anderson had already decided Castillo's fate. "He's a happy guy in the clubhouse," Anderson told Joe Durso of the *New York Times*. "But, basically, he's my backup catcher and third baseman."

The next season, hard times befell Marty Castillo and the Detroit Tigers. Detroit dropped to third place in their division, winning twenty fewer games. As for Castillo, he may have been hitting with a bat made from pizza boxes, finishing with a .119 average and just ten base knocks in fifty-seven games.

He never earned another big league opportunity. Marty finished his career in the Twins' organization, hitting .251 with Triple-A Toledo. In 1990, Marty returned to playing ball with the short-lived Senior Professional Baseball Association, also known as the "Geezer League." He currently owns a restaurant in Florida called (fittingly) Marty Castillo's Upper Deck.

Marty's two brothers, Art and Dave, also played minor league ball in the Twins' organization. Dave Castillo provided the following insight, "Marty was signed by the same Twins' scout that signed myself and my older brother Art to a contract. We are proud to say that all three of us were released by the Twins...yeah right!"

Of the following Hall of Fame ballplayers, winners all, with well over 100 years of experience, none of them ever played on a World Series champion: Ty Cobb, Ted Williams, Ernie Banks, Harmon Killebrew, and Willie McCovey. For while baseball's enduring charm has always featured the compelling matchup between pitcher and batter, it takes the sum of the parts of a team to sustain the success needed to win a division, pennant, and World Series. The 1984 Detroit Tigers exemplified that tenet. Not a single player on the squad may ever be inducted into the Baseball Hall of Fame, yet everyone on these Tigers seemed to come through with games on the line, to the point where victories seemed routine. And, for one glorious season, Marty Castillo typified that spirit and solid role-playing function.

The Big Johnson
Bobby Johnson, C
1959-

One member of *Mendoza's Heroes* was a teammate of Mario Mendoza himself. That honor belongs to Bobby Johnson, who had a brief three-year hitch as a catcher/first baseman with the Texas Rangers in the early 1980s. Though just a .197 swinger, Johnson was hardly an easy out. The numbers reveal Bobby could hit (9 HR), catch (two career errors), and even run (three stolen bases).

When Bobby was born in 1959, his Uncle Ernie was making quite a name for himself. Uncle Ernie was Cubs' legend Ernie Banks, on his way to his second straight National League Most Valuable Player Award. A ninth round pick of the Texas Rangers' 1977 free agent draft, tall Bobby Johnson enjoyed his biggest year in pro ball with Wausau of the Midwest league in 1979. That year, Johnson hit a ton, slamming 24 home runs and securing a .303 average. He also led league catchers in putouts, assists, and double plays.

Bobby saw his first major league action in 1981. Hailing from Dallas, Johnson did not have to drive too far to get to the game as the Rangers played in nearby Arlington. In a six game trial, Johnson impressed Texas management with two home runs and a .278 batting average. On September 29, rookies Johnson and Wayne Tolleson both earned their first-ever major league base hits in the same inning.

The prized prospect Johnson looked like the heir apparent to longtime Rangers' catcher Jim Sundberg. After a tremendous spring training in 1982, Johnson seemed ready. He led the team in all three Triple Crown statistics. Unfortunately, Johnson could not translate his Florida success when the games counted in the standings, batting a disappointing .125 in a score of appearances. Sent back to the minors, Johnson responded by leading American Association catchers in fielding percentage.

Rangers' manager Doug Rader gave Johnson some playing time in 1983. Johnson's moments in the sun included six doubles, a triple, and five home runs in only 175 at bats. He also was catcher deluxe, going without an error in 62 games behind the dish. Johnson did mishandle a couple at first base—the only two of his major league career.

That season, Bobby Johnson was involved in a pair of 15-inning marathons over eight days. On July 3 against Oakland, the teams were tied at four apiece when the Rangers exploded for a record twelve tallies in one extra inning frame. Johnson came to bat twice in the busy inning, drawing a walk, hitting a single, batting in a run, and scoring. A week later, Johnson earned his biggest hit in major league togs. On July 11th, he crashed a dramatic 15th inning home run to give the Rangers a 5-4 verdict over the Milwaukee Brewers. The game-winning blast momentarily put Texas atop the American League West standings.

With Jim Sundberg shipped to Milwaukee in December 1983, Johnson seemed poised to compete for the starting job behind the plate for the new season. However, Johnson never got the chance. The Rangers waived Johnson during spring training, with the move sending shock waves throughout the organization. What happened? At 24-years-old, Johnson seemed productive enough. Yet, a series of factors led to his premature departure. Although Johnson outhit Sundberg in 1983, the front office took pause to his high strikeout ratio. Even Johnson's stellar glove work behind the plate was offset by the fact that he had some trouble throwing out base runners. Johnson's release was a *fait accompli* when he vocally expressed his dismay of Doug Rader's decision to declare Ned Yost, acquired in the Sundberg deal, the team's starter behind the mask. "He [Johnson] had more than one opportunity last year," was Rader's rebuttal. "For one reason or another, I tried to give Bobby Johnson the job on a silver platter. He just wouldn't take it."

Johnson's stock dropped measurably when he left his winter ball team in the Dominican Republic, after just two weeks, then came to training camp running the slowest mile of any player on the roster. One of Bobby's final statements before leaving the Rangers was, "They basically went out and got a guy [Yost] who had the same type of year I had last year and made him the number one catcher. They'll live or die with Yost."

Johnson's statement proved prophetic. Ned Yost batted a miniscule .182 and the Rangers dropped from third place to the basement of the American League West division. Johnson played in the Yankees' organization following his tour in Texas, but never appeared in another major league game.

The Minister Of Defense
Orlando Mercado, C
1961-

Orlando Mercado, the former Defense Minister of the Philippines, had the daunting task in protecting his island nation against guerrillas, insurgents, and other subversives. Although no relation, baseball's Orlando Mercado has some things in common with his namesake. He too is from an island nation—Puerto Rico. In addition, Mercado, a catcher, protects the plate and is also a "minister of defense."

Orlando Mercado enjoyed great days in baseball before puberty, as his led his Mickey Mantle League team to a world title. Just sixteen years of age when acquired by the Seattle Mariners as a free agent in 1978, Orlando had a steady rise to the majors. He hit ten home runs and sported a .257 batting average for San Jose in the Class A California League in 1979. Mercado followed that up with eleven circuit clouts and 71 batted in for Class AA Lynn of the Eastern League in 1980. After faltering to a .215 mark in his first year of AAA ball, Mercado rebounded with a sensational 1982 season for Salt Lake City. Orlando totaled his personal bests in home runs (16) and batting average (.280). That earned him a September trip to Seattle.

Initially, Orlando Mercado looked like Orlando Cepeda. In his first big league start, on September 19, Mercado crashed a Grand Slam off Steve Comer of the Texas Rangers. Only three other players can claim a grand salami as their first hit: Bill Duggleby in 1898, Bobby Bonds in 1968, and Creighton Gubanich in 1999. That same game, young Mercado (age 20) teamed with Edwin Nunez (age 19) to form the youngest battery in Mariners' history. No ancient mariners here.

Mercado saw most of his action with the 1983 squad, batting only .197 in less than 200 times to the plate. *The Sporting News* critically observed "Mercado and [Rick] Sweet played in 159 games last year but combined to hit barely .200. Their success in throwing out base runners was about as high." After three years with Seattle, Orlando was on the move for the next six years, never spending more than one season with the same team. Included as stops in the Mercado odyssey were the aforementioned Seattle, Texas, Detroit, Los Angeles, Oakland, Minnesota, New York Mets, and Montreal Expos. Altogether, Mercado strapped on the tools of ignorance in America's great northwest, west coast, east coast, midwest, southwest, and Canada.

In 1986, Mercado batted a career best .235 and committed just a single error for the Texas Rangers. On June 16, Orlando watched a potential career highlight turn into a nightmare. Orlando was catching knuckleball specialist Charlie Hough and calling a brilliant game. Hough took a no-hitter into the ninth inning against the California Angels. With Texas leading 1-0, and just two outs to go, left fielder George Wright (in the game as a defensive replacement) muffed Jack Howell's fly ball for a three-base error. The next batter, Wally Joyner, singled to break up the no-hitter and tie the game. Hough threw the following batter, Doug DeCinces, a flutterball that eluded Mercado for a passed ball. That allowed Joyner to advance to second base. The next batter, George Hendrick, struck out. But, unfortunately, that knuckleball also slipped far past Mercado. Before the catcher could recover the ball, Wally Joyner scored from second base. Using some heavenly luck, the Angels prevailed 2-1. Hough, Mercado, and the Rangers walked off the field dejected losers.

In his final big league season, Mercado blasted a career high three home runs for the New York Mets in 1990. Orlando spent the final four seasons as a player in the minor leagues in the Mets, Cubs, Indians, and Anaheim Angels' organizations. With the Angels, Mercado made the transition to player-coach. When it was all over, Mercado played a total of seventeen seasons for twelve different organizations. As a major leaguer, Mercado appeared in 253 games in the uniforms of eight different ball clubs.

Orlando Mercado remains active in baseball. From 1994-1999, he served as a minor league coach for the Anaheim Angels. Mercado has returned to the majors as the Angels' bullpen catcher. Orlando's ability to work well with pitchers has always been his strong suit, both as a player and a coach. Easy job? Don't bet on it. During a simulated game, Mercado, catching Tim Belcher, got hit underneath his right eye by the bat of Orlando Palmeiro during the batter's follow-through. The catcher received a gash that required four stitches to close.

Orlando still lives in his hometown of Arecibo, Puerto Rico. Mercado remains a local legend in Puerto Rican winter league baseball, being a member of the 1982-1983 hometown club that captured the league championship. With Mercado and Candy Maldonado supplying the power, they became Arecibo's version of the Mantle & Maris boys. In 1987, Mercado played on the Puerto Rican national team that won the Caribbean Series.

Laga Beer
Mike Laga, 1B
1960-

While many players herein struggled with largely mediocre teams, such was not the case for slugging first baseman Mike Laga. The burly muscle man with a devastating long-ball stroke played for some of the best teams of the 1980s; teams all with great first basemen. Had Laga played regularly for an also-ran, he likely would have been a much more successful hitter. Nevertheless, Mike responded to that possibility with, "I dream about that a little bit. But, it never happened, so I'm not going to worry about it."

Laga did plenty of slugging in professional baseball with 271 home runs. Sixteen round-trippers were hit in the majors and 220 in the minor leagues. Mike also lugged his potent stick all the way to the Far East where he crashed 35 more home runs in Japanese baseball. Laga's 16 major league shots occurred over bits and pieces of nine seasons.

Hailing from Ramsey, New Jersey, Mike developed his keen swing from playing the popular east coast game of stickball. Being able to bench press 300 pounds didn't hurt. Though undrafted out of high school, he starred as a collegiate player at Fairleigh

Dickinson University and Bergen Community College. That attracted scouts for a second look. Laga became the Detroit Tigers number one pick in the 1980 winter draft.

After two long ball seasons at Class AA Birmingham and Class AAA Evansville, crushing 65 total home runs, Laga received a late-season call to the 1982 parent club during the September roster expansion.

Brash about his abilities, Laga soon told the Detroit baseball writers that he would launch at least ten rockets *out* of Tiger Stadium. He somewhat lived up to his boast, taking a Jim Palmer 0-and-2 pitch clear over the right field roof into a neighboring lumberyard. Again, against the Orioles, Laga knocked in three runs on two hits in the same inning, during an eight-run frame. Detroit gave Laga a good look and he responded impressively, batting .261 with twelve extra-base hits. Three went yard.

On defense, Mike made first base play routine, catching 163 putouts. However, his best catch occurred during his first road trip to Boston. While dining at a seafood restaurant in the Fanueil Hall marketplace before a Red Sox game, Laga met his future wife.

Possessing all the tools and moxie of a phenom, Mike Laga seemed destined to break into the Tigers' starting lineup. However, Detroit, with a succession of veteran players from Enos Cabell to Rick Leach to Darrell Evans, would always deny Mike a starting spot or even a reserve role. From 1983 to 1985, the big portsider would earn only limited play as a late-season call-up.

Though he spent most of 1984 destroying American Association pitching (30 HR and 94 RBI), Mike did make the most of his brief opportunity with the 1984 World Champion Detroit Tigers, going 6-for-11 for a .545 batting average. He and some other members of the squad did not get World Series rings. "They were giving rings to Domino's Pizza store owners but not to the players," Laga lamented.

In 1986, Mike continued bashing the long ball. First, he slammed three homers with Detroit in just 15 games. Then, coming over to the St. Louis Cardinals, Laga belted another three circuit blasts in 18 games. All told, Laga crushed the ball over the fence six times in only 91 at bats that year.

As a Cardinal, Laga did something no player, not even Mark McGwire, can claim. On September 8, 1986, Laga became the only man ever to hit a ball *out* of Busch Stadium. So what if the shot was a foul ball, pulled wide of the right field foul pole? Mike recalled the blast clearing the light towers on its way out. The ball landed and came to rest in a flowerbed. According to Mike Taylor, a witness to Laga's misguided missile, "He [Laga] was surprised when he got a standing ovation for a foul ball." Laga later told *Northampton Gazette* writer Andrew Ayers, "I'd rather have had a single," after eventually going down on strikes—via a forkball by the Mets' Ron Darling. The ball now resides in the St. Louis restaurant of former Cardinal third baseman and announcer Mike Shannon.

Over the 1987 and 1988 seasons, Mike Laga bounced up and down between St. Louis and their Triple-A affiliate in Louisville. Two words kept Laga from securing bigger opportunities in the big leagues: Jack Clark. In 1987, Laga still enjoyed one of his finest in professional baseball. In just 116 games, Laga walloped 29 home runs, drove in 91 runners, and batted .304. During the Cardinals' 1987 pennant-winning club, Mike appeared in 17 games but batted only .138. However, this time Laga could slip the ring of a National League Champion on his finger. Laga appeared in 41 games with exactly 100 at bats for the 1988 Cards—both career highs. Although he secured only 13 hits, Mike earned some extra playing time by virtue of his flawless play at first and backing up oft-injured Bob Horner. However, after the Cardinals acquired Pedro Guerrero in mid-season, Laga became expendable.

Mike Laga closed out his major league career with the San Francisco Giants in 1989-1990. Once again, another prominent first baseman, Will Clark, kept Laga from appearing in more than a handful of games. Coincidentally, Laga played for his third pennant winner as a member of the 1989 Giants.

Mike factored in some victories for San Francisco. The Giants trailed the Reds 8-0 entering the seventh inning in a September match in Cincinnati. Giants' manager Roger Craig began to remove many of his starters and inserted Mike Laga into the game. Suddenly, the Giants' reserves started scoring. Thanks to Laga's two-run clout in the eighth, San Francisco cut the lead to 8-4. The Giants surged ahead 9-8 on Laga's ninth-inning single. San Francisco's Steve Bedrosian escaped a bases-loaded jam in the bottom of the ninth for the victory.

Against Orel Hershiser of the arch-rival Dodgers, Mike delivered what he calls his finest moment as a major leaguer. During a crucial September game against Los Angeles in their pennant drive, Mike pinch-hit for Matt Williams with the Giants trailing 2-0 and the bases loaded. After observing several tough pitches from "Bulldog" Hershiser, Laga lashed a bases-clearing double off the wall to give San Francisco the win.

Tired of waiting for his chance to be a regular, Mike Laga packed his bags and moved his family to the Far East. In Japan, Laga played two seasons as a *gaijin* with the Fukuoka Daiei Hawks. Finally getting a regular chance in 1991, Mike knocked 32 home runs, with 82 batted in, and a .236 average. Unlike most American players, who quickly feel unwelcome in the Land of the Rising Sun, Mike quickly built a great rapport with his teammates and the fans in Fukuoka. Laga didn't experience the severe culture shock too badly other than "getting acclimated to driving on the other side of the road and eating with chopsticks." Unfortunately, Laga could not match his numbers the next season. In a brief 12-game stint with the Hawks, Laga's saga ended unceremoniously. He may as well have been hitting with chopsticks. Mike Laga soon returned back to his homeland.

Throughout the 1980s, Mike Laga sipped enough cups of coffee to open a Starbucks franchise. While Laga could powder the ball a country mile, his high strikeout totals and low on-base figures precluded him from being an everyday ballplayer. Perhaps, with more game experience, Laga could reasonably garner Rob Deer-like numbers (20-30 HR/70 RBI/.210 BA).

One surprising aspect in Mike Laga's game was his crisp fielding. In six of his nine seasons, he played whole campaigns without committing a single error. In 123 games at first base, Laga owned a .996 fielding percentage. Although he didn't meet minimum qualifications, that would have tied him with Wes Parker, Steve Garvey, and Don Mattingly for the best mark ever by a first sacker.

Mike currently lives in Florence, Massachusetts and is the father of three children. While finishing his degree at UMass, Laga served as an assistant baseball coach for the school. While family commitments curb his desire of being a coach or manager in professional baseball, Laga does coach the Little League team in Florence simply known as "Local."

In looking back, Mike Laga understands why he never received a fair shake at being an everyday performer: "I was always the player stuck in the minor leagues hitting 20 or 30 home runs a year. In the big leagues, you can't move that front-line guy. Not when they're perennial All Stars. It's hard to get playing time behind them. But, don't get me wrong. I don't begrudge baseball at all. I had a great career out of it and I loved it."

Despite being a first-round draft pick, a nine-year veteran, and a member of three pennant-winning teams with the Tigers, Cardinals, and Giants, Mike Laga's claim to fame is twofold. One, of course, is smashing one of the most prodigious moon-shot foul balls in baseball history. The other is his sudsy nickname. First uttered with gusto by Chris Berman of ESPN, Mike's sobriquet is Mike "Laga Beer."

The Reverend
Ron Tingley, C
1959-

Ron "Tingles" Tingley, a backup backstop, grabbed a lot of bench over his long career in baseball. From 1982-1995, Tingley toiled for six different major league teams, mostly pacing their dugouts and bullpens. Every now and then, Tingley made it into a game. His career batting record showed ten home runs, 55 batted in, and a .195 average over 278 contests.

One of only a handful of players hailing from the "State o' Maine," the San Diego Padres made Ron their 10th round pick in 1977. After serving a long six-year apprenticeship in the minors, the Padres began to take notice after a 13-homer, .288 season in the Texas League. Tingley even dinged 10 triples to lead the league—a rare feat for catchers in any professional outfit. With a solid 1982 campaign for Triple-A Hawaii, Ron earned his first ticket to "The Show," going 2-for-20 in eight games.

Tingley spent the entire 1983 season with the new Triple-A affiliate of the Padres, the Las Vegas Stars. With Las Vegas, Tingley put together a solid campaign with 10 homers, 48 RBI, and .282 in 92 games. Cast by his role as a clubhouse clown, Tingles achieved near-legend status with the Stars. Tingley greatly enjoyed the backslapping camaraderie of being a baseball player, and hanging out with the guys. For his positive attitude, Tingley quickly earned a mocking nickname of "The Reverend." This moniker offered nothing in the way of Tingley's piety, but he earned the handle because of his irreverent way of treating teammates. As turnabout was fair play, Reverend Tingly made it his solemn duty to give each man an appropriate nickname. Bruce Bochy, who shared catching duties on the Stars, earned a doozy. Tingley affectionately dubbed Bochy, "Bucket Head."

"That was because of the size of my head [he wears a size-8 baseball cap]," Bochy said. "I have a big head, but, believe me," he laughed, "it wasn't because of all the base hits I got. It was just something I was born with," Bochy said of his spacious cranium. "But, 'Bucket Head?' The Reverend could have done better than that."

Little did Bochy know, his last statement unwittingly described Tingley's next several seasons in baseball. Entering a "lost years" phase, Tingley bounced around in the Angels and Braves' organizations, missing large stretches of time with aches and pains. When he did play, Tingley suffered through hitting droughts and self doubt. Most players would have called it quits at this nadir. However, Tingley somehow persevered, being acquired by Cleveland as a free agent in June 1986. For the next three years, Tingley toiled in the Indians' farm system, hoping for another chance in the majors. Ron's keen sense of humor helped.

After twelve years of playing professional ball, and six years since his first appearance, Ron Tingley made a remarkable return with the Indians in 1988. Wearing Cleveland flannels, Tingley celebrating by hitting a home run in his first trip to the plate.

Traded back to the Angels in 1989, Ron saw spot duty with the Halos until 1991. Given a chance finally to step out of his minor league shadow in 1991, Ron backed up an aging Lance Parrish and batted an even .200. More importantly, Tingly demonstrated his experience behind the plate. He began to earn kudos as a defensive catcher. At age 32, Ron was voted the team's Rookie of the Year. The 1991 Angels, with an even 81-81 record, were the only last-place team in history with a non-losing record.

With Lance Parrish traded away to the Seattle Mariners early in 1992, California played musical catchers with Tingley, Mike Fitzgerald, Greg Myers, and John Orton. Tingley played a career high 71 games that year. Batting .197, Tingley was still the most effective of this catcher syndicate.

After a fine defensive year in 1993, fielding his position near flawlessly, Tingley backed up Benito Santiago in the early stages of the 1994 campaign with Florida's Marlins. Then, as a mid-season acquisition, Tingley donned White Sox flannels. Catching for losing ball clubs throughout his career, Tingley maintained his sense of humor. But, the White Sox were winners and Tingley received a benediction of sorts. However, one game ahead of Cleveland, the baseball strike wiped out the rest of the season.

After the conclusion of the work stoppage, Tingley found himself with the Detroit Tigers. Ironically, in his last season in the majors, Tingley enjoyed his finest year, crushing four home runs, with 18 RBI, and a .226 average. All career highs. Tingley's crowning achievement was his dramatic Grand Slam in the ninth inning that drew the Tigers into an 8-8 tie with the Indians. In his final major league game on September 27, Tingley smashed two doubles. His second two bagger drove in a run. Tingley later scored to provide the margin of victory in Detroit's 7-5 triumph over Boston.

For the cost of $280,000, small change relative to major league salaries, the Detroit Tigers earned a good investment off Ron Tingley. However, the Tigers' front office purged players up for salary arbitration shortly after the conclusion of the 1995 season. Ron was one of four players scheduled for arbitration. All received their release. Why would Detroit release Tingley after Ron doing such a good job? Age likely was a factor. Ill will by Tigers' management over salary increases was probably another underlying determinant. Whatever the reason, the 1996 Tigers could have used Ron's, or anyone else's help for that matter, finishing an appalling 53-109.

In 1996 Ron had his third go around with the Angels' organization as a non-roster invitee to spring training. Tingly did not make the squad. Relegated down to Class A ball in Lake Elsinore, Ron became a real-life Crash Davis. In a game against the front-running Lancaster JetHawks, Ron walloped a two-run homer in the ninth inning to give his team the lead. Then, just two days shy of his 37th birthday, Ron Tingly gave himself last rites, retiring his mask and glove for good. All told, Tingley laced up his spikes for 20 years for 21 different professional baseball teams. After a long fifteen years of bushes and buses, Tingley finally earned a look longer than ten games in the major leagues.

Sten The Man
Mike Stenhouse, OF
1958-

Holding a degree in Economics from Harvard, Mike Stenhouse could be the only ballplayer in major league history with an IQ higher than his career batting average. That being said, Mike could swing the bat as proven by his college and minor league records. Even one of baseball's most astute judges of talent, statistical guru Bill James, blamed questionable personnel management in Stenhouse's three big league stops. Neither Montreal, Minnesota, nor Boston gave Stenhouse a legitimate opportunity to succeed. Stenhouse added that a peculiar string of tough luck also hampered his career in baseball.

Born in Pueblo, Colorado, Mike and his family traveled often with their father Dave Stenhouse, a pitcher in the Cincinnati Reds' organization. Despite seven years in the minors and a no-hit game in 1958, Dave still had not made it to Cincinnati. The Reds' organization traded Dave to the Washington Senators, desperate for any live arms after coming off the throes of an expansion season in 1961.

Early on, Dave Stenhouse did not disappoint. The rookie quickly established himself as the ace of the Washington staff, compiling a 10-4 slate halfway into the season. Stenhouse earned the honor of becoming the first rookie ever to start an All-Star game. Squaring off against Dodgers' World Series hero Johnny Podres, Dave Stenhouse pitched the second All-Star game of 1962, played at Wrigley Field.[11] In two frames, Stenhouse allowed one run in the 9-4 American League victory. Unfortunately, from that date forward, Stenhouse's pitching career took a reversal of fortune. Losing eight of his his last nine decisions, Stenhouse closed at 11-12. After two more losing campaigns, Dave Stenhouse suffered an arm injury and finished 16-28. Following his playing career, Stenhouse returned to his old haunts, taking a position as head baseball coach at Rhode Island College and later Brown University.

Already well known for being the son of a major leaguer, Mike Stenhouse carved his own name as a baseball and basketball star after a stellar prep school career at Cranston East High. Though heavily recruited by typical college baseball factories like Arizona State, Mike chose to be a scholar-athlete, attending Harvard. With Harvard's success in athletics generally limited to their crew rowing team, during Mike's term at the hallowed campus, Harvard experienced a renaissance in mainstream sports. As Stenhouse slugged away on the baseball team, the Crimson became one of the northeast region's best ball clubs. A two-time All-Ivy League and Eastern Intercollegiate Baseball League selection,

---

[11] From 1959 to 1962, baseball presented two All-Star games each year.

Stenhouse finished second in the nation in batting average with a .475 mark as a freshman. Stenhouse joined future major leaguers Kirk Gibson and Bob Horner as college All-Americans the next season.

During the summer, Stenhouse also performed in the highly competitive Cape Cod League. After hitting a home run in one game, the same pitcher attempted to bean Stenhouse the next at bat with a high and tight pitch to the head. In order to protect himself, Stenhouse put his hand up to his helmet. The ball shattered bone and Stenhouse's Cape Cod days were placed on hold.

In his junior year at Harvard, Stenhouse quit playing basketball to concentrate on playing baseball. "All my life, I waited for this year and this draft," said Mike Stenhouse in an interview with the author. What follows is Stenhouse's odd tribulations in being drafted #1 on two different occasions. The Seattle Mariners sent their head scout to look at Stenhouse take batting practice. But, just as Stenhouse was about ready to take his cuts, an American Legion team came on the field for a scheduled game. Stenhouse's chance to impress the Mariners ended before it started. Seattle ended up picking Al "Choo Choo" Chambers instead. Still convinced he was a high draft choice, Stenhouse preferred being selected by any club except Cleveland or Oakland. The Indians were perennial doormats. But Oakland, with owner Charles Finley trying to sell the club, wasn't buying and indeed, selling off what players he had. Yet, the Athletics picked Stenhouse as the last pick in the first round, despite not even scouting Stenhouse and relying on scouting bureau reports.

"It was just a mess of an organization. Most late picks in the first round were getting $40,000 to $60,000 bonuses. Finley offered me $12,000." Mike Stenhouse's father, handling the negotiations said, "That's not good enough." In response, Finley said, "I can't spend any more money."

As a result, Stenhouse returned to play the outfield back in the Cape Cod League. However, Dave Stenhouse and Mike Stenhouse quickly filed a complaint with the Office of the Baseball Commissioner to make Mike a free agent. The Stenhouse's were convinced that Finley wasn't negotiating in good faith. "We understand what Finley is doing but we can't do that," argued the Commissioner's office. Distraught over his dwindling options, Stenhouse realized he had to sign with Finley on the owner's terms. If however, Stenhouse did not sign a contract, according to the rules, Stenhouse would have to wait until his senior year to be selected again. Stenhouse could not go into the winter draft. This left Stenhouse in a quandary.

"Boy, I don't mind missing this year. But I don't want to miss spring training and the first half of next year just to wait to get drafted [again]," related Stenhouse. Working with a local lawyer on interpretation, the Stenhouse's received free legal advice. The rule basically stated that if a student attending a four-year college, gets drafted after his junior year, and does not sign a contract while eligible for a senior year of playing ball, the student could not be drafted again until June of his senior year.

In the meantime, Charles Finley, desperate for the lethal Stenhouse bat, called to say that he could not offer more money. Finley did promise a September call-up to the majors. Initially, Harvard's best batsman agreed. "Great! Let's sign." Stenhouse's Cape Cod squad threw a party for the soon-to-be major leaguer. The next day, after reading the contract, Dave Stenhouse called back to the Oakland owner stating, "OK, we have the contract here but there's nothing in here about...*that*.[12] Finley replied that he could not place the roster promise in the body of the contract. "Sorry, if you don't put that in writing, we don't sign," argued the Stenhouse clan. "Are you calling me a liar?" Finley responded. Then, he hung up. Stenhouse did not sign, but got a free party out of it.

"What if I became ineligible for my senior year?" thought young Stenhouse aloud. So, the Stenhouse triumvirate read the rule carefully and called the Commissioner's office. "If the way the rule reads, obviously it's not the way it's intended, but it's how it reads, if he becomes ineligible for his senior year, will you let him go into the winter draft?" asked Dave Stenhouse to baseball's ruling body.

"How would he [Mike Stenhouse] become ineligible?" questioned the Commissioner's office.

"We could pay our agent a dollar and that would make Mike a professional by NCAA standards."

"You just get it done and we'll turn our back on it and let you go through a loophole," remarked the Commissioner's office.

Then, Dave Stenhouse paid the lawyer a single dollar. The lawyer sent a letter to the Commissioner's asking the office about the eligibility status of Mike Stenhouse. The office sent a quick response that Stenhouse was indeed ineligible for his senior year to play baseball at Harvard. Thus, Mike Stenhouse entered the winter draft.

The fourth pick overall in the 1980 winter draft, Stenhouse became the property of the Montreal Expos. The Canadian club gave Stenhouse a $32,000 signing bonus. Ironically, the Oakland team may have been a better move for Stenhouse. Very thin in their farm system and weak in their major league outfield, a better opportunity may have existed for Stenhouse to break into Oakland's lineup. Conversely, the Expos boasted a solid outer garden of stars with Andre Dawson, Tim Raines, and Warren Cromartie.

The Expos' potent outfield and personal differences with manager Bill Virdon limited Mike Stenhouse's opportunities to excel in Montreal. Over three seasons, he appeared in only 105 games with Montreal, never earning enough at bats to develop a rhythm against major league pitching. Stenhouse admitted that he tried too hard and told *The Sporting News*, "It was impossible for me to play that way. There's aren't too many players who can succeed under those conditions."

One of Mike's earliest and most amusing memories in a major league uniform occurred during his first spring training camp in 1981. Stenhouse walked to the clubhouse the very first day and observed a dilapidated old Volkswagon bus in the parking lot. Stepping out of the van was a man resembling an old hermit. He sported a scraggly beard, ragged old shorts, worn-out sandals, and a torn T-shirt. Incredibly, the same man pulled a baseball bag from the van and walked into the clubhouse. That man was hardly a hermit. It was Bill "Spaceman" Lee, a 34-year-old veteran pitcher. As it happened, Mike Stenhouse, his brother Dave Jr., a standout catcher and hitter at Holy Cross, and several former Red Sox players—including Dalton Jones, Dave Stapleton, and Jim Lonborg—later became members of Lee's barnstorming baseball troupe called the

---

[12] "That" being Finley's promise for Mike Stenhouse to make the 40-man Oakland roster in September.

Grey Sox. Unlike major league players, who fly in jet airplanes, and minor leagues, relegated to air-conditioned buses, Lee's Grey Sox traveled together in something resembling Ken Kesey's Magic Bus—Lee's old Volkswagen van. These traveling baseball bedouins were less about winning and more about swapping tall tales and laughter.

Mike finest year as a professional came in 1983. At Wichita, Stenhouse led the American Association in batting (.355), on-base percentage (.490), and slugging percentage (.681). Stenhouse claimed league Most Valuable Player honors and Topps honored Stenhouse as their Minor League Player of the Year. That earned him a couple of brief call-ups with Montreal.

One of his first major league at bats came against the St. Louis Cardinals. In a critical situation with a ballgame in the balance, Mike came into pinch hit with one out in the ninth inning of a tie game. With two runners on base, forkball reliever Bruce Sutter made a mistake and hung the first offering chest-high and right in Stenhouse's hitting zone. But, Stenhouse anxiously swung early and "pool-cued" the ball off the end of the bat, spinning the sphere into the third base dugout. Stenhouse resigned himself to a missed opportunity. Yet, Sutter's next pitch is a split-finger in the exact same location. Again, an excited Stenhouse swung too soon and hit the ball off the end of the bat. Unfortunately, Stenhouse did not know where the ball went. Thinking the ball foul, Mike peered into the third base dugout again. But, no bodies scattered or appeared to have even moved. By the time Stenhouse regained his situational awareness, the Cardinals' second baseman was wheeling to first to complete an around-the-horn double play. Stenhouse barely made it out of the batter's box. Needless to say, the play did not endear Stenhouse to manager Bill Virdon.

In 1984, Stenhouse set an Expos' spring training record for home runs, finally positioning himself for a promising career. Taken north to Canada with the club, Stenhouse stayed around the whole year, but his regular season turned sour. He hit just .183 in limited duty. Stenhouse did show flashes of brilliance and power, with twelve extra base hits and four home runs. When he wasn't playing, which was all too often, Stenhouse made some good friends. Two would later become big league managers, including the Phillies' Terry Francona and Pete Rose of the Reds. Rose and Stenhouse became gin rummy rivals.

One manager duly impressed with Stenhouse was Billy Gardner of the Minnesota Twins. In the 1984 off-season, Gardner coveted a left-handed bat between Tom Brunansky and Kent Hrbek. Remembering that Stenhouse had belted a monstrous tape-measure home run against his team in the Grapefruit League, Gardner made a deal to get Mike to Minnesota. Given the role of designated hitter against right-hand pitchers, Stenhouse got off to a great start. Then, as Mike put it, "A couple of goofy things happen." First, Roy Smalley went down with a groin injury in the first week of the season. After Smalley healed a bit, he could run and bat, but not move laterally. Smalley was unable to play the infield. Billy Gardner informed Stenhouse that Smalley would DH for just a "few games" until Smalley could return to his shortstop position. Gardner may have been pressured to play Smalley due to the incumbent infielder's large salary. In the meantime, Minnesota started a new shortstop named Greg Gagne. Unfortunately for Stenhouse, that "few games" turned into weeks which turned into months. Out of the lineup, Stenhouse appeared only as a spot-starter or a replacement for Brunansky, Hrbek, or Mickey Hatcher. "So, somebody gets hurt, and I lost my job," lamented Stenhouse. "Billy Gardner might have made it up to me, but he got fired two months into the season."

Still, his 1985 season with the Twins was Mike's best in the majors. In 81 games, Stenhouse hit .223, yet his bat was exceptionally productive, as evidenced by his power numbers. One of Stenhouse's five home runs that year was a game-winner that ended a ten-game losing skid for the Twins. Perhaps, Mike's most fearsomely hit ball that year occurred on July 9th. Against the Baltimore Orioles, Stenhouse hit a laser beam that smashed into pitcher Nate Snell and broke a rib.

In 1986, Stenhouse achieved a dream that every New England lad fantasizes over— wearing the uniform of the Boston Red Sox. As a pinch hitter and temporary fill-in for Jim Rice, Stenhouse looked like the reincarnation of Eddie Yost, The Walking Man. In 21 games Stenhouse drew 12 bases on balls, yet managed only two his. As luck would have it, major league owners reduced team rosters to 24 men. Stenhouse started the year in Pawtucket, as the likely 25th player on the big league roster. Called up to the Sox in May, Stenhouse was sent down in late July and not around when Boston made their fateful journey into the 1986 post-season. Mike led the club in on-base percentage when optioned back to Pawtucket.

With Boston, Mike did receive a pennant ring but this was tempered with a big disappointment. Veteran Red Sox players broke with tradition when voting on shares. Part-time Red Sox players like Stenhouse, Rey Quinones, Rob Woodward, and Jeff Sellers, despite their respective time with the club, received only partial shares.

Although Stenhouse tried to jump-start his playing career with Toledo in the Tigers' organization, the comeback really wasn't meant to be. In hindsight, Stenhouse lamented on the hitting training he received at baseball's highest level.

"The worst hitting instruction I got was when I got to the big leagues." For obvious reasons, Stenhouse did not mention names.

"It's politics basically. When people have a theory that worked for somebody, they feel it will work for everybody. They should be working with individuals but many are hooked on theory."

Incredibly, Stenhouse also recalled one particular instructor's pet theory. "We had a hitting instructor, who while in the locker room saw someone flick a rolled-up towel at another guys butt." Thinking this a brilliant way to teach hitting, the coach "had all the extras go out and bat like we were flicking a towel—with no follow-through. It was ridiculous."

Like many players in the pages herein, Stenhouse owned a beautiful, natural swing, hardly cultivated by snapping towels. But, such a long and rhythmic stroke requires the timing that can only be gained with experience—and that experience gained only by facing major league pitching day in and day out. Without that timing, the high-performance swings misfires like some untuned engine on a Jaguar XKE. And, according to Stenhouse, it's essential that young players establish their skills immediately. Would Stenhouse have been a better hitter with 400+ at bats every season? Could he hit .260, .270? He replied, "Higher. A lot higher, I could hit."

Kiefer Madness
Steve Kiefer, SS
1960-

Just about the time actor Kiefer Sutherland made a name for himself on the silver screen, Steve Kiefer played bit parts for three different American League teams. Although he never appeared in more than 40 games in any of his six seasons, Steve Kiefer proved that he could hit the long ball. A career .341 slugging average in the majors and blasting three home runs in a single Winter League game provide evidence.

The Chicago native played ball at Fullerton College in California. Steve was the Oakland Athletics' No. 1 selection in the 1981 winter draft. A power-hitting shortstop, Oakland envisioned Kiefer as their version of Cal Ripken. Most observers felt Steve won the starting shortstop position in spring training 1983, when he hit .269 with 6 doubles, 7 runs, and 10 RBI in Cactus League tune-ups. Instead, he spent the season with Albany of the Eastern League. With Albany, Kiefer showed pop, hitting .246 with 19 home runs and 81 RBI.

After a .268 and 16 HR campaign for Triple-A Tacoma, Oakland called up Kiefer for the final month of the 1984 season. Steve played two years and only 63 games for the men in green, batting below .200 each season. Seeing enough, the A's dealt Steve Kiefer, along with catcher Charlie O'Brien and two other prospects, to the Milwaukee Brewers for pitcher Moose Haas on March 30, 1986. The change of scenery did Steve some good.

In 1987, baseball witnessed resurgence in home run slugging not seen in years. Leading the way were the Chicago Cubs' Andre Dawson, bludgeoning out 49 blasts, and A's rookie Mark McGwire, also with 49 circuit clouts—a harbinger of things to come. On a far more modest scale, Steve Kiefer belted five home runs in just 99 at bats. For a few moments, in early August of 1987, Kiefer was on top of his game and the results were phenomenal. Steve joined the Fraternal Order of the Grand Salami, hitting a bases-loaded blast off the Baltimore Orioles' Scott McGregor, at County Stadium on August 4th. It was the Brewers first Grand Slam in two years, but, incredibly, Kiefer's fifth slam of the season. He blasted four bases-loaded dingers at Triple-A Denver before being called up. Kiefer hit a two-run homer the next day to out the Brewers ahead for good. In closing out a sweep of the Orioles, Kiefer doubled and scored three runs in an 11-8 win. Those three great efforts were part of a 7-game hitting streak by Kiefer.

After a brief seven-game trial in 1988, Steve Kiefer hit well with a .300 average. It seemed that at 28 years of age, Kiefer was finally coming into his own. Milwaukee management didn't quite think so. Moving on to the New York Yankees in 1989, Steve's bat became barely a whisper, ending his playing career. For what it's worth, Kiefer earned $95,500 for his solitary base hit that season.

A 34-year-old Kiefer made one last run to secure a spot on a major league roster during the strike-marred quagmire that distinguished spring training 1995. A member of the replacement Kansas City Royals, Kiefer never played due to the end of baseball's labor-management hostilities.

Steve Kiefer presently resides in Moreno Valley, California and works as an orthotist (an orthopedic braces and support specialist). Steve Kiefer's kid brother Mark pitched for the Milwaukee Brewers from 1993-1996. Mark Kiefer sports a handsome 4-1 record and a save in 44 relief appearances.

What If?
Jose Oliva, 3B
1971-1997

For many ballplayers, some twist of irony or bad luck kept them from being successful hitters in the major leagues. What if budding Red Sox first sacker Harry Agganis not died during the 1955 season? What if promising Cubs' second baseman Ken Hubbs did not perish in plane crash in 1964? What if Mike Miley, the star quarterback from LSU, later an infielder for the California Angels in the 1970s, had not been killed in a car crash in 1976? Would Miley have gone on to be the star everyone predicted?

As for Jose Oliva, the Dominican third baseman who played in Atlanta and St. Louis, the same painful question begs for asking. What if? Perhaps, Oliva still might be playing today, and chances are he would have boosted his average well above .200.

One of over 190 players hailing from the Dominican Republic, Jose Oliva was born in San Pedro de Macorís, the hardscrabble sugar mill town that is also the birthplace of Sammy Sosa. Originally, Jose played shortstop and catcher. Felipe Alou managed Sosa and Oliva in the Dominican winter leagues. Too often, to their detriment, Sammy and Jose would show up late. Alou suspended the younger and not yet established Oliva, while saving choice words for the veteran Sosa. "I suspended Oliva, but I did not suspend Sosa. I really got angry with Sosa. But, I needed him on the team," Alou said.

Signed as a free agent, Jose Oliva started his professional career in 1989 as a member of the Texas Rangers' organization. Jose had a real predicament after the Rangers broke spring training camp in 1992. Assigned to their Double-A affiliate in Tulsa, Oliva did not have any transportation to travel to Oklahoma. His friend, Sammy Sosa, helped Jose out by purchasing him a car. Oliva went on to be a Texas League All-Star that season.

The Rangers traded Oliva to Atlanta for veteran pitcher Charlie Leibrant in December 1992. The Braves immediately moved Oliva from his natural shortstop position to third base. First off, with Oliva's erratic glove, he was never going to make people forget about Ozzie Smith or even Jeff Blauser. However, Oliva did possess an extremely strong arm well suited for the hot corner. Of more concern was the fact that Chipper Jones was ordained as the shortstop of the future by the Braves' organization.

After clubbing 24 homers in 1994 for Triple-A Richmond in just three months, Oliva earned his invite to Atlanta. A formidable presence at the plate, Oliva reminded some as looking more like an NFL linebacker than an infielder. Early on, Jose Oliva hit like Tony

Oliva. He quickly zoned in on .300 and was averaging a home run every ten at bats. No pitcher could stop him. Only owners, union representatives, and lawyers could. The baseball strike of 1994, abruptly ended what could have been a spectacular rookie half-season for Oliva.

In 1995, Jeff Blauser remained the incumbent at shortstop. Chipper Jones emerged as the Atlanta third baseman over Oliva, during the abbreviated spring training following the strike. Yet, Jose began the season as the Braves' starting third baseman while Jones played left field as a fill-in for the injured Ryan Klesko. Oliva got off to a decent start, hitting .375 with a couple of home runs by early May. Then, several unfortunate things happened to Jose Oliva. First, Klesko healed and returned to the outfield. Consequently, Chipper Jones wrested third base out from under Jose. No longer an everyday player, Oliva lost his edge. A 5-for-59 slump drove his average down as if attached to a falling boulder.

Even while struggling at the plate, Oliva displayed gutsy play. In a May 20 game against the Florida Marlins, Oliva came into pinch-hit in the bottom of the eighth with one out and the bases loaded. Jose grounded into what looked like a sure double-play ball. But, Oliva made a hard, headfirst dive into first base and barely beat the throw from second. That scored Ryan Klesko to tie the game. The Braves eventually won 8-7. Oliva finally busted out of his elongated slump on July 29, going 2-for-5 and belting a homer to break open a game against the Giants.

After 48 games and a lowly .156 batting average with the Braves in 1995, Jose Oliva was off to St. Louis, traded on August 25 for minor league outfielder Anton French. Jose played another 22 games for the Cardinals during their drive to the National League Central title.

While no one questioned Oliva's ability to send the ball rocketing out of the park, with seven long balls in 183 at bats, both the Braves and Cardinals probably concluded that his talent remained quite raw. He batted only a composite .142 for the year, fanning every four times to the plate. Oliva's defense also made him a liability as he suffered through a spate of six errors over 11 games at third base.

Oliva spent the entire 1996 season at Triple-A Louisville, slugging 31 circuit blasts. He was with the Mets briefly in 1997, but never played a regular season game in New York flannels. Strikeouts bothered Oliva and big league brass. Four times as a minor leaguer, Oliva managed to be punched out on strikes 100 times in a season.

With the 1997 season in the books, Jose went to play winter ball with the Estrellas Orientales team of San Pedro de Macorís. Performing on a hometown squad and happy, things were looking up for Jose Oliva. He was leading the Dominican winter league with a .287 batting average, socking eight home runs, and knocking in 40. *Baseball America* honored him with winter league All-Star status. In the Dominican All-Star game, Oliva helped the Eastern Stars to a 9-5 victory over the Cibaena Eagles. Just before Christmas, Jose had a verbal agreement for a minor league contract with the Seattle Mariners.

What if Oliva buckled his seatbelt to his convertible on that fateful date in December 1997? Oliva was driving with a female companion from Santo Domingo to San Cristobal, 30 miles to the south, when a horrible accident occurred. The impact catapulted Oliva from the vehicle. The distraught woman, who was not injured, told doctors at the Centro

Medico Hospital in San Cristobal that she waited by the side of the highway for an hour before she was able to get help. They laid Jose Oliva to rest in San Pedro de Macorís.

Oliva's death instantly wiped out a promising career in baseball. In tribute, friend and former teammate Cardinals' pitcher Manny Aybar inscribed the numerals "123" on his ball cap. Oliva wore that number on the back of his T-shirt in winter ball. However, controversy quickly ensued when San Diego Padres' manager Bruce Bochy asked the umpires to tell Aybar to change his cap, citing a rule that disallows altered uniform items. The cap went. But Bochy should have thought twice. Now earning the ire of Tony La Russa, the St. Louis skipper forced the umps to chastise Padres third base coach Tim Flannery, who was caught outside the boundaries of the coach's box—a seldom enforced rule.

And, as for Jose Oliva, what if?

EPILOGUE
The 51ˢᵗ Hero

One of the pratfalls of writing a book based on a finite list, is the dismay of not being able to add that one additional player. The caste of below .200 hitters has many other fascinating stories besides the men that you read about here. But, like some NFL coach just before final roster cuts, I could hear myself muttering in front of the computer monitor, "Tommy Dean, meet me in my office; and bring your play book," as I made my final cutdown to fifty players.

In actuality, the list is objective, based on a complex algorithm for determining who the 50 *highest* ranking below .200 hitters were. It even had square roots in it! But the empirical model also had a bit of subjectivity. A parameter for intangible value proved crucial in getting Japanese League legends (Manuel), great managers (La Russa), and World Series stars (Doyle) over some more obscure players whose major league batting statistics might have been quantitatively better. As for the formula, my editor's ears bled profusely after he read through it in my original manuscript, so we left it on the cutting room floor. It still resides in cyberspace. If you really have the urge, the URL is http://members.tripod.com/~alpepper/mendoza50.html.

Who were some of the 51st men? The unkindest cut was Charlie Sweasy, the "father of all below .200 hitters." He was one of the ten members of the unbeaten 1869 Cincinnati Red Stockings. Sweasy later batted a dainty .190 in the National League from 1876–1878. An infielder, he was a true savior when the Red Stockings came closest to losing that year. With his team trailing 27–25 in the bottom of the ninth, Sweasy, though he never hit a major league home run, blasted a game-winning Grand Slam that day.

I could have picked several obscure old-time ballplayers. None of which, you probably ever heard of. Mike Heydon, the Dead Ball Era backstop, extinguished himself with a rather mediocre career average of .179 with five teams.

But, Baby boomers, like myself, may recall Mike Miley, the sensational quarterback at LSU and a hard-luck (.176) hitting shortstop for the Briggs-Garrett era California Angels. Al Moran, the starting shortstop for the 1963 Mets, had a career worth interest. Moran's greatest hitting days occurred years later as one of the best senior softball players in the country. For Moran, pitched balls really did resemble grapefruits. One could make a case for Joe Morgan—not the arm-flapping two-time MVP for the Reds, but the Joe Morgan who hit two homers and batted .193 for five different clubs in the "Far and Few Between" era, and later managed the Boston Red Sox to a couple of American League East crowns.

Other players, who would make great stories, were excluded for failing to meet the minimum 200 plate appearances criterion. Mike Adams, the 1970s-vintage player for the Twins, Cubs, and A's, batted .195, but reached base with incredible frequency. A .375 on base percentage (nearly equal to Pete Rose) is proof positive of this. Adams' father, Bobby Adams, played in the majors for 14 years.

Two others, with less than 200 plate appearances, included Ross Moschitto and Doug Gwodsz. I liked their names. Moschitto carved a niche as Mickey Mantle's late-inning outfield replacement during the twilight of "The Mick's" career. Joe Garagiola once commented, "When I covered the Yankees in the '60s, they had players like Horace Clarke, Ross Moschitto, Jake Gibbs and Dooley Womack. It was like the first team missed the bus." If Greg (The Bull) Luzinski was known for hitting "Bull Blasts," then Ross' lone homer can be referred to as "The Moschitto Bite."

As for Gwodsz, he owns one of the most unusual nicknames in baseball. Doug's sobriquet was "Eye Chart." Doug Rader gets the credit here. Whenever Rader saw the young catcher, he would invariably cover one eye with his hand and start uttering, "G–W–O–D–S–Z" as if he were reading an eye chart for an optometrist at Lenscrafters. Gwodsz hit a scant .144, exclusively for the Padres. However, the stellar defender had a 19–4 win-loss record in games he started in 1983 and contributed in the Padres' 1984 pennant-winning season. Pronounced phonetically, his last name sounds like "GOOSH."

Recent vintage players include Kevin Roberson, who hit 20 home runs and batted .197 from 1993–1996. Then there is hard-hitting J.R. Phillips, with 23 career homers, and a .188 career batting average through the 1999 season. Had I recalculated my algorithm today, both of these players would rank high.

A couple of longtime below .200 hitters broke through the Mendoza Line in 2000. Tom Prince raised his career batting average to .203. After the 2001 season, it is up to .206. At least for now, Prince is no longer the all-time leader in seasons played by a below .200 hitter (15 years). Juan Castro batted .241 in 2000 to boost his lifetime batting average from .188 to .206. Castro is now up to a robust .210. These examples justify my position to wait five years to nominate a player—just like the Hall of Fame. It also leaves me with a moral quandary: Should I root for these men to slide back below .200? Would this be no different than the person who goes to NASCAR races hoping to see a crash?

Below .200 hitters of the 21st century may be a contradiction in terms. With the glut of 11–9 and 8–7 games played today, the chances of a .195 hitter hanging around in the majors—no matter how good defensively he is—are slim to none. Purists call for a return of rules that will give shell-shocked pitchers a fighting chance. However, as long as attendance figures remain at record highs, I do not see the upper echelon of baseball's hierarchy "fixing something that works."

As the self-proclaimed guardian and chief curator of below .200 hitters throughout history, I will maintain a taut watch of players in baseball's third century. If fortune favors me, I will draft a second edition of *Mendoza's Heroes,* with more players featured. You can be a stakeholder here. If you see factual errors, incorrect assumptions, false generalizations and other outright examples of author ineptitude that escaped the editors, please set me straight. Likewise, if you know of some interesting facts and data of a player featured here or some other sub-.200 hitter I unjustly undervalued, I solicit your input.

Thank you readers. Thank you Heroes.

"Batting is the first thing a player thinks about when he crawls out of bed, and it's the last thing on his mind when the lights go out."

-Jimmy Johnston, versatile infielder-outfielder, 1911-1926

Statistics

NAME	YEARS AND TEAMS	G	AB	R	H	2B	3B	HR	RBI	SB	BB	SO	BA	SA
Gair Allie	1954 PGH	121	418	38	83	8	6	3	30	1	56	84	.199	.268
	MINOR LEAGUE TOTALS	827	2665	379	670	107	13	52	304	24	527	485	.251	.360
Frank Baker	1970-71 NY Yankees, 1973-74 BAL	146	288	28	55	8	3	1	24	4	40	60	.191	.250
	MINOR LEAGUE TOTALS	576	1909	268	480	56	24	11	170	22	243	277	.251	.323
	1973-74 ALCS with Baltimore Orioles	4	0	0	0	0	0	0	0	0	0	0	.000	.000
Charlie Bastian	1884 WIL & KC (UA), 1885-88 PHL (NL), 1889 CHI (NL), 1890 CHI (PL), 1891 CIN (AA) & PHL (NL)	504	1806	241	342	49	26	11	144	57	179	308	.189	.264
Cramer Beard	1948-1952 PGH, 1957-58 CHI (A)	194	474	80	94	11	6	6	35	16	78	107	.198	.285
	MINOR LEAGUE TOTALS	1834	6185	1339	1754	288	139	128	732	255	1296	1015	.284	.437
Bill Bergen	1901-03 CIN, 1904-11 BKN	947	3028	138	516	45	21	2	193	23	88	81	.170	.201
Dan Briggs	1975-77 CAL, 1978 CLE, 1979 SD, 1981 MON, 1982 CHI (NL)	325	688	67	134	20	6	12	6	12	53	133	.195	.294
	MINOR LEAGUE TOTALS	1123	4067	682	1212	234	56	125	717	52	435	831	.298	.472
	JAPANESE LEAGUES 1982-83 Yakult Swallows	176	581	62	150	30	1	18	68	3			.258	.406
Fritz Buelow	1899-00 STL (N), 1901-03 DET, 1904 DET & CLE, 1905-06 CLE, 1907 STL (AL)	431	1334	125	256	25	18	6	112	20	69		.192	.251
Doug Camilli	1961-64 LA (NL), 1965-67, 1969 WAS	313	767	56	153	22	4	18	80	0	56	146	.199	.309
	MINOR LEAGUE TOTALS	485	1673	259	443	85	14	48	295	12	176	277	.265	.418

NAME	YEARS AND TEAMS	G	AB	R	H	2B	3B	HR	RBI	SB	BB	SO	BA	SA
Marty Castillo	1981-85 DET	201	352	31	67	11	2	8	32	3	19	76	.190	.301
	MINOR LEAGUE TOTALS	718	2430	333	630	124	13	76	338	34	276	500	.259	.415
	1984 ALCS with Detroit Tigers	3	8	0	2	0	0	0	2	1	1	3	.250	.250
	1984 World Series with Detroit	3	9	2	3	0	0	1	2	0	2	1	.333	.667
C. Coleman	1961 PHL, 1962-63, 1966 NY Mets	201	462	51	91	8	2	9	30	7	37	85	.197	.281
	MINOR LEAGUE TOTALS	932	2888	445	758	107	34	77	427	76	302	384	.262	.403
	1970 Mexico City Reds	142	511	85	150	23	7	14	75	1			.294	.440
Bill Conroy	1935-37 PHL (AL), 1942-44 BOS (AL)	169	452	45	90	13	3	5	33	3	77	87	.199	.274
	MINOR LEAGUE TOTALS	800	2297	280	580	122	25	47	341	29	254	253	.253	.389
Bob Davis	1973, 1975-78 SD, 1979-80 TOR, 1981 CAL	290	665	50	131	19	3	6	51	0	40	118	.197	.262
	MINOR LEAGUE TOTALS	695	2435	359	678	105	20	70	403	25	193	484	.278	.424
Brian Doyle	1978-80 NY Yankees, 1981 OAK	110	199	18	32	3	0	1	13	1	10	13	.161	.191
	MINOR LEAGUE TOTALS	760	2547	335	647	84	21	17	225	66	266	185	.254	.324
	1978 ALCS with New York Yankees	3	7	0	2	0	0	0	1	0	1	1	.286	.286
	1978 WORLD SERIES with New York Yankees	6	16	4	7	1	0	0	2	0	0	0	.437	.500
Oscar Dugey	1913-14 BOS (NL), 1915-17 PHL (NL), 1920 BOS (NL)	195	279	45	54	10	1	1	20	17	31	38	.194	.248
	1915 WORLD SERIES with Philadelphia Phillies	2	0	0	0	0	0	0	0	1	0	0	.000	.000
Henry Easterday	1884 PHL (UA), 1888 KC (AA), 1889 COL (AA), 1890 COL PHL LOU (AA)	322	1128	141	203	23	15	9	92	42	112	57	.180	.251

NAME	YEARS AND TEAMS	G	AB	R	H	2B	3B	HR	RBI	SB	BB	SO	BA	SA
Ernie Fazio	1962-63 HOU, 1966 KC	141	274	37	50	10	4	2	8	5	33	85	.184	.270
	MINOR LEAGUE TOTALS	634	2249	332	542	93	25	58	248	6	277	449	.241	.382
Frank Fernandez	1967-69 NY Yankees, 1970 OAK, 1971 OAK WAS CHI (NL), 1972 CHI (NL)	285	727	92	145	21	2	39	116	4	164	231	.199	.395
	MINOR LEAGUE TOTALS	792	2339	351	564	94	10	94	407	16	479	686	.241	.427
Herman Franks	1939 STL (NL), 1940-41 BKN, 1947-48 PHL (AL), 1949 NY Giants	168	403	35	80	18	2	3	43	2	57	37	.199	.275
	MINOR LEAGUE TOTALS	766	2385	288	652	120	23	50	372				.273	.406
	1941 WORLD SERIES with Brooklyn Dodgers	1	1	0	0	0	0	0	0	0	0	0	.000	.000
Jim French	1965-71 WAS	234	607	53	119	17	4	5	51	3	121	78	.196	.262
	MINOR LEAGUE TOTALS	582	1871	295	477	84	9	54	252	26	381	236	.255	.396
Jim Fuller	1973-74 BAL, 1977 HOU	107	315	24	61	17	0	11	41	1	19	130	.194	.352
	MINOR LEAGUE TOTALS	820	2811	458	714	133	31	170	554	12	388	919	.254	.505
Adrian Garrett	1966 ATL, 1970 CHI (NL), 1971-72 OAK, 1973-74 CHI (NL) & CAL, 1975 CHI (NL) & CAL, 1976 CAL	163	276	30	51	8	0	11	37	4	31	87	.185	.333
	MINOR LEAGUE TOTALS	1530	5182	897	1344	210	59	280	961	65		297	.259	.465
	JAPANESE LEAGUES 1977-79 Hiroshima	384	1302	193	338	37	2	102	247	6	186		.260	.526
John Gochnauer	1901 BKN, 1902-03 CLE	264	908	94	170	32	8	0	87	18	87		.187	.240
Bob Johnson	1981-83 TEX	98	249	24	49	8	1	9	27	3	20	80	.197	.345
	MINOR LEAGUE TOTALS	590	1903	302	486	96	12	84	333	35	338	490	.255	.451

NAME	YEARS AND TEAMS	G	AB	R	H	2B	3B	HR	RBI	SB	BB	SO	BA	SA
Steve Kiefer	1984-1985 OAK, 1986-88 MIL, 1989 NY Yankees	105	229	34	44	7	3	7	30	0	12	68	.192	.341
	MINOR LEAGUE TOTALS	1006	3563	579	922	191	37	141	564	131	316	857	.259	.452
Mike Laga	1982-85 DET, 1986 DET & STL, 1987-88 STL, 1989-90 SF	188	423	39	84	18	0	16	55	1	22	115	.199	.355
	MINOR LEAGUE TOTALS	1121	4018	622	1072	220	42	220	723	20	416	886	.267	.507
	JAPANESE LEAGUES 1991-92 Fukuoka	136	485	57	112	19	1	35	87	1	35	122	.231	.491
Tony La Russa	1963 KC, 1968-70 OAK, 1971 OAK & ATL, 1973 CHI (NL)	132	176	15	35	5	2	0	7	0	23	37	.199	.250
	MINOR LEAGUE TOTALS	1295	4418	696	1172	194	26	69	491	99	629	581	.265	.368
Charlie Manuel	1969-72 MIN, 1974-75 LA	242	384	25	76	12	0	4	43	1	40	77	.198	.260
	MINOR LEAGUE TOTALS	979	3187	468	915	164	40	117	560	35	414	502	.287	.474
	1969-70 ALCS with Minnesota Twins	2	1	0	0	0	0	0	0	0	1	1	.000	.000
	JAPANESE LEAGUES 1976-78 Yakult Swallows, 1979-80 Kintetsu Buffaloes, 1981 Yakult	621	2127	368	644	69	2	189	491	6			.303	.604
James McAvoy	1913-15 & 1917-19 PHL (AL)	235	674	38	134	18	8	1	53	6	38	87	.199	.254
Mike McCormick	1904 BKN	105	347	28	64	5	6	0	27	22	43		.184	.222
Tom McLaughlin	1883-85 LOU (AA), 1886 NY (AA), 1891 WAS (AA)	340	1183	142	227	28	19	2	81	16	75		.192	.253
Orlando Mercado	1982-84 SEA, 1986 TEX, 1987 DET & LA, 1988 OAK, 1989 MIN, 1990 NY Mets & MON	253	562	40	112	17	4	7	45	4	42	82	.199	.281
	MINOR LEAGUE TOTALS	954	3035	355	784	188	18	82	453	20	294	543	.258	.413

NAME	YEARS AND TEAMS	G	AB	R	H	2B	3B	HR	RBI	SB	BB	SO	BA	SA
Charlie Metro	1943 DET, 1944 DET & PHL (AL), 1945 PHL (AL)	171	358	42	69	10	1	3	23	3	36	55	.193	.257
Rich Morales	1967-73 CHI (AL), 1973 CHI (AL) & SD, 1974 SD	480	1053	81	205	26	3	6	64	7	95	150	.195	.242
	MINOR LEAGUE TOTALS	697	2485	287	589	100	10	12	276	27	205	306	.237	.300
Larry Murray	1974-76 NY Yankees, 1977-79 OAK	226	412	49	73	16	4	3	31	20	49	74	.177	.257
	MINOR LEAGUE TOTALS	769	2617	476	664	102	30	42	282	306	443	501	.254	.364
Jose Oliva	1994 ATL, 1995 ATL & STL	89	242	24	43	10	0	13	31	0	19	56	.178	.380
	MINOR LEAGUE TOTALS	765	2606	346	624	126	39	111	426	32	223	722	.239	.446
John O'Neill	1902-03 STL (NL), 1904-05 CHI (NL), 1906 BOS	303	945	74	185	24	5	1	74	20	52		.196	.235
Larry Owen	1981-83 ATL, 1985 ATL, 1987-88 KC	171	358	42	69	10	1	3	23	3	36	55	.193	.257
	MINOR LEAGUE TOTALS	864	2639	294	582	98	10	61	298	14	336	448	.221	.335
Ray Oyler	1965-68 DET, 1969 SEA, 1970 CAL	542	1265	110	221	39	6	15	86	2	135	359	.175	.251
	MINOR LEAGUE TOTALS	781	2500	389	590	88	21	59	276	12	408	577	.236	.359
	1968 WORLD SERIES with Detroit Tigers	4	0	0	0	0	0	0	0	0	0	0	.000	.000
Bill Plummer	1968 CHI (NL), 1970-77 CIN, 1978 SEA	367	892	72	168	37	1	14	82	4	95	191	.188	.279
	MINOR LEAGUE TOTALS	686	2180	240	530	66	17	49	276	16	244	480	.243	.356

NAME	YEARS AND TEAMS	G	AB	R	H	2B	3B	HR	RBI	SB	BB	SO	BA	SA
Luis Pujols	1977-83 HOU, 1984 KC, 1985 TEX	316	850	50	164	27	6	6	81	1	52	164	.193	.260
	MINOR LEAGUE TOTALS	694	2302	216	556	91	10	28	267	12	133	418	.242	.326
	1980 NLCS with Houston Astros	4	10	1	1	0	1	0	0	0	0	0	.100	.300
	1981 NLDS with Houston Astros	2	6	0	0	0	0	0	0	0	0	1	.000	.000
Mike Ryan	1964-67 BOS, 1968-73 PHL, 1974 PGH	636	1920	146	370	60	12	28	161	4	152	370	.193	.280
	MINOR LEAGUE TOTALS	447	1391	172	315	44	5	32	163	2	213	313	.226	.334
	1967 WORLD SERIES with Boston Red Sox	1	2	0	0	0	0	0	0	0	0	1	.000	.000
Dave Schneck	1972-74 NY Mets	143	413	32	82	14	4	8	35	4	27	73	.199	.310
	MINOR LEAGUE TOTALS	776	2585	408	645	121	17	121	421	48	292	522	.250	.450
Bill Shipke	1906 CLE, 1907-09 WAS	186	552	59	110	11	10	1	29	21	55		.199	.261
Anthony Smith	1907 WAS, 1910-11 BKN	170	500	46	90	12	2	1	26	13	90	60	.180	.218
Mike Stenhouse	1982-84 MON, 1985 MIN, 1986 BOS	207	416	40	79	15	0	9	40	1	71	66	.190	.291
	MINOR LEAGUE TOTALS	688	2238	417	652	128	27	101	408	44	508	342	.291	.508
Ron Tingley	1982 SD, 1988 CLE, 1989-93 CAL, 1994 FLA & CHI (AL), 1995 DET	278	563	52	110	27	3	10	55	3	54	165	.195	.307
	MINOR LEAGUE TOTALS	922	2845	410	740	99	43	73	421	44	363	707	.260	.402
Bill Traffley	1878 CHI (NL), 1883 CIN (AA), 1884-86 Bal (AA)	179	663	85	116	13	12	1	28	8	34	1	.175	.235

NAME	YEARS AND TEAMS	G	AB	R	H	2B	3B	HR	RBI	SB	BB	SO	BA	SA
Bob Uecker	1962-63 MIL, 1964-65 STL, 1966 PHL, 1967 PHL & ATL	297	731	65	146	22	0	14	54	0	96	167	.200	.287
	MINOR LEAGUE TOTALS	619	1922	308	528	89	19	86	345	6	331	431	.275	.475
John Vukovich	1970-71 PHL, 1973-74 MIL, 1975 CIN, 1976-77 & 1979-81 PHL	277	559	37	90	14	1	6	44	4	29	109	.161	.222
	MINOR LEAGUE TOTALS	1118	4047	467	1050	191	17	91	576	50	332	612	.259	.383
Eddie Zimmerman	1906 STL (AL), 1911 BKN	127	431	31	80	10	7	3	37	9	37	37	.186	.262

NAME	YEARS AND TEAMS	G	AB	R	H	2B	3B	HR	RBI	SB	BB	SO	BA	SA
Mario Mendoza	1974 Pittsburgh Pirates	91	163	10	36	1	2	0	15	1	8	35	.221	.252
	1975 Pittsburgh Pirates	56	50	8	9	1	0	0	2	0	3	17	.180	.200
	1976 Pittsburgh Pirates	50	92	6	17	5	0	0	12	0	4	15	.185	.239
	1977 Pittsburgh Pirates	70	81	5	16	3	0	0	4	0	3	10	.198	.235
	1978 Pittsburgh Pirates	57	55	5	12	1	0	1	3	3	2	9	.218	.291
	1979 Seattle Mariners	148	373	26	74	10	3	1	29	3	9	62	.198	.249
	1980 Seattle Mariners	114	277	27	68	6	3	2	14	3	16	42	.245	.310
	1981 Texas Rangers	88	229	18	53	6	1	0	22	2	7	25	.231	.266
	1982 Texas Rangers	12	17	1	2	0	0	0	0	0	0	4	.118	.118
	1982 Mexico City	34	100	6	24	2	0	0	7	2			.240	.260
	1984 Mondava/Aguascalientes	96	369	61	120	23	4	2	51	1			.325	.425
	1985 Aguascalientes	111	402	56	115	14	4	4	49	5			.286	.368
	1987 Aguascalientes	107	386	66	122	19	2	5	55	1			.316	.415
	1988 Jalisco	122	389	44	107	10	4	1	38	0			.276	.329
	1989 Monterrey	109	381	47	113	20	0	1	40	2			.297	.357
	1990 Monterrey	81	247	20	60	6	0	3	18	1			.243	.304
	MAJOR LEAGUE TOTALS	686	1337	106	287	33	9	4	101	12	52	219	.215	.262
	MEXICAN SUMMER LEAGUE TOTALS	660	2274	300	661	94	14	16	258	12			.291	.365
	MEXICAN PACIFIC WINTER LEAGUE TOTALS	986			830				244				.239	

SOURCES: *Total Baseball, Patric Doyle, SABR*

KEY: Italicized numbers represent partial statistics.

blank space reresents incomplete statistics.

BIBLIOGRAPHY

Books

Anderson, David. *More Than Merkle: A History of the Best and Most Exciting Baseball Season in Human History*. Lincoln, Nebraska: University of Nebraska Press, 2000.

Bench, Johnny, and William Brashler. *Catch You Later: The Autobiography of Johnny Bench*. New York: Harper and Row, 1979.

Blake, Mike. *The Minor Leagues: A Celebration of the Little Show*. New York: Wynwood Press, 1991.

Boswell, Tom. *How Life Imitates the World Series*. Garden City, New York: Doubleday and Co., Inc., 1982.

Bouton, Jim. *Ball Four*, Twentieth Anniversary Edition. New York: Macmillan, 1990.

Bready, James H. *Baseball in Baltimore*. Baltimore: The Johns Hopkins University Press. 1998.

Caren, Eric C. *Baseball Extra*. Edison, New Jersey: Castle Books, 2000.

Cataneo, David. *Peanuts and Crackerjacks*. Nashville: Rutledge Hill Press, 1991.

Cepeda, Orlando, and Bob Markus. *High and Inside*. South Bend, Indiana: Icarus Press, Inc., 1983.

Coleman, Ken, and Dan Valenti. *The Impossible Dream Remembered*. New York: Viking, 1987.

Creamer, Robert. *Baseball and Other Matters in 1941: A Celebration of the Best Baseball Season Ever*. New York: Viking, 1991.

Dark, Alvin, and John Underwood. *When in Doubt, Fire the Manager*. New York: E.P. Dutton, 1980.

Dickson, Paul. *The New Dickson Baseball Dictionary*. New York: Harcourt Brace & Company, 1999.

Faber, Charles F. *Baseball Ratings*. Jefferson, North Carolina: McFarland & Company, 1985.

Foley, Red. *Topps Baseball Cards: Update 1988*. New York: Warner Books, 1988.

Fulton, Bob. *The Bernice Gera Story*. Cleveland: Society for American Baseball Research, 1999.

Gewke, Cliff. *Day By Day In Dodgers History*. New York: Leisure Press, 1984.

Golenbock, Peter. *Bums: An Oral History of the Brooklyn Dodgers*. New York: Putnam. 1984.

Harmon, Merle with Sam Blair. *Merle Harmon Stories*. Arlington, Texas: Reid Productions, 1998.

Hetrick, J. Thomas. *Chris Von der Ahe and the St. Louis Browns*. Lanham, Maryland: Scarecrow Press. 1999.

_____. *MISFITS! Baseball's Worst Ever Team*. Clifton, Virginia: Pocol Press, 1999.

Hickock, Ralph. *A Who's Who of Sports Champions*. New York: Houghton Mifflin Company, 1995.

James, Bill. *The Bill James Historical Baseball Abstract*. New York: Villard Books, 1988.

Kiner, Ralph, and Joe Gergen. *Kiner's Korner*. Westminster, Maryland: Arbor House Publishing Co., 1987.

Lane, F.C., *Batting: One Thousand Expert Opinions on Every Conceivable Angle of Batting Science*. Cleveland: The Society for American Baseball Research, 2001.

Lansche, Jerry. *Glory Fades Away: The Nineteenth-Century World Series Rediscovered*. Dallas: Taylor Publishing Company, 1991.

Luciano, Ron, with David Fisher. *Baseball Lite*. New York: Bantam Books, 1990.

Lyons, Jeffrey and Douglas B. Lyons. *Out of Left Field*. Times Books, 1997.

Mandel, Brett H. *Minor Players, Major Dreams*. Lincoln, Nebraska: Bison Books, 1997.

Mandelero, Jim. *Silver Seasons: The Story of the Rochester Red Wings*. Syracuse, New York: Syracuse University Press, 1996.

Marazzi, Rich and Len Fiorito. *Aaron to Zipfel*. New York: Avon Books, 1985.

Martinez, David. *The Book of Baseball Literacy*. New York: Plume Books, 1996.

Metro, Charlie with Thomas L. Altherr. *Safe by a Mile*. Lincoln: University of Nebraska Press, 2002.

Miller, Jeff. *Down to the Wire*. Dallas: Taylor Publishing Company, 1992.

Nash, Bruce M., and Alan Zullo. *The Baseball Hall of Shame*. New York: Pocket Books, 1989.

Nemec, David. *Great Baseball Feats, Facts & Firsts*. New York: Signet, 1997.

_____. *The Great American Baseball Team Book*. New York: Plume Books, 1992.

Nemec, David, and Saul Wisnia. *Baseball: More Than 150 Years*. Lincolnwood, Illinois: Publications International, Ltd, 1997.

Okkonen, Marc. *Baseball Memories, 1990-1909*. New York: Sterling Publishing, 1992.
_____. *Baseball Memories, 1930-1939*. New York: Sterling Publishing, 1994.
Okrent, Daniel, and Steve Wulf. *Baseball Anecdotes*. New York: Oxford University Press, 1989.
Owens, Tom, et. al. *Great Book of Baseball Cards*. Lincolnwood, Illinois: Publications International, Ltd., 1990.
Pietrusza, David, Silverman, Matthew, and Michael Gershman, eds. *Baseball: The Biographical Encyclopedia*. Kingston, New York: Total Sports Publishing. 2000.
Reichler, Joseph L., ed. *The Baseball Encyclopedia*. New York: Macmillan, 1985.
Reynolds, Bill. *Lost Summer*. New York: Warner Books, Inc., 1992.
Rhodes, Greg and John Erardi. *Big Red Dynasty*. Cincinnati: Road West Publishing Co., 1997.
Ritter, Lawrence S. *The Glory of Their Times*. New York: Macmillan, 1966.
Shannon, Mike. *Tales from the Ballpark*. Chicago: Contemporary Books, 1999.
Shatzkin, Mike, ed. *The Ballplayers*. New York: William Morrow, 1990.
Slocum, Frank. *Classic Baseball Cards - The Golden Years 1886-1956*. New York: Warner Books, 1987.
Smalling, Jack. *The Baseball Autograph Collectors Handbook, Number 10*. Durham, North Carolina: Baseball America, Inc., 1999.
Thorn, John. *The Relief Pitcher*. New York: E. P. Dutton, 1979.
Thorn, John, Palmer, Pete, Gershman, Michael, and David Pietrusza, eds. *Total Baseball: The Official Encyclopedia of Major League Baseball*. New York: Viking, 1996.
Uecker, Bob, with Mickey Herskowitz. *Catcher in the Wry*. New York: Jove, 1982.
Van Hyning, Thomas. *Puerto Rico's Winter League: A History of Major League Baseball's Launching Pad*. Jefferson, North Carolina: McFarland & Company, Inc. 1995.
_____, *The Santurce Crabbers: Sixty Seasons of Puerto Rican Winter League Baseball*. Jefferson, North Carolina: McFarland & Company, Inc. 1999.
Various. *Minor League Baseball Stars: Volume III*. Cleveland: Society for American Baseball Research, 1992.
Various. *Official Baseball Register*. St. Louis: The Sporting News, 1979 and 1984 editions.
Various. *The Series: An Illustrated History Of Baseball's Postseason Showcase*. St. Louis: The Sporting News, 1993.
Waggoner, Glen, ed. *Rotisserie League Baseball*. New York: Bantam, 1984.
Ward, Geoffrey, and Ken Burns. *Baseball: An Illustrated History*. New York: Alfred A. Knopf, 1994.
Whiting, Robert. *You Gotta Have Wa*. New York: Vintage Books, 1990
Will, George F. *Men at Work: The Craft of Baseball*. New York: Macmillan, 1990.
Williams, Ted. *My Turn At Bat: The Story of My Life*. New York: Simon and Schuster, 1970.
Wisnia, Saul, with Dan Schlossberg. *Wit & Wisdom of Baseball*. Lincolnwood, Illinois: Publications International, Ltd., 1997.
Zminda, Don. *From Abba Dabba To Zorro: The World of Baseball Nicknames*. Morton Grove, Illinois: STATS Publishing, 1999.

Periodicals and Other Sources

Ayres, Andrew. "Laga a Big League Slugger," *Northampton Gazette*. December 4, 1999.
Boggs, Frank. "Miracle Braves' Oscar Dugey Recalls Feats of 50 Years Ago," *The Sporting News*. October 10, 1964.
Brett, George, with Luciana Chavez. "George Brett: Daily Diary," *The Sporting News*. June 10, 1998.
Clifton, Merritt. "Pardon My French," *The National Pastime*. Cleveland: Society for American Baseball Research, 1987. Winter edition.
Daley, Arthur (p. 152).
Edgar, W. W., "Fred Buelow Is Dead After Long Illness," *Detroit Free Press*. December 28, 1933.
Farber, Michael. "The Case for Pedro Martinez," *Sports Illustrated*. September 10, 1997.
Fimrite, Ron. "The Yankee D Boys Did Double Duty," *Sports Illustrated,* October 30, 1978.
Frassinelli, Mike. "Dave Schneck," *The Allentown Morning Call*. March 1, 1998.

Fuller, Mike. *Seattle Pilots Baseball Team*. Seattle: Fuller Vision Web Site, www.brandx.net/pilots. 1997-2000.

Grantz, Marty. "10th Spectacular Season," *Colorado Springs Sky Sox Web Site*. Colorado Springs: www.skysox.com/history/index.shtml. 1998.

Greene, Sam. "Buelow Thorn in Ed Barrow's Side," *Detroit News*. January 11, 1934.

Gross, J. Scott. "1884 Wilmington Quicksteps," *The Baseball Research Journal – 15*. Cleveland, Society for American Baseball Research. 1986.

Hamilton, Brian. "Sammy Sosa Timeline," *Target 61 - The Home Run Chase*. New York: Time Warner, www.cnnsi.com/mlb/1998/target61/timeline/sosa/. September 28, 1998.

Hawk, Joe. "Padres Manager Bochy Recalls 'Bucket Head' days with Stars," *Las Vegas Review-Journal*. February 12, 1999.

Henneman, Jim. "Thundering Drive Hospitalizes Snell." *The Sporting News*. July 22, 1985.

Konotopetz, Gyle. "Garrett's Passion is Hitting," *Calgary Herald*. June 19, 1999.

Lewis, Ethan. "A Structure To Last Forever:" *The Players' League And The Brotherhood War of 1890*. www.empire.net/~lewisec/Players_League_web1.html. April, 1995.

MacDonald, Ian. "Stenhouse Making Noise with his Bat," *The Sporting News*. March 26, 1984.

McDermott, Barry. "Few Things Come to Him that Waits," *Sports Illustrated*. July 18, 1977.

McGrath, John, New Season Calls for an Old Line: Mendoza, *The Tacoma News Tribune*, December 20, 2000.

McKissic, Rodney. "Uecker's not 'Mr. Baseball' for Nothing," *The Detroit News*. May 12, 1999.

Ocker, Sheldon. "The Tigers get to Mesa, then Tribe gets to Tigers," *Akron Beacon Journal*. September 4, 1995.

Reeves, Jim. "Johnson's Release was a Shocker." *The Sporting News*. March 26, 1984.

Reusse, Patrick. "Metrodome May Suit Stenhouse." *The Sporting News*. February 18, 1985.

Scott, Barry. "Interesting Battle Looms at Catcher." *The Sporting News*. March 5, 1984.

Smith, David, Lahman, Sean, et. al. *Retrosheet Newsletters*. WWW.Retrosheet.Org. Vols. 1-7.

Pluto, Terry. "From the Heart," *Akron Beacon Journal*. August 14, 1998.

Wulf, Steve. "Detroit Jumped All Over 'em," *Sports Illustrated*. October 22, 1984.

Zimmerman, Eddie. "Eddie Zimmerman Thinks Training Trip is Important," *The Newark Evening Star*. March 12, 1914.

Zimmerman, Hy. "M's Singing Praises of Mendoza's Glove Magic," *The Sporting News*, August 8, 1979.

Interviews

Beard, Cramer, Telephone interview with Al Pepper, January 14, 2001.

Briggs, Dan, Telephone interview with Al Pepper, February 7, 1999.

Carroll, Tom, Telephone interview with Al Pepper, October 7, 2000.

Doyle, Brian, Telephone interview with Al Pepper, February 19, 2000.

Franks, Herman, Telephone interviews with Al Pepper, July 6, 2000, and December 23, 2000.

French, Jim, Telephone interview with Al Pepper, January 11, 2000.

Garrett, Adrian, Telephone interview with Al Pepper, December 27, 1999.

Howard, Frank, Telephone interview with Al Pepper, as call-in guest on *Afternoon Sports Talk with Tony Mercurio*, December 10, 1999.

Laga, Mike, Telephone interview with Al Pepper, March 3, 2000.

Mendoza, Mario, Radio interview with Sean McCall, May 9, 1999.

Metro, Charlie, Telephone interviews with Al Pepper, December 18, 2000, and March 29, 2001.

Owen, Larry, Telephone interview with Al Pepper, November 9, 1999.

Soria, Oscar, E-Mail interview with Al Pepper, January 30, 2001.

Stenhouse, Mike, Telephone interviews with Al Pepper, November 20, 1999, and November 22, 1999.

Index

(Mendoza's Heroes in **bold**)

ABOUT THE AUTHOR

Hailing from Philadelphia, Al Pepper is a 1982 graduate of Temple University. While at Temple, Al was a member of the school's rowing team and College Bowl trivia team. After college, Mr. Pepper became an officer in the United States Navy. He has served aboard five different ships and various shore commands. His first published work was a Master's Thesis on the feasibility of using blimps for military command, control, and communications. Mr. Pepper is presently a communications systems Test Director for the Navy's Test and Evaluation Force.

A member of the Society for American Baseball Research (SABR), Pepper dedicated nearly four years researching the records and careers of over 200 players while writing *Mendoza's Heroes*. Al Pepper currently lives in Virginia Beach with his wife, Janice, and two children, Ian and Kylie.

ABOUT THE ARTIST

Jonathan D. Gordon has been a professional artist since he was 16 years old. Just 21 years of age, Jon is renowned for his black-and-white portraits of minor league baseball players and rookie athletes from other sports. He has since moved to living color and broad action. He is the owner of *Artofjon Studios* (www.artofjon.com).

Mr. Gordon is active in charity work for numerous organizations, including Firefighter Ministries and "Visual AIDS," which supports artists with HIV. Jon resides in Virginia Beach, VA.

Mendoza's Heroes: Fifty Batters Below .200 by Al Pepper, Pocol Press, 250 pp., 2002, $17.95. Baseball's honor rolls are filled with legendary deeds of batting prowess. Crowds have risen in unison from their seats to loudly cheer the majestic trajectory of a white sphere "crushed" by the likes of Babe Ruth, Mickey Mantle, Willie Mays, and Barry Bonds. But, what about players who repeatedly produced little more than pathetic squibbers to third base, infield pop ups, and ego-bruising strike outs? What could possibly be their value to a baseball club? Plenty. Virginia Beach-based baseball author Al Pepper reveals their unique, offbeat, and unusual tales in *Mendoza's Heroes: Fifty Batters Below .200.* You may be familiar with Brian Doyle, Choo Choo Coleman, and Bob Uecker. Others, forgotten in the mists of time, are brought back to life. Using eye-opening statistics, interviews with players, and anecdotal biographies, Pepper's *Mendoza's Heroes* serves as a rollicking tour through baseball history — from the nineteenth century through today. Illustrations by Jon Gordon. ISBN: 1-929763-11-5.

Celebrate this doubleheader of bizarre ball playing! $32.95 for both books.

MISFITS! Baseball's Worst Ever Team by J. Thomas Hetrick, Pocol Press, 200 pp., 1999, $17.95. All aboard the train for the wackiest rail ride in baseball history. Presenting the strange-but-true odyssey of the 1899 Cleveland Spiders, a baseball team possessing such cosmically bad karma that the *Cleveland Plain Dealer* pondered, "How did they get so bad? And once they got there, how did they manage to make it through an entire season without committing mass suicide?" These questions are finally answered in this exhaustive tale of baseball woe. Filled with game accounts, anecdotes, statistics, and biographies of the men behind the madness. Meet some of the most colorful individuals ever to wear baseball uniforms—like Foghorn Tommy Tucker, Buttermilk Tommy Dowd, Chief Sockalexis, Crazy Schmit, and Ossee Schreckengost. Hysterical and historical. Illustrated by Michael D. Arnold. ISBN 1-929763-00-X.

TO ORDER: Specify book and send check. Add $2.00 S+H per book. Priority mail $4.00 per book. Foreign orders extra. Payable to: **Pocol Press.**

name: _____   street: _____

city: _____ state: _____ zip: _____ email for updates: _____

copies: _____ amount: _____ book titles(2) _____